GIORGIO ARMANI

Exploring 35 years of creative output, this richly illustrated book offers an unprecedented look into Giorgio Armani's unique aesthetic, corporate and cultural strategies. More than any other designer, Armani best represents the global success of the 'Made in Italy' label. His impact is palpable not simply in women's fashion and red carpet glamour, but is also inseparable from the evolution of the menswear industry. Written in a lively and accessible style, the book includes thoughtful and provocative chapters exploring: the evolution of the man's suit; boutique culture in a global reality; the influence of Orientalism; the designer's ambivalent relationship with the fashion press; the business of vertical branding; the use of the evening dress to construct the house's history; power dressing for the modern woman; the relationship between textiles, film and the contours of masculinity; the continued dialogue with early twentieth-century aesthetics; as well as the spaces and bodies of the theatre of fashion. The first holistic and critical investigation of one of the most influential fashion houses in the world, *Giorgio Armani: Empire of the Senses* is a must read for anyone interested in the history and theories of fashion.

John Potvin is Associate Professor at Concordia University, Montreal. In addition to several essays and articles, he is the author of Material and Visual Cultures Beyond Male Bonding, 1880–1914 (2008). *He is also the editor of* The Places and Spaces of Fashion (2009) *and co-editor of* Material Cultures, 1740–1920: The Meanings and Pleasures of Collecting (2009) *and* Fashion, Interior Design and the Contours of Modern Identity (2010).

Giorgio Armani

Empire of the Senses

John Potvin

ASHGATE

Published by
Ashgate Publishing Limited
Wey Court East
Union Road
Farnham
Surrey, GU9 7PT
England

Ashgate Publishing Company
110 Cherry Street
Suite 3-1
Burlington, VT 05401-3818
USA

www.ashgate.com

British Library Cataloguing in Publication Data
Potvin, John.
  Giorgio Armani : empire of the senses.
  1. Armani, Giorgio. 2. Fashion design--Italy. 3. Men's
  clothing--History--20th century.
  I. Title
  746.9'2'092-dc23

  ISBN: 978-1-4094-0668-6 (hbk)

Library of Congress Cataloging-in-Publication Data
Giorgio Armani : empire of the senses / by John Potvin.
    p. cm.
  Includes bibliographical references and index.
  ISBN 978-1-4094-0668-6 (hardcover) 1. Armani, Giorgio. I. Title.
  HD9940.I84A767 2012
  746.9'2092--dc23

2012017880

Printed and bound in Great Britain by the
MPG Books Group, UK.

Contents

List of illustrations

14   Armani on his via Borgonuovo runway with staff in 1990; 2, Rosanna Armani; 3, Gabriella Forte; 4, Silvana Armani; 5, Leo Dell'Orco; 6, Noona Smith; 7, Dreda Mele; 8, Caterina Salvador

15   Mafalda von Hesse, Cate Blanchett, Giorgio Armani, Claudia Cardinale, Elsa Pataky, Megan Fox and Kasia Smutniak attend the Giorgio Armani Privé haute couture autumn/winter 2009 fashion show in Paris

16   Roberta Armani and famed Spanish bullfighter Cayetano Rivera Ordóñez walked the runway as the last exits of the Giorgio Armani men's autumn/winter 2007 collection

17   The New Man in leather trousers. Aldo Fallai. From the autumn/winter 1980 advertising campaign

2   Armani/America: Haptic Pleasures

18   Spring/summer 1979. Inspired by the golden age of debonair film stars, Armani's new film-star look was based on his fascination with the classic images and identities of Hollywood masculinity. This suit lends a broad V-shape to the male physique; the trousers are deeply pleated

19   Autumn/winter 1979

20   The evolution of Giorgio Armani collection labels through time. From top to bottom: 1, first Giorgio Armani collection label;

2, first diffusion line 'white label' introduced in Milan in 1978 and the USA in 1979–1980 and produced by GFT; 2 to 5, the gradual evolution of the Giorgio Armani black label collection since the designer moved his design atelier from the company's inaugural headquarters in via Durini to via Borgonuovo

21   Unconstructed, unpadded and unlined blue linen jacket; white linen trousers from the spring/summer 1979 collection

22   Richard Gere in an Armani suit as Julian Kay in a publicity photo for *American Gigolo* (1980)

23   The spring/summer 1990 men's and women's collections share similar ideals and shapes, premised on the gender-blending use of fluid and textured textiles

24   Model from the autumn/winter 1990 menswear collection presenting a more humble and casual sense of masculine luxury

25   Spring/summer 2003. Armani's research into textiles and surfaces has never abated

3   Armani/Industry: Fashioning Finance

26   In the same year that Armani is represented symbolically ripping the stuffing out of a jacket in *Made in Milan*, home sewing magazine *Threads* (August/September 1990) deconstructs the Armani jacket to look inside and see how

sources of influence for Armani's menswear. The period remains a consistent source of inspiration

82   Spring/summer 1995

83   1998 Indian summer for menswear

5   Armani/Womenswear: Hybrid Modernity

84   Spring/summer 1989

85   A c.1979 suit once worn by Lauren Bacall and gifted by the actress to the Costume Institute, New York

86   Autumn/winter 1981. The jacket, in heavy and textured tweed coupled with a narrow lapel in leather, is reminiscent of a kimono. Many jackets, like this one, were also minimally embellished with double-track ridges from shoulder to sleeve, here cuffed in leather like the collar. The jacket is paired with pleated culottes in the same fabric

87   Gian Paolo Barbieri. From the autumn/winter 1983 advertising campaign

88   Spring/summer 1985

89   A look from autumn 1986 featuring power shoulders met with feminine pink fabric and unusual styling

90   Aldo Fallai. From the autumn/winter 1986 advertising campaign, shot in the designer's

via Borgonuovo palazzo before it was remodelled by Peter Marino

91   Spring/summer 1987: a softened version of the traditional man's tailored suit, made light and fluid for the summer months in Capri and Deauville

92   Aldo Fallai. From the spring/summer 1987 advertising campaign

93   Peasant-inspired and simplified glamour for spring 1988

94   Aldo Fallai. From the spring/summer 1988 advertising campaign

95   Bohemian chic from autumn/winter 1988

96   Autumn/winter 1988

97   Spring 1989 formed part of a period of fluid femininity which had not characterized his designs prior to 1987

98   Autumn/winter 1989

99   Spring/summer 1990

100   Evening for spring 1990 inspired by Poiret and Nijinsky

101   Evening looks from spring 1990 that seem as if a woman threw on a piece of fabric over herself and draped it according to the natural contours of her body

102   Interwar chic inspired this lush and full velvet coat, collarless silk man's shirt and beret for the autumn 1990 collection

121   Dreadlocks and kimono sleeves: autumn/ winter 1998

122   Peter Lindbergh and Paolo Roversi. For the spring/summer 1997 advertising campaign

123   Seeing double: repetition and the modern art of Armani from autumn 1988. Armani customarily gave buyers options for each garment with three to four different colours and/or fabrics, highlighting the modernist fetish for repetition, but also lengthening his runway presentations considerably

124   Autumn/winter 1988

125   Eveningwear from his spring/summer 1989 collection

126   Evening ensemble from spring 1991. Grid-like structure over a feminine and fluid fabric. Eveningwear which plays with concealing and revealing: Armani is adept at giving the appearance of transparency, nudity and revealing skin in various though not offensive ways. Here it is done through a zipper, a unique choice for an evening garment.

127   Embroidered dress from autumn/winter 1994

128   Final exit from the autumn 2007 collection which made its way directly into the final stop of the itinerate Giorgio Armani exhibition at the Trieannale in Milan. Fitted Giorgio Armani Privé evening gown with flared skirt embellished all over in horizontal rows of faceted Swarovski crystal beads in graduated sizes from neckline to hem and smaller crystal rhinestones. Sleeveless with scoop neckline, sculpted décolletage at back and tank top straps. Apart from Christian Dior, Armani is the only designer to have a specially designed crystal for his exclusive use, the 'Diamond Leaf' seen here in this floor-length dress

129   Left: 1993 worn by Katie Holmes; Right: 1995 worn by Victoria Beckham at the 2008 Metropolitan Museum's Costume Institute Annual Gala

130   Dress in the immediate right-hand foreground seen here in the Guggenheim exhibition and taken out of the Armani archive to be worn by Katie Holmes at the 2008 Met Gala

131   Peter Lindbergh. From the spring/summer 2002 advertising campaign

132   Mert Alas and Marcus Piggot. From the autumn/winter 2004 advertising campaign

6   Armani/Space: Boutique Cultures

133   Outside shot of the stately façade of the Place Vendôme location

134   View of the menswear floor of the London boutique designed by Claudio Silvestrin

135   Mannequins reminiscent of the silent beauties of the 1920s as

for the various labels which comprise the Armani brand

156   Interior entrance to the Giorgio Armani portion of the Hong Kong Armani/Charter House emporium, designed by Claudio Silvestrin

157   Interior shot of the Giorgio Armani boutique at Armani/Charter House

158   Façade of the Armani/Ginza Tower designed by Massimiliano and Doriana Fuksas featuring the LED light bamboo leaves

159   Interior view of the Armani/ Ginza Tower, the Giorgio Armani womenswear floor

7   Armani/Theatre: In the 'Church of Armani'

160   Armani posing in his via Borgonuovo palazzo, before it was redesigned by architect Peter Marino. The space was likened to a Zen monk's cell, with little decoration save for patterned pillows

161   Jean-Michel Frank-designed salon that resembles nearly identically Armani's own, which included numerous pieces from the French designer. The interior is from the Vicomte Charles de Noailles's Paris residence, 1923–26. Picture from: Todd, Dorothy and Raymond Mortimer. *The New Interior Decoration.* London: B. T. Batsford, 1929

162   Image from the controversial *Time* spread featuring the autumn 1982 collection

163   While Armani side-stepped the regularity of the runway during the early to mid-1980s for his own collection, he continued to hold wildly successful runway shows for both Erreuno and Mario Valentino. The press and buyers were starving for Armani shows at the time, which only served to heighten the presentations of these other collections. Here an exit from his autumn 1984 Erreuno collection

164   Still-life presentation style which marked the display of Giorgio Armani collections in the early 1980s. Spring/summer 1984

165   Intimate and animated presentation off the runway for his autumn/winter 1984 collection

166   From the September issue of *Esquire*: Armani poses with models displaying his autumn/winter 1987 collection on his basement runway in via Borgonuovo

167   The designer posing in front of one of his models cum Adonis cum living sculpture from the spring 1997 presentation at the Stazione Leopolda in Florence as part of the *G. A. Story*, the showcase of the Pitti Imagine Uomo

168   Various scenes from the *G. A. Story* choreographed and orchestrated by American theatre director Robert Wilson,

Acknowledgements

Sigmund Freud once wrote:

> biographers are fixated on their heroes in quite a special way. In many cases they have chosen their hero as the subject of their studies – for reasons of the personal emotional life – they have felt a special affection for him from the very first.[1]

Indeed, like Freud's own interest in Leonardo da Vinci, I too, despite this not being a biography, am charged with this alleged crime. However, in this cultural biography of the house of Giorgio Armani I wish to follow the lead taken by queer and feminist scholar Eve Kosofsky Sedgwick, who has called upon scholars to release themselves from the tyranny of the 'hermeneutics of suspicion' and replace it with a sustained 'reparative' project in which a scholar's response to the objects they narrate are not guided 'by hatred, envy and anxiety', but are evoked through a 'love' stemming from experiences of 'affects, ambitions and risks'.[2] Sedgwick's suggestion is quite liberating and leaves open the possibility of scholarly joy and pleasure, rarely admitted to or openly acknowledged.

If I am completely honest, this book has been a long time in the making, 25 years to be exact. It began back in 1987 when I purchased my first *GQ* which featured the now iconic black and white Giorgio Armani advertisements by photographer Aldo Fallai. The men and the sole female companion in those images embodied power, a nostalgic nod to the interwar period, an intelligence coupled with self-assurance and an old-world European glamour tinged with a soupçon of a jet-set lifestyle filled with holidays in Deauville or Capri. The affect that the memories of these images hold for me today is as powerful as they were when I was a teenage boy growing up in Alberta, Canada. The images still call out to me: to dress well, to dream, to travel, to fly off to

---

[1] Freud 1985: 223.

[2] Sedgwick 1997: 126; 138.

fashion's imaginary lands. For me, the fact they still hold such resonance not only attests to the power of visual representation, but to Armani's longevity and steadfast potent aesthetic vision. Since that first defining moment, I have never stopped being fascinated, mesmerized and even at times perplexed by the man, his single-minded vision, strength and above all his creative output. Throughout this project I was continuously and at times unceremoniously reminded how many people only see what they want to see or are stuck in a politics of insularity and exclusion. In the end I am grateful for these moments: they allowed me a greater degree of clarity, stamina and reminded me to chart my own course, perhaps, dare I say, not unlike the man whose partial story is discussed within these pages.

There are a number of photographers and indiviuals who freely and generously gave me permission to reproduce their work here in good faith. There are, however, two Toronto-based photographers in particular who need to be signalled out. It was a pleasure to be able to work with a close, respectful and patient friend, Scott Young, whose beautiful pictures helped to personalize these pages. Finally, the lion's portion of thanks in this regard must go to Ola Sirant whose overwhelming generosity and gorgeous runway pictures helped me to visualize ideas, arguments, stories and beautiful memories. There are also a number of people who helped in large and small but equally important ways: Hugh McPherson for his endless technical assistance and humorous and treasured debates which usually got me hot and bothered; Gillian Carrera for the treasure trove of CD-Rs of past runway shows; Alexandra Palmer for her encouragement at the very early stages of this project; Varounny Chanthasiri, Jennifer Farley and Molly Sorkin at the FIT Museum for their help with garments and images and allowing me to see that very special Armani Privé dress discussed in Chapter 5; Christine McGarry, Katie Green and Angela Dalton who all worked diligently as my research assistants; Constantino Muscau who, without any hesitation, attempted to pry open some impossibly heavy doors for me; Meredith Norwich and Margaret Michniewicz from Ashgate for their faith in both me and the project and especially for their patience, professionalism and risk taking; my dear Mama and Papa G as well as my closest friends who have indulged me, with great humour, along the many phases before and during the creation of this book; and finally, to my husband, Dr Dirk Gindt who helped immensely in innumerable ways throughout this process and who was always by my side with love, friendship, intelligence, devotion, humour and on research/ shopping trips; to him, those listed above and those who may have been inadvertently forgotten go my most heartfelt gratitude.

Parts of my text were first published elsewhere, and I am grateful to the following publishers for allowing me to reprint the material here. A substantial portion of Chapter 2 first appeared in *Fashion Theory* 15.3 (September 2011). Parts of Chapter 6 were published in *The Places and Spaces of Fashion* (Routledge

2009). A small portion of Chapter 5 was culled from an essay I published in *Fashion, Interior Design and the Contours of Modern Identity* (Ashgate 2010).

Image Credits

It's all one process. Searching for elegance, knowing where to look for it, then finding it.

Giorgio Armani's final words in *Made in Milan*

Elegance doesn't mean being noticed, it means being remembered.

Giorgio Armani in 'Armani Disarmed'

Introduction: Made in Milan

'Milano'.

This is the first, singular and solitary utterance by the film's narrator, Italian designer Giorgio Armani in Martin Scorsese's slow-moving and unassuming documentary *Made in Milan* (1990). Long before their collaboration, Armani has always maintained that the city is 'stupendous, but with human dimensions. It's a city that gives you absolutely nothing but work. But at the same time, it has an elegance all its own that's so subtle'.[1] The opening monologue of the film is worth quoting in full for how it evokes the designer's intimacy with and admiration for his adopted city, and how it offers a spatial network through which life and work merge seamlessly.[2]

> Milan is my chosen city, where I live and work. It's a city that allows you to express yourself, and respects you if you have something to say. Exceptional qualities for a metropolis, and Milan is a metropolis ... Milan seemed so cold, and so big. Then suddenly it is welcoming, rich in unexpected beauty to discover day by day. The buildings here are not imposing and opulent like the ones in Rome. But they have a discreet elegance that almost whispers. Milan is not a city on the grand scale, like Paris and London. But if you go beyond the narrow streets and past the house façades you discover fantastic interiors. The small intricate gardens and intimate refined settings are reminiscent of something exclusive and private. Something from the past. The beauty of the city is in harmony with my style of work, my way of life, my way of seeing things. Milan has changed a lot since I first came here. But it hasn't lost the atmosphere that can absorb and protect you while you work and play. Here, you can participate in the life of the city in whatever way is best for you. I have only a few hours in the day for myself because I've chosen work as my way of life. But Milan still allows me to feel that I am a part of the city, and that the city is a part of me.[3]

Produced to target an American audience, *Made in Milan* is as much about the hidden beauty and protection the city offers the designer as it is about the design process and a lifestyle fashioned by hard work. Nonetheless, this narratological intertwining reveals a sort of manifesto for Armani's design ethics; an ethics fuelled entirely by a complicated relationship to the metropolis. Yet, as with every partnership, limitations present themselves, and for Armani Milan is both 'snobbish' and 'restrictive'. 'However, Milan is my home,' he concedes. 'I enjoy the way the future, present and past mix together.'[4] While Italy can boast a centuries-old textile and craftsmen tradition, Milan, as Armani characterizes it, stands at the edge of time. Italian fashion in the two decades following the Second World War was governed by increasing feuding between the fashion centres of Florence (which produced largely hand-made objects and avoided introducing industrial strategies into the mix) and Rome (the centre of *Alta Moda* but which continued to be ruled by Parisian patterns and styles), leaving the door wide open for the Lombard city to become the modern centre of fashion, drawing on past tradition and present industrial know-how to forge a future of success.

1   The designer at home in his via Borgonuovo palazzo
in 1986, initially designed by Giancarlo Ortelli

The fashion industry in Italy has a rather short, but impressive history. In the 1930s, neither prêt-à-porter nor a substantive consumer base existed, and as a result no real fashion industry, as we might understand it today, could take hold. Fashionable young women either made their own clothes or if they were from the middle and upper classes went directly to their local tailors and seamstresses or Roman and Parisian couturiers, while their male counterparts turned to tailors for sartorial needs. Clothing styles were either dominated by Paris or the visual culture of Hollywood circulating in mass appeal periodicals and films. In his biography of the city, John Foot declares Milan to be the 'capital of the miracle',[5] and he claims it was in large measure due to foreign journalists, particularly from the USA and UK, that Milan soon began to be thought of as a fashion capital and 'the city of the future'.[6] Following the Second World War, Milan became Italy's economic hub, propelled by industrial know-how as well as through the relocation of important media and communication company headquarters. In post-war Milan the desire was to 'redesign the urban environment from top to bottom' or as Ernesto Rogers characterizes it, 'from the spoon to the city'.[7] Every aspect of social, economic and cultural life was scheduled for renewal and growth. The first so-called 'Italian miracle' of the late 1960s and 1970s transformed Italy into an industrially and culturally savvy nation. Fashion houses sought to distinguish themselves from their French neighbours through an ability to translate the quality and high fashion aspect, once the exclusive privilege of haute couture, to a prêt-à-porter garment destined to a substantially broader market. The international success of the Made in Italy label was thanks in large part to the numerous satellite industries implicated in the creation, production, distribution, advertising and consumption of fashion, now centred around the northern Italian city known for its greyness and industrially inspired, unadorned façades. Marketing theorist Claudio Stroppa noted the economic possibilities of fashion when he claimed that '[f]ashion has become one of the great powers of our times. It determines the character and direction of consumer demand, because to be out of touch with fashion is like being out of touch with the world'. Textile manufacturer Gritti financed *La psychologia del vestire* (*The psychology of clothing*), a project whose findings Stroppa published in 1967 and in which it was determined that clothing serves to 'express our selves [sic], realize our selves [sic] and our hidden desires, to exalt our personality and our culture'.[8]

Adam Arvidsson importantly submits that the political turmoil and terrorism that bracketed the 1970s led to an image of Italy as singularly depicted through the political, obscuring a more complete, holistic picture of the country. The period, he contends, marked an important moment in the 'affirmation', and I would add transformation and consolidation, of consumer culture.[9] The oil crisis set in motion a number of economic imperatives, new directions within cultural and economic networks; throughout the 1970s politics gradually as if imperceptibly gave way to economics, fuelled by increasing identification with consumer cultures and fashioned objects. Prosperity in Italy in the 1980s was a result, in large part, of greater American demand, as well as the increase in flexibility spurred on by subcontracting, offshore production and the automation of factories. In addition, the then socialist government led by Bettino Craxi (1983–1987) skilfully deployed state policies infused with an aesthetic and cultural rhetoric propelled by commodity culture as a means toward forging social consensus particularly among the middle class which was enjoying increasing wealth, prosperity and a newfound joy of consumerism.[10] Craxi's increased government spending propelled the Italian economy to the point of garnering a spot among the G7 while simultaneously precipitating an out of control and skyrocketing national debt. The politician's moves were evidently not without a hefty price, and by 1992 it was clear that numerous politicians had been implicated and subsequently sentenced in the *Mani Pulite* (Clean Hands) bribery scandal, in which Craxi and many others were convicted of giving preferential treatment and contracts to deep pockets in private companies.

Throughout its tenure in office, the Craxi government found inspiration by looking over its shoulder, turning its gaze back to Italy of the 1930s to offer a politics of change, distinct from the previous regime it had replaced. The visual and political link between Mussolini and Craxi was satirized by cartoonist Giorgio Forattini, who depicted the socialist leader in riding boots and black shirt, clearly reminiscent of the former dictator's unique and identifiable sartorial uniform. Style (an aesthetic cum political strategy) fuelled and propelled Craxi's conviction that the public must be convinced that the large entrepreneurs indelibly linked to his (socialist) party were jointly responsible for the 'economic miracle'. As Philip Willan noted in his obituary for *The Guardian*, '[p]arty conferences were not gatherings of earnest socialist working men, but theatrical productions frequented by a social elite of fashion designers, architects, financiers and intellectuals'.[11] In contradistinction to Mussolini's attempts to reinvigorate the image and importance of traditional folk costumes,[12] youth culture in 1960s and 1970s Italy helped to precipitate a new and emerging fashion industry, even if only obliquely. In the mid-1980s, the socialist administration was at the forefront of courting fashion designers as important allies in the redesign and rejuvenation of Milan. Craxi was keen, in particular, to have Milan shed its industrial past and embrace a more glamorous future that would revolve around notions of self-fashioning and cultural design. It was within this new Italian ethos that the concept of autonomy and the eventual desires for lifestyle would emerge. Youth culture shied away from the long-held hierarchical associations with fashionable clothing and instead adopted fluid attachments to consumer goods; objects which facilitated group affiliation, patterns of communication and personal identity were adopted to avoid any semblance of the hierarchical and hegemonic structures of their fathers and grandfathers. Social cohesion no longer determined the performances of consumption, that is to say, the correlation between advertising and consumption was no longer clearly prescribed, but determined by individual and group affinities.[13] Identities were increasingly recognized as volatile rather than simply and exclusively based on clearly ascribed class differences and traditional gender codes.

The figure of the professional Italian fashion designer was a relatively new entity charting equally new territory. This development in the clothing sector was fuelled by a textile industry which appropriated the ideals of the anti-fashion movement of the early 1960s and applied them to spice up their new prêt-à-porter collections. Among the characteristics of the anti-fashion movement was a desire to move beyond the dictates established by bourgeois cohesion, the creation of a boutique culture which was less about sales and more about sociability and where street culture and social interactions promised fashions for the future with seemingly endless possibilities. At the centre of this movement was the consumer-self, in charge of his/her sartorial and cultural identity, no longer waiting to be dictated to. The new set of *stilisti* (Italian for designer) was typified, in large part, by what they were not, *couturiers* prescribing a staunch style ethos and unitary look. Rather their task was to 'interpret the micro-movements of a diffuse consumerist effervescence and translate these into a distinct lifestyle centred on the particular label'.[14] The *stilisti* formed a new breed somewhere between Parisian haute couturier and the traditional Italian tailor. At once designer (in the purest sense of the term) and stylist, the *stilisti* possessed the ability to engender entire lifestyles that from their inception coupled creativity with industrial *savoir-faire* at every level.

The initial rise of the Made in Italy label and what would become an ambiguous, if not slightly clichéd Italian Look reached unprecedented heights in the second half of the 1960s when Italy experienced its first (economic) miracle. However, it was not until the early 1970s, amidst a backdrop of social unrest and political turmoil, that Milan distinguished itself as the centre for fashion when a number of important fashion houses moved to show their collections in the industrial city. In 1972 Walter Albini migrated from Florence to Milan to exhibit his collections there, shortly followed by Missoni and Krizia. By the late 1970s the image of Milan as the centre of the Made in Italy label was shored up by five core fashion houses: Ottavio and Rosita Missoni, Mariuccia Mandelli (Krizia), Walter Albini, Gianfranco Ferré and Giorgio Armani. Throughout the 1970s and especially the 1980s, these five design houses enjoyed sizeable increases in sales and revenues, especially from the USA. While their popularity and success soared in the 1980s, the height of the Made in Italy phenomenon, Armani above all has remained the most successful. Editor-in-chief of *Vogue Italia*, Franca Sozzani, stated: 'Surely, we had Walter Albini, Pucci and Valentino, but the real explosion of the Made in Italy starts with Armani.'[15]

TAXI
FASHION TRAVEL & LEISURE LIVING

Armani
The Pursuit of
Excellence

2   The man and the myth: *Taxi* cover from August 1986

These new barons of consumer culture were now responsible for helping to construct a new cultural paradigm. Albini,[16] for example, was at the forefront of developing ready-to-wear, while collaborating with numerous houses responsible for countless lines. He was also among the very first to conceptualize the notion of a total lifestyle, when he started to design fabrics, furniture and accessories among others. His first collection under his own name appeared as late as 1973, and given his premature death in 1983, it is hard to surmise the success he would have enjoyed alongside his compatriots. Not unlike the anti-fashionistos of the 1960s, this new breed of designers drew inspiration from myriad and ostensibly unlimited sources. On the heels of the oil crisis (1973–74), consumers set out to pull into their orbit free-floating associations, objects and images, which then helped to forge their newly contrived identities. In 1978 Modit, founded by Bepe Modenese, began the process of organizing and systematizing the runway presentations of Milanese fashion to buyers and the international press by inaugurating the twice a year runway presentations. Modit,[17], under the steady guidance of public relations executive Modenese, centralized and focused journalists' and buyers' attention on the Milanese showings in a concerted way throughout the 1980s placing the city on the fashion circuit alongside Paris and New York. In the wake of this conjuncture of various economic and cultural forces, *stilisti* like Albini and Armani created more than clothes, they evoked novel conceptual life-worlds, both cohesive enough to lead to eventual brand identity and yet fluid enough to lend the consumer a degree of agency. Set against the industrial backdrop of Milan, this book sets out to narrate the cultural biography of one of its citizen's most important and successful fashion houses.

To Fashion a Cultural Biography

This book seeks to make a significant historiographic and methodological intervention into the study of fashion. It tacitly queries the extent to which we can usefully move beyond a staid, moribund and conservative modernist approach to contemporary creative production and designer fashion that privileges the avant-garde,[18] often regionally circumscribed, as only and singularly worthy of scholarly and critical analysis. Today the avant-garde is eulogized as quickly as it becomes famous, not providing for the richness of the *longue durée* of time, experience and longevity. The mid-nineteenth-century poet and art critic Charles Baudelaire set in motion what would ultimately prove to be the call to arms to galvanize generations of artists and critics. His desire was for artists to capture at once the ephemerality of contemporary life, while at the same time portraying universal qualities and ideals which seemingly transcended both time and place. The conceptual force of modernity, while concerned with a distinctly contemporary sense of dislocation, fragmentation and ambiguity, locates itself within a more general experience of the aestheticization of everyday life, as exemplified in the ephemeral and transitory qualities of an urban culture shaped by the imperatives of fashion, consumerism and constant innovation, facets of what was to become the ethics of the avant-garde. Since then, many ideals espoused by modernists have been subsumed within fashion's expanding matrix. We owe much of our own understandings of Baudelaire's nineteenth century to the German philosopher Walter Benjamin, who attempted to recapture the cultural life of that period. However, by the time Benjamin was writing in the 1920s and 1930s modernity was no longer an aspect of avant-garde culture, the preserve either of a cultural or economic elite, but an important force that had trickled down to the masses. Commodity culture formed an increasingly greater aspect of the quotidian for greater numbers of people, as commodities began to flood the market and possibilities of consumption appeared endless. Benjamin's vision of the nineteenth century speaks, I contend, as much about his own conditions of time and place as to the cultural turn the French poet witnessed and helped to propel. As a consequence I am less concerned with Benjamin writing about fashion, commodity and urban culture in the nineteenth century as most fashion scholars are. What intrigues me are the conditions in which he wrote and how his own corporeal and intellectual perambulations were definitively rooted in the 1920s and 1930s, the period to which Armani himself returns repeatedly, incessantly, compulsively. Benjamin is not simply a chronicler of the nineteenth century, *après le fait*, if you will, rather than a product of the culture of the 1920s and 1930s, particularly as it concerns a discussion of fashion. I suggest that Armani has provided for an alternative means to attend to the needs and pleasures of the body and in so doing has not returned to the so-called embryo of modernism, the mid-nineteenth century, but importantly has reinvested the signifying potential of the interwar period, the moment of modernity's and modernism's zenith. Michel Foucault has queried what modernity really is and whether, according to him it is more apt to refer to it 'as an attitude' rather than 'as a period of history'. By 'attitude' Foucault suggests '[a] mode of relating to contemporary reality; a voluntary choice made by certain people; in the end, a way of thinking and feeling; a way, too, of acting and behaving that at one and the same time marks a relation of belonging and presents itself as a task'.[19] It is precisely this way of thinking, feeling, acting and behaving that resides at the centre of Armani's endless returns to the interwar, and which inspires the explorations throughout this book.

The challenges and pitfalls of working on a living designer are many, particularly when the designer in question is the most powerful, richest and controlling in Europe, invested in safeguarding his image and managing his house's cultural legacy. Despite my numerous requests and countless manoeuvres, access to the house's archives were denied. As a result, this book tacitly queries how possible it is to conduct research on a single living designer whose image is tied to very real economic and material realities. Here, then, I wish to underscore the heretofore unmentioned relationship between brand image and the power of the archives, an issue that has become all too prescient in light of how other Italian fashion houses like Gucci and Valentino, for example, have recently inaugurated their own centres for research. I hope this book, however, is a testament to my resilience, what can be done without gaining entry into the archives and my belief that there was and will surely continue to be many stories waiting to be told in the on-going cultural history of Giorgio Armani. As this book demonstrates to the researcher and student of fashion, access to the archives enables a certain type of material, but not the only one of importance. As attested to by the various themes of the chapters which comprise this book, I do not limit the notion of cultural biography to one definition or to one act of translation: rather its scope is broad as it permeates into the domains of architectural space, design, culture, gender, the body and various forms of media. Fashion is more than the presentation in magazines or a favourite blog, conceptual spaces which more recently seem to determine the value and worth of a designer. Because fashion is the sum and negotiation of cultural, economic, political, aesthetic, moral and corporeal technologies, confluences, resources and beliefs, the cultural biography of Giorgio Armani this book offers is the first holistic approach ever undertaken on any one single living designer on such a scale. By cutting across both time and space, I offer my reader a truly global perspective, allowing fashion to travel by not limiting Giorgio Armani to one city, country or continent. In these terms, beyond the trends and whims of what is 'in' today and 'out' tomorrow, Armani remains unparalleled as a force beyond the obvious. Fashion studies as a young discipline is richly divided between the care for and attention to the material object itself, a visual analysis of the images of fashion, the praxis of consumption whether in purely spatial or economic terms, the sociological attention to the systems of its various agents and finally the corporeal dimensions of fashion's embodied practices. This book ambitiously seeks to bridge the often artificial boundaries which demarcate these varied scholarly methodologies.

On several occasions when discussing the proposed book, many people were under the erroneous impression that much had been written on the Italian designer. After much reflection I realized that what this spoke to was how Armani's name had become so ubiquitous in popular culture, his influence so palpable to the point of indifference, that because of the countless stories and reports which flood the public domain through various media (Internet, newspapers, television, film and magazines), everyone felt either they *knew* *Giorgio*, or that everything had already been said about him. In fact, to date only one weighty tome has been published resulting from the controversial travelling exhibition begun in 2000 at the Guggenheim Museum in New York which served as a twenty-fifth anniversary retrospective of the designer's oeuvres.[20] Previously, in 1982, Richard de Combray was commissioned along with Arturo Carlo Quintavalle and Anna Piaggi to each contribute an essay in a volume on the designer alongside rarely seen sketches from several of his women's collections. This trinity of essays, while fascinating documents of the period, simply served to create part of the hagiographical narrative of the designer and the man.[21] What such books gain in breadth and visual sumptuousness, they tend to lose significantly in interpretive depth. In a series of essays for *Textile and Text*, Richard Martin wrote on various historical facets and the visual culture of the Emporio Armani magazine and advertising campaigns on the occasion of the 1990 Fashion Institute of Technology exhibition *Images of Man* he and Harold Koda curated, and for which they wrote a short introductory essay to the advertising images featured in the show.[22] More recently journalist Renata Molho has written an unauthorized biography on the designer, relying exclusively on unsourced, previously published material.[23] No other designer in the twentieth century, when the concept took shape, has impacted both women's as well as menswear as has Armani, and while Chanel, Christian Dior and Yves Saint Laurent have earned their privileged and deserved place of honour in the pantheon of greats, every year now countless volumes and glossy tomes explore and/or eulogize their life and work.

This book is more than a simple and limited case study, but a blueprint to explore the exhaustive parameters of creative production, through the affect of translation and the holistic approach to a very wide-ranging series of issues and themes. My hope, then, is that the researcher and student of fashion's multiple histories and ever-expanding personalities realizes that it is not limited by the social, cultural and aesthetic ethos of the avant-garde or so-called 'alternative' of a given time, but that living designers who engender entire life-worlds and global powerhouses are worthy of exploration within the annals of modern fashion, because they reveal much more than the

3   Entrance to the 2000 *Giorgio Armani: Retrospective*, Guggenheim Museum

machinations and ideals of a small elite coterie, but affect the economic, cultural and aesthetic lives of millions. While some material I present here might exist within the public domain the task, as I have established, is to critically evaluate and engage with it in a manner that, to date, has yet to be undertaken. As a point of departure, I have investigated the rich visual (advertising campaigns, editorial content, runway presentations and films), material (the spaces and garments themselves) and textual (catalogues, reviews, press releases, interviews with sales staff and consumers, magazines and newspapers) culture surrounding the designer since he founded his house in 1975. These three separate though entirely interdependent facets of a fashion enterprise are mitigated by and cut across the modalities of aesthetics, gender, economics, space and time. These are, after all the source material of the discipline of fashion studies and the very stuff of the empire of the senses.

The Affect of Translation

By paying more detailed attention to the complex possible relationships between specific objects and images within a given space and the attitudes, perceptions and contexts they may relate to or purport to embody, this book also develops considerably upon current understandings of the fashion system as a multidisciplinary outcome. It does so by establishing for the first time the methodological importance of translation both in the networks of creation, production and distribution of fashion and its study, research and theorization. Structural linguistics and semiotics have long held sway in the study of fashion since the seminal work of Roland Barthes.[24] Yet it is intriguing how the notion of translation has yet to come to bear on this field of research. Taking the lead from the material itself, this book proposes translation (as transition, transformation and tailoring) as an important and formative framework to unpack, analyse and narrate the complexities of an historical juncture in fashion. To best facilitate this, I have elected a holistic view of the work of one designer as a means to explore the modalities of gender, ethnicity, performance, space, economics, design, aesthetics and historicism that through various interpretative functions of translation enact myriad dynamics and patterns of communication that dominate the empire of fashion. As the economic, aesthetic and cultural core of the Giorgio Armani enterprise, the designer, in his own unique and powerful way, has forged a career of translating the urban energy and design rigour of Milan to a global audience that for 35 years has been all too eager to adopt and adapt. The *Oxford English Dictionary* offers numerous definitions of the term, and below are listed six interconnected yet distinct meanings, which variously appear throughout this book.

1. transformation, alteration, change; changing or adapting to another use; renovation
2. *rhetoric.* transference of meaning; metaphor
3. *fig.* to interpret, explain; to expound the significance of (conduct, gestures, etc.); also, to express (one thing) in terms of another
4. to change in form, appearance, or substance; to transmute; to transform, alter; *spec.* in industrial use: of a tailor, to renovate, turn, or cut down (a garment); of a cobbler, to make new boots from the remains of (old ones)
5. to transport with the strength of some feeling; to enrapture, entrance;
6. to express the sense of (words or text) in another language.

Affective as much as it is cognitive, the performative acts of interpretation, examination and translation are not only indicative of my own role in the narration of the material, visual and textual culture of the house, but it is also suggestive of the mode of cultural communication endemic to Giorgio Armani's cultural heritage. The affect of translation, as I wish to propose here, is not limited to, yet remains dependent on, a transformational movement of and through time, language, space, appearance and meaning, localized through the sensory experiences and embodiment fashion necessarily entails. By affect I mean to suggest the sensory, aesthetic and phenomenological responses to the spaces, objects and sensations of fashion encoded in the various and varied acts of translation I weave throughout. At its most basic, translation appears repeatedly and often unconsciously in the writings and critical reception of Armani's work; however unreflexive these references might have been, they nevertheless point to the way the designer has set out to communicate his aesthetic ideals to various constituencies. Put in simple terms, Armani's harnessing of the affective forces of translation has led him to build an global empire, as translation also, and simply, refers to the transmission and migration of foreign ideas materialized in objects and through images. Peter Burke, who maintains that there is something lost in the process of translation, submits that 'the close examination of what is lost is one of the most effective ways of identifying differences between cultures. For this reason the study of translation is or should be controlled to the practice of cultural history'.[25] Burke also notes that the praxis of 'cultural translation' unfolds the two processes of 'decontextualization and recontextualization'.[26] While in every act of translation something is lost, I wish to submit that something new and unforeseen is gained producing in its wake a hybrid state, space, object or cultural force.

We might also do well to recall James Clifford's admonition that 'translations' are always and can only hope to be 'approximations ... built from imperfect equivalences'.[27] Armani has been keen to limit the possibilities of false and unequivocal translations of his work, preferring, for instance, to keep his publicity in-house, avoiding third-party gatekeepers to translate his work beyond repair. For, as Benjamin eloquently submits, 'in its afterlife – which could not be called that if it were not a transformation and a renewal of something living – the original undergoes a change'.[28] Transferred here for our purposes, Benjamin's notion of transformation might reveal fashion as a living, growing, expanding and finally morbid entity, one that lives on after it has served its purpose in the ambiguous and incomplete space between word, image and material object. By controlling the visual and material culture of Giorgio Armani, the designer consciously seeks to ensure that once morbidity sets in, the image will be consistent in its afterlife, the aesthetic ethos and corporate structure will outlive the man and the legacy will be maintained in perpetuity. Whether positive or negative, third-party interpretation, like this book, is seen as a threat to safeguarding the cohesiveness and univocality of brand image as well as the man's aesthetic and the house's gatekeepers' single-minded control. In light of this, it is not entirely surprising I was not given access to the archives.

Lawrence Venuti claims that 'a translation emerges as an active reconstitution of the foreign text by the irreducible linguistic, discursive, and ideological differences of the target-language culture'.[29] The 'original' is an act of genius, an 'unchanging monument of the human imagination', while the translation 'can be no more than a copy, a derivative, simulacral, false, an image without resemblance'.[30] Like Venuti I wish to problematize this binary through the myriad experiences, spaces and times of fashion. Are not all designers caught uneasily between these two poles, particularly within a postmodern world, where all has already been done save for the products of hybridity which emerge from loose and uneven translations from various sources, what might be glibly called 'inspiration'? The success of a translation, whether of the written word or of fashion, resides in the very erasure of its own activity, that is, when it appears not have been the result of translation.[31] Here authenticity and originality assume new meaning and burden. It has been said that Armani's temporal and ethnic sources of inspiration can rarely be detected, producing modern interpretations of seemingly familiar shapes and silhouettes. 'I've always tried to make clothes that are without references', claims Armani. 'That has sometimes been my problem with the fashion press. There haven't been easy references to explain what I've done'.[32] Translations, like garments, must appear seamless, the labour involved rendered invisible, the mystery upheld at all costs, the mystification of genius clung to. The translator – interpreter – possesses much power. Translation must also appear seamless in order to facilitate the act of consumption, allowing the consuming-subject to assuage fears of unintelligibility or otherness within the target market, Middle-Eastern shapes translated for Western audiences, for example.

Actor–Network Theory (ANT), often referred to as the 'sociology of translation', concerns itself with the mechanics of power. Following along from ANT, the sewing machines in a designer's atelier are equal in importance to the creation of the social order of the fashion system itself. The mills, the press and the Internet, for example, have aided in propelling Giorgio Armani to its status. While social order is a product 'generated by a network of heterogeneous, interacting, materials', compelling is how Armani transforms these various mechanisms by ostensibly single-handedly controlling his empire, not entirely unlike the Wizard of Oz, unwilling to reveal the truths which might lurk behind the velvet Armani/Casa curtain. In this theory, translation 'concerns itself with how actors and organisations mobilize, juxtapose and hold together the bits and pieces out of which they are composed; how they are sometimes able to prevent those bits and pieces from following their own inclinations and making off; and how they manage, as a result, to conceal for a time the process of translation itself and so turn a network from a heterogeneous set of bits and pieces each with its own inclinations, into something that passes as a punctualized actor'.[33]

Armani perfectly performers his role as a 'punctualized actor' whose empire is fashioned in such a way as to ensure the single-mindedness of the designer's vision, the singularity of his control and the aesthetic culture of his power; it is hard to forget, but easy to take for granted his auratic presence. To best achieve my own act of translation, I have ordered the chapters in such as a way as to begin with this investigation of the designer and the mystique of empire building, gradually migrating thematically from his design philosophy and financial savvy, largely premised on an ideologically driven aesthetic programme, toward the public spaces of consumption and performance, spaces peopled by the very constituency Armani professes to direct his efforts toward. In other words I suggest a centrifugal movement from the heart to the outposts of where control is exercised, but where the presence of the designer is made palpable and omnipresent nonetheless.

As an act of translation from the material and visual to the textual, this book, by my own admission, remains incomplete. After all, given how translation, and by extension hybridity, acts as the guiding metaphor permeating the pages of this text, the act of interpretation and movement is never complete or finite, but a continuous deferral of meanings, gaps, fissures and absences, ever open to future explorations and investigations. Though necessarily and understandably incomplete, and perhaps at times overlapping, each chapter tells of a unique facet of Armani's design empire, while at the same time forming part of a larger on-going aesthetic narrative. With over 140 Giorgio Armani collections (to say nothing of his other labels, and what the designer produced for firms like Mario Valentino, Erreuno and Hitman to name a few), hundreds of film wardrobes, dozens of licenses, numerous collaborations and countless sponsorships and patronage, one book could not exhaust the

4   Aldo Fallai. From the autumn/winter 1986 advertising campaign

vastness of his empire and output. As a result, I wish to offer snapshots of what has occupied me for many years. Some of the themes and events may not necessarily be new to my readers, but my hope, nevertheless, is to offer a different perspective from the current and rather limited one.

My reader may have noted the repetitive, stylized chapter titles. These are meant to self-consciously mimic Armani's via Manzoni megastore in Milan whose doors he opened at the turn of the millennium as an attempt to create a whole environment where all the senses are attended to. Each new brand he created in 2000 paralleled the opening of the Milanese megastore and offered a panoply of fashion, furniture and services, from chocolates (Armani/Dolci) to floral services (Armani/Fiori) to fine dining (Armani/Caffè) all within a clearly streamlined brand identity, as a means to reinforce his aesthetic and impact on numerous cultural and economic domains. While various Armani labels are considered throughout, the book focuses its gaze on Armani's so-called 'black label' or Giorgio Armani (Borgonuovo) label. 'Borgonuovo (or mainline)', as Armani has always asserted, 'is the utmost of my creativity, to use a modern term. In Borgonuovo, I put the height of what I consider sophistication, that which I dedicate to a woman [and a man] that I would like to spend time with, live with, love'.[34] Elsewhere he also asserts that with this collection he develops one singular idea, 'imposes one concept which in turn is carried through from beginning to end. The deep morality, the sainthood, is limited to Giorgio Armani'.[35]

I have identified four key periods in the history of the house. The first, from the house's inauguration to the death of co-founder, partner and former lover Sergio Galeotti in 1984, were years marked by considerable growth and a severe focus on honing the image and identity of the brand. The second period between 1984 and 1995 characterizes another moment of intense growth and success, but at a point when the Armani aesthetic was at its most sublime, most perfected and perhaps even its most original and liberated, reaching its zenith. It also begins the classic era of runway presentations the world is most familiar with, shown in the basement of his via Borgonuovo palazzo. When asked in an interview which period of his career he most cherished Armani offered 1985 to 1990, explaining:

> In the 1970s and early 1980s I can't say I was having fun. I was working all the time and was unaware of so many things... In the years 1985–90, I began to be a reality in the marketplace, but I was still able to make decisions with a certain freedom. There was something magical about those years. I was very sure of myself when I designed my collections. The period after that was a very important one. I could no longer take risks like I used to, and I couldn't afford not to sell – I couldn't even afford a drop in sales. My designing became a commercial responsibility.[36]

After Galeotti's death the designer felt the burden of having 'something to prove'. It was also in this second period that Armani realized he was on the 'right path' for the house, one premised on the idea that what appears in the stores and consequently in the streets is that which appeared on the runway, fashion which 'may not be the trend of the year', but which 'confirms' his single-minded 'ideas [and] products'.[37] Loosely bracketed between 1995 and 2000, the third stage of the house's history witnessed increasing financial responsibility and prosperity, but declining cultural cachet. It marks a period when numerous fashion houses were bought and sold on the open market, ushering in the era of the global fashion conglomerate. It is also characterized by a sense of renewal with the return to prominence of such venerable Italian houses as Gucci and Prada, whose heritages were reinvigorated by a new generation of media-savvy designers. Both rejuvenated houses also stole the spotlight from Armani, who by then no longer had his rival Gianni Versace for public sparring sessions that only served to heighten their visibility and sales. The advent of minimalism in fashion, despite the label being erroneously attributed to Armani, was an initially uneasy bedfellow to his previously sumptuous and rich Orientalist-inspired garments. As a result, Armani was widely portrayed by the press as out of sync with what women, in particular, wanted. This lead to a visibly disgruntled, obstinate and protectionist designer. The final and current period, then, marks an important and yet neglected sense of rejuvenation for the house and the designer, despite his age. Armani of the twenty-first century is more lean, focused, active and fit than he has ever been. In 2000, as a way to celebrate the house's 25 years, Armani embarked on numerous and various projects: a retrospective exhibition; new product lines; the first multi-brand megastore; and the reacquisition of production and distribution networks. Since the turn of the millennium the designer has also been creatively clearer and more direct about his sources of inspiration, more often than not turning to Asia and the glamour of the interwar period. These four periods, as I have outlined them, feature differently throughout this book, and reveal how the case of Armani, the man and brand, suggests an important force of resistance and struggle as much as success, power and control.

One final word should be devoted to my title, which I arrived at through various sources of inspiration. First and foremost is Giorgio Armani's dramatic, though limited, advertising campaign for its trio of fragrances Onde, each inspired by a different region of the 'Orient' (India, China and Japan). The campaign read 'a trilogy of fragrances, an empire of the senses' with a photograph of a bobbed dark haired model unabashedly recalling the 1920s *garçonne*. The self-conscious and blatant reference to empire coupled with the exoticism of the East as well as the nostalgic nod to the interwar period colluded to perfectly visualize the themes explored throughout this book, the hallmarks of Giorgio Armani's aesthetic ideal. The advertisement also evoked the way in which the designer has elaborated a complete sensorium of fashionable experiences. Here then, the notion of somatechnics is a useful term to apply to the various technologies of fashion inseparable from, grafted onto and embedded into the performing consumer body. My title, *Giorgio Armani: Empire of the Senses*, refers back to the myriad strategies indebted to the phenomenological, sensorial, corporeal and material experiences and expressions of being-in-the-world. *Empire of the Senses* for me suggests the fashions of embodiment while simultaneously alluding to Giorgio Armani's global reach, whether by way of the spaces he has constructed or through his impact on or input in various media, be it music, television, art, theatre or cinema. As I will elaborate in this book, clothing and design, that is the empire of fashion, orients the embodied subject through various mechanisms. Empires, as with the human sensorium, imply a relational dynamic between subjects and objects, as well as a power structure, which, within the phantasmagoric realm of fashion is not easily discernable, but rather rendered opaque to safeguard the mystery and aura of the house they faithfully serve. At the centre of this empire, lest we forget, is one man and one man alone whom the Italian press has affectionately crowned King Giorgio.

Notes

1   *W* 8 May–15 May 1981.

2   Armani was born in Piacenza in Emilia-Romagna, and moved to Milan early in his life.

3   Armani in *Scorsese* 1990.

4   'Giorgio Armani' 1986: 107.

5   Foot 2001: 1. By 1999, Foot also notes that 6 out of the 10 most successful fashion houses were Italian, and of these 4 headquarters were located in Milan: Armani, D&G, Prada and Versace.

6   See Foot 2001: 128.

7   Rogers in Foot 2001: 109.

8   Stroppa in Arvidsson 2003: 117.

9   Arvidsson 2003: 121.

10   Arvidsson 2003: 135.

11   *The Guardian* 20 January 2000.

12   See for example Paulicelli 2002.

13   Arvidsson 2003: 118–9.

14   Arvidsson 2003: 127.

15   Sozzani in Ferrero-Regis 2008: 13–4.

16   For more on Albini see Frisa and Tonchi 2010.

17   By 1990 the organization changed its name to Momi-Modit Milano.

18   For an excellent discussion of the development of fashion studies and its debt to art history among other disciplines see Breward 2000.

19   Foucault [1978] 2004: 33.

20   See *Giorgio Armani* 2000.

21   See de Combray 1982 and Quintavalle 1982.

22   Martin 1990a; 1990b; 1990c; Martin and Koda 1990.

23   Molho 2007.

24   See Barthes 1967: 2006; see also Calefato 2004.

25   Burke 2007: 38.

26   Burke 2007: 10.

27   Clifford 1997: 11.

28   Benjamin 1999b: 73.

29   Venuti 1992: 10.

30   Venuti 1992: 3.

31   Venuti 1992: 4.

32   *Giorgio Armani* 2000: 13.

33   Law 2003.

34   *WWD* 21 April 1993.

35   Witter 1989: 101.

36   *DNR* 17 June 1996.

37   *DNR* 18 January 1995.

1

Armani/Mystique: Building Empire

> They say he doesn't drink or smoke; that he eats only plain food, like unadorned pasta; that he owns two suits, two ties and two hundred pairs of shoes; that his days are divided up into hour-long instalments with an allotted objective for each. They say that he doesn't like to travel, and instead gets his view of the wide world from television; that he is a demanding taskmaster who fills his staff with equal measures of devotion and fear; that the Armani girls who populate his offices and shops – scrubbed, groomed, minimal make-up, upright posture – are not allowed to wear dark tights or high heels with their regulation Armani clothes; that he requires the hangers on the rails in his outlets to be precisely defined, identical distance apart. And there are weirder, wilder stories. Apparently he swims in a pool shaped like a thin channel which is only wide enough for one man's breaststroke; all the cutlery in his kitchen is hermetically cling-wrapped; he wears rubber gloves to shake hands.
>
> To my certain knowledge, the part about the gloves is untrue.
>
> GQ (UK)

> I cannot distinguish any longer what is Armani and what is the Armani mystique.
>
> Gabriella Forte

As the story goes, after five successful years as a freelance designer, Giorgio Armani sold his blue Volkswagen in 1975 to help toward the paltry $10,000 start-up funds he and his partner (and then lover) Sergio Galeotti used to establish Giorgio Armani SpA in the heart of Milan. Despite how lucrative and exciting freelance designing and consulting proved for the designer, spurred on by Galeotti, the duo established their own label. Launched in a small office at 37 Corso Venezia and with the help of a part-time secretary (Irene Pantone), Armani and Galeotti set in motion what would develop into a global design enterprise, officially registering the company on 24 July 1975. Three short months later, the newly inaugurated house showcased its first menswear collection for the spring/summer season in their tiny showroom; this collection would forever solidify Armani's pre-eminent position in the annals of fashion history.

As with every inevitable 'great' designer story, Armani's grand narrative moves from obscurity to fame and fortune. His is the story of a legend. However, like most legends, stories more often than not are steeped in mythologizing grandeur, highly protected and recited by press staffers as easily as they are created, narratives known for their opacity as much as for their simplicity, purposefully cloaking its protagonist in an aura of (often tortured) creative genius. Fact, fiction, fashion and fantasy work equally to conjure importance and mystique. There are those stories that a fashion house constructs and those retold by a designer himself, both seamlessly folded into the narrative of the brand which often transcend the man himself. For instance, the now infamous and iconic 1982 cover of *Time* featuring a young and dashing Armani has become part of the designer's mythology; the cover is repeatedly cited as the first time a designer has been on the cover of the weekly magazine since Christian Dior in 1957, conveniently ignoring that French designer Pierre Cardin had already been featured in 1974. It is also retold how Armani's success, in hindsight, began when he was quite young when his mother set the table for a very rare and special chicken Christmas dinner; feeling there was too much on the table, Armani edited the arrangement by removing the simple floral bouquet. This simple act of removal, of subtraction, coupled with the designer's humble yet influential beginnings marked the embryo of what Armani would become famous the world over, simple, unadorned, comfortable and yet luxurious modern clothes.[1] Mythology is both inevitable and useful, endlessly repeated stories born from a desire to construct a solitary heroic creative figure and brand image indelibly collapsed into each other.

Fashion scholar Yuniya Kawamura has attempted to strip the solitary figure of the designer's long-held significance within the fashion system, claiming designers are only one of a number of fashion's many actors. While her proposal to look beyond the designer is important given the numerous agents involved in the life story of a fashioned garment, we would do well not to lose sight of the fact that the rise to prominence of Italian fashion in the 1970s was entirely premised on clearly identifiable and celebrated designer identities, houses whose labels were quickly associated with a definitive and distinctive lifestyle. Kawamura sites journalists, editors and buyers as fashion's key gatekeepers, powerful agents of meditation between what designers produce and display and the consuming public. As this chapter will establish, however, Armani deploys his press office and ambassadors to act as gatekeepers of the house itself, distinct from and at times at odds with the gatekeepers Kawamura claims possess immense power. Co-curator of the controversial 2000 Guggenheim Museum Giorgio Armani retrospective, Harold Koda asserts that for the exhibition they wanted to give the viewing public an alternative perspective on his work, distinct from the one regularly proffered by the press, work rarely or ever reported on by the media. As the designer himself asserts: 'Most of the stuff the public sees is filtered through buyers and fashion editors', well-positioned gatekeepers of the fashion system. The retrospective, he claims 'is expressive of a side of Armani that people didn't know but consistent with' what they thought they knew.[2] Through various means, such as the retrospective, Armani attempts to sidestep the industry's gatekeepers and engender his own system of meaning-making and a material and visual culture premised exclusively on his own moralizing aesthetic programme. The sections of this chapter, focusing first on the designer's relationship with the press and second on the creation of a network of ambassadors, feature as modes of translation that attempt to reach Armani's preferred audience, the customers themselves, and counter the industry's so-called gatekeepers. I wish then to challenge and extend Kawamura's definition to importantly claim that while fashion has its many gatekeepers, so too does a powerful designer like Armani who works tirelessly to maintain the value and worth of the remote creator. What ensues in its wake is a rather fascinating and compelling site of perennial tension: after all, a gatekeeper's endless struggle is one over the authority of translation.

I am reminded of the auratic power of a designer's name in one of the most revealing moments in the 1989 Win Wender's documentary *Notebook on Cities and Clothes* in which the film's protagonist, Japanese designer Yohji Yamamoto, is filmed on the eve of opening a new boutique in Tokyo. Equipped with a piece of chalk Yamamoto proceeds to sign his name on the stone plate that serves as the store's signboard. He fails to successfully replicate with exactitude his own signature, used in every pre-made label sewn into each garment, not only on his first attempt but on several subsequent efforts. The humour of the situation quickly leads to frustration, at which point it becomes painful to watch. This poignant moment of frustrated repetition highlights several interrelated aspects of designer culture: (1) the auratic presence of the designer's 'signature' – and signature style; (2) how the label has become bigger than the man himself to the point he can no longer faithfully sign his own name, the marker of personal signification and (3) the importance the act of repetition has in the conceptualization of brand identity. In his discussion of the 'author function', Michel Foucault complicates how the author becomes 'characteristic of the mode of existence, circulation, and functioning of certain discourses within a society'.[3] The name of the man and name of the designer (the authorial subject of the designed object and brand image), reside somewhere 'between the two poles of description and designation', to a point where they are all too easily collapsed – the man and the brand – in other words are inseparable to the point where the man, Armani himself, ceases to exist.[4] For Sigmund Freud, on the other hand, the public is more invested in the myth and personality of the artist (or designer) than the work of art (or design) itself.[5] In this respect Armani fails to deliver, given that scandal and excess rarely figure in the press reportage of the designer; only aggrandizing mythology services the public appetite. However, as Silvia Giacomoni maintains, 'Armani does all he can to destroy the myth of the creator and to present himself as a first-class professional active in the clothing industry: but it doesn't come off.'[6] Herein lay public interest in the designer, one premised not so much on the personal, but on the political, economic and cultural power attached to his designs and his at times provocative pronouncements.

To deconstruct the work and the myth, then, is also to threaten to expose the wizard behind the red velvet curtain, a revelation on par with the downfall of the notional heroic figure. No other designer in Italy better embodies the solitary paternal and hero figure, who not only ensures that every and all decisions come back to him, but also that the image of the company remains a centrifugal focus on the man, which in turn attenuates his remoteness. While the house of Giorgio Armani currently employs a staff of slightly over 5,000 there can be no question that the house's decisions come down to Armani's decisions, a man who is said to design every object that bears his name.

5   Aldo Fallai. From the spring/summer 1988 advertising campaign

Armani and Advertising

Images, for me, are storytellers, oracles. They must communicate emotions. I have always thought that the image (the principal means of communication for fashion) should translate and embody my style.

Giorgio Armani

Reportedly unsatisfied with the results of *Made in Milan*, the designer's discontent was largely derived from the criticism from the press. According to Armani: 'I'm a revolutionary, and I'm unwilling to accept the way the system works. I am fed up with overemphasis, contrivance, and insincere enthusiasms.'[7] Perhaps it is fair to say that in the last quarter of the twentieth or the first decade of the twenty-first century no other designer has held more of an ambivalent or equivocal relationship with the press than Armani. As gatekeepers of an Italian house (read patriarch's home), governed by an internal family-inspired system, press offices are ferociously protective and often deny 'strangers' entry into the inner sanctum. After all, as Galeotti once claimed: 'Our image is the only thing we have in assets and that's what I spend most of my time guarding.'[8] The relationship between advertising and the press is a mutually beneficial one, though tacitly precarious as it marks the site of inevitable power struggles between those invested in a singular aesthetic and those cultivating a larger fashion system which hosts myriad and often competing images and ideas. To preserve his mystique, the designer is usually surrounded by a circle of intimates charged with safeguarding the genius behind the velvet curtain. Armani is certainly no exception to this rule, and is in fact a perfect exemplar of how the house begins to take over the individual. As an assertive and domineering father figure, Armani is so guarded and protected that all his ideas, themes and emotions are communicated by way of a translator – he chooses to speak exclusively in Italian and French – an affect which only serves to enhance his mystique and persona while distancing him from those outside the core.

In the late 1970s Gini Alhadeff was hired to handle the house's public relations and advertising, but was replaced by the designer's sister Rosanna in 1982 when Alhadeff left to pursue a writing career. Until the mid-1990s Rosanna directed all advertising campaigns, was head of public relations and acted as liaison between the house and the Camera della Moda (Chamber of Fashion). Under her direction many of the leading photographers of the era were employed to create what would become a highly identifiable and iconic visual culture. No one better embodies the Giorgio Armani branded imagery than Italian photographer Aldo Fallai. While numerous photographers were hired to capture the essential core of each Giorgio Armani collection, Fallai was hired for a record 34 seasons, the effect of which certainly created a homogenous, clear and identifiable image for the brand. In 1993 Peter Lindbergh assumed the mantle until 2002, though not as exclusively as had Fallai. It is long held that Armani's advertising campaigns have been nearly exclusively in black and white, seemingly better suited to his neutral colour palette. In fact, on inspection of the numerous campaigns over the course of the 35-year history of the Giorgio Armani label, one sees innumerable examples of advertisements and fashions in bold and striking colour. However, there can be no doubt that the black and white images from the mid-1980s to the mid-2000s in particular have left an indelible mark on fashion's visual landscape. Under Rosanna's direction and Armani's guiding hand all

6   Aldo Fallai. From the autumn/winter 1988 advertising campaign

advertising campaigns were and continue to be conceived and delivered in-house rather than outsourced to a second- or third-party advertising firm. The reason is a rather simple one: someone from outside 'cannot be expected to truly understand the sensibility, atmosphere and vision that [the house is] trying to convey'.[9]

Armani's campaigns have, for the most part, been 'consistent' and avoid provocation by remaining 'true to [his] values' to create what he believes to be 'elegant and positive' imagery, especially given that he sees advertising as rather 'intrusive'.[10] Campaign imagery from the late 1980s to the early 2000s resoundingly taps into a nostalgic return to the golden era of Hollywood

7   Aldo Fallai. From the spring/summer 1991 advertising campaign

(1930s and 1940s), a period which was itself characterized by its glossy black and white imagery. Armani however claims that 'it's not a love of the past... It's a search for an image that's less violent than what people normally show today – something less aggressive, less avant-garde ... I don't like what I see around me at this point. What I'm taking from the past is a sense of reassurance'.[11] Imagery resoundingly offers its viewers a sense of comfort and control, core tenets of the Armani aesthetic empire. The images often possess a cinematic quality and an air of mystery created through the mastery of fastidious detail. Unlike some houses whose focus in campaigns is ambiguous at best, displacing the object in favour of a mood or feeling alone, Armani's campaigns' focal point is unwavering attention to the atmosphere the clothing itself conjures in its surroundings. The product is placed front and centre rather than obscured by art house pretension or deflected by big name models, which the designer has mostly avoided, on the premise that it detracts from *his* core message. Celebrity photographers are also generally avoided because, according to Rosanna, Armani asserts that their photographs end up viewed by and pleasing only the elite, and limited, fashion crowd.[12] While this may well be true, Armani has never employed obscure photographers either, even if they were up and coming when he employed them. From their debut, Armani's advertisements have always printed the photographer's name on the side of the image when they appeared in magazines. However, in 2000, when Armani launched his global Giorgio Armani website, and also began to work with star photographers, their names disappeared in print ads and were replaced by the Internet address. This shift asserts the power of a monolithic brand identity over creative collaboration in a cultural climate obsessed with identifying, honing and simplifying a brand's so-called DNA, the unique components that distinguish a designer from the others within an increasingly populated and competitive fashion landscape.

By referring back in time to a specific (and consistently repeated) era and by side-stepping contemporary trends in fashion and its photography Armani not only referenced the era he loves most, but was staking a claim for the timelessness of his clothes, seemingly placing them outside of history and time itself. The pictures, after all, had to reinforce the ideal of universal style rather than localized fashion, which he portended through his main line. According to Armani the use of black and white photographs, the contrasting effect of this limited range, 'bring[s] out form', which can also 'accentuate the dramatic effects of lighting'.[13] The move must also be seen in light of a larger campaign of disdain toward the fashion system. In a now infamous collection of quotes, collectively entitled 'Armani Disarmed', the designer spoke of his distaste for 'leafing through fashion magazines that think they are promoting change or indicating new paths, that believe they are presenting the avant-garde, supporting the vacuous self-assertion of certain decidedly useless trends … the idea that every collection must break the rules clears the way for all sorts of foolishness'.[14]

In line with the advent of the new millennium, for the autumn/winter 1999–2000 campaign Armani decided to shake off his own by then staid traditional imagery and hired Ellen von Unwerth to shoot a colour-rich campaign on location in Palm Springs and Los Angeles. Von Unwerth was chosen precisely for her sense of colouration which brought an entirely new and contemporary feeling to the photographs. 'I wanted someone able to photograph my clothes', Armani noted of the sea-change, 'able to "forget" about the traditional Armani style icon. It was important to me that she give

8   Peter Lindbergh. From the autumn/winter 1993 advertising campaign

the pictures a modern attitude and not conform so much to the "the Armani style".'[15] This was followed-up by a spring/summer 2000 campaign, also shot by the edgy photographer, featuring disco-inspired scantily glad women and seductive men uncharacteristically, oddly and provocatively posed on a dance floor, a markedly radical departure for a man who once railed against the alleged 'foolishness' he witnessed in magazines and advertisements. Another hint that Giorgio Armani attempted to 'modernize' itself came when the house hired former editor-in-chief of *Dutch* magazine Matthieu Vriens as creative director. Before joining the firm Vriens had quickly gained a reputation for pushing the avant-garde magazine into uncharted territory with provocative, specially themed issues. Vriens reported directly to Armani and was charged with the house's creative studio and worldwide creative direction, a position which oversaw advertising campaigns, retail merchandising and design, packaging and special events. However, within a year Vriens resigned from his post, reportedly due to frustration over his inability to move the image of the house into edgier territory. As Lisa Armstrong from *The Times* noted, the episode 'illustrates the difficulties faced by any big fashion house wanting to tweak its image'.[16] In more recent years, Armani has also done an about face electing to work with more recognizable 'it' models for both his menswear and womenswear campaigns, as well as turning to external stylists like Katy England, best known for her work with Alexander McQueen and so-called edgier and well-known fashion photographers like Mert and Marcus (spring/summer 2010; autumn/winter 2010) and Nick Knight (spring/summer 2011).

Press and the Fashion System

As early as 1981 Armani was already openly displaying his resentment to the fashion press. In an interview with Paris-based *L'Officiel*, the designer professed to his supposed naivety of the nature of the relationship between himself as a designer and the press.

> I always thought the fruit of one's labour would be published for what it was without taking into account the pages of publicity. The idea that 'I give you this amount, and you owe me this amount' shocked me and it shocked me precisely because I am sure of my own work... What I mean to say is that in this profession there is a tension which has no relation to creativity. It has nothing to do with making beautiful clothes.[17]

According to fashion critic and Armani's unofficial biographer Renata Molho, by the late 1990s the 'days of spontaneous coverage' on the part of large and influential magazines like *Vogue* and *Harper's Bazaar* were gone and replaced with a sort of quid pro quo wherein editorial content was directly proportionate to the advertising revenues the magazine gained from each designer.[18] However, as Giacomoni asserts: 'The great upholder of the industrial project refuses to admit that he is only one wheel in it'.[19]

Gradually as Italian designers prospered in the early 1980s, so too did they gain greater control over their companies. A crucial part of this control was the power over their image through advertising and the subsequent power struggles that ensued. The Italians were the first in the 1980s to pay enormous sums for advertising with the clear expectation that in the end their clothes would feature, proportionally, in editorial content.

> For designers it is seductive, since it allows a large degree of control. At the start of each season, they can predict precisely their level of exposure, and also influence the clothes shown ... This effectively leaves the fashion editor impotent, since the pages no longer reflect her choice, only the merchandising strategy of the advertiser.[20]

By 1988, Armani was creating an average of 3,000 objects for the various labels he designed for under his and other names, making him not only an important creative force but also a vital member of the fashion advertising community, to say nothing of the impact of perfume and cologne.

Armani usually sent large 18" × 24" photographs to fashion editors expressing the mood, idea and image he wanted to articulate with the collection. These photographs, like those of his advertising campaigns, bore his mark in every way. Notorious for his micromanaging style, Armani would loom large over the photographers, leaving very little space for their own interpretive agency. The resulting demand was a way to guarantee that editors and journalists adhered to and perpetuated the combinations and styling he had fastidiously devised, which in turn reinforced the exits he presented on the runway, a fashion ideal at its purest form. However, not all editors succumbed to the pressure. Nina Hyde of the *Washington Post*, for example, used to go 'through the streets to see how women in Milan and New York carry off their Armani jackets, what kind of a pullover was beneath the jacket that the Armani look had envisaged as being next to the bare skin'.[21] The transition and tension between the street, embodied by the polyvocal consuming public, and the purity of the Armani vision will resurface throughout this book.

Competition for editorial space has become increasingly fierce, driving many designers to count the number of pages in which they and their competitors' designs appear. Perhaps not since Coco Chanel and Jean Patou (who also reportedly counted how many times his rivals appeared in leading magazines) has there been a better and more dramatic rivalry in the fashion press than the one between Armani and his compatriot Gianni Versace. There is no denying that the very public sparring matches between the two helped, at least in part, to fuel the usually fickle international press's interest and insatiable appetite for the Made in Italy phenomenon throughout the

1980s and 1990s. Apart from their clear aesthetic and design differences, each residing at the opposite ends of the Milanese fashion spectrum, they were fierce competitors over press coverage. Anna Zegna, member of the illustrious textile family, recalls how when she worked in Versace's press office from 1979 to 1982, Versace 'used to have [her] count the number of [magazine] covers Armani had and how many he had'. Press buzz was no small matter for Milanese designers. By the mid-1990s, for instance, Versace's promotional budget for special treatment to VIPs rose to a staggering $70 million.[22] Armani, on the hand, expects all licensees to funnel 5 per cent of retail sales to fund the house's advertising and public relations expenses. In addition, the house also stipulates a commission on handling the $28 million that licensees spent on marketing in 1991 alone. For most this would be an expense, not an income: not so for Giorgio Armani.[23] Typically the house's annual budget for advertising is between 4 and 5 per cent of annual sales, which in 1998, for example, reached $40 million of the $830 million in sales; however for 1999 this number rose to 7 per cent in line with sales increases in both 1997 and 1998.[24]

The highly public sparring matches between Milan's then extremes often meant that Armani did not shy away from poking fun at his rival and spending publicity money to do so. Thanks to then Armani fashion director Wilfredo Rosado,[25] the designer was put in touch with photographer and filmmaker David LaChapelle in 1996. The two settled on collaborating on a film for the Emporio Armani collection, which *The New York Times* described as both 'pointed and hilarious'. *Salvation Armani* stars Jennifer Tilley as the heroine who overcomes an assault by 'bad guys' wearing hip-hop styled clothes resplendent in Versace-like gold medallions dangling from their necks. Tilley's character is further 'assaulted' by a campy, drag send-up of Donatella (Gianni's peroxide blonde sister, muse and future designer for the house). In the end, Tilley's unfortunate character is taken charge of by six handsome, chiselled-faced models, clad in white Armani suits, which offer her salvation by way of a complete makeover. With its clear moralizing undertone, despite its tongue-in-cheekiness, the film represents Armani as fashion and by extension cultural saviour. As LaChapelle stated of the two designers' on-going feud: 'I always read about Versace saying things about Armani, like, "He's tired, he's finished, he's through". He gets vicious over there in Italy'.[26] The film nonetheless displayed a light-hearted side to a designer best known for his serious Milanese greys and beiges.

Comedy aside, publicity and advertising are big business, and in 2002 Armani unceremoniously pulled his fashion adverts from *Vogue* (USA). The tragedy, according to the designer, was the way and the infrequency his clothes appeared in the magazine's editorial spreads and reviews of runway shows. As a response to growing antagonism between the magazine's chief editor, Anna Wintour, Armani reinforced his irritation by seating her nearest to the model's exit rather than front and centre at his October show.[27] Armani's growing grumbling over the frequency – or lack thereof – with which his shows were being covered in magazines was taken up by *Daily News Record*, which reported that between May and October 2002, in 15 different men's magazines covering the collections, Armani ranked third with 65 instances of reportage, closely behind fellow compatriots Dolce and Gabbana (75) and Gucci (70).[28] Although in no way does this speak to the situation Armani felt was occurring at *Vogue*, it does show Armani's continued importance in menswear, which I suggest has been far greater in significance and long-term impact than in womenswear. It also tacitly presages the increasing competition levelled at him from a new generation of Italian designers, which blossomed in the 1990s.

9   Aldo Fallai. Hollywood glamour meets desert sands, on set in Morocco for the spring/summer 1989 advertising campaign

However, frequency has not been the only issue taken up by Armani. As a response to a negative review of his spring/summer 2005 collection in the 5 July edition of *The New York Times*, Armani pulled his advertising from the bedrock of the American periodical news. Two years later, surrounded by a vortex of negative press over his collections, Armani displayed his frustration when he snapped that

> [t]he press is never happy. If I had not sometimes taken some chances, the press would have accused me of being too steady. I am interested in what the press says, but contest it if I think it's wrong and accept it without pleasure if it's correct. In any case, I have seen some of my ideas which the press disliked, copied much later.[29]

When asked how designers respond to negative press, Cathy Horn of *The New York Times* reported that 'Armani's conduct was absolutely impeccable, and I've always felt free to say whatever I wanted.'[30] By 2008 things had clearly changed between the reporter and designer when Horn was banned from attending Armani's autumn/winter women's show. Despite having received her invitation, Robert Triefus, who took over from Rosanna as head of international communications, informed the journalist she was no longer invited to attend. The reason was that the designer felt she had made 'belittling' remarks about friends and family members in her review of his previous spring/summer Giorgio Armani Privé haute couture collection in Paris.[31] It might be worth noting that Armani, contrary to what numerous bloggers seem to believe, has not been the only designer to bar Horn from his show. Carolina Herrera, Dolce & Gabbana, Helmut Lang, Nicole Miller and Oscar de la Renta have all refused her entry to their shows at some point. There are, however, instances when editors and journalists have come to the rescue of designers. In response to one particularly 'mean-spirited' review by fashion writer Colin McDowell, chairman and editorial director of Fairchild Publications, Patrick McCarthy, who has covered the Milan shows since the late 1970s rebuked Armani's detractor by stressing that

> McDowell ignores the scope of [Armani's] continuing power, both commercially and artistically, and the fact that many of the runways in Milan and Paris, upon some of which he heaps praise, were filled with obvious references to Armani's designs ... The relevance of any designer has to be judged on whether he or she influences the way real people look. The answer, for the vast majority, is no, but in Armani's case, it is a resounding yes.[32]

Editors (like Wintour) and even journalists (like Horn), the gatekeepers of large multi-billion dollar conglomerates, benefit directly from advertising revenues, an important fact even Italian designers failed to remember in the recent attempts by Wintour to squeeze Milan fashion week into fewer days. Perhaps the fault does indeed lie with the Italian designers themselves, who notoriously decline to co-operate with each other. While the same should be said for editors and journalists, as creative, headstrong, visionary and entrepreneurial, designers ought not to feel so easily compelled to bend to the whims of one editor. Wintour's relationship with Italian designers came to a head in 2008 on the occasion of the autumn/winter 2009 Milan fashion week. The Metropolitan Museum of Art, Costume Institute's 2008 blockbuster exhibition and annual gala, *Superheroes: Fashion and Fantasy,* was co-hosted by Wintour, Armani, Julia Roberts and George Clooney and opened in May with much fanfare. However, the real drama, apart from what was worn and by whom on the red carpet, has been limited to the exhibition's press conference, which fuelled an internal yet highly public industry catfight. On 20 February 2008 in a press conference for the exhibition held during Milan's fashion week, Armani stunned the fashion press when, standing beside Wintour, claimed he did not understand why so many people disliked the editor, declaring he was simply 'indifferent' to her. Perhaps, it was thought, Armani was responding to Wintour's alleged assertion that 'the Armani era is over'. Contrary to Wintour's supposed position vis-à-vis the designer, in 2006 research company A C Nielsen reported that Armani and Gucci were listed as the top two designer labels that people would most want to buy if money wasn't an issue. The company's findings were based on a survey of 21,000 people in 42 countries. According to Deepak Varna, senior vice-president for the international company, both houses 'have consistently reinforced and updated their brand values'.[33] For the past decade or so, Wintour has been a huge advocate for the Costume Institute, to the point of exerting direct pressure on curatorial independence by placing the full force of *Vogue,* considered by many as the world's most powerful fashion magazine in terms of both influence and advertising dollars, behind the annual exhibition and gala. Although Wintour didn't speak at the media conference, the tension in the air was palpable to every journalist who reported on the event ringside. Given the theme of the exhibition, one would think Armani was channelling Batman while Wintour assumed the role of Catwoman.

Perhaps Armani's statement was also a response to the growing animosity shared by many Italian designers who were enraged by Wintour's pressure to significantly shorten Milan's fashion week from seven to four days. The request was expressed in a letter by Wintour asking the designers to be considerate of American editors who had to make their way to Milan at a time when the dollar was so weak. The demand provoked a considerable backlash. Roberto Cavalli for example told reporters backstage of his showing that: 'If we [Italian designers] pull our advertising, editors are sure to be less in a hurry to leave Milan.' Referring to Wintour, the flashy designer is reported to have dismissed her importance altogether: 'I don't need her in my front row.'[34] While the individual quips and attacks between the designers and Wintour may be passed off as merely anecdotal, it underlines the power struggles

10   The spider web dress from the spring 1990 collection, one of two Giorgio Armani dresses in the MET *Superheroes* exhibition (2008)

between editors and designers and in particular showcases the power and presence commanded from within the fashion system. In a temporary show of good faith, however, for the spring/summer 2008 season Armani resumed his advertising campaigns of the Giorgio Armani label in *Vogue*; this only lasted for the one season.

Cult(ures) of Celebrity

The first recorded international celebrity to wear Armani's clothes at an awards ceremony occurred in 1978, at the precise moment when the Italian house was hitting its stride. On the evening of 4 April 1978 Diane Keaton accepted her Academy Award for her role in Woody Allen's iconic and career-defining *Annie Hall* wearing an Armani jacket. While the designer's name would not become indelibly associated with Hollywood and the media saturated red carpet hype for another decade, the event marked a decisive moment in the growth of the house's prospects and the visibility of its womenswear in the USA. Since that fateful evening, Armani has clothed countless celebrities around the world for red carpet and special events. Following the subsequent release of *American Gigolo* in 1980, Armani reportedly stated: 'I like to create clothing for people who work, and that includes actors and actresses, inasmuch as they are people who work, and not just as stars.'[35] The designer has forged important, long-lasting friendships with celebrities, best exemplified by his relationship with Michelle Pfeiffer. More recently, Armani reminisced how since he first saw her *Scarface* (1983)

> she has become a muse, an inspiration and a loyal and dear friend. I will never forget her elegance and sophistication on the red carpet at the Academy Awards in 1990. The sleek black long-sleeved column dress she wore that night helped to usher in a new era in Hollywood dressing, where simplicity and natural beauty could be the winning combination.[36]

She, on the other hand, recalls thinking: 'Why do I want someone to dress me? I can dress myself, and who is Giorgio Armani?' Now, however, Pfeiffer refers to him as her 'soul mate' and an 'artist'. Part of the attraction for the actress is how Armani 'is versatile and flexible enough to adjust to [her] sometimes schizophrenic personality ... You don't see the whole design until it is actually on your body. So much of fashion today is unwearable'.[37] To memorialize their relationship the designer asked the actress to model for the spring 2005 Giorgio Armani advertising campaign. Pfeiffer is among a select few celebrities who have made appearances in advertisements for the designer's mainline collection. These have included Laura Hutton for the spring/summer 1981 campaign, who was herself already a model, and Kristin Scott Thomas and Olivier Martinez who were both photographed by Paolo Roversi for the spring/summer 2003 campaign.

While Armani's relationships with actresses likes Pfeiffer, Jodie Foster, Glenn Close and Julia Roberts span decades, he has come under fire in more recent years for what has come to be perceived as a pandering to the obsession with celebrity endorsements leaving some feeling cynical, or less than convinced. The point was driven home on the occasion of the controversial retrospective of Armani's work. Elsewhere I have investigated some of the criticisms and the cultural implications of the Armani exhibition; however, here I wish to single out two issues raised by the critics as a means toward outlining, in part, one of this book's ambitions.[38] Referring specifically to the weighty

11   Michelle Pfeiffer for Giorgio Armani, spring/summer 2005 advertising campaign

catalogue, one critic chastised it for 'tend[ing] toward celebrity endorsement', rather than providing readers with 'scholarly critique', a resounding criticism also levelled at the exhibition's sixth section, which displayed Armani's various Hollywood and celebrity garments.[39] The apparent lack of critical content was also vehemently taken up by critic Judith Thurman when she declared that '[t]his so-called retrospective invites you to worship Armani's virtuosity in a vacuum', a product of the decontextualization that occurred when the garments were meant to stand in as purely aesthetic objects.[40] By the twenty-first century, Armani's relationship with the celebrities who fill his front-row at his twice-annual runway shows has come under increased scrutiny by the press, leading one reporter to query: 'Why does Armani have to bother with so many celebrities at his show? Is Armani so desperate to divert attention away from his clothes? You can hardly blame Armani. This is after all the designer who has been tied to film since he dressed Richard Gere in *American Gigolo*.'[41] These critical remarks point to the ways the fashion press have bound Armani with celebrity so tightly as to obscure any attention to the clothes themselves. This has only served to reify the very relationship to celebrity they criticize. The comments are also slightly ironic given how celebrity's increased symbiotic, and perhaps at times parasitic, relationship to fashion not only helps to sell designer products and fashion magazines, but increasing newspapers and more critically respected journals like *The New Yorker* as well. Fashion and celebrity have long enjoyed a profitable and

12   The 'Hollywood Room' at the 2000 Guggenheim exhibition, in which garments worn by celebrities at red carpet events or in films were displayed

complicated relationship,[42] and if reports of Armani's front row reads like a Who's Who of the film, music and sports industries it underscores his ongoing and relentless forays beyond the fashion system and into other terrain, relationships he is not alone in profiting from.

In many ways, this book aims to rectify this and provide a much-needed investigation of a designer whose place in fashion and design history has yet to be taken up by any serious or scholarly text. In no way, however, does this book purport to be the last or definitive word on the designer and his *oeuvre*. Given that my lens remains focused on the cultural narratives that form the

13   Like the 'Hollywood Room', this final room at the Guggenheim exhibition caused controversy because it featured the designer's then current collection. Critics railed against it, claiming it suggested the spaces of the museum were merely an extension of the designer's Madison Avenue boutique

life-worlds of fashion in addition to the networks of power that facilitated Armani's expansion and success, I am less preoccupied with the notion and expressions of celebrity despite Armani's involvement with its visual culture. After all, according to many critics, the Guggenheim Museum has already provided a venue for this exploration. In large part much – at times too much – attention has been paid to the house's relationship to the cult of celebrity obscuring the designer's *oeuvres*, aesthetic ideology, contributions and the myriad facets of its material and visual culture. This is not to say celebrities will not figure or make cameo appearances in my discussions, however, their inclusion is simply to corroborate a holistic understanding of the house.

Armani/Ambassadors

Here I wish to focus on a phenomenon Armani was the first among his compatriots to tap into early on, the figure of the ambassador-muse. While there can be no doubt that Tina Turner, Sophia Loren and especially Claudia Cardinale embody the ideal woman for whom he designs, these women have never been on the payroll. Marisa Bulleghin and Gini Alhadeff were the first of these so-called Armani/Ambassadors to have an impact and play a seminal role in the aesthetic culture of the house in the early years. Armani and the blonde-haired Bulleghin met in 1975. At the time she was 32 and maintaining a successful retail career which she gave up to work for him as the 'Armani filter' as well as a 'highly trusted "assistant" who has', as Armani claimed, 'a good eye and a good sense of what women want and what will sell.' Her presence in those years was vital, often providing Armani with sound advice and knowledge of how women were living, and what they were wearing and experiencing outside of the rarefied confines of the Armani sanctuary. According to Bulleghin 'Armani hired me because I know what women want to wear. In the meantime, I've learned a lot of other things as well ... At first it was a bit of a shock to my system'. On average she would spend ten hours a day at work, with weekends spent, on occasion, at the Armani palazzo.

> The funniest part about it [reflects Bulleghin] is that I am really very rarely not at his side. We look at sketches, fabrics, toiles, everything... Giorgio would love to know everything about me – who my boyfriends are, where we go – everything ... He asks me tons of questions and teases me endlessly. He won't leave me alone. And I couldn't be happier.

Bulleghin stayed with the company until 1985.[43]

When Alhadeff joined the house in the late 1970s, Bulleghin was Armani's assistant, Adriano Giannelli was placed in charge of international marketing

14 Armani on his via Borgonuovo runway with staff in 1990; 2, Rosanna Armani; 3, Gabriella Forte; 4, Silvana Armani; 5, Leo Dell'Orco; 6, Noona Smith; 7, Dreda Mele; 8, Caterina Salvador

and Cesare Giorgino headed the menswear division, which was soon taken over by Leo Dell'Orco who today remains in charge of the menswear studio. Alhadeff provided the house with a decidedly international flair. Born in Egypt and raised in Japan, Alhadeff studied in New York at Pratt and soon after moved to Milan where she served as both muse and translator, equally important responsibilities within the Armani orbit. According to her she does 'a lot of things at Armani. I am, I suppose, the resident clown, the getter of aspirin when Giorgio has a cold, the official weirdo representative, a provider of encouragement and a travelling companion, and I rarely say "no" to his ideas' a diverse job ideally suited to a self-professed eclectic woman.[44] Despite how Armani would repeatedly shout that she was 'too cerebral',[45] she is believed to be the inspiration behind what industry insider *Women's Wear Daily* in 1980 was heralding as the 'new, witty and feminine clothes that Armani' was beginning to design. Although the niece of Italian house Krizia's founding and head designer Mariuccia Mandelli, Alhadeff's plans were never to work in fashion. According to Alhadeff, she met Armani over lunch when he asserted: 'We need someone like you'. Like Bulleghin, she proved herself to be a well of endless stimulation and outside information and quickly learned to 'understand his moods and his rhythms'. She considers what she does as not 'banal work – we experiment, we provoke ourselves – it is a thoroughly, thoroughly modern experience'.[46] When Alhadeff left Armani in the early 1980s, she turned to writing, becoming a novelist and contributing writer to magazines and journals around the world, and in 2003 published a fictional account of her years working in the Italian fashion capital. In *Diary of a Djinn*, her male protagonist, referred to as the 'master', bears an uncanny resemblance to her former employer.

> I looked at his short straight nose, the exposed nostrils like those of a calf, the blue eyes, unlipped mouth, strong stocky body. I knew that he had few friends, that he liked to eat white food such as chicken and mashed potatoes, that he always dressed in blue – blue sweatshirt and pants – and seemed impervious to fashion's ephemeral revolutions.[47]

Despite how the narrator, clearly Alhadeff herself, falls under the 'spell' of the 'master' described above, she portrays a bleak environment seeped with torment and cynicism.

> He put an eagle insignia on the glass door to the offices [a striking resemblance to the company's via Durini headquarters] and it was clear from that time on that we worked for a regime, of perfume, menswear, womenswear, sportswear – and it was only the beginning. The more money there was, the more success, and the more dissatisfied the master seemed to become. He read of other designers in the papers and envied whatever recognition they got. A lot of exposure had little to do with recognition and everything to do with money. The partner took fees the master got for designing other companies' collections,

gave the master and himself a small stipend and invested the rest in four-to-eight page ads in fashion magazines. It was a flaunting Milan had not seen before and soon copied.[48]

If we take the novel at face value, Alhadeff's characterization of the 'master' might well prove to be Armani himself in light of his equivocal relationship with the press, let alone the numerous less than subtle material details she includes. Her choice of title for her protagonist alludes to the 'master's' controlling ways, but also conjures a man with wisdom to impart, charting new territory for Italian industry, part of the so-called miracle. The title may also, at least obliquely, refer to his common nickname in the industry, 'Milan's Master Tailor'. Although she has denied 'the master' is Armani, claiming that the character 'is a combination of people',[49] in these excerpts, amongst numerous others, which swerve uncomfortably between fact and fiction, Alhadeff is trading on the mystique cultivated around the designer in the early years of the house.

As a way to engage with the American consuming public, where his mystique was reaching epic proportions, Armani hired Jacqueline Kennedy's sister Lee Radziwill in 1986 as supervisor of special events, the realization of a dream Galeotti had before his death. Radziwill had been wearing Armani

15   Mafalda von Hesse, Cate Blanchett, Giorgio Armani, Claudia Cardinale, Elsa Pataky, Megan Fox and Kasia Smutniak attend the Giorgio Armani Privé haute couture autumn/winter 2009 fashion show in Paris

for the past seven years, which she purchased at Bergdorf Goodman in New York, and in the early 1980s Armani invited her to attend his runway presentations. She quickly became a regular fixture at Armani-sponsored events, leading to her role as the first woman to truly, officially assume the position of ambassador. In her new position Radziwill confessed publicly: 'I rarely wear anything but Armani … And that's the way it has been for seven years. Once you get used to Armani you really don't like wearing anything else. It simplifies life enormously. I feel particularly at ease in his clothes.'[50] With her connections, social graces and legendary status, Radziwill helped to increase Armani's social and cultural presence in the USA, hosting numerous special events and parties on his behalf.

While no man has assumed the privileged role of paid Armani ambassador, Pat Riley became the first living testimonial for the house, one of many men he has collaborated with in various forms from within the physically demanding world of sports. As head coach for the Los Angeles Lakers from 1981 to 1990, Riley was a highly visible and flamboyant personality in his own right. Widely credited with raising the awareness on the part of coaches and numerous players to concern themselves with clothing and personal grooming, his relationship with Armani was not simply one of endorsement but of friendship and admiration, so much so that Riley has accepted awards on his behalf. Regardless of the friendship, reports indicate that Riley and his wife Chris receive Giorgio Armani clothing valued at $125,000 (at retail) a year.[51] It is no surprise that Riley contends it takes him two minutes each morning to select his clothes for the day, given that 80 per cent of his closet was stocked with items from the designer's collection. While Spanish bullfighter Cayetano Rivera,[52] Italian actor Raoul Bova, American actor Samuel L. Jackson and Ukrainian footballer Andriy Shevchenko have paraded down Armani's runway in Milan or have appeared in special advertising campaigns, no other man has benefitted from such an explicitly commercial and long-lasting relationship as Riley.

Gender clearly plays a significant part in the role these ambassadors enact in what is ostensibly an alternative theatrical venue for the performances of fashion. Despite how menswear is so pivotal to Armani's global success, Armani's move to deploy a female aggregate as ambassadors speaks to the overall importance placed on and the impact of womenswear in the industry and to the designer's subsequent desire to proselytize his aesthetic message through strategically placed women. The fact that Armani has elected to work almost exclusively with women speaks to the importance of womenswear within the industry, but also alludes to a gender notion of the art of social hostess and cultural doyenne, roles largely assumed by women over the past century. In 2004, Armani moved to make his female ambassadors a decidedly more official and prominent facet of his public relations throughout Europe. Spanish model Eugenia Silva joined Lady Helen Taylor, Princess Mafalda von

Hessen, the designer's niece Roberta Armani, Celine Charloux, Jamie Tisch and Princess Alexandra of Greece became 'world ambassadors' functioning as walking embodiments of the Armani aesthetic ideal, living out the Armani lifestyle within the public eye. As part of his initiative, Armani also planned to contribute more to these women's various charities: 'It's about becoming a part of local communities'.[53] Of her new role, Silva stated that

> Armani is very big in Spain, and the press is really proud that I've become an ambassador ... This job is a challenge, because Armani is not necessarily known for his young image. But I think you can be young and fashionable in Armani – and there are so many different ways of wearing the collections.[54]

These ambassadors attenuate the social and cultural cachet of the designer, and translate his more abstract ideals and lifestyle propositions into an embodied performance on various local and regional stages. Through them the global and the local collude.

16   Roberta Armani and famed Spanish bullfighter Cayetano Rivera Ordóñez walked the runway as the last exits of the Giorgio Armani men's autumn/winter 2007 collection

Lady Helen Taylor claims responsibility for the designer's move. The daughter of the Duke and Duchess of Kent, Taylor became an Armani ambassador to the UK in 2000, although her devotion to the designer goes back to 1992 when he designed her wedding dress. Since then she has continued to wear his clothes. Her association with the designer was heavily surveyed in the British press, when in 1994, for example, *The Times* reported how when Taylor stepped out twice in a week for separate public functions sporting a lace skullcap, the designer's Sloane Street boutique sold out of them immediately.[55] According to the designer: 'Helen is the personification of modern elegance: Natural, charming and thoroughly captivating. She has always enjoyed my fashion philosophy, and I have always greatly enjoyed her company'.[56] Taylor has since become an important member of Armani's international entourage accompanying him on trips to various locations, most notably on his 2004 tour of China, when actress Mira Sorvino also accompanied the designer. 'I'd like the collaboration to continue', Taylor claimed. 'I've developed a great personal

17   The New Man in leather trousers. Aldo Fallai. From the autumn/winter 1980 advertising campaign

relationship with Armani, and I want to work hard for him. He commands so much respect, and seeing the way he works is very inspirational'.[57] Their formal relationship ended, however, in 2009 when the designer cut what were seen to be extraneous costs as a result of the global economic crisis.

However, perhaps no one within the current Armani stable best embodies and works harder within the public eye for Armani than his niece Roberta who, in 2004, became director of international VIP relations whose job it is to ensure A-list celebrities wear Armani at events, herself since becoming a highly photographed woman. Daughter to Armani's older brother Sergio, Roberta began working for the company in the first Emporio Armani boutique in the USA, located in Lower Manhattan. She soon realized the mystique hovering around her uncle when at work shoppers would go up to her and want to touch her once they heard her last name. According to Roberta: 'It was the first time I realised, "My God, I have a very important heritage to live up to".'[58] She returned to Milan where she served as an intern in the house and soon became a key member of staff when she assumed the role of public liaison. The relationships she has forged with celebrities run deep and have become crucial to the public face of the house. In 2006, Roberta took over the planning of the Tom Cruise and Katie Holmes wedding two weeks before the nuptials, relocating the event to Castello Odescalchi, a dramatic, medieval castle located just outside Rome. While rumours of Giorgio Armani's future fill countless pages of magazines and newsprint, there is no doubt that Roberta has been groomed to take on a formidable role in the future, and the attention to detail she exhibited at the Cruise–Holmes wedding will surely put her in good stead for her inevitable future role within Armani's ever-expanding theatre of fashion.

Notes

1   *Newsweek* 3 September 2001.

2   *Time* 18 December 2000.

3   Foucault 1998b: 211.

4   Foucault 1998b: 209.

5   Freud 1985.

6   Giacomoni 1984: 21.

7   Armani in Molho 2007: 147.

8   *W* 28 August–4 September 1981.

9   *WWD* 31 January 2005.

10   *WWD* 31 January 2005.

11   Brantley 1988: 172–3.

12   'In the court of Armani' 1994: 150.

13   'Armani Disarmed' 1995: viii.

14   'Armani Disarmed' 1995: vii.

15   *WWD* 18 June 1999.

16   *The Times* 13 December 1999.

17   Fallaci 1981: 176. Translation author's.

18   Molho 2007: 187.

19   Giacomoni 1984: 21.

20   *TS* 4 April 1988.

21   Giacomoni 1984: 133.

22   Ball 2010: 310.

23   *Forbes* 28 October 1991.

24   *WWD* 18 June 1999.

25   Rosado has since left Giorgio Armani to pursue a career as a luxury jewellery artist.

26   *NYT* 15 September 1996.

27   *WWD* 5 November 2002.

28   *DNR* 23 December 2002.

29   *WWD* 6 November 2007.

30   *NYT* 5 February 2007.

31   *NYT* 18 February 2008.

32   *The Times* 2 December 2001.

33   *TS* 21 February 2006.

34   Cavalli in *New York* 21 February 2008.

35   Armani in Molho 2007: 79.

36   *Armani Press Release* 12 January 2004.

37   *The Times* 22 January 2005.

38   For more on the exhibition see Potvin 2011; Potvin and Gindt 2013.

39   Heartney 2001: 62.

40   *The New Yorker* 6 November 2000.

41   *Independent* 29 June 2001.

42   For a more recent discussion of the relationship between fashion and celebrity culture see Gibson 2012.

43   *WWD* 18 January 1980.

44   *WWD* 18 January 1980.

45   *NYT* 25 August 1985.

46   *WWD* 18 Jan 1980.

47   Alhadeff 2004: 15.

48   Alhadeff 2004: 64.

49   *NYT* 29 December 2002.

50   *TS* 17 September 1997.

51   *DNR* 17 December 1997.

52   Rivera is the great-grandson of Dominguin whom Pablo Picasso based his tauromaquia paintings on. For generations his entire family were renowned bullfighters in Spain and in 2008, surrounding much controversy instigated by animal rights activists, Armani designed Rivera's *Goyesco* (bullfighting outfit).

53   Comita 2004: 78.

54   Comita 2004: 78.

55   *The Times* 19 July 1994.

56   Clifton-Mogg 2006: 36.

57   Comita 2004: 78.

58   *The Telegraph* 31 August 2010.

2

Armani/America: Haptic Pleasures

In 1992 Armani was bestowed the prestigious Fiornio d'Oro award by then mayor of Florence Giorgio Morales. The award recognized the designer's significant contributions to the Made in Italy label globally. The success of the label in the 1970s and 1980s, when it gained considerable currency and cultural capital, has been to translate a celebrated and respected centuries-old tradition of textile manufacturing into a marketable, iconic fashion image to such an extent that visual image has superseded material object. Much has been made of Armani's involvement with American and European cinema and the ensuing proliferation of the red carpet moment as symptom of the cult of celebrity, both of which have been instrumental in the perpetuation of the Made in Italy image. Since Armani's clothes made their filmic debut in the now iconic *American Gigolo* in 1980, the designer has collaborated on countless films. So, it should come as no surprise that the organizing committee for Hollywood's Rodeo Drive Style Walk of Fame Award elected Armani as its first recipient in 2003. On the occasion of the presentation Jodie Foster recounted to a full audience of Hollywood elite her first personal fitting with Armani, likening it to 'being painted by Picasso, or directed by Visconti, in other words it was working with a master'. Harrison Ford, on the other hand, stated that Armani is now a part of everyday language, while devotee Samuel L. Jackson claimed that '[t]he man made [him] look good in purple velvet' referring to the designer as both fearless and a genius.[1] This chapter focuses its lens on the first decade of Armani's long and impressive relationship with the USA through the intersecting textures of the filmic surface and the narratological potential of textiles. This period, approximately marked out between 1978 and 1988, evinces a pivotal moment in the development of Armani's own history and that of his relationship with what has long been his most important market, North America. Bearing in mind that texture, text and textiles share a common etymological origin in Latin (*textere*: to weave), I wish to explore how both the aesthetic and commercial disciplines of fashion and film attempt to construct three-dimensional life-worlds through two-dimensional surfaces elicited by virtual haptic and optical involvement on the part of the spectator.

Surface is not meant to conjure a superficial lack of depth purportedly endemic to the postmodern condition. Rather, it refers here to the deep and meaningful inscriptive surfaces both textiles and the filmic screen extend. Like Anne Hollander, I too wish to suggest that 'dressing is an act usually undertaken with reference to pictures – mental pictures which are personally edited versions of actual ones. The style in which the image of the clothed figure is rendered … governs the way we create and perceive our own clothed selves'.[2] Textiles, I assert, provide the material of and for narrative itself, and hence identification both with on-screen characters as well as the narrative discursively attributed to Giorgio Armani's branded identity and early success. Armani resonated with a global audience in those earlier years he appeared on the fashionable landscape precisely because he managed to move from an Italian idiom premised on craftsmanship and textiles to an American language premised on the surface images that a medium like cinema provides for.

In addition, I also wish to expose how Armani's menswear was the leading protagonist of two, eventual intertextual narratives: first, the development of a notional Italian Look (a look distinct from Paris and New York) which in turn propelled the global phenomenon of the Made in Italy label to new heights; and second, the challenges and crisis faced by masculinity in a period characterized by on the one hand gender trouble and on the other greed, excess and a steady rise in the consumerist ethos which saw the emergence of a softer, caring and self-expressive New Man as *the* preferred male consumer identity in the English-speaking West; an identity precipitated by advertisers and marketers and manifested specifically through fashion.[3] With the emergence of Italy as a leader in sportswear coupled with the designer's involvement with textile development and his much-cited involvement with *American Gigolo* (1980), Armani showed himself to be an astute and agile translator across space, place and surface. The designer mobilized film not simply as a marketing tool, though a clearly successful strategy, but also deployed textiles within the filmic visual text to elicit a 'haptic visuality', that is, an alternative form of surface reading I see as endemic to his success.

Translating the Italian Look, Armani Style

As I outlined in the previous chapter, an act of translation insinuates, among other things, a movement from one place, space or situation to another as well as a migration of meaning from one (form of) language to another. As Benjamin suggests, in the act of translation 'the mother tongue of the translator is transformed as well. While a poet's words endure in his own language even the greatest translation is destined to become part of the growth of its own language and eventually to be absorbed by its renewal'.[4] Through fashion, Italians in the 1970s '"lost their accent", and in the process they transformed their image from the most proficient manufacturers of textiles and fashion goods which bore the prestigious Made in Italy label, but translated their talents to construe an idiomatic Italian Look'.[5] These idiomatic expressions, visual as much as sartorial, clearly required translation across international markets. The implication of the affect of translation on the mother tongue is that the desire for Armani to achieve recognition and success within an American audience effectively transforms the very nature of the implied Italian-ness of his aesthetic, one born from within a national design ethos that since the Second World had been inspired by Hollywood glamour. In her extensive investigation of the emergence and culture of the Italian Look, Silvia Giacomoni suggests that consumers buy into and purchase an Italian fashion object 'on the basis of the overall image they want to give themselves [and that] for the public at large, the general idea of Italy is connected with images: of art, of the cinema, of design and now of fashion'. She asserts that

> Italian fashion designers won the world over when they came up with clothes that could underline men's physical, economic, intellectual and social power … In general terms it is reasonable to say that in the second half of the seventies the Italian Look offered images that corresponded to social evolution.[6]

The Italian Look is a rather ambiguous term, however, Giacomoni describes it as 'proteiform', while American publisher John Fairchild dismisses it altogether, arguing for global rather than national styles.[7] In my use of the term here, I side more in favour of Giacomoni's definition, for the look offers an ever-changing and ephemeral Italian quality. While it may change over the years and decades, it does, nevertheless, seem to point to a distinctly Italian combination of traditional tailoring, regional textiles and a search for luxurious comfort, a combination distinct from other Western fashionable clothing. It also weds industrial knowledge, traditional craftsmanship and creative ingenuity more effectively.

Nicola White has shown how in the two decades immediately following the Second World War, Italian fashion had already made significant inroads internationally, namely and specifically in the USA, largely through American cultural and economic involvement in Italy.[8] Prior to the emergence in the late 1970s of the visual and material cultures associated with the Italian Look, Italy had already refashioned its national identity, in large part through American interests in the textile industry and fashion sector. In short, the USA and Italy had already entered into a cultural and economic symbiosis long before Armani designed the wardrobe for *American Gigolo*. However well documented and well-argued White's research has proven to be, it limits its purview to womenswear alone. I wish to expose how, at least in terms of menswear, a cohesive Italian fashion system with global impact did not occur until the mid to late 1970s, again, in large measure thanks to American interests and imports. In part, what contributed to the impact of Italian fashion in the USA in the latter half of the decade was how accessories and fashion were visually and discursively brought together under the neologism of the Italian Look, a marketable global concept. According to *The New York Times*, while the Italian Look had caused quite a sensation in Europe by 1979, and even to some extent in the USA, it had not yet made a substantial impact on American retail sales. This new aesthetic impulse was nonetheless being adapted – or translated – by a number of then influential American designers, such as Bill Kaiserman and Lee Wright among others.[9] By September 1979, realizing the future potential impact and inevitable success of the new Italian designers, Bloomingdale's in New York played host to *Bavura d'Italia*, an event to celebrate and generate interest in Italian fashion at which some of that country's key designers propelling the decisive new look were featured and were even in attendance, including Fendi, Missoni, Versace and Armani (the latter markedly absent due to illness). Surely, at least in part, as a response to initiatives such as those by Bloomingdale's and the growing cultural currency of the Italian Look, it is significant to note that in the same year Armani founded Giorgio Armani Men's Wear USA as a way to make inroads mainly into the American (male) buying public, which he had up to that point failed to achieve.

Heralded as a revolution, Armani's first men's collection for spring/summer 1976 not only stripped the jacket of its moribund and stiff associations, making it sexy and desirable again, but also marshalled an entire new way of dressing for men. Armani moved the buttons of his unlined jacket down, the lapels were given a lower notch, the shoulders were sloped, its inner structure symbolically and materially disembowelled. In the infamous *Time* cover story from 1982, film scriptwriter, journalist and eventual collector of Armani garments, Jay Cocks conjures Fred Astaire's legendary way of breaking in a new jacket by throwing it against the wall until it yielded to its toe-tapping owner. According to Cocks, what Armani did was to 'translate this same energy and desire' to make the clothes appear, through cut and textiles, to have already been lived in.[10] When Barney's introduced Armani into its store in New York and subsequently to Americans, the store's president Fred Pressman was charged by manufacturers with 'trying to ruin the industry, [by] promoting wrinkles'. According to him 'they didn't see the collection in terms of lifestyle, only some kind of fashion statement, or misstatement. They couldn't understand why people would want things wrinkled like that or draped like that'.[11] Pressman secured the exclusive rights to sell the Giorgio Armani collection for $10,000 a season, which by contemporary standards was an impressive amount for a fledgling designer. Within two years of introducing the label, Barney's was selling $400,000 a year worth of both the men's and women's collections.[12]

In his discussion of Baroque art Gilles Deleuze has theorized how the fold (whether of fabric, space or subjectivity) produces a forward-moving energy, dynamism and vitality. Like the wrinkles and creases misunderstood and feared by the American press and retailers, the Deleuzian fold provides a means to think through subject-actualization in a new way. The fold does not presume a difference between interiority and exteriority – or between appearance and essence – rather it is suggestive of how the inside is nothing but a fold of the outside, or what Deleuze calls 'forces of the outside'.[13] During the golden age of Hollywood cinema, the costumes worn by leading male actors were seamlessly folded into their identity on and off the celluloid screen. Numerous examples illustrate this symbiosis. From the authority maintained by Robert Montgomery's elegant dinner jackets to James Cagney's meaningful and compact gangster suits to debonair William Powell in plaid, these men conveyed a clear-cut image and an identity constructed, maintained and perpetuated by the film studios themselves. Reading the old adage *you are what you wear* through Deleuze's notion of the fold might have new resonance when one considers the protean masculine ideal and identity emerging at the end of the 1970s. Subjectivity and identity, like the fold itself, is created at a point in time. Outward appearance, then, can suggest a folding into one's self, where one's public exterior is folded into and reveals the interiority, that is, one's supposed private self. 'Giorgio Armani's style, though unspectacular, is distinctive, and the "Armani look" has an eponymous identity which transcends the designer's own creations and has become a byword for a certain type of man'.[14] The folds, so feared by Americans who coined his look 'Sloppy Chic', were the product of the natural fibres of linen, cotton and silk that lent the appearance of being 'schlepped in' and whose 'distinction may at times be more in the eye of the wearer that the beholder'. Regardless of the beholder, these suits embodied the so-called Italian Look. The creases and wrinkles re-emphasize the effect of movement and the body on fabric, for rather than denying these effects, Armani reinforces them. A more permanent press image for the ideal male of the day stood in as a protective armour in a cultural atmosphere in which creases and wrinkles materialized masculine immorality and denial of social cohesion. According to *Time*, Armani was to be given the dubious honour of 'the greatest evangelist of male unkempt'.[15] Noting the designer's popularity in the USA, the magazine reveals how the look is endemic to the way men were functioning culturally and socially.

From an entirely different vantage point, *Vogue* likewise declared that 'the whole world shops Italy for fabrics'. The biggest news for fabrics in 1978, according to the bible of the fashionable American woman, was 'texture. Interesting, appealing-to-the-eye-and-hand textures. Texture that gives modern fabric its character.'[16] According to David Tessler, owner of San Francisco's City Island Dry Goods Co. boutique, '[p]eople today are willing to be comfortable, both physically and socially ... They have no use for constraints

18   Spring/summer 1979. Inspired by the golden age of debonair film stars, Armani's new film-star look was based on his fascination with the classic images and identities of Hollywood masculinity. This suit lends a broad V-shape to the male physique; the trousers are deeply pleated

or formality'. Geraldine Stutz, president of Manhattan's Henri Bendel, also saw the crumpled look as 'the ultimate declaration of independence, the last statement of revolt against fashion dictatorship'.[17] However these folds and wrinkles that many in the industry disliked, would become the stuff of show business and the material success of Armani and the Italian textile industry. Armani's initiatives between 1978 and 1980 must also be folded into the moment when the Made in Italy phenomenon was riding high off the coat-tale of the swelling Italian economy and its increasingly favourable global position.

For many in the American menswear industry Armani's gesture for his first season was a radical enough revolution and many suggested, and quite correctly, that American men would need time to take to the new silhouette. Armani was himself unsatisfied however, and between 1978 and the 1980 seasons the designer introduced two imbricated yet ostensibly separate sartorial and corporate initiatives. First, he helped to usher in anew the male peacock, which, as women had done for some time, wanted to embrace fashion's latest propositions at a voracious pace, or at least twice a year. To this end, Armani penned a new sartorial gesture for men known as 'Armani slouch' for autumn/winter 1978, a season in which he took inspiration from American actors from the 1930s and 1940s, namely Cary Grant and Gregory Peck. This was then quickly changed for the 1979 seasons when he fashioned a much narrower cut. According to *Los Angeles Times* fashion reporter Timothy Hawkins, '[j]ust when the American consumer is beginning to understand the new narrowed-down proportions … generally fathered by Armani, the designer is widening his fall horizons for 1980'.[18] While the designer claimed his customers wanted something new, speculation was that this final shift in silhouette hinted at the introduction of his new diffusion line, commonly referred to as the 'white label', (to be discussed later) due to make its debut in the USA. The widening of the silhouette, it was anticipated, would be more in keeping with how American men wore their suits; after all, the American consumer did not wholeheartedly support the previously narrower silhouette. For retailer Larry Chrysler, however, the shift from narrow to a more full cut was too fast for men to accept, and would threaten American manufacturing. He suggested that '[m]en won't accept their wardrobe becoming obsolete every few months … It's not healthy for the menswear industry'.[19] Armani himself acknowledged that his changes were received with a 'very strong reaction' by the American press and buyers. According to the designer he had only changed the silhouette twice in four years, including the purported present fiasco. Asserting his nationality and obliquely reifying the newly coined Italian Look, Armani defiantly claimed that what he designs is 'pure Italian', even if it 'creates a stir and controversy in certain foreign markets', tacitly referring to his American detractors.[20] However, according to one American report, the move was even too fast for the Italians. As one store owner in Bologna decried: 'This is crazy. I can't keep up'.[21] What industry insiders did agree on was that Armani's new move was certainly directional, ahead of its time and that manufactures were already always following his lead. Looking back on that fateful period Bill Flink, vice-president of men's retailer Hickey-Freeman insists that '[t]he whole world was changed by Giorgio Armani in 1979 ... He revolutionized clothing by making suits bigger, easier, more comfortable and fluid. Every manufacturer got the message – even traditional people.'[22]

The second and crucial initiative from this short period was that the designer was among the very first to realize the potential of niche marketing through the creation of lower-priced diffusion collections, and created, as previously mentioned, what would commonly be referred to as his 'white label', today labelled Armani Collezioni.[23] The strategy was a means to captivate a broader spectrum of the middle-class, North American audience. The new enterprise

19   Autumn/winter 1979

was to compete with American retailers and producers who, according to Giorgio Armani sales director Andriano Gianelli, were 'cheaply copying the Armani style'. As a result, the Italian fashion house 'wanted to make them have to compete with the original'.[24] The diffusion line made its initial debut in Milan in 1978 and was then marketed strategically in the USA under the directional auspices of the newly inaugurated Giorgio Armani Men's Wear Corporation where Armani's fiercest protector and right hand, Gabriella Forte, joined the company. According to many, it was Forte who laid 'down the Armani law to the outside world'.[25]

Given that parts of the collection were produced by Gruppo Finanzario Tessile (GFT) in Hong Kong for the American and Canadian markets, many of the hand-made elements of the Giorgio Armani collection as well as the impeccable choice in fabrics were reigned in. The use of natural fibres, such as cotton and linen, continued to play a vital and distinctive role in the new line; these were textiles, which importantly retained perceptible textures. From its inception the 'white label' line was sold in department stores that could house it in a separate in-store boutique, removed and distinct from its competitors under the same roof. The collection targeted men between 25 and 50, particularly those who had already purchased designer menswear. The creation of this line speaks to Armani's desire to expand his influence within the highly lucrative American market, conscious of the fact that while he had received high praise and numerous accolades since his debut under his own name, his access to the American customer was still rather limited.

Despite its more commercial trajectory, ticketed at half the price of the Giorgio Armani collection, the diffusion line was to retain many of the features which were said to distinguish Armani: 'very classic, elegant, relaxed and truly Italian'.[26] Following along from Benjamin, 'the great motif of integrating many tongues into one true language is at work' here in this comingling of creative sources.[27] It is with this collection that Italy meets the USA, where commerce meets pure aesthetics and wherein the narrative potential of the translation begins to unfold. Benjamin once asked: 'Is a translation meant for readers who do not understand the original?'[28] Edward Glantz, formerly of Barney's New York and who joined the Giorgio Armani USA team as product-development coordinator, states that his role is to

'translate' some Armani designs into wearable clothes for the American man. [Giorgio Armani USA assured its buyers that] there will be no loss in the translation: 'Giorgio is a fashion designer ... we will faithfully translate what he creates for our American customers'. What the translating will entail is hard to tell, but it will probably involve some substitution of fabric and a tendency to smooth out a bit of the Armani rumple to suit the more permanent-press American sensibility.[29]

Underlying Glantz's discussion of the new label and following on from Benjamin's incisive query, American men had yet to clearly understand the so-called original or authentic Giorgio Armani label. As I will discuss in the following section, this translation occurred across both nationality and medium, as the line made its spectacular debut in *American Gigolo*, for which Armani designed a 40-piece wardrobe for John Travolta who was originally to play the title role. Importantly, the clothes in the film are 'identical' to those in the new line, which is 'significant' according to Arnold Fishbein, then president of the American operation.

The increase in changes to the clothed male contours along with the creation of this diffusion line also helped to incite men to think more concertedly about how they dressed and shopped. In a feature article on the designer in 1979 *Esquire* confirms my assertion of Armani's desire to accelerate the pace of the men's fashion system: Armani 'wants men to like new clothes … The result of his 1975 revolution in menswear was that he proclaimed to the world that the wearer was in the business of enjoying himself, that his affairs, however lucrative they might be, were not high-serious, or formal, or stately.'[30] Sex and Armani are often not words one would associate with each other today. However, early on in his career Armani made clear what his goal was for menswear when he unilaterally declared: 'I wanted men's jackets to be sexy … I wanted to change the look of men. It has taken 10 years and four of them were spent working on fabrics.'[31] It was while working at Cerruti that he cut his teeth and contrived what would become his iconic and revolutionary unstructured, unlined men's jacket. What Armani achieved in turn in his own dramatic fashion was to beat the jacket into submission, to force it to adhere to the particularities of the body, to its contours, to its natural movement, allowing the body to breathe, loosen up and reveal itself a little more. Already by 1982 Armani had introduced jackets that fit more intimately like a cardigan or shirt for the GFT-produced line. 'Armani's unstructured

20   The evolution of Giorgio Armani collection labels through time. From top to bottom: 1, first Giorgio Armani collection label; 2, first diffusion line 'white label' introduced in Milan in 1978 and the USA in 1979–1980 and produced by GFT; 2 to 5, the gradual evolution of the Giorgio Armani black label collection since the designer moved his design atelier from the company's inaugural headquarters in via Durini to via Borgonuovo

look makes even his English wool suits feel as comfortable as silk pyjamas. "He has changed the whole concept of menswear in the '70s," says designer Bill Blass, while Pierre Cardin credits Armani with "worldwide impact"'.[32]

21   Unconstructed, unpadded and unlined blue linen jacket; white linen trousers
from the spring/summer 1979 collection

To celebrate and expand his increasing success in the USA, Armani was
invited to New York by his newly acquired retail friends and growing legion
of devotees. At the time of his trip *The New York Times* declared that Armani
'still has the feel for what young American men like to wear', despite, the
author noted, his grey hair.[33] If ever there was a moment when Armani defied
what his grey hair signified it was on that trip to New York in September 1980.
To begin his first major visit to the city, he staged a large-scale, open to the
public, runway presentation of his men's and women's collections silhouetted
by the famed statue of Prometheus on the Rockefeller Center grounds just off

Fifth Avenue. The event was hosted by Bergdorf Goodman, and also served as a benefit for the Film Preservation Society at the Museum of Modern Art and George Eastman House, though these organizations were clearly not the main attractions or the topic of discussion. Lauren Hutton arrived wearing an Armani pantsuit topped off with a baseball cap – an image numerously reproduced by the press. Of the event's overwhelming success, Dawn Mello of Bergdorf commented: 'Leave it to Giorgio to bring out a crowd like this ... Look how he handles mink. For him it's just another fabric. He is a total, uncompromising perfectionist'.[34] Carlo Rivetti of the eponymous family-based GFT also recalls his own trip to the USA for Armani's first showing in New York:

> The show was at seven in the evening, as I said, but there was already a line at six. And there's nothing like a line to attract more people, curious about what's happening. We expected four hundred people, but there were four thousand. This was truly the birth of what the Italians call 'Il Made in Italy'. No one expected it ... There were no strategies, no planning, only the power of this one man.[35]

The event was followed by an intimate dinner for 40 hosted by Giorgio Deluca of the Dean & Deluca gourmet food emporium. In addition, another smaller runway presentation of the collections was held at Saks Fifth Avenue in honour of and benefit to the NYC Ballet, where a photographic retrospective of Armani's work since 1976 was also exhibited while 15 male models (some of the ballet's own dancers) showed off his designs. To top off his whirlwind trip, Armani invited 400 guests to celebrate at Studio 54. The night's theme was a Viennese Waltz, in which the iconic nightclub was 'transformed with crystal chandeliers, white slip-covers and 20 violinists in white tie'. The discotheque under Armani's direction was redesigned into a ballet stage with the dancers of the Trockadero ballet (all transvestites) performing Tchaikovsky's *Swan Lake*, followed by the *Nutcracker Suite* which soon segued into disco tunes. Such a juxtaposition, one of many odd assemblages, showed Armani's humour and modernity, but also as Molho points out in her biography, it 'modernized the image of Italy'.[36] Armani would later declare that 'New York is the only city in the world. It defines the idea of what a city is.'[37] Of Armani's New York extravaganza and design acumen, *The New York Times* concluded:

> While Armani clearly has the authority to effect a dramatic fashion change, this does not seem to be his aim. He is, at the moment, basing his appeal on such elements as style and taste. It is a far more enduring approach. At 45, he has a sense of control. He wants men to look and feel at ease in their clothes, not pompous or stuffy.[38]

By October 1981, *Women's Wear Daily* had affectionately dubbed him Gorgeous Giorgio, as a result of a second important USA trip for the designer. This time, the four-day trip was to California, and included stops in Beverly Hills and San Francisco. As in New York, the goal was to win over customers and visit important retail outlets like I. Magnin, which had just opened the largest Giorgio Armani in-shop boutique in the USA. In San Francisco he replicated a small-scale showing of his runway collection for 2,000 guests, while in Los Angeles he staged a more intimate though similar showing for 700 VIPs. Staged at the Dorothy Chandler Pavilion at the Music Center (LA), proceeds from the $50 a head tickets went to support the local public television station KCET. Armani, the consummate perfectionist, was dissatisfied with the results, however, declaring that the 'room was too big for this kind of show'.[39] These visits were meant as diplomatic missions on the part of the designer to foster a closer relationship with retailers and customers at a moment when the Italian Look was set to take over from traditional Parisian chic.

American Gigolo and the Textures of Film

> What Hollywood designs today, you will be wearing tomorrow.
>
> Elsa Schiaparelli

> But they [Armani's creations] were also part of a fantasy image that transcended any single film. The clothes had become, indelibly, a part of the actor's mystique – perhaps the only part that was imitable.
>
> Jay Cocks

The two parallel and colliding creative initiatives orchestrated by Armani in the late 1970s previously outlined made their debut on 1 February 1980 with the release of Paul Schrader's *American Gigolo*,[40] for which Armani designed the wardrobe for the lead character of Julian Kay played by Richard Gere. The story's protagonist is well-toned, speaks five or six languages, is familiar with the best restaurants and bars in Southern California and most importantly knows how to bring a woman to orgasm that hasn't experienced one in over ten years. What marks Gere's character as suspect is that he assumes a traditionally female role as sex worker, is exposed as a sex object left vulnerable to a scopophilic gaze, is fetishistically associated with fashion, is feminized consistently throughout the film by his power brokers, that is, his pimps who refer to him as Julie, and finally that throughout the film and certainly in the quiet, unassuming climax, Julian is in constant need of support and assistance, turning to women and an African-American pimp, themselves marginalized by society and the media. As a male protagonist Kay is consumed as much as he consumes, a sexy embodiment of the New Man.

In the first scene immediately following the introductory credits, through which we recognize his materialistic and sensualist existence, Julian is working out, a subtle yet effective reminder of the traditional phallic male body powered by American cinema. However, Gere's character is denied full power. Not only he is dependent on a woman to save him from his wretched condition, the movie also marks the first time a Hollywood actor was seen in full frontal nudity in a film. Together these aspects only served to emasculate the lead character, removing his phallic presence and traditional male power. From the film's opening credits when we see Julian driving his black convertible Mercedes, followed by being bought tight-fitting Italian suits by one of numerous female patrons to the iconic scene in which we witness the pleasurable ritual a shirtless Julian performs in the selection of his jacket, shirt and tie, we realize the materiality and materialism through which he celebrates his life and supports his lucrative career. As a film, I suggest, American Gigolo has lost any cinematic relevance it might have once possessed, but it is the fashion coupled with Gere's alluring performance in the clothes, themselves protagonists, which have marked it as a significant film for fashion history. What is important, as previously mentioned, is that the clothes featured in the film are 'identical' to those of the new so-called 'white label' line making its debut in the USA at that time. For this film, Armani's selections from the American-destined line were not nostalgic in any way, but very much of the moment, directional, sexy and slightly less Italian and a little more Americano. Menswear designer Glenn Laiken (recently made famous for his seven-year collaboration with television pop psych guru Dr Phil McGraw) made his own career debut on American Gigolo and was reportedly commissioned to 'modify' Armani's designs to better suit an American male audience.[41]

According the Giovanna Grignaffini, the USA had already become familiar with Armani by the time of American Gigolo, and as a result, the signifying potential of the clothing in the movie was apprehended through their verisimilitude. In her work on the relationship between Italian fashion and cinema since the 1950s Grignaffini maintains that Armani's fashions in films used early in his career did

> not just represent themselves as items of 'designer clothing' but simultaneously a realm of values and a life style that turn on the notion of *informality* ... This means that they [the characters] can bring it onto the scene through the clothes they are wearing ... In fact, within a narrative and scenographic structure ideally suited to the repertoire of designs on which Armani's work is habitually based, the stylist has produced a visual symphony in which the contrasts of colour, form and material constitute the principal indication as to the nature of the characters and the shifts that occur in their stories.[42]

22   Richard Gere in an Armani suit as Julian Kay in a publicity photo for
American Gigolo (1980)

As the movie progresses and suspicions mount, Julian's clothes noticeably articulate his stress and anxiety. By the film's end the iconic sexy and powerful Armani suits are gone at the precise moment when he is saved and redeemed by his female benefactor. What might this suggest about the relationship between Armani and the representation of contemporary masculinity?

The film flirts with growing fears of white middle-class heterosexual men at the turn of the decade, in which affirmative action, the gay liberation movement and women's increased incursion in the corporate world threatened emasculation. However, and perhaps more importantly, the film helps to usher in the significant re-emergence of consumerism, and the New Man, which Gere's character, despite his questionable profession, represents. Amid the numerous characteristics of the protean figure was a sense that the traditional and once stable gender definitions and scripts were being challenged in a period of increased socio-cultural instability. The student riots, the Vietnam War and turbulence in the infrastructure of the UK and USA are generally cited as cultural forces and precursors to the significant emergence of a new male type, one which capitalism sought to redress as a male peacock, ostensibly in hiding since John Carl Fluegel's 'great masculine renunciation' from over a century-and-a-half before. In the 1980s '[t]he consumer', according to Don Slater, 'was the hero of the hour … the very model of the modern citizen'.[43] The New Man placed emphasis on a well-groomed and gym-toned body, a knowledge of all things fashionable, a man who was more approachable and yet slightly vulnerable, less rigid in his gender performances, a man in touch with his emotions. But it is also important to note how the rise of the New Man paralleled the economic and cultural shift from product-based to lifestyle-based advertising.[44] The emergence and rise of this purported New Man was recorded by *The New York Times* in late 1979 in an article that clearly suggested that an interest in looking good and sporting fine clothes no longer carried with it a stigma. The New Man, soon marked as an homogenous ideal, was a controversial figure to be sure, and while some might have advocated the protean figure as a new and improved masculinity, the reality was that it was primarily a consumer-driven typology propelled largely by savvy marketing agents unabashedly flirting with accelerating the growing male consumer base no longer afraid to display pleasure and desire through clothing in a period of rapid economic prosperity and expansion.

In the 1980s, sexy and Armani were terms neatly folded together following the success of *American Gigolo*, which proved to be less interesting as a film than as a lifestyle proposition. For Armani, '[s]ociety changes, and my clothes change with it. But I try to filter my own ideas through a daily reality. It's as if I were on a movie set. Life is the movie and my clothes are the costumes.'[45] Gere's gigolo cum model swaggers between his roles, seemingly unafraid and unaware of the scopophilic pleasure he engenders. The sexuality that Armani's jackets and form-fitting yet loose trousers connoted possessed a *soupçon* of the feminine and were certainly novel. Yet Kay is also keen to ensure that his celluloid and cinematic audience is aware of his heterosexuality, and like the New Man of the period and despite his ambivalent expressions of and experiences with consumption, he is resolutely heterosexual. Kay's homophobic comments peppered throughout the film only serve to reinforce the cinematic and social heterosexual matrix.

Nonetheless Gere's hero was armoured not simply with Armani but with the new Americanized (read globalized) version of the Armani aesthetic. By desiring to make inroads in the North American market, Armani deployed his new label to pierce the texture of the filmic text, screen and surface, translating his material aesthetic into a visual image and new corporeal identity. At the time men's apparel was already a significant business, with between $16 and $17 million a year worth of suits sold at retail. Interestingly, by 1977 one out of every three suits sold in the USA were imported.[46] The significant difference between an Italian suit made by designers like Armani and his mentor Cerruti and those produced by American manufacturers was a matter of one inch. The 'seven-inch drop' favoured by the Italians is arrived at by the difference between the waist and chest measurements and produced a leaner and more body conscious fit, while the six-inch drop is a more traditional and comforting size for North American men. The Italian suit connoted not only modernity but also a degree of corporeal and social risk, a look distinct from the mainstream. A man's desire for sartorial differentiation is long held to be contrary to homosocial male bonding and aggregation, and as such leaves the so-called fashionable male vulnerable.

Early on Armani deployed textiles traditionally and exclusively used for women's wear to suggest greater movement and an inner life to the garments as well as a more sumptuous sensuality to men's sartorial experiences and expression. As I have suggested elsewhere, through the Italian textile system, Armani worked with textiles like wool crepes, linens, viscose and synthetic blends, tweeds, silk, cashmere and velvet – fabrics with unique textures that are never harsh or stiff – as an important antidote to the ocularcentrism of American mass and popular culture.[47] Farid Chenoune, in his expansive tome on menswear, claims that Armani's feminine use of fabric treatment was also coupled with collections throughout the 1980s that made men 'sexy ... [and] broad-bottomed ... shifting the centre of masculine anatomical interest from the front to the back' a move which earned him 'favour among the homosexual clientele that constituted some of Armani's earliest fans'.[48] By gradually introducing lighter textiles, such as wool crepe for a man's suiting, previously exclusive to womenswear, Armani provided a more 'humble posture'[49] and understated luxury by the 1990s, and as a result men's bodies read differently in narratives on as much as off the screen. Feminist scholar Luce Irigaray has posited that a 'woman takes pleasure more from touching than from looking'.[50] Irigaray's gendering of the haptic brings us back to the feminine qualities both Armani and Kay purportedly brought to the screen and men's fashion. The film, like most of its generation, moves rather slowly, leaving ample time for the viewer to appreciate the tactile quality and value of Kay's extensive, coveted wardrobe. Armani's designs, Arturo Carlo Quintavalle posits, suggest 'systematic narrative'.[51] Textiles themselves also help to slow down the visual apprehension of the film; they act as signposts to narratological development, either to mark continuity or ruptures in the fabric of the story.

At the intersection between cinema and fashion visual materiality and haptic visuality are tantamount. As early as 1978, designer Egon von Fürstenberg insisted that the phenomenological experience of clothes involves the senses of sight and touch.[52] Film scholar Susan Buck-Morss has evocatively proposed the cinematic screen as 'a prosthetic organ of the senses'. When 'exposed to the sensual shock of the cinema', she asserts, 'the nervous system is subject to a double, and seemingly paradoxical modification'. The senses are at once heightened and yet at the same time dulled to the point of 'corporeal anaesthetization'.[53] On the other side of things, commenting on the apparent three-dimensionality of the clothing in *American Gigolo* less than one year after the film's debut, Richard de Combray noted how the designer seemed to have 'discovered [that] the eye was genuinely capable of discerning ten

23   The spring/summer 1990 men's and women's collections share similar ideals and shapes, premised on the gender-blending use of fluid and textured textiles

million variations in colour, hue, tone, and intensity'.[54] The relationship between the haptic and the optic when choosing the right elements of the 'power look' was outlined by von Fürstenberg when he imparted that '[t]he way the fabric feels to your hand is the acid test in selecting a suit... Even before reading the fibre-content information on the label', he suggested, one 'should handle the fabric'. Additionally, sight was also central to the selection process; '[a] trained eye seeks those small details that characterize the quality suit'.[55] The phenomenological play of the camera in *American Gigolo* that glides over Julian's finely tailored garments elicits an eroticism through folds, subtle gradations of colour and the fabrics themselves.[56] Lighting and the camera itself must manage to 'handle the fabric' for the viewer, to elicit the fullness of the intermingling of haptic and visual experiences which would eventually prove to be the true success of Schrader's film and Armani's new male propositions. The tactility of Armani's garments, which help bring out their sophistication and presence on the screen, draws the viewer in closer, as a sort of indexical rapprochement that the filmic space offers. According to film scholar Stella Bruzzi:

> In the cinema work of Giorgio Armani it is possible to detect a use of couture clothes based on an intrinsic, subtle fetishism of detail, a desire to highlight the qualities of the clothes themselves, an emphasis which does not prioritise the body or character wearing them.[57]

The textures of the textiles, also as compelling driving forces in the narrative, improve and enhance the mimetic impulse of cinema, that is, they are conductive agents that allude more thickly to the three-dimensionality of real life that cinema portends to represent through a two-dimensional surface, and thus assist in a deeper phenomenological fulfilment for the human sensorium.

Film theorist Laura Marks's theorization of haptic visuality might prove, in part, insightful to new ways of unpacking the Armani affect on the Italian Look and menswear in general through cinema. While Marks is preoccupied with examples of video art and films that already include haptic visuality in the production process, she defines the term as 'the way vision itself can be tactile, as though one were touching a film with one's eyes'.[58] Through the two-dimensionality of the screen's surface, the eye must do the handling and touching for the embodied spectator. It is here, in this important act of translation, where visuality and the haptic cavort, and where gender is troubled. According to Marks:

> Haptic visuality is distinguished from optical visuality, which sees things from enough distance to perceive them as distinct forms in deep space: in other words, how we usually conceive of vision. Optical visuality depends on a separation between viewing subject and the object. Haptic looking tends to move over the surface of its object rather than to plunge into illusionistic depth, not to distinguish form so much as to discern texture [and] emphasizes the viewer's inclination to perceive them.[59]

What Marks proposes is a rapprochement of sorts, decidedly anti-Cartesian and anti-Kantian in process and outcome, by coaxing the subject and object into a closer, more intimate relationship. It also supposes a way to address the textures of both film and textiles as texts. I wish to extend her discussion by suggesting its importance for Armani's incursion into both cinema and the North American market; after all, like the body, film too needs to be clothed in order to signify in the world of meaningful objects. The focus for Marks, as I suggest is the case with Armani, are the haptic forms of representation, rather than the optical. Or, posed as a question, how might textiles within the cinematic narrative prove to be an equally powerful textural gesture in the construction of static or moving images? Marks focuses attention, in particular, on filmmakers who attempt to reconstruct and transmit a physical sense of place and culture, long distant from the cinemagoer. These artists, like Armani I posit, engage in forms of translations across both cultural and spatial boundaries.

An important factor that contributed to the emergence of the New Man of the 1980s and new, more advanced forms of consumption was the onslaught of flexible specialization, or post-Fordism.[60] Sean Nixon argues that flexible specialization allowed for a number of 'new men' to emerge, variously spatialized through flexible and specialized retail outlets, each catering to specific, identifiable lifestyle images or market niches.[61] What materialized, according to Nixon, were three distinct stylistic trends in menswear imagery in men's fashion magazines: 'street style', 'Italianicity' and 'Edwardian Englishness'.[62] Most relevant here is how this second stylistic category was enabled by the rise of Italian menswear designers in the late 1970s and early 1980s, impacting directly the editorial content of leading English-language magazines. The models used for this aesthetic lifestyle possessed 'physical features [that] signified both sensuality and hardness'.[63] In addition to this gender ambivalence, another defining feature of the visual culture associated with the Italianicity prototype was to be found in the textural pleasure of such sartorial offerings.

Buttressed by advertising, consumer goods and fashionable features, the acute desire to create *the* ideal lifestyle magazine catering to this preferred consumer would also assist in the further elucidation and representation of the new and improved man. In this context, fashionable goods generally and Armani more specifically feature prominently in East Midlands Allied Press Metro Group's advertising director Zed Zawada's comments from 1986:

> Publishers look at women's magazines, their circulation figures and bottom line and they think: if we put together a road test of a new Porsche with an in-depth interview with Giorgio Armani and some stuff about personal finance, then we'll hit some sort of composite male who has all these interests.[64]

By 1990 Armani was not only associated with the New Man that emerged and evolved throughout the 1980s but more specifically with a look that became expressive of the dominant culture of power. In an article from *The New York Times* outlining Italy's allure in the USA, where anything from Armani to Zabaglione is all the rage, the author notes that 'when it comes to fashion, no designer has more cachet right now than Giorgio Armani'.[65] By the late 1980s Italian style, power and Armani were inextricably linked, best exemplified in the by now iconic and infamous example of New York artist Jean Michel Basquiat. The skyrocketing success for the once down and out graffiti artist was marked with certain key lifestyle signifiers. Early on in his career, upon receiving a cheque for $20,000 from the sale of one of his paintings, the artist immediately 'went out shopping and purchased six Giorgio Armani suits', recalls his close friend Vincent Gallo.[66] After all, the 'power look' according to von Fürstenberg,

> is a ticket to the winner's circle. It is a passport to the world where men enjoy privilege and pleasure, take command, and seem at ease everywhere. These men receive courtesies without having to ask for them. They get quicker and greater attention from waiters and clerks, more favourable looks from women; colleagues, clients, customers, and friends listen to them more readily because of their air of authority.[67]

Von Fürstenberg further claims that through his manual, aptly titled *The Power Look*, a man will be able to 'communicate power and derive pleasure' through the clothes he chooses.[68] Unburdened pleasure and the power look are fused together and form the aesthetic and cultural DNA of the 1980s New Man. Given the context in which the protean masculinity emerged, one must ask whether *American Gigolo* could have appeared in the latter part of the 1980s or later still, especially in an era dominated by a body politic informed by the onslaught of AIDS and right-wing conservativism. While Gere may have been the first Hollywood actor to expose himself fully to the cinematic lens, *Top Gun* (1986) featured a blatant and self-conscious homoeroticism, easily digestible for the American and world audiences, made possible and plausible through the aggressive auspices of war and male aggregation. The irony, to a degree, is how the film's lead actor, Tom Cruise, would soon become friends and associated with the Italian designer, who provided a specially designed wardrobe for his wedding to Katie Holmes in 2006. Despite endless rumours of Cruise's sexuality, he stands as the personification of the straight male hero in Hollywood in a protracted era of aggressive expansion of American global commercial interests.

In his films from the 1980s and 1990s, Schrader has returned to the questions of gender trouble and the new masculinity and his collaborations with Armani tested the waters one more time by using film as a mimetic device for emulation and to incite desire. By the time of Schrader's 1990

24   Model from the autumn/winter 1990 menswear collection presenting a more humble and casual sense of masculine luxury

filmic adaption of Ian McEwan's *Comfort of Strangers,* Armani had become discursively and materially conflated, as a brand, adjective and identity, with the power look. Not unlike the odd portrayal of sexual decadence exhibited in Schrader's *American Gigolo,* the director once again portrays declining male authorial power. In this second film, the central male character Robert is solely responsible for propelling the sexual and thrilling intrigue of the narrative, portrayed by the elegant and charming Christopher Walken who, throughout the film, sports fluid, crumpled linen suits by Armani. Part of what compels Robert is his need to reassert male power, evidently in crisis where ostensibly *American Gigolo* left off. The story takes place in Venice, a haunting stage that infuses each scene of the film with a sense of 'grandeur, decay, and corruption', and of course Italianicity.[69] Our innocent protagonists, the unmarried English couple Colin (Rupert Everett) and Mary (Natasha Richardson) are in Venice less on a holiday than trying to decide what to do about their complicated and troubled relationship. While on a quest to locate a restaurant for dinner, they meet the sophisticated and enticing Robert by chance, and he takes them to a bar, diverting them off their course. The next morning fate has mysteriously brought them back together in Piazza San Marco when Robert extends to the couple an invitation to nap and dine at his home. The art-filled apartment on the Grand Canal he shares with his Canadian wife Caroline (Helen Mirren) is both grand and impressive. Robert and his wife become increasingly peculiar, and when Colin makes a remark about the museum-like atmosphere of the odd couple's home, Robert deliveries a brutal punch to his guest's solar plexus. Meanwhile Helen confesses to having watched Colin and Mary sleeping and discloses her theories on the connection between pain and sexual pleasure. The couple leave their hosts after dinner, and spend the remainder of their holiday happier than ever, love rekindled with plans to marry. Their fate changes drastically when one night they pass the apartment one last time and are invited once again to join the couple for dinner. Things turn decidedly unpleasant and quickly get out of hand, leading to a psychological thriller whose outcome is less than compelling.

As the critic for the *Los Angeles Times* noted in his review of the movie, the moral of the story is at best ambiguous, and he wonders whether to '[w]atch out for twitchy foreigners wearing linen Armani suits when on holiday abroad' might prove to be the entire point of the film. With full movie credits prominently given to Armani, the reviewer concludes that the 'wardrobe upstages the actor'.[70] Here, ten years after Schrader's *American Gigolo*, sexuality and clothes cavort in a filmic world devoid of true clarity and meaning. However, the infusion of power and aggression, rather than the vulnerability seen in the early 1980s, in the relationship between sexuality and fashion reveals a decade of corporate aggression and masculine virile power. In the final decade of the century protection became a guiding metaphor. In the same year the film made its lacklustre debut, feminist theorist Judith Butler also published her now infamous track on gender trouble. Butler's work spawned an important method for exploring and deconstructing the codes and strictures of gender and by extension sexuality itself.[71] However, we would do well to remember that while it was published in 1990, her theories were the product of the sexual politics of the 1980s rather than a new methodological guide for the 1990s. In this way her text embodies some the developments I have been discussing. It is also important to recognize how capitalism has helped to shape gender categories and typologies particularly evident since the 1920s and acutely so in the 1980s; the New Man, after all, was nothing more than a consumer category. Butler focuses her attention on the subversive (that is the anti-normative) performances of drag as an example to illustrate how all gender categories are performative acts. However, might there not be more trouble created in the codes underpinning gender's myriad performances throughout the 1980s? On another level, in both films men take centre stage in a way that troubles normative understandings of their respective positions within society, namely within the sexual realm of gender roles. In these two films by Schrader, the stories and wardrobes are decidedly contemporary, where the past and history take no part. However, as Cocks also noted, Armani's quiet revolution and very contemporary adaptation of modern classics 'is very much a matter of the moment, and what may now seem like a temporal fancy can become, decades hence, a tactile key into the past. Clothes are the fabric of history, the texture of time. And this time, right now belongs to Armani'.[72]

25   Spring/summer 2003. Armani's research into textiles and surfaces has never abated

Conclusion: Paris 0, Milan 1

It is always interesting that it is the French and not the Italians who have been considered stylish, though in truth it is the other way around.

Richard de Combray

Paris was the capital of the nineteenth century and undisputed epicentre for all things fashionable, feminine and female. However, the insertion of menswear into the accelerated fashion system, I conclude, needed a new location, an unchartered space of protean modernity and a blind hope in an unknown future. This space is at once tangible and immaterial and yet exists at the point of collusion between Milan specifically and the USA more broadly. The emergence of Milan, particularly as it concerns menswear, points to the on-going decentring of control of fashion that began following the Second World War, which paralleled similar if not identical patterns in the visual arts and industrial design. The new democratic reformative zeal of the late 1960s and 1970s, which spilled over into the realms of industry and aesthetics, was the very same principle on which Milanese prêt-à-porter was predicated.

It was the English-speaking world, expressly the UK and the USA, which were at the forefront of declaring the end of haute couture and Paris's uncontested reign. Referring to Milan as a design centre, British reporter Sally Brampton in 1981 declared it to be 'a city of the future rather than of the past. Milanese attention to visual detail and beauty is part of a living, developing style.'[73] Then director of the Conran design museum Stephen Bayley also stated that the Italian city was 'the unrivalled fashion capital, not just of Italy but of the world'.[74] He also noted that in the USA the Italian Look was more widely and better received that in the UK. Brampton nevertheless asserts that the Milanese designers were 'now influential enough [to] threaten the French fashion industry'.[75] In Cocks' 1982 article in *Time*, published in the same week as the French prêt-à-porter collections in Paris, the author began by asking Yves Saint Laurent's partner Pierre Bergé about the impact the Italians and Armani have had on the world of design. Bergé responded by biting back, rhetorically querying: 'Give me one piece of clothing, one fashion statement that Armani has made that has truly influenced the world',[76] to which, as a response, Cocks not only wrote an entire eight-page feature article on the Italian designer's contributions, but also outlined the work of numerous American designers legibly influenced by the Italian designer.

Notably less than two years after *American Gigolo* made its debut in cinemas, de Combray, in his lush and sumptuous volume on Armani, also posited that the days of the 'Old Rich' and of women flying off to Paris to go the haute couture salons were over. In short, he declared the death of haute couture.[77] Even as early as 1978 *Newsweek* reported on the escalating migration away from Parisian to Milanese fashion houses with the former's 'narcissistic forms of fashion creation [and its] rude treatment on Parisian showroom floors'.[78] These remarks highlight a decisive cultural turn at which point Paris's uncontested supremacy was officially challenged by both New York and the Made in Italy label, which successfully fused industrial sense with aesthetic sensibility. At its centre was a strong ally, as White has noted – the USA. Cinema has serviced as a democratizing force in American culture, while prêt-à-porter for Armani was also meant to do the same, supposedly devoid of the moribund charm of Old World haute couture. Today it seems ironic, on some level, that Armani was omitted from Robert Altman's biting satire of the (mostly French) fashion industry, *Prêt-à-Porter* (1994). Given that Altman focused his attacks and dismissive lens on the purported ridiculous hyperbolic world of haute couture, Armani was omitted for not being outrageous and eccentric enough. Referring to Altman's choice not to include him, Armani stated: 'I detest the atmosphere from which, perhaps Altman created his film, which I'm not in … I heard that he said Armani is too serious to involve him in this escapade', he surmised.[79] However, Armani quickly returned to (fashion) business as usual, and in 2005 charted his own foray into haute couture with the inauguration of Giorgio Armani Privé.

Notes

1   *DNR* 9 September 2003.

2   Hollander 1994: 349–50.

3   For more on the New Man and his relationship with fashion see Mort 2009.

4   Benjamin 1999b: 74.

5   Giacomoni 1984: 9.

6   Giacomoni 1984: 9.

7   Giacomoni 1984: 9.

8   See White 2000b.

9   *NYT* 16 September 1979.

10   *Time Magazine* 5 April 1982.

11   *Time Magazine* 5 April 1982.

12   *NYT* 2 June 1978.

13   See Deleuze 1993.

14   Bruzzi 1997: 30.

15   *Time* 3 July 1978.

16   'Italian Fabrics '78' 1978: 119.

17   'Italian Fabrics '78' 1978: 119.

18   *LAT* 27 July 1979.

19   Chrysler in *LAT* 27 July 1979.

20   Piaggi 1979: 236.

21   In *LA Times* 27 July 1979.

22   *DNR* 31 November 1991.

23   The first lower-priced ready-to-wear collection for women introduced in America is for fall 1983 and is priced at 30 per cent less than his 'couture' line. Semi-couture practices were used for the primary, couture line; the firm boasted that 40 per cent of the garments were made by hand, likely, in part a desire to retain the quality of Italian craftsmanship as well as a product of limited and exclusive distribution. The two 'original' white labels for Giorgio Armani and Collezioni were only slightly different. When the diffusion line (meant for department and speciality stores and a larger and slightly less fashion-oriented clientele) was initiated, the press officers and journalists wrote of and discussed it as a slight variation on the Italian version, made to be produced for a larger market. In effect, the strategy was similar to what Dior implanted decades earlier, with his CD London and Christian Dior-New York lines which also had regional headquarters, see Palmer 2009.

24   Gianelli in *People Magazine* 30 July 1979.

25   Brantley 1988: 130. In 1994 Forte, who had been Armani's right hand for 15 years, unceremoniously took a job at his then biggest competitor Calvin Klein. Referring to his competitor, Armani lashed out: 'He recruits my people, my collections. Next he will be calling me up to head his design studio!' *WWD* 24 May 1994.

26   *LAT* 27 July 1979.

27   Benjamin 1999b: 77.

28   Benjamin 1999b: 70.

29   *Esquire* 22 May 1979.

30   *Esquire* 22 May 1979.

31   Armani in *NYT* 4 March 1979.

32   *People Magazine* 30 July 1979.

33   *NYT* 13 January 1980.

34   *NYT* 18 September 1980.

35   Rivetti in Molho 2007: 83.

36   Molho 2007: 84.

37   *DNR* 19 June 1989.

38   *NYT* 22 January 1980.

39   *W* 9–16 October 1981.

40   It is interesting to note that Ferdinando Scarfiotti was employed as the visual consultant for *America Gigolo*. Scarfiotti had worked with Bernardo Bertolucci on a number of films, notably on *The Conformist*, one of Armani's all-time favourite movies.

41   www.wbir.com. Accessed 10 January 2010.

42   Grignaffini 1987: 23–4.

43   Slater 1997: 10.

44   Chapman 1988: 229.

45   Armani in *Made in Milan* 1990.

46   *NYT* 16 September 1979.

47   Potvin 2007: 93.

48   Chenoune 1996: 294.

49   *NYT* 8 April 1990.

50   Irigaray 1985: 26.

51 Quintavalle 1982: 139.

52 von Fürstenberg 1978: 53.

53 Buck-Morss 1994: 55.

54 de Combray 1982: 168.

55 von Fürstenberg 1978: 53.

56 Bruzzi 1997: 26.

57 Bruzzi 1997: 30.

58 Marks 2000: xi.

59 Marks 2000: 162.

60 See Nixon 1996: 21–2.

61 Nixon 1996: 59.

62 Nixon 1996: 168.

63 Nixon 1996: 186.

64 Zawada in Mort 2009: 456.

65 *NYT* 10 August 1988.

66 *NYT* 27 August 1988.

67 von Fürstenberg 1978: 4–5.

68 von Fürstenberg 1978: 6.

69 *LAT* 29 March 1991.

70 *LAT* 29 March 1991.

71 Butler 1990.

72 *Time* 5 April 1982.

73 The *Observer* 6 October 1981.

74 Bayley in *The Observer* 6 October 1981.

75 Brampton in *The Observer* 6 October 1981.

76 *Time* 5 April 1982.

77 de Combray 1982: 151.

78 *Newsweek* 23 October 1978.

79 *WWD* 25 October 1994.

3

Armani/Industry: Fashioning Finance

> Decadence is what goes down well in Paris; Milan is the present and the future. The French disguise the industry–designer relationship. We make it quite clear that the concrete side of the make-believe is achieved today through industry.
>
> Bepe Modenese

> I don't think you can separate the notions of creativity and commerce ... I do not think you can say that an item of clothing or an accessory is truly fashionable unless it is bought and worn.
>
> Giorgio Armani

Threads, a magazine devoted to 'home sewers', published a series of descriptive 'how to' articles between 1990 to 1999 in an attempt to systematically translate Armani's fabrication and design for a broader audience of women capable of crafting their own versions of his famous jackets and trousers. According to one of the articles' author, Ann Hyde, despite Armani's use of exclusive fabrics, similar textiles equal in quality are apparently available to home sewers. For her North American readers, Hyde adds the proviso that location (generally limited to major urban centres), price and selection bear considerable weight in the final choice of fabric. After examining numerous jackets and suits, she concludes that '[b]ecause [Armani] subtracts the underpinnings, his fabrics must also be of stand-alone quality, capable of expressing his message without stiffeners or backing'.[1]

Textiles alone provide the interface between the body and the outside world. Articles written for a magazine like *Threads* reinforce the relationship between on the one hand the regional and personal desire to replicate the original and, on the other, the realities of a global aesthetic. To understand this complex of realities, Hyde suggests a trip to an Armani boutique, if only to 'feel the fabrics'. The author's recommendation is not to *see* the colours, shapes or textiles per se, but rather to *touch* the fabrics. According to Hyde, the suggested visit to an Armani boutique provides 'the best way to experience Armani's exquisite fabric judgement'.[2] As we saw in the previous chapter, the haptic, the sense of touch, becomes the locus of knowledge of being-in-the-material-world. It is precisely through the haptic that the home-sewer is able to translate global industrial design into a domestically crafted version: through translation, the global becomes personal. As part of her project of dissection and deconstruction, Hyde takes apart a jacket from the designer's spring/summer 1990 collection – coincidentally the same year Armani would disembowel one of his own jackets in *Made in Milan*. Through the fabric (in this particular case a woven check) the author is able to discern the 'grain of the ultra-light jacket, making it easier to see the actual shape and orientation of seam lines'.[3]

By treating textiles as texts loaded with meaning, both Hyde and Armani reaffirm the inevitable relationship the jacket has with on the one hand the body and on the other the implied labour attached to the final product. Armani himself has noted the significance and vitality of the haptic:

> My energies are concentrated in my hands when I touch fabric. I think that my constant, almost maniacal research on fabrics is one of the reasons behind my success. To model a fabric around a body is one of the most sensual experiences on earth. You have to feel it; it has to become one with the body.[4]

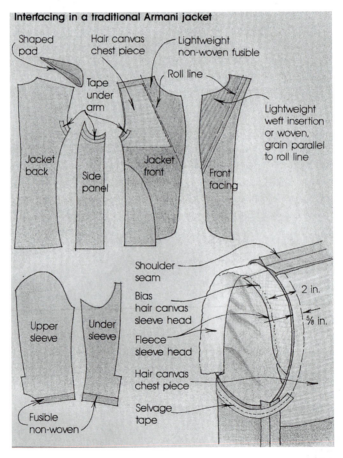

Interfacing in a traditional Armani jacket

Shaped pad — Hair canvas chest piece — Lightweight non-woven fusible — Roll line — Tape under arm — Jacket back — Side panel — Jacket front — Front facing — Lightweight weft insertion or woven, grain parallel to roll line

Upper sleeve — Under sleeve — Fusible non-woven — Shoulder seam — Bias hair canvas sleeve head — Fleece sleeve head — Hair canvas chest piece — Selvage tape — 2 in. — ⅝ in.

26   In the same year that Armani is represented symbolically ripping the stuffing out of a jacket in *Made in Milan*, home sewing magazine *Threads* (August/September 1990) deconstructs the Armani jacket to look inside and see how Milan's master tailor achieves his fluid, unstructured looks

'Touch is our most social sense';[5] it suggests deep and profound opportunities for the self to engage with others providing for long-term meaning, memories and stories. However, cultures differ markedly in their customs of touching, that is, the intensity, degree and frequency with which people use the sense to negotiate the quotidian and inter-personal relations. Derived from the Greek, *haptein*, meaning to grasp, the haptic marks the territory where we might negotiate the world of objects, of things, of people. Since the eighteenth century, as exemplified in the writings of Immanuel Kant, the visual occupies a place of honour within the human sensorium, allowing the image to take hold of our sensual experiences and our understanding of the material world. Even today, the image on the computer screen overrides the sensory tedium and sterility of our fingers' constant tapping against the hard plastic keyboard, a material increasingly ubiquitous in the working lives of many people. Perhaps the antidote might be textiles; after all, they 'speak to us, and its language is ... seductive and current'.[6]

In his exploration of Armani's various stages of the design process, journalist Marco Romanelli posited that an Armani garment, despite its status as a 'manufactured object',

> has a technical and communicative valency so as to permit ... a renewed capacity for dialogue with an unspecified number of users. Users who can personally re-interpret the object itself, taking possession of it and so making it ineffably and infinitely different ... Because in his work it is possible to see a sign of this attainable Utopia which today is politically and poetically forgotten. Armani's prêt-à-porter as a paradigmatic 'design series' ... contrast[s] high fashion which is the equivalent of high craftsmanship (neo-craftsmanship or antique craftsmanship, with no substantial difference) and a current prêt-à-porter which oscillates between an excess identifiable with high fashion and a basic condition of low production.[7]

The notion of the 'design series', a serialized set of objects, resides somewhere between excess and the quotidian, between industrial production and creative imaginings and places the designer squarely within the democratic ethos Armani claims to want to provide his various segmented constituencies of customers. Within Armani's moralizing aesthetics the personal and the industrial override the fashion system and its inherent need for dramatic change. He asserts: 'The only reason you throw away a jacket should be because it doesn't fit. It's anti-democratic to assume people have money to waste every six months, and immoral to design so that something looks wrong the next year and will have to be thrown away'.[8] It is at the moment of the selection of fabrics for each collection that pleasure is tinged with inevitable self-doubt. As Armani recounts, 'all of a sudden I realize that to touch a beautiful wool crepe – the gesture seems old'. It is also at this decisive juncture in the creative and industrial process when he realizes his vision is his own and that while he 'may not be in the trend of the year' he reaffirms the path that asserts his ideas, products and the singularity of his vision.[9] As part of that vision, each season's new propositions became less about silhouette and more concerned with research into textiles and hybrid fabrications. As a self-declared and proud industrialist, Armani has designed and produced textiles as a means to bridge fashion and finance, which as for many Italians has proven to be a winning formula only made possible by the country's formidable textile industry. Armani's success, like that of his compatriots in the late 1970s when the Made in Italy label began to garner serious cultural capital around the world, was predicated on the assistance and know-how of key textile industrialists. However, the symbiotic relationship between finance and fashion in the emergence of Italian fashion system is sadly neglected by historians and scholars, particularly those in economics and business. As Elisabeth Merlo and Francesca Polese explain, these scholars, and we might also add fashion historians to the list,

> have shown little interest in tracing the cause and origins of the success of Italian fashion. This lapse can be partly explained by the paucity of primary sources on the subject. The relatively few archives of the many companies active in the Italian fashion system generally contain sketches of dresses and textile samples, rather than paperwork or business records.[10]

This chapter seeks to bring fashion and finance closer together by highlighting how Armani moved from simply being a *stylisti* designing for numerous labels including his own to an industrialist in his own right, a process that has guaranteed his own success and has helped to safeguard the Made in Italy label for which Armani has become its beacon in the global landscape of design. Of the Made in Italy label, Armani defined it ostensibly through his own aesthetic paradigm as not 'too traditional, too dull, too commercial – because "Italian taste" can be a little old-fashioned, a bit BCBG. It means making things that are new, in a spirit everyone can understand and wear.'[11] This chapter frames certain key collaborations and developments in the designer's single-minded vision of creating a completely self-sufficient, vertically integrated fashion empire in the 'spirit everyone can understand and wear'.

Made in Italy: The Case of GFT and Armani

Founded in 1930 by the Rivetti family, Gruppo Finanzario Tessile (GFT) had become the leading manufacturer of men's clothing in Italy by the 1950s, and by the 1970s it began to enter into the designer fashion sector with an initial agreement with Emanuel Ungaro to produce the house's Parallele boutique line. Given the then declining state of clothing manufacturing in France since the war, it makes perfect sense that GFT manoeuvred itself into a position to fill the widening gap in the market. At the same time Carlo Rivetti (GFT founder Silvio's son), was also keeping an eye on Milan's most promising designer and at first offered Armani a contract to design its lower-end Mix and Match line, which sold upwards of 50,000 pieces a year. With the success of this line already guaranteed, GFT shrewdly entered into one of the most lucrative long-term licensing agreements in fashion history. 'It was Marco who first came to us,' recalls Armani. 'We had reservations about them, but from the beginning we had an excellent collaboration with Rivetti. He understood our product right away. He's in love, a bit, with fashion.' Armani noted how GFT's mentality was 'slow to move but sure to win the race in the long run'; not unlike his own philosophy, we might also conclude.[12] Despite Armani's early success and continued freelance work for numerous firms, Giorgio Armani's own industrial capacity in the late 1970s was virtually non-existent, unable to keep up with demand from international buyers. The licensing agreement included the creation of the Giorgio Armani 'white label' diffusion line, primarily destined for the North American market as well as the production of the more exclusive Giorgio Armani collection, a collaboration that single-handedly paved the road for Armani's global success.

On the heels of the agreement with Armani, GFT signed lucrative deals with leading European designers such as Valentino and Louis Férraud, followed by American designers. Rivetti recently noted that in the late 1970s, faced with the oil crisis and a general and significant decline in textile production and fashion consumption, GFT was compelled to think of new ways to increase sales and fill what he identified as the void left by French prêt-à-porter manufacturers in the 1960s and 1970s.

27   Spring/summer 1989

According to Rivetti, what they did was to 'incorporate "fashion"' into the mix to increase desirability of the clothing lines.[13] In fact, it was not until the deal with GFT that Armani became a cultural and economic force to be reckoned with outside of Italy. In terms of menswear, what it meant was a significant acceleration of its system. With 'fashion' (or aesthetic ephemerality) brought to bear more directly upon the industrial manufacturing of men's clothing, obsolescence began to accelerate the cycle and diminished the lifespan of a man's suit, once tailor-made and meant to last for decades. In 1979 the two companies formed a subsidiary in the USA known as Giorgio Armani Men's

GIORGIO ARMANI

24 South Molton Street, W1 Tel: 493 9847

28   Aldo Fallai. From the spring/summer 1983 advertising campaign

Wear Corporation. The new corporation would serve to launch Armani to a broader North American audience and would be responsible for the manufacture and distribution of the new label launched as part of their 1978 agreement. In 1983 Armani modified his contract with GFT to produce a second (more limited) diffusion line, known as Mani for men in Canada and the USA and for women in Europe. GFT's goal for these and other diffusion lines within its growing stable was to create designer or fashionable ready-to-wear within a manufacturing system, all the while under the creative control and quality direction of each house to ensure a sense of independence, uniqueness and an authentic identity, the embryo of the brand DNA taken for granted in more recent years. By 1983 exports for GFT rose a staggering 23 per cent, due almost entirely to the increase in sales of the Armani and Valentino lines in the USA, which comprised 25 per cent of the company's exports.[14] By 1984 the USA imported $551,800,000 worth of Italian clothing, and only two short years later that number rose to a stunning $851,200,000.[15] The boom that GFT and Italian designers experienced in the first half of the 1980s neatly coincided with the Craxi socialist government between 1983 and 1987, a period coincidently known as the second 'Italian miracle'.

Two central ingredients can be ascertained in the development of Milan as a global fashion capital: first, the emergence of a global marketplace and second, the urban aggregation bringing together various enterprising individuals and institutions that could provide the necessary know-how to market, produce and distribute the fashion object.[16] Lucrative deals with textile manufacturers enhanced the public fame and private fortune of Milanese designers whose status was also greatly enhanced by the proliferation of new and exciting fashion magazines coming out of Milan. Within the pages of *Vogue Italia* Franca Sozzani was – and remains – a proud and staunch supporter of Made in Italy, championing the work of leading and young and up-and-coming designers. *Vogue* along with magazines like *Uomo Vogue, Mondo Uomo* and *Donna* emerged in the 1980s amidst the rise of the Made in Italy phenomenon and became instrumental in the perpetuation of the Italian Look and the image of Italian designers.[17] Throughout the 1970s, 1980s and 1990s Armani advertisements in these Italian magazines also listed the names of the textile mills and manufacturers he collaborated with in the creation of the collection. The same could not be said when he used identical advertisements in foreign magazines. On a national level and beyond the objects themselves, the symbiosis between designer and textile manufacturer was made visually legible through the adjacent sector of marketing.[18] Throughout the 1980s Italy, and Milan at its centre, experienced an unprecedented design explosion in all satellite disciplines. With most industries coming together toward a collective, yet unknown, goal, Milan seamlessly systematized the production of commodities with potent signifying potential, objects of no real practical merit, but which possessed enormous symbolic value to a new and different generation of consumers.

As early as 1986, however, the international press began to question the longevity of Made in Italy and Milan as a true and worthy fashion capital. In Canada, for example, national newspaper *The Globe and Mail* asked whether, despite their manufacturing know-how and textile mills (also used by designers outside of Italy), 'signs of a downturn in Italian fashion [were] already apparent. Apart from the sharply rising costs, which have given many retailers pause, the major problem is a dearth of fashion talent. Put simply, there are too few designers designing too many lines'.[19] The fact remained that throughout the 1970s and 1980s designers like Albini, Versace and Armani designed numerous lines for various textile manufacturers and family-run fashion houses, leaving some buyers and press with a feeling of creative déjà vu. With no institutional structure to facilitate fashion design education, Italy

29   Autumn/winter 1988. Editorial image from Connoisseur magazine

was forced to look further afield for design expertise by the mid-1980s. Labels like Byblos hired design duo Keith Varty and Alan Clever, while Fendi turned to Karl Lagerfeld to salvage its illustrious reputation. With no apparent rising stars on the horizon coupled with increases in production and labour costs, the industry went on the offensive to promote the Made in Italy ideals abroad less by featuring new or unknown names, but by turning the spotlight once again onto the Milanese stars like Armani, Versace and Ferré who had gained success in the mid-1970s.

In 1988, sponsored by the Italian Trade Commission Concept and Organization and the Milan based Domus Academy, the *Moda Italia: Creativity and Technology in the Italian Fashion System* exhibition in New York showcased the work of Italy's leading designers. Included were Ferré, Krizia, Missoni, Fendi, Armani and Versace. In addition, Italy's top five textile and fashion manufacturers were also featured: Benetton, Fila, GFT, Marzotto and Zegna. According to the Italian Trade Commission in New York City, the USA accounted for 10 per cent of Italian fashion exports.[20] Located at Pier 88, the $1.5 million exhibition was to pay witness to both technology and creativity. Ampelio Bucci wrote in the catalogue that '[t]he exhibition is not meant as a celebration but as an opportunity to illustrate the unique characteristic of Italian fashion: a production model capable of meeting man's growing third millennium demand for quality. The exhibition is designed to present a record of its great development in recent years'.[21] Globalization is all too often seen as either an antidote to or antithesis of nationalism. However, turning to the advertising campaigns of the past thirty years, the case of the Made in Italy phenomenon, as just one example, eloquently demonstrates how nationalism is effectively not out of sync with globalism, but rather imbricates itself within its narrative as a means to create a highly recognizable and coveted object specifically destined to the global landscape.

While recent threats from China loom large over the future of Italian fashion, the Made in Italy label has long struggled to position itself as *the* pre-eminent purveyor of quality luxury accessories and fashion in the world, often having to stave off various economic and cultural antagonistic forces. The timing of the 1988 exhibition revealed itself to be fuelled by growing fears of the rising costs for foreign buyers due to Italy's rampant inflation largely a result of Craxi's various initiatives. In the accompanying catalogue, quality, craftsmanship and technical prowess were cited as the core ingredients of Made in Italy, qualities that set it apart from others within the landscape of fashion. The catalogue importantly drew attention to how foreign designers like Donna Karan, Ungaro, Christian Lacroix, Sonia Rykiel and Claude Montana not only sourced their textiles in Italy but had their accessories and garments manufactured there as well, underscoring the country's industrial acumen. Given that its target audience was a country that single-handedly defined the language of casual and nonchalant fashion, an Italian understanding of sportswear was evoked as a way to communicate why their design was best suited to modern American needs. Dawn Mello, then president of Bergdorf Goodman and highly influential doyenne of American luxury fashion, also emphasized how 'Italian fashion is so comfortable and perfect for active Americans. They really understand sportswear so well, and Americans, who naturally gravitate towards sportswear, love it.'[22] Ellis Saltzman, senior vice-president and director of fashion and product development of Saks Fifth Avenue, stated that 'Italian designers revolutionized the whole American sportswear look ... They out-Americaned the Americans.'[23] Despite the clear American-centricism of the catalogue, at the time of the exhibition, West Germany remained the leading European buyer of Italian clothing goods with an equally important 24 per cent of the total Italian exported value; Italian sales in Germany however decreased by 6.3 per cent over 1987. The USA was the second leading nation of customers of Italian goods with 13.8 per cent, with a notable increase of 5 per cent over the previous year.[24]

According to Bucci, at the heart of the hope for the Made in Italy label was Armani; 'If there is someone who is able to galvanize Italian fashion it is a shy and modest star who is considered one of the most esteemed designers in the entire world.'[25] One year after Armani made his appearance on the Milanese catwalk under his own name, a British newspaper reported how 'Armani meant for fashion what Picasso meant for painting; he emancipated and revolutionized fashion and in this way he established thoroughly new and bold patterns of behaviour.'[26] The catalogue was not alone in its synthesis of the transformative power and mystique of the designer and with much riding on Armani's impressive, yet newly founded reputation, the hopes of Made in Italy rested heavily on his shoulders.

Along with Armani, Italy's success was also predicated on manufacturing powerhouses like GFT whose sales had gone from $7 million in 1980 to $230 million by 1988. Cognizant of the impending decline in sales with the economic downturn in the USA and abroad, Rivetti took the opportunity to stretch GFT into new territories. In an attempt at global expansion he began to consider moving into retail, rather than limit the company to production and distribution. For the first time in its history GFT allocated a substantial budget of $2.5 million in advertising and promotional campaigns for their stable of designers, largely in keeping with the continued Made in Italy campaign being waged in the USA and further afield. As part of its initiative toward greater global expansion, GFT became the first producer of luxury goods to pen a joint venture to operate in China with direct participation from the Chinese government. The venture with Tianjin-Jin Tak Garments Co. Ltd was to produce menswear in a factory in Tianyin, outside Beijing, and began production in 1988 manufacturing some 20,000 pieces a year for distribution in the Far East.

30   Spring/summer 1988

With Armani accounting for 20 per cent of GFT sales and Valentino comprising an additional 25 per cent, GFT grew to become a significant purveyor of the Italian Look abroad. By 1986, it was the largest exporter to the USA of Italian-made apparel, and constituted 15 per cent of the Italy–USA clothing trade. Italy provides not so much a 'look' per say, claims Rivetti, but 'a capacity to produce things with quality – it's part of the Italian culture'.[27] As a function of GFT's initiative to diversify and move further abroad, Rivetti took the company downmarket by developing cheaper American men's and women's designer collections, marketing Andrew Fezza, for example, as America's Armani. According to Guido Petruzzi, president of GFT/USA and the Giorgio Armani Fashion Corp. (formerly Giorgio Armani Men's Wear Corporation), Armani was 'the wedge' for their business and design approach to the USA. The success of the Armani diffusion line, Petruzzi claims, 'was the marriage of a good designer and a strong manufacturing organization'.[28] Although GFT's model success in the 1980s was predicated on its Armani business, the GFT-produced Armani line was initially a tough sell in a country noted for its rather conservative notions of tailoring and sportswear. As Petruzzi notes however, 'everybody tries to copy Armani' and the menswear customer 'wants fashion faster'.[29] In an article aptly and significantly titled 'The Americanization of GFT', Petruzzi was made to defend his company's decision to become more global by designing clothes more American in inspiration, while increasingly producing more of its garments in Hong Kong, China, Mexico and Canada, countries where production and labour costs were significantly lower than in Italy. According to Petruzzi, 'the company's design and merchandise teams use the same model, but interpret it for America. The sizes are different ... also the weight of the fabric'.[30] While today industry insiders and scholars debate the future of Made in Italy with Prada, for instance, claiming a global Made in Prada label to replace the former prestigious national one, GFT was the first to recognize the challenges of a global product, designed in one country, while being produced in another. By 1988, prices at Armani, for example, were up from between 12 and 15 per cent while at Valentino increases were between 20 and 24 per cent. Additionally, labour prices simultaneously rose 10 per cent accounting for a portion of the swell in fabric and final garment costs. These economic realities were further impacted by a declining American dollar, significantly crippling buyers' purchasing power.[31] As Petruzzi was quick to claim, 'Made-in-Italy is becoming less important than styled-in-Italy ... We try to tell our costumer that it doesn't matter where the clothing is produced if it has our quality'.[32] According to the Milan based *Associazione Italiana Industriali Abbiglimaento* (Italian Association of Clothing Manufacturers), imports of fashion goods increased by 14.1 per cent in 1988 after a fifth consecutive year of growth. At the time, imports from other EEC countries accounted for 43 per cent of the total imports into Italy while countries such as Hong Kong, Korea, Taiwan and Singapore had modest imports; China notably increased its imports into Italy by 14.2 per cent reaching 9.7 per cent of the total imports into that country in 1987.[33]

31   Spring/summer 1990

Despite GFT's various initiatives within and beyond Italy, by 1990 Rivetti was the first to complain that the 'fashion stage' had become 'too crowded'. He remarked that '[a] lot of undeserving people jumped on the train during the good years, not only in fashion but in the business around it ... Some need to disappear, and only the best will survive'. By 1991 the manufacturer warned that '[t]he partnerships between Italian design and industry has finished its period of vertical growth. Periods like 1983 to 1986 [under the Craxi government] will never be repeated again, and in a sense that's good', concluded Rivetti.[34] He spoke of the need to 'turn a label into a brand', a commercial and symbolic strategy crucial for secondary, diffusion or bridge lines. 'Couture works equally well from Switzerland to South Africa. Ready-to-wear is always more difficult. But bridge lines must be one way in Italy and another in France and Germany, both in men's and women's, and this is transforming the label into a brand.' Rivetti cited the GFT-Armani collaboration as an example of a product designed expressly for the American market while maintaining the aura of the designer, a brand in itself rather than simply a label.[35] Fundamentally Rivetti was ahead of the times: the concept of brand identity did not come into the foreground until the late 1990s. Previously, strategies we now group together and identify as branding were a rather dispersed set of practices and only later were they combined to consolidate a marketing, financial whole. Marzotto, the manufacturing giant responsible for labels such as Missoni, Biagotti and Ferré, found itself making similar claims to Rivetti. Pietro Thiella, general managing director for apparel at Marzotto, also made dire predictions for the industry when he lamented that '[i]f costs continue to go up, we'll have to think about producing outside of Italy where the price of production is lower. We'll have to go someplace where prices are competitive'. This would have been unthinkable in the so-called heyday of the Made in Italy label in the mid-1980s.[36]

The situation was dismal indeed and after several quarters of declining profits, GFT, for the first time in its illustrious history, plunged into the red in the first half of 1991. The world's largest manufacturer of designer men's apparel lost $11.8 million with sales decreasing by 1.2 per cent. In part, the decline in growth was not only a result of a slowdown of western economies, but also the result of a restructuring plan which the company had initiated the previous year, 'with the aim of getting closer to market needs'.[37] Despite its decline in sales and profit losses, the company maintained its course by 'creating separate operating companies for its various sectors, rationalizing its product range, redefining relationships with designers for closer cooperation on commercial lines, cutting expenditures and decreasing structural costs'.[38] However, with reported net losses of $28.7 million in the first six months of 1992, the company continued to haemorrhage and by 1993 Rivetti began the arduous task of trying to sell a controlling share of his family-run company.[39]

In September 1993 *Women's Wear Daily* reported that Rivetti was asking designers 'to give [them] a hand' and according to him they were responding positively.[40] It seemed, at least for the time being, that his stable of high-profile designers would not jump from his ailing ship. At the same time rumours began to circulate that Armani had not renewed his contract with the troubled manufacturer, and by September Armani had yet to make any public statement as to the future of their licensing collaboration. After a failed plan to sell GFT to Miroglio SpA, the powerful Milan merchant bank Mediobanca stepped in to rescue the company. By 1994, however, Armani had still not yet decided its relationship with the company that had once lent the necessary industrial structure needed to grow it into a global brand. Throughout the year more rumours circulated in the industry that Armani was looking for the necessary financing to procure a significant stake in the still haemorrhaging GFT and called an audit of its business and financial holdings. The reason the fashion house gave was that it suspected the possible unauthorized sales of its GFT-produced line. The suspicion was that a former GFT executive sold $6.25 million worth of clothes to Japan between 1992 and 1993 without paying royalties to Giorgio Armani.[41] By 1997, with their relationship still intact, Armani and GFT planned a strategic overhaul of the Giorgio Armani Fashion Corp. name as a symbolic though important move to ensure the Armani brand identity while at the same time enhance GFT's manufacturing presence; after all, the Giorgio Armani Fashion Corp. was then entirely controlled by the manufacturer. According to one GFT spokesperson, the move was simply 'a question of a name change, but it is an important move for the corporate identity of GFT ... In the United States everybody knows Giorgio Armani, Calvin Klein, and Joseph Abboud, but not everybody knows GFT'. Meanwhile Pino Brusone of Giorgio Armani maintained that it is a good idea not to have

33   Autumn/winter 1998

Armani's name on 'companies that are not part of the Armani group'.[42] The designer nonetheless realized the power his name and products possessed, the benefits some manufactures experienced because of his success and the weight which came to bear on him as a result, asserting that manufacturers 'have progressively become more important because I realize that some manufacturers rely on the success of the Armani lines. This was not my choice and it is a great responsibility.'[43] The final outcome was a simple label change for the so-called 'white label' – it now read 'Giorgio Armani Le Collezioni'.

34   Emporio Armani spring/summer 1991. The line's success was immediate and expanded rapidly

However, as part of Armani's millennial drive to gain greater and more complete control over his empire, he severed its once lucrative relationship with GFT from 31 December 2000 and took the formerly known 'white label' in house. In the process Armani acquired two GFT menswear-manufacturing factories in Settimo Torinese outside Turin and one in Metelica in the Marches region, which in its wake saved countless jobs at the precise moment when many were being lost to China. In addition, the house also acquired the distribution company formerly owned and controlled by GFT and responsible for the Armani lines. As we shall see later in this chapter, 2000 proved to be a benchmark in the designer's desire to consolidate and control a more integrated Armani brand name and image. The Le Collezioni collection began production in house for the autumn/winter 2000 season. This line as well as the Emporio Armani women's collection is today produced at the wholly owned Antinea factory outside of Milan, while smaller factories in the Florence region produce the accessories lines. Armani also hired 700 of GFT's employees, and stated: 'This is a symbolic moment for the Armani Group, since the GFT license was the first we entered into.'[44]

Emporio's Soaring Eagle

In touch with a new Italian prosperity and an increasingly savvy youth culture, Giorgio Armani started a secondary line by opening an inaugural boutique in via Durini in 1981, down the street from the company's then headquarters. When they opened the first store, the number of items displayed in the shop window could be counted on one hand; these included a rubber belt, a blouson jacket in quilted cotton and a simple pair of jeans. The store only sold jeans, t-shirts and what we now identify as fast-fashion, targeted at Milanese youth. The new label, however, engendered some concern for Galeotti who worried the collection would not only instil confusion among consumers, but might also jeopardize the cultural cachet the Giorgio Armani label had already garnered. This sparse denim collection, which would come to be known as Armani Jeans and from which the large Emporio Armani line was born, was more a spatial and cultural concept premised on bringing democracy to fashion than a designer label. 'Emporio is freer', according to the designer, 'it takes into account the Armani style as well as the current trends, it offers the freedom to mix the clothes according to one's own imagination. It's for everybody, not just young people, but the young at heart.'[45] The relationship between Giorgio Armani and Emporio is, according to one fan of the designer, an act of 'translating ... It's an evolutionary process'.[46] Armani's reputed evolution from season to season is also a product of a trickle-down process from his high end Giorgio Armani collection to his various subsidiary lines. The timing of the label could not have been better. Italy had suddenly been transformed into a country no longer looking to buy durable or permanent goods but rather yearning for fashionable objects that lent status and signifying potential. Armani was there at the right time and with the right product and rode the wave by opening numerous Emporio boutiques throughout Italy.[47]

Soon after Armani and Galeotti opened the doors to their emporium in via Durini, the Burghy Bar opened on the nearby Piazza San Babilla and began to attract a group of mainly young Milanese men. These self-proclaimed Paninari (derived from the food offered at their preferred hangout) soon became walking billboards for the Emporio Armani name, sporting the bomber jackets and jeans easily identified by the streamlined, minimal eagle logo on the right back pocket. Riding around on their motorinos and Vespas, they embodied the new post-1970s youth culture of the city.[48] Londoners soon picked up the distinctive city look of the Paninari in a much more watered-down and urbane way. In London baggy jeans were coupled with black leather and suede jackets, leather gloves and Paraboots to construct a decidedly 'urban uniform' of youth, an image that also helped accelerate the designer's presence in that city.[49] In 1986, British Pop duo The Pet Shop Boys, who had themselves started to wear the Armani-eagle emblazoned clothes, released what was initially intended only as a B-side paean to these boys of

35   Emporio Armani autumn/winter 1995 collections for men and women. Since its inauguration in 1981, the Emporio Armani line has expanded to encompass the full gamut of sartorial needs

Milan. In the video for the song, not only were *Paninari* included, but so too was the Emporio Armani eagle logo, helping to chart the intersection between brand identity, fashion, popular music and Armani's impact on Milanese street culture. The date of the release of their song and video importantly coincided with a significant period of development and growth when the via Durini store was no longer merely a concept providing youth with fun and cheap fashion basics, but became a full-fledged label, showcasing a complete sportswear collection which it had been doing since 1984. According to Dylan Jones: 'Emporio wasn't just a weekend thing, it was sign that you were totally in control of your life, a sign that you didn't need to "dress up" in stiff, conventionally formal clothes in order to impress someone.'[50] Armani was no longer for a select elite, but intended for everyone.

It was only when Galeotti died prematurely in 1984 that Armani single-mindedly brought the label to a new level by beginning a women's line. In 1987 Armani closed its original location and relocated it down the street to 24 via Durini, an address included in the Armani Jeans label until only recently. In addition, he shuttered a number of smaller stores he had opened throughout Italy and relocated them to more fully developed retail spaces on a much larger scale. The initiative became the impetus for the global

36   The via Borletto billboard curated by Emporio Armani in collaboration with the citizens of Milan. The billboard is changed regularly. In this instance the designer poses with the Milan-based Armani Jeans basketball team which Armani is the primary patron and sponsor

expansion of this more youthful-oriented line into a network of boutiques that at last count comprises 185 free-standing stores in 40 different countries. What is remarkable is how the inauguration of the first full-fledged Emporio Armani store received more press attention than did his Giorgio Armani flagship boutique at 9 Sant'Andrea. While Yves Saint-Laurent was the first to start a secondary line (Rive Gauche) in 1966 sold in specialized same-named boutiques, in Italy Armani was the first of the big name designers to create a secondary line with more affordable prices and destined for a younger, hipper and more fiercely style-conscious customer. Not unlike how Prada has positioned Miu Miu as a separate and unique collection, Emporio Armani was meant to be an entity of its own, a label in its own right, targeted at an entirely different constituency to his primary Giorgio Armani collection, yet with the same unmistakable Armani aesthetic. Menswear industry insider *Daily News Record* reported seeing Armani trimming and merchandising the Milan store window displays himself, as he reportedly did each and every week; Armani 'is once again light years ahead of the crowd', the periodical

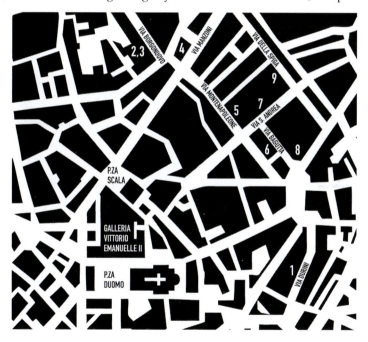

37   Armani's Milan: 1, via Durini, design headquarters in the 1970s and early 1980s, the site of Armani's first Emporio Armani Store and short-lived Armani/Casa store; 2, 21 via Borgonuovo, residence and design atelier; 3, 11 via Borgonuovo, the current press headquarters; 4, the Armani/Manzoni mega-store; 5, the Armani Junior boutique; 6, the current location of the Giorgio Armani boutique; 7, 9 Sant'Andrea, the inaugural home of the Giorgio Armani boutique and currently the Armani/ Casa boutique; 8, the Armani Collezioni boutique; 9, home to the only free-standing Giorgio Armani accessories boutique in the world

announced. 'He is convinced that this is the only way to get his message across to the customer.' In those early years Armani's direct involvement and attention to detail, even within the spaces of his Emporio boutique, reflects a desire for complete control as well as an important means through which he and his single-minded message and image can have a direct rapport with his customer on the street. As the former daily concluded optimistically: 'Obviously, he's on to something.'[51] Three years after its founding Armani's niece Silvana joined the company and over time she has assumed the position of head of the Emporio women's studio, a position she holds to this day. On several occasions, the designer has shared the spotlight with his niece when he has taken his final bow at the end of the runway show, which already in 1997 was viewed as a hint of 'Armani's intention to control his own legacy'.[52] A logical and natural choice given that even Armani himself views Silvana as more of 'a staunch Armanian' than he.[53]

To further extend his visual presence in Milan, the first Emporio Armani billboard was erected in 1984 at the intersection of via Borletto and via dell'Orso, in the heart of the city. The now iconic billboard has become not merely an advertisement for the Emporio Armani and Armani Jeans labels, but also a visual testimonial to the designer's impact on the physical, visual and cultural landscape of the city of Milan. In the fenced-in small garden patch foregrounding the billboard is posted a small sign indicating that Emporio Armani curates the space with the collaboration of the citizens of Milan.[54] In addition to this 'curatorial', civic initiative, Emporio, rather than the Giorgio Armani label, is the channel through which the designer frequently sponsors restoration programmes and cultural and sporting events in the city and beyond. Like the eagle soaring above, with Emporio Armani the designer's presence is made tangible and omnipresent within the city's cultural fabric, and for this reason, he ensures that the Giorgio Armani boutique in Sant'Andrea remains a subtle and quiet glamorous (international) destination within Milan's famed *quadrilatero*, appealing to a more sophisticated rather than younger hip, clientele.[55] Today, however, the landscape of Milan's fashionable core is architectural evidence of Armani's design and cultural presence, with numerous Armani boutiques and headquarters peppered throughout the city's centre. In cities like Milan, where there are numerous boutiques, the company offers black, glossy folding map cards indicating the location of each Armani boutique, a cartographic allusion to the designer's customer as a sort of (single-minded) fashion tourist. In addition to the famed via Borletto billboard and the numerous boutiques, Armani's omnipresence in maintained by way of numerous forms of advertising that dominate the cityscape. Whether with the large EMPORIO ARMANI sign that greets every visitor arriving at the city via Linate airport or the overwhelming advertising campaign displayed in the via Montenapoleone underground metro station, from which one walks out into a small piazza whereupon one is faced with a

38 Milan's metro at via Montenapoleone where the Emporio Armani underwear ads featuring David and Victoria Beckham were prominently displayed on every wall of the exit

large Armani billboard announcing a restoration project he co-sponsors with the city, itself located beside the Armani/Manzoni megastore housing several of the house's brands, one is never too far away from his presence or quotidian impact on the city. The megastore, the first of five such boutiques the house would eventually open in the twenty-first century, opened its doors in 2000 to celebrate the house's 25-year anniversary. In addition, it was also importantly opened to showcase the designer's expanding lifestyle empire. In this store the designer includes: Emporio Armani, Armani/Jeans, Giorgio Armani Cosmetics, Armani/Casa (accessories for the home and furniture), Armani/Dolci (confectionery), Armani/Privé (members only nightclub), Armani/Caffé, Armani/Sony (music and equipment),[56] Armani/Fiori (flowers), Armani/Libri (books) and as of November 2011 it also houses the designer's second luxury hotel and spa. Notably the Giorgio Armani label was kept in its own, separate and distinct location.

New Frontiers: The Case of A/X and Simint

In 1984, as part of Galeotti's drive to expand the company into new ventures and having reached a prominent position within the industry, Giorgio Armani signed a long-term deal with Vivienne Westwood to produce and distribute a collection for the British designer. Completed and signed in two days by the formidable and shrewd Galeotti, this was to be the first diversification project for the house. The licensing agreement between the two designers was to last seven years, an agreement Westwood herself claimed would turn 'underground overground for sure'.[57] The deal penned by Galeotti was meant as a strategy to infiltrate the more avant-garde fashion market, and granted Armani exclusive rights to the former punk designer's name around the world. The Italian house would be responsible for producing and marketing the collection, while Westwood herself would retain complete artistic autonomy. According to Westwood: 'We both have very clear formulas. Armani gives status to relaxed clothes. He will always look like Giorgio Armani, and I will always look like Vivienne Westwood.'[58] With the untimely death of Galeotti, Armani was, at least initially, at a loss for direction and the contract with Westwood was quickly shelved. By 1987 Westwood brought the case against Giorgio Armani SpA to civil court in London alleging breach of contract and seeking $3 million in damages. According to Armani's heavy-handed Gabriella Forte, 'Westwood herself broke the contract by failing to produce designs that could be reproduced in a factory.' Westwood's agent, on the other hand, claimed that he tried to get in touch with the Italian designer, however, according to him, 'it's easier to get Ronald Regan on the phone'. An arbiter was called in, but the Armani camp retaliated by asserting it had plans to pursue a counter-suit.[59] In the end there was no counter-suit, nor did the initial case go forward. The Westwood licensing initiative was the first and last of its kind that the house entered into.

Among the numerous previous and subsequent licensing agreements, Armani seemed content not to chase his late partner's dreams of the avant-garde, but rather became increasingly focused on licensing agreements, which completed, enhanced or extended his own brand portfolio. When he signed the licensing of his eyeglass collections over to Luxottica Group SpA in 1987, the brand's sales rose from $24 million in 1988 to $64 million by 1991, while the eyewear manufacturer's stocks more than doubled within a little over a year and a half. Soon thereafter the designer also entered into a contract with American based MIG-90, Inc. to manufacture his Armani Calze collections (socks and hosiery). With this deal Armani designed and oversaw all the packaging, continuity and marketing of the product, whereas MIG-90, Inc. was placed strictly in charge of manufacturing and distribution. As with most other things entered into by the Italian designer, Armani's keen sense of control has meant a unique and privileged position vis-à-vis licenses. These generally include a maximum limit in dollars and units each licensee can and must sell, and as Mello has noted this is a rather unique position for a designer to be in.[60]

By 1989 Armani had begun to acquire manufacturing companies and factories as part of a gradual process of taking complete control over his various clothing lines that did not fall under any of his then current licensing agreements. With a stake of 51 per cent in Intai, the Italian accessories manufacturer,[61] Armani began staking a 10 per cent claim of SIM (Societa Manufatti SpA), valued at $9 million with an option to purchase an additional 10 per cent in the future, which he later acquired in 1990. SIM manufactured the men's and women's Armani/Jeans collections for Europe and abroad and in 1988 it had sales of $117 million with losses of $7.7 million.[62] Industry insiders heralded the move as 'a new strategy for the firm which until [then] had limited its business involvement to design and distribution of Armani's men and women's collections'.[63] The house had depended on licenses to produce its various collections: however with this investment it was now poised to move beyond designing and marketing into the spheres of production and distribution. The strategy was to invest into manufacturers already producing various lines. In addition to its production of the Armani lines, SIM also held the distribution licenses for jeans and children's collections for Moschino, Krizia, Versace and Nikos. In a vote of confidence on the new development, Santo Versace, chairman of Gianni Versace stated: 'I am very pleased that Armani has taken an interest in SIM. [It] is a great company, and Armani's participation would only serve to strengthen the other labels.'[64]

As part of his push into manufacturing, Armani purchased a factory once owned by Sicons and placed on auction by bankruptcy courts. The apparel portion of Sicons, located in Veneto, was renamed Antinea by Armani who

once designed on a freelance basis for the ailing firm. Sicons produced its own label in addition to holding the license to produce Emporio Armani womenswear, which it continued to do under the new owner. In addition to the factory Armani also hired 150 of its former 200 employees. The goal of the purchase, according to the designer, was not simply to acquire factories that produce his goods, but rather 'to create a greater integration', between the designer, manufacturer and financier, to bring the cultures of fashion and finance into a greater intimacy.[65]

Comprising 25 per cent of Armani's then retail and wholesale revenues, by 1991 the USA was still deep in recession, and designer fashions no longer ranked high among key priorities for the average consumer as they once had throughout the 1980s. With Calvin Klein, for example, floundering with a staggering debt load of $68 million it is no wonder that magazines like *Time* were declaring the death of designer clothing.[66] On the heels of his recent investments and acquisitions and in the wake of a decidedly more conservative consumer ethos, Armani declared that 'consumerism ha[d] been taken to the limit'. According to him, '[p]eople are tired of being bombarded by all the names in fashion. They don't want crazy things anymore. They look to simple things from the past because they provide a kind of reassurance.'[67] The solution, as Armani saw it, was to open a chain of stores in the USA that featured a lower-priced, basic causal and denim collection; in short, it was meant to be Armani's answer to The Gap. The stores, known as A/X, stocked items from his already profitable Armani/Jeans line, founded ten years earlier. The new venture would also provide some much-

40   Spring/summer 1990

needed revenue to buttress the house whose sales for 1991 were predicted to decline, the first decrease after over a decade of steady and significant growth.

Reiterating Rivetti's claims that the luxury and designer markets had reached the point of saturation, Armani asserted that '[t]here's no more space for new ready-to-wear stores and names. We reached a maximum in the '80s and now you're going to see who has real value – who can survive in a recession – and who is linked only to the well-being of the market.'[68] The new chain of stores was not without critics, most claiming that it would dilute the cultural cachet and symbolic currency of the Giorgio Armani name. Some marketing analysts suggested that the designer was breaking one of the golden rules of the industry, that is, never use an exclusive brand name to sell another product. Throughout the 1980s numerous designers created cheaper bridge lines as a means to capture a broader audience, fearful or tired of the high prices of designer products many have come to expect as a seemingly inherent right. However, many designers like Donna Karan and Calvin Klein have also wanted to disassociate their names directly with these new lines, opting for abbreviations like DKNY and CK. However, the need to disassociate one's name directly from a line also points to a lack of control. For Emporio Armani, one of the first secondary lines created by a designer, the distribution is so tight that unlike CK and DKNY, the merchandise rarely, if ever, shows up in uncontrolled downmarket retail environments and in bargain bins in discount chains. Quality control of the A/X stores, according to the company, would be guaranteed by way of a limited distribution and retail network, initially 200 stores were forecasted to open in the USA alone within the first three years, a number it has yet to achieve.[69] Moreover, despite what is truly a stretching of the Armani name and brand, the designer was not selling objects he did not already design in house. However, for most, this was not enough. 'In a way, he's attacking himself', claimed Jack Trout of Trout and Ries, a marketing consulting firm in the USA. Citing the downfall of Cadillac as a perfect case of the syndrome of moving downmarket, Trout continued: 'I have no doubt that he'll have some success selling cheaper clothes, but marketing is littered with brands that have been cheapened by line extensions. Once you go downscale with a brand name, you can't ever come back up'.[70] Surely, at least in part it also signalled another facet of the on-going threat to the Made in Italy image and quality.

Given that the client who shops at Giorgio Armani is not the same as the one stepping into an A/X emporium, cannibalism within the various labels was and remains of no concern. Armani astutely noted that '[p]eople are not going to give up dressing expensively. But because of momentary reasons and because of the overeating of fashion, the orgy of fashion that happened in the late 1980's, people want not to be so obvious.'[71] Indeed the early 1990s spawned an era of inconspicuous consumption coupled with the rise of minimalism, with flashier labels left to flounder or reinvent themselves altogether. Although from the standpoint of the house, it was maintained that the new American-based venture was to complement rather than compete with the designer's own pre-existing lines, loyal customers increasingly became unclear as to the identity of each vertically integrated Armani label. While numerous sales associates I talked to in both Canada and the USA confirmed the state of confusion, *The New York Times* took the question to the streets, when its reporter interviewed four different people who were all devoted to the Giorgio Armani collection; all agreed to be interviewed only on the condition of anonymity. The reporter's findings were not entirely surprising, but certainly revealing nonetheless. All four of the respondents maintained that despite the new A/X line, they all planned to continue purchasing the Giorgio Armani black label collection. One interviewee mentioned, 'I do think the line is proliferating too much', while another claimed needing assistance to differentiate between the various collections, stating, 'I had to get a definition from the sales person as to the difference between the black label ... the white label ... and Emporio Armani. It's all getting really complex.'[72]

The first A/X store located in SoHo opened in December 1991, and its mass appeal translated at the cash registers with line ups around the block for the opening weekend and sales double what was projected. Opening day sales totalled $130,000 with 5,514 shoppers passing through the 3,500 square foot store.[73] This first and all subsequent boutiques designed by Naomi Leff were meant to recall a P/X shop, utilitarian and pared down to industrial simplicity. For the chain, the house claimed from the beginning that 80 per cent of the products would remain under $100. However, *The New York Times* took the designer to task by noting how there was much more over the alleged $100 mark.[74] Equally affected by the recession, department stores were also eager to get a piece of the downmarket segment, after all Armani consistently drew large sales for them. Saks Fifth Avenue opened two freestanding A/X boutiques in Chicago and Boston in March 1992. The initiative marked the first time the department store had ever opened an outlet under a name other than its own and the first agreement of its kind for Armani.

A/X was not only meant to increase revenue for Giorgio Armani, but also for the beleaguered manufacturer Simint SpA, formerly SIM, and its subsidiary Simint USA. In 1993, the American operation reported losses of $8.2 million in a six-month period ending 31 October, while Simint SpA lost an equally troubling $7.6 million. By this point the company was heavily indebted to the sum of $142 million, half of which was incurred by the USA operation directly responsible for A/X. On the heels of such losses Armani and his sister Rosanna purchased an additional stake in the company for $20 million. The purchase meant Armani now owned a 22.5 per cent of Simint SpA, while Rosanna held a 17 per cent stake. With a combined total of 39.5 per cent, it now left the designer holding the single largest interest in the company. News of the acquisition by the Armani siblings boosted the value of the stocks slightly.[75] However, by May 1994, Rosanna had reduced her stakes in Finar Srl, a financial holding group that controlled 16.8 per cent of Simint SpA, from 90 to 9 per cent. The move was a result of a much-needed infusion of capital into the company from Singapore tycoon Ong Beng Seng who already held a 5 per cent stake in Simint SpA and an additional 10 per cent of the USA subsidiary. Seng was not new to the Armani enterprise, distributing the Armani/Jeans line throughout the UK. Meanwhile a buyer was being sought for Simint USA. By June Simint had announced it had sold its A/X operations to Seng, which by then comprised 41 stores in the USA.[76] The desire to bring Simint SpA out of financial ruin, a move that would signify more than simply the newly acquired manufacturing power of the designer, but also, if only in a small and symbolical way, the health and well-being of the Italian garment manufacturing industry located in the area. Brusone announced that

> [t]he significant financial effort we are making for Simint shows the desire of Giorgio Armani to bring the company out of the troubles ... This is a company that is not only of importance to the industrial reality of the city of Modena where it employs a significant amount of people, but also for the small shareholders that risk losing everything they had invested.[77]

By 1995, as a means to stave off additional losses Armani embarked on a major restructuring programme. First he moved to close the few A/X outlets owned by Saks and focused solely on company-owned freestanding stores. Armani then hired Maurizio Caciatore to manage and oversee the transformation of the company. In September he proceeded to cut the work force from 475 to 228 workers and discontinued the production of the Moschino Jeans license as well Versace childrenswear, Best Company and Marina Yachting.[78] Simint also continued doing the cutting for the Emporio Armani and Giorgio Armani collections, which it had been doing since 1994, in addition to producing all the jean lines and some of the knitwear for Emporio Armani. By August 1995 Simint could finally claim to be back in the black with a net profit of $2 million in the first half of the year. The company concluded that the stronger performance had mostly to do with a strong performance of Armani products rather than the other labels they produced; sales of Armani Jeans and sportswear alone rose 21 per cent for the autumn/winter 1994 season.[79]

Having provided the much-needed influx of cash, by early 1996 Armani and Ong mutually decided to discontinue their collaboration on the Simint USA operation. Armani cited the possible conflict of interest that Ong now faced with his move toward diversifying into different designer labels, including the production and retail of Donna Karan.[80] By April Armani had purchased another 16.8 per cent shares in Simint (raising his total to 53.1 per cent) from Finar Srl, the holding company used by Seng to purchase Simint USA two years earlier. Armani committed $78 million to help save Simint, and by 1998 the company produced its second year of large gains when its net earnings shot up by 77 per cent to $32 million. The designer noted how

> Simint depended on Armani alone. My hope is that now that weight will be lifted with the help of other partners, other labels, and that Simint will become autonomous. In the old sort of relationship between designer and manufacturer, one person created the clothes and the other sold them. Now there is intense collaboration between the two for distribution, sales points, everything that has to do with the business. In the future, designers will become increasingly tied to their manufacturers, to the needs of industry, to the final result, to the sales figures.[81]

The rocketing sales and earnings were a result of the restructuring initiated by both Caciatore and Brusone as well as vigorous sales of the Armani/Jeans line, which by that time comprised 90 per cent of Simint's revenues.[82] By 2001, Armani again acquired 39.5 per cent shares in Simint, bringing his total to a 92.7 per cent stake.[83]

In 2005 Giorgio Armani SpA and Como Holdings owned by Christina Ong in Singapore signed a joint venture to be called Presidio Holdings for the management and global expansion of A/X. No longer selling the Armani/Jeans line, the A/X stores that had already begun a global push into South East Asia and South America were not merely a 'store' any longer, but a full-fledged independent label, A/X Armani Exchange. It that same year, Armani also began his seemingly impromptu foray into haute couture in Paris. With these two labels, on either extreme of fashion's spectrum, prestigious and elite haute couture and fast fashion, Giorgio Armani was 'effectively closing the circle on [its] unique multi-brand approach, whereby [it was] reaching all levels of the marketplace with carefully differentiated fashion collections under the Armani master brand'.[84] The brand within brand strategy has been successful at attracting numerous different economic segments. When in the UK in 2005, Armani was once again questioned as to whether he was overextending his name and brand identity with the launching of A/X in that country. He responded by reminding the reporter that everyone in the industry thought he was foolish in 1981 to create a secondary and jeans line.[85] Today A/X Armani Exchange, Emporio Armani and Armani/Jeans are flourishing labels, part of the dream once shared by Galeotti to see his partner's designs on more backs than those of the rich and famous.

Manufacturing Legacy in the New Millennium

What is luxury? Although largely elusive in terms of acquisition and meaning, within our global brand-obsessed context, luxury, I surmise, constitutes a number of key components as brands attempt to universalize it and its experience. These primarily include: the spaces of display and consumption and the boundaries of access that heighten the aura of the object in question; the rituals and performances of service and display around it; and finally the object itself which is defined by way of its material, preciousness and rarity, aesthetic appeal and signifying potential, qualities temporally and geographically relative and dependent. However, often there can be a lack or a rupture within one or more of the experiences listed above, which tarnish the illusory sparkle of luxury's phantasm. On one such occasion at the new Giorgio Armani boutique in via Montenapoleone (Milan) in 2009, a salesperson was sent into a tizzy when asked what sort of leather was used for a business card holder. Her apparent lack of knowledge was quickly followed by a dismissive nonchalance toward both the client and the object. In addition, it was also apparent she had no way of finding out. The outposts of luxury sell a rather limited amount of objects; only a select few of the Giorgio Armani boutiques around the world even sell the entire collection. It would seem like a basic supposition, therefore, that product knowledge is not only feasible, but also necessary and highly desirable within the visual and material economy of luxury especially in the rarefied space of the designer's Milanese boutique.

If, as the designer himself has alluded, Armani desires his house to be regarded akin in stature to a luxury brand like Hermès, then the micro-management he is so infamous for might be at a crossroads, at which point perhaps a back-to-basics ethos might better service not so basic objects. Respected fashion journalist Dana Thomas has tracked how luxury fashion has lost its sheen through the incessant search for ever greater global market share, the accelerated onslaught of the 'it' bag of the season within the financial culture of accessories, the downmarketing of exclusivity for the masses and finally the ubiquity of perfume as a means to sustain a house's clothing segment. In her book, *Deluxe: How Luxury Lost its Luster* Thomas argues that

> [t]he luxury industry has changed the way people dress. It has realigned our economic class system. It has changed the way we interact. It has become part of our social fabric. To achieve this, it has sacrificed its integrity, undermined its products, tarnished its history, and hoodwinked its consumers. In order to make luxury 'accessible', tycoons have stripped away all that has made it special.[86]

As large corporate enterprises, luxury conglomerates like LVMH and PPR, and to a lesser extent the Prada Group, have contributed to the ideal that, even if only through perfume or a bag, one can attain the notional lifestyle exhibited in the advertisements and tacitly coded within the spatial regime of boutiques and outposts around the world. Although his perfumes and colognes are among the highest selling in the industry, unlike many of his peers Armani has built an empire primarily on clothing (which boasts lower profit margins than accessories) and as a result has never relied on the sales of accessories or perfumes to compensate for, sustain or buttress his fashion collections. [87]

41   Spring/summer 1990

As we have already seen, the designer has sought out every possible market segment through his stable of various labels, moving from A/X Armani Exchange all the way to his more recent foray into haute couture, catering to the desire to possess a piece of the so-called democratic Armani ideal. Despite moving downmarket with the creation of his A/X line, Armani has also had a rather equivocal relationship with luxury over the decades. Throughout the 1970s and 1980s and even into the 1990s Armani has always expounded on the merit of the industrial process of fashion within the more democratic system of prêt-à-porter. As he asserts: 'High fashion for the wealthy and the very rich still exists, but the rule is that the articles shown on the runway, with a few corrections and a few modifications, must be capable of becoming clothes for everyone.'[88] Within this aesthetics of realism, luxury becomes anathema, an object that can have no impact on the world of quotidian design. In 2002, however, Armani ruffled some feathers when he declared after he presented his menswear collection that luxury disgusted him.[89] The press picked up on the irony of his statement and were quick to charge him with hypocrisy. The designer however contended that the press, as they often do, missed entirely the point he was attempting to make. According to him: 'When the press came back after the men's show they said "we like this image of the worker and a return to the values of the past". So I said, joking, "Well, I'm glad you appreciate this because I am sick of hearing about luxury." And being good journalists they wrote it.'[90] Later, when asked again about the nature of luxury and his controversial comments, Armani told *Corriere della Sera,* 'I thought about it. And I correct myself: luxury is something that goes beyond fashion. It's an object that will last forever.' And, with a sense of humour, tinged with irony, he gives the 'blue-shirted Armani' as an example to illustrate his definition.[91]

By 2002, as Thomas argues, so-called luxury[92] fashion houses were performing a virtual blitzkrieg of marketing the must-have 'it' bag and hottest accessories, pouring millions of dollars into advertising. 'Status symbols are not luxury', Armani contends. 'Luxury must be top quality, and very exclusive'.[93] For the designer, American *Vogue* in particular focuses too much attention on the avant-garde for the moneyed eccentric few, rather than accessible fashions for working people. As we have already seen, his position largely stems from his lack of return on his American advertising expenditure. Armani and *Vogue* are fundamentally no different, however, each invested in the cultivation of certain products, images and ideals, which in turn translate into either advertising revenue or sales. As editor of *Vogue* (UK) Alexandra Shulman pointed out following Armani's remarks, 'Armani is very successful at marketing. They are big advertisers, and it is not as if they are a low-key operation. They are hugely successful and know very well how to market themselves.' She also noted how '[i]t's a rather odd remark because Giorgio Armani collection clothes are extremely expensive. He does have his jeans line and Emporio Armani, which are less expensive but still by no means cheap.'[94] Nonetheless, Armani maintains it is largely a question of respect, expectations and hard work, something the new generation does not possess. 'Today's youth', he noted at the time, 'which has suffered neither deprivation nor war, does not value sacrifice, having the newest watch is what people care about.'[95] Luxury, as many might agree, is less about the price tag, which often connotes rarity and exclusivity, and more about quality. By 2008, after years of speculation as to the future of the house, even Armani was tempted to consider a merger with luxury house Hermès. 'Hermes has such class, such prestige', the designer is reported to have said.[96] Despite his desire to up the luxury ante with such developments as his haute couture collection and bespoke men's tailoring atelier, neither Armani nor his Italian counterparts can boast that they guarantee their goods and provide impeccable service, something Hermès can. In a recent shopping trip to Milan, one person I interviewed claimed that within a week of wearing a belt he had purchased at the flagship boutique it was ruined with white discoloration ingrained in the leather. When he approached the boutique in London (a franchised store), the sales staff simply suggested he could call the Milan store, offering no other advice, service or assistance. Despite fashion houses' global pretensions, franchising and mass production has meant a loss, to some extent, of quality and service, the latter fundamental to the culture of luxury. A knowledgeable and customer-oriented staff is also essential to this culture. On several occasions I have witnessed sales staff ignoring customers because they were themselves too busy trying on clothes or chatting with each other, an experience decidedly antithetical to a man that stipulates the distance between each hanger. In this instance one must ask is image more important than service in the new cultural economy of luxury?

In March 1999 the *International Herald Tribune* ran a story contemplating the future of Italian fashion houses, querying whether they could sustain themselves in the encroaching new millennium.[97] While the health and longevity of Made in Italy has been doubted numerous times before, millennial fever and superstition was to some extent justified. By the end of the 1990s most Italian houses seemed to lack long-term vision. Given that 33 per cent of Italian houses are only first generation, with few possessing an heir apparent, fears abound that their futures seem unsure at best. Italian houses have subsequently had to redefine themselves not on the aesthetic level, but in financial terms. Sergio La Verghetta, deputy commissioner of the Italian Trade Commission in New York, claims the Italians are not good at evaluating the markets they are in. 'Italian companies have been successful in the U.S.

42   Spring/summer 1994

because of their image, fashion, quality and the magic of the Made-in-Italy label. And this was with much higher duties. But the situation is very different now with the growing competition from North America and Asia'.[98]Armani, for instance, has always maintained he does not adjust his practices to suit the needs of any given country, despite the creation of two distinct labels which were initially targeted at the American and subsequent Asian markets.

Prada, a house which has virtually dominated the fashion scene since the late 1990s, has repeatedly made the covers of design magazines as well as trade and financial papers with headlines of its internal turmoil, rapid acquisition woes and financial ill-health. At the turn of the millennium and beyond in both Paris and Milan numerous houses were hiring and quickly firing star designers, leaving companies to flounder and lose client faith. Perhaps, in part, the fears were generated by Italy's most successful house when it made a shocking announcement in July 1998 that Armani was actively searching out Italian or international partners for collaborative ventures to increase the potential of the company. The assumption was that these moves were an indication he was either looking to sell the company or float it on the stock market. With every passing collection Armani has been dogged by questions not of his collections but of the financial direction he was planning to take with his company. Cool, calm and collected as ever, the designer usually simply responded by claiming he was thinking over his options.

The collaborations Armani began to search out were fundamentally to ensure the health and future well-being of the company beyond its sun-baked emperor, whether he floated it on the stock market or declared an heir, thought to come from within the company. The process, however, was to make the company less emotional and more professional, setting people up for their future roles within the house. The strategy was clear and decisive: consolidate power by bringing manufacturing and distribution in house; expand the brand into new territories; consolidate, enhance and segment each label by offering more comprehensive and complete collections; and spread globally by opening or redesigning retail outlets across the various Armani labels. According to Armani, his and his company's 'golden moment' had yet to come.[99] Since 1990 Armani's profit increases averaged high double-digits per year, a figure unusually robust for a designer brand, and interestingly double that of luxury-power house LVMH.[100] The sales figures and profit margins throughout the 1990s reveal the designer's incredible staying power among his highly loyal clients, said by some, however, to be ageing along with their designer of choice. Armani's limelight has been stolen away by Prada and Gucci, while his designs were often dismissed and at times attacked by the fashion press. However, Sara Forden, editor-in-chief of *Luna*, a woman's magazine based in Milan, has noted how '[a] few years ago, everything in fashion was hot and sexy – that was Gianni Versace's style in particular – but Armani stuck to his stylistic beliefs, to clean lines and beautifully cut clothes.

It cost him a lot of headlines, but he wouldn't bend. And now fashion has come his way again'.[101]

By 1998 consumers were spending a staggering $3.28 billion on Armani products at retail, with apparel accounting for 58 per cent of that total. In the same year the house also increased its interest in Giorgio Armani Japan Co., by 25 per cent, bringing his total to an 85 per cent stake in the company, with his partner Itochu holding the remaining 15 per cent. In addition to Japan, Armani began buying back or not renewing franchising contracts for his Giorgio Armani and Emporio Armani stores. In Hong Kong, for example, Armani took control of three out of four of that city's boutiques (one Giorgio Armani and two Emporio Armani) from Joyce Boutique Holdings Ltd so that by 1999, 49.8 per cent of the company's revenues came from wholly owned boutiques, then totally 81.[102] By June 2000, with cash reserves of $335 million and new ventures in the works, it became clear that Armani was no longer interested in selling to LVMH, rumoured to be the most likely candidate, but rather in expanding and building the brand. It is rumoured that Pino Brusone's sudden departure early in 2000 was likely the result of his proactive pushing of an IPO or partnership with the French luxury conglomerate. Later, when asked if he was looking to acquire other labels, as many of his largest competitors had done in their shopping sprees of the 1990s, Armani simply responded: 'We already have the best one'.[103]

43   Left: men's jacket/coat with thick stretch wool collar made from wool, viscose and elastoide (*c*.2006); right: men's alpaca coat with wool scarf (*c*.2006)and leather saddle bag (*c*.2004)

The late 1990s were clearly troubled and unfocused times for the designer, whose unsure future spilt over into his vacillation with the press regarding his future as well as into his designs. However, with a renewed focus on building and expanding the horizons of his company, Armani began to chart new territory to conquer. First, the house moved aggressively into accessories, an area he had never fully developed and neglected. Intai, a wholly owned subsidiary of Giorgio Armani, began producing all leather goods and accessories for the house, and Dawn Mello formerly of Bergdorf Goodman and chief consultant at Gucci was hired to consult on the new accessories division. By 2000, runway shows for the men's and women's collections featured the new accessory lines, especially the purses, briefcases and handbags, in almost every exit. The house also introduced a critically acclaimed and highly successful make-up line as well as Armani/Casa, a furniture line and interior design service, all of which feature prominently in Armani's mega-store in Milan at 21 via Manzoni.

In tandem with these new design initiatives, Armani also began to bring the production and distribution of his various labels in house. In 1999, a significant 32.3 per cent of the company's revenues came from the seven factories he then owned, with royalties from licenses accounting for around 14.5 per cent of the revenue and 2.2 per cent assured from interest.[104] In July 2000, Giorgio Armani and Emernegildo Zegna Group, which by then had become one of Armani's leading competitors in the menswear sector, announced they had

44   The accessories wall at the Guggenheim Museum retrospective, less than one year after the designer moved to create an accessories line and increase his presence in this lucrative segment of the fashion market

entered into a collaboration to produce and distribute the Le Collezioni (white label) collection for men. The agreement was touted as one 'that might alter the balance of the men's wear industry'.[105] Under the new agreement Giorgio Armani still retained 51 per cent of the Milan-based manufacturing and distribution business once owned by GFT, leaving the remaining 49 per cent to Zegna. John Hooks of Giorgio Armani was placed in charge of the new venture, which the designer reported was valued at $222 million at wholesale for both the men's and women's line.[106] 'In the market we compete', noted Zegna CEO Gildo Zegna. 'In the back office, we help each other. We want to keep Italian brands Italian.'[107] Next on the list was Armani's prized black label manufactured by Vestimenta. Founded in 1962 in Trento, in northern Italy, the small company was best known for manufacturing the Hilton line in Europe, distributed in North America as Vestimenta. Having produced the collection since 1979, by 2000 60 per cent of its $125 million in sales was generated by Giorgio Armani's Borgonuovo (or black label) collection.[108] By 2001, eager to take over the manufacturing of his primary namesake collection, Armani formed another joint venture with the Trento based company. In a statement announcing the renewed collaboration, Armani claimed that his vision to diversify into the spheres of 'manufacturing, distribution and retail, is proving to be a winning strategy'.[109] The newly formed company, Borgo 21, headed by Massimo Mosterts (owner of Vestimenta) as chief executive officer gave 60 per cent ownership to Giorgio Armani with the remaining 40 per cent to Vestimenta. In addition, the latter sold the designer the three factories producing the Armani collection. 'The focus on owning our manufacturing and our stores has allowed us to increase and improve our margins considerably', said a Giorgio Armani spokesperson.[110] In 2006 Armani would acquire the remaining 40 per cent of Borgo 21 held by Vestimenta, leaving the designer with complete control over the companies that manufacture and market the Giorgio Armani label.

Following the attacks on the USA on 11 September 2001, fashion's two largest conglomerates Gucci and LVHM reported 15 per cent decline in sales, while Armani, thanks in large part to increasingly diversified revenue channels, posted a 23 per cent increase of sales on $1.2 billion at wholesale.[111] The results of the attacks on the luxury and fashion industries were deep and significant and did not leave even Armani unscathed, though he came out significantly better than most. In the USA the designer had to lay off 28 employees from its retail, communication and merchandising divisions due to the lagging USA economy and in an attempt to streamline operations following the acquisition of Le Collezioni from GFT.[112] However, of these 28 positions, 5 were already vacant and 3 employees were relocated. These lay-offs compare with Gucci, for example, which terminated 130 positions in the USA.[113] While sales had increased by 23 per cent, net profits at Giorgio Armani were down by 9.1 per cent in 2001. This was largely due to Giorgio Armani's continuous aggressive acquisition pace; the house spent $270 million on investments in retailing and acquisitions including the joint venture with Vestimenta, putting a crimp on the company's profits. Despite the decline in profits the company nevertheless went ahead in 2002 and bought four additional factories, including I Guardi, which specializes in footwear.[114]

45　Autumn/winter 1994. Silk and plastic jacket paired with silk dress

By 2004 American journalists seemed particularly poised to launch a new campaign against Made in Italy, and were once again declaring its death. In a particularly biting and condescending article in *The New York Times* featuring Milan's men's fashion week, reporter Guy Trebay dismissed the cultural and economic importance the fashion and textile industries play in the life of Italy. He stated:

> Ever since this country joined the European Union, a current nostalgia has emerged here for an Italy that is swiftly passing out of existence, a mythical place amalgamated from local cultures that, however deep-rooted, may not prove strong enough to resist the global market juggernaut ... there is a move afoot to replace the treasured Made in Italy label with one that reads Made in Europe, so that manufacture can be cheaply outsourced throughout the European Union ... In reaction, Italian designers seem mobilized to reclaim their cradle culture.[115]

The underlying negative connotations of nostalgia belies the fear that numerous European designers, manufacturers and governments were grappling with in the wake of the impending 1 January 2005 deadline when the world trade in textiles was freed of all previous import and tariff restrictions, a date expected to open the market to a tidal wave of Chinese products. However indifferent were Trebay's comments, they did presage, to a small degree, Prada's initiatives of two years later. At the 2006 Business of Luxury summit in London, Prada CEO Patrizio Bertelli announced that the company was planning to outsource production of some of its main label, and in 2011 it replaced the eponymous Made in Italy label with Made by Prada; a response to the global context of textile and industrial production, offering instead to list the various countries involved in the production of each designed garment.

However, in January 2005, key figures in the Italian industry began to speak out. Notable among them was Mario Boselli, chairman of the Italian Chamber of Fashion in Milan, who warned not to underestimate the potential threat of China in a context of lifted tariff restrictions. 'I'm tired of hearing China is an opportunity', Boselli lamented. 'While true in theory, it is a practical lie. It is an opportunity for a few and a problem for many. We must be aware that we will go through a terrible moment because China follows a predatory strategy with predatory prices and without respecting our rules'. Again he warned: 'Once China has destroyed our western production cycle, it will raise its prices and we are dead.'[116] At the same time, Didier Grumbach, president of the French federation for prêt-à-porter and haute couture called for greater co-operation between the two fashion capitals, while also requesting greater defence of intellectual property of designers' work. The issue of safeguarding intellectual property has long been an on-going saga ever since Paul Poiret attempted to protect his unique couture creations from poaching by American manufacturers. The problem has never fully been resolved, nor is it likely to be given that designer's themselves 'borrow' freely from myriad sources, including their own colleagues.

46   Autumn/winter 1997

The effect of the new global climate spelled disaster for many in the French and Italian industries. Five years into the new millennium *The Economist* reported Ungaro was up for sale, LVMH was attempting to offload Christian Lacroix, Givenchy and YSL and Versace was still reporting crippling losses, noting that even mass-market producers cannot sustain continued long-term problems.[117] The World Trade Organization predicted that within the short span of two years, however, China alone would control 50 per cent of the world's fashion market. European Union imports of Chinese textile and clothing almost doubled between 2001 and 2003. By mid-decade 60 per cent of French brands were already produced abroad, and now Italy was going through what France experienced eight years before, when approximately one-third of the industry's jobs disappeared.[118] However, the obverse is also true and relevant. With numerous textile factories in ruin throughout northern Italy, such as Biella, those remaining and producing Italian designer fashions and accessories one at a time, were given a modicum of job security with the rise of the Chinese market.[119] However, Italy's economic malaise was also fuelling fears of a disintegration of their role within the EU, given its continued lagging economy. In large part, Italy's greatest challenge are the thousands of family-owned companies which helped the country to prosper and larger companies to flourish in the 1970s and 1980s, but are ill-suited to the realities of globalization. In the twenty-first century the question for Italian houses must revolve around how they manage the China 'problem' while maintaining the house's image and the luxury quotient intact. With the knowledge he has no direct heir to take over the house despite three family members functioning in key roles, Armani continues to structure the firm in such a way that it becomes less dependent on family ties and more reliant on an internal network that is self-sustaining as a global enterprise.

Noteworthy about the previously cited article in *The Economist* was how it pinned the hopes of the industry on Armani. On the heels of a successful debut haute couture collection in Paris (in January 2005), the final word on the topic saw the magazine suggesting: 'Now that Mr. Armani has at last been to the Paris shows, he must return again and again.'[120] Indeed, Giorgio Armani's successful brands within brand strategy (avoiding the expensive and mostly non-lucrative acquisitions of other labels) coupled with the push in 2000 to diversify its complete lifestyle package in addition to its move into manufacturing and distribution has meant that while Giorgio Armani has experienced decline in sales since the global recession hit in 2008, the house has not only rebounded in 2010 but it remains in significantly better health than many since 2005.[121] In an interview with British designer Stella McCartney Armani was asked about what the independence of his house has offered him and his company, to which he responded: 'It gives me the freedom to pursue projects and initiatives that I feel passionate about, even if in the short term they may not deliver a financial return.'[122]

47   Autumn/winter 1997

With Giorgio Armani listed as only one of three Italian companies in the top 100 global brands, the designer's power remains impressive enough to attract not only the likes of AC footballer Andriy Shevchenko and Italian entertainer Andrea Pezzi to his menswear autumn/winter 2006 collection runway show, but also the cultural and economic symbolic presence of Peter Mandelson, the European trade commissioner for external trade, an unlikely attendee at the runway shows. 'Actually I am here to make a political point', Mandelson stated when asked by reporters why he was attending the Armani show. 'There is an argument that Italian manufacturers cannot stand up to international competition, but I believe that Italians have the most powerful fashion industry, and I'm here to make the case for European competitiveness.'[123] Clearly the move was to signal, if only obliquely, that Made in Italy retains its importance as a cultural and economic force and that at the heart of the national cum global label was Armani. While conglomerates PPR and LVMH continue to absorb smaller design firms, Karan, Lauren and Klein have all either sold or floated their companies on the stock market, Lacroix has filed for bankruptcy, Viktor and Rolf have closed their one and only boutique (in the heart of Milan) and even in the wake of the current global crisis Armani remains fashion's greatest success story of creative and commercial independence.

Notes

1   Hyde 1990: 27.

2   Hyde 1990: 27.

3   Hyde 1990: 28.

4   Armani in 'Armani Disarmed' 1995: iii.

5   Field 2001: 19.

6   Segre 2005: 126.

7   Romanelli 1988: 63–4.

8   Witter 1989: 101.

9   *WWD* 25 October 1994.

10   Merlo and Polese 2006: 416.

11   *DNR* 25 June 1992.

12   *WWD* 23 February 1987.

13   Rivetti 2009.

14   *WWD* 20 January 1984.

15   Aragno 1988: 8.

16   Merlo and Polese 2006: 418.

17   See Ferrero-Regis 2008.

18   In the wake of the new millennium and Armani's expansion into production and manufacturing, these previously crucial relationships began to appear less important when he stopped including the names of textile manufacturers in his advertisements. This absence also parallels Armani's move not to include the names of the photographers of campaigns in the advertisements as well. The result is a pure and unadulterated focus on the work of the designer alone.

19   *G & M* 16 April 1986.

20   *NYT* 5 April 1988.

21   Bucci in Aragno 1988: 12.

22   Mello in Aragno 1988: 8.

23   Saltzman in Aragno 1988: 8.

24   France came in at 12.8 per cent, Switzerland at 7.2 per cent, UK at 6.8 per cent and finally Japan at a low 6.2 per cent. Aragno 1988: 3–4.

25   Bucci in Aragno 1988: 81.

26   Aragno 1988: 81.

27   *WWD* 23 February 1987.

28   *DNR* 5 December 1988.

29   *DNR* 5 December 1988.

30   *DNR* 5 December 1988.

31   *NYT* 14 December 1988.

32   *DNR* 5 December 1988. However, the relationship between customer and price also became a sore issue for GFT when in 1987 an independent personal shopper charged Saks and GFT with conspiring to eliminate any GFT apparel being sold for less than a suggested 220 per cent mark-up from the wholesale price. The personal shopper, Susan Roth, who conducts her services under the corporate name of Trims Unlimited alleged that GFT stopped doing business with her in August to save business for Saks Fifth Avenue. GFT accounted for 50 per cent of her merchandise sales. In turn Saks Fifth Avenue threatened to terminate their relationship with GFT if they did not cut off their links with other personal shoppers, who charge a significantly lower mark-up percentage. *WWD* 7 December 1987.

33   In Aragno 1988: 4.

34   Rivetti in *WWD* 11 June 1991.

35   *WWD* 1 May 1990.

36   *WWD* 11 June 1991.

37   *WWD* 10 October 1991.

38   *WWD* 10 October 1991.

39   *WWD* 20 January 1993.

40   *WWD* 7 September 1993.

41   *DNR* 30 November 1994.

42   *DNR* 16 July 1997.

43   *DNR* 17 June 1996.

44   *DNR* 12 June 2000.

45   *WWD* 21 April 1993.

46   *G & M* 15 August 1991.

47   In 1988 the GNP per capita of Italy overtook that of Britain. By 1989 the company had opened 65 Emporio Armani store doors in Italy, 9 throughout the rest of Europe, 1 in North America and 12 in Asia.

48   For more on the *paninari* see Muscau 2009.

49   Dylan Jones in 'Armani Disarmed' 1995: xiii.

50   Jones in 'Armani Disarmed' 1995: xiv.

51   DNR: *The Magazine* October 1985.

52   *G & M* 11 October 1997.

53   *G & M* 22 November 1997.

54   Today the sign reads: *Qui il verde è curato da Emporio Armani* [and in slightly smaller print at the bottom right hand corner] con la collaborazione dei cittadini.

55   The *quadrilato* consists of three central shopping streets: via Montenapoleone, via Sant'Andrea and via della Spiga, all of which today boast an Armani boutique.

56   While the Armani/Sony has since closed, Armani has curated a numerous of CD volumes through the Armani/Caffé and A/X Armani Exchange labels.

57   *WWD* 16 January 1985.

58   *WWD* 16 January 1985.

59   *WWD* 19 March 1987.

60   *Forbes* 28 October 1991.

61   *WWD* 8 October 1990.

62   *WWD* 19 September 1989.

63   *DNR* 19 September 1989.

64   *WWD* 19 September 1989.

65   *DNR* 9 October 1990.

66   *Time* 11 November 1991.

67   *W Europe* October 1991: 23.

68   *W Europe* October 1991: 23.

69   This number never materialized. With every new retail venture Armani embarks on, overly generous numbers are always given initially, with a significantly smaller number of actual openings. Today, the A/X Armani Exchange retail network comprises less than 200 stores globally.

70   *NYT* 9 September 1991.

71   *NYT* 9 September 1991.

72   *NYT* 9 September 1991.

73   *DNR* 17 December 1991.

74   *NYT* 29 September 1991.

75   *DNR* 4 February 1994.

76   *CDS* 4 May 1994.

77   *DNR* 8 November 1994.

78   *DNR* 14 September 1995.

79   *DNR* 13 October 1995.

80   *DNR* 4 March 1996.

81   *DNR* 17 June 1996.

82   *DNR* 29 July 1998.

83   *DNR* 9 July 2001.

84   Armani press release 3 November 2005.

85   *Telegraph* 10 December 2005.

86   Thomas 2007: 13.

87   I give as only one example, in 2008 clothing comprised a 56 per cent share of the total wholesale turnover including licensed products. This is lower than it was in the 1980s for instance, but clearly significantly higher than other luxury brands in its category which usually boast 70 to 80 per cent turnover stemming from accessories and perfumes. Eyewear comprises the house's second largest category, coming in at 26 per cent. See Giorgio Armani Annual Report 2008.

88   'Armani Disarmed' 1995: iv.

89   *Corriere* 15 January 2002.

90   *Corriere* 15 January 2002.

91   *Corriere* 5 March 2002.

92   For Thomas Hermès remains the only exception to the downmarketing of luxury, given that every handbag is still hand-made in France. See Chapter 6 Thomas 2007.

93   *Evening Standard* 11 February 2002.

94   *CDS* 14 January 2002.

95   *CDS* 14 January 2002.

96   *Bloomberg* 12 December 2008.

97   *IHT* 11 March 1999.

98   *DNR* 22 January 1999.

99   *WWD* 2 August 1999.

100 Unfortunately, no official figures of the company have been made available before 1994.

   1994 net profit, net sales, $278.71, net profit $27.24 million

   1995: net sales $441.06 million; net profit $77.12 million +58%

   1996: net sales $549.58 million; net profit $82.96 million +25%

   1997: net sales $651.42 million; net profit $101.30 million +19%

   1998: net sales $694.15 million; net profit $111.78 million +7%

   1999: net sales $775.99 million; net profit $97.95 million +12%

   2000: net sales $924.79 million; net profit $108.74 million +19%

   Source: *IHT* 9 April 2002.

101 Forden in *Forbes* 12 December 2001.

102 *DNR* 16 June 2000.

103 *Forbes* 12 December 2001.

104 *Forbes* 12 December 2001.

105 *CDS* 25 July 2000.

106 After 11 years with the company within the inner core of the operation, John Hooks left in 2011. Speculation is that he staunchly disagreed with Armani's latest expansion of the lower-priced labels, rather than focusing on his primary Giorgio Armani collection a move Hooks believed would serve to further enhance the luxury of and sustain the future reputation of the house long-term. Hooks's resignation came as a personal and professional blow to the designer.

107 *Time* 18 December 2000.

108 *DNR* 10 January 2001.

109 *DNR* 17 January 2001.

110 *DNR* 17 January 2001.

111 | Sales ($US billion) | | Sales/employee | Gross margin % | Operating margin % |
| --- | --- | --- | --- | --- |
| Armani | 1.0 | 28,667 | 66.3 | 18.7 |
| Gucci | 2.3 | 24,500 | 65.8 | 14.4 |
| H Boss | 0.9 | 25,616 | 50.1 | 17.8 |
| LVMH | 10.9 | 23,000 | 68.2 | 16.9 |
| POLO | 2.0 | 19,063 | 41.4 | −1.3 |

Source: Forbes 12 December 2001.

112   In 2001, Armani employed 945 staff in the USA alone.

113   WWD 4 December 2001.

114   DNR 15 April 2002.

115   NYT 18 January 2004.

116   WWD 18 January 2005.

117   The Economist 29 January 2005.

118   The Economist 29 January 2005.

119   Reuters 9 June 2006.

120   The Economist 29 January 2005.

121 | | Sales | Net profit | Net worth |
| --- | --- | --- | --- |
| GA SpA | 1, 298, 983,000 | 133,005,000 | 858,845,000 |
| Ferré | 709,741,000 | −7,641,000 | 163,420,000 |
| Versace Holding | 319,737,000 | −99,834,000 | 39,121,000 |
| Valentino | 169,749,000 | 2,540,000 | 80,966,000 |

All figures in Euro: 1$ = 0.8040, Euro 2004 figures.

Source: AIDA.

122   The Independent 16 May 2006.

123   The Guardian 20 January 2006.

4

Armani/Menswear: Tailoring Masculinity

> First the drawing. That is the essential basis of everything. Then the tailleur.
> Then I modify. Disegno. Tela. Modificare ... When I have it made up in fabric
> I will perhaps modify again. Or perhaps the fabric will inspire something
> quite different, in which case I start again: Disegno. Tela. Modificare.
>
> Giorgio Armani

In 1992 John Birt was promoted to Director-General of the BBC where he had worked since 1987, a move that sparked immediate outrage. Soon reports surfaced revealing that while in the position of Director-General Birt was also employed as a private consultant, a way for him to write-off numerous personal expenses against his income tax, including secretarial services provided by his wife. That this was occurring in the public sector only served to fuel the fires of controversy. Birt's contentious if profitable career is not of interest here, however I am fascinated by how Armani was seen as guilty by association in the British press. In an aptly titled article 'Armanigate: John Birt and the Armani suit', *The Sunday Times* queried whether ten years after the scandal had passed Armani would have become a casualty of the Birt scandal. The connection between the two men was a rather simple one. Birt was a big fan of the designer's suits and went so far as to claim them as tax deductions, arguing that they were 'an expense wholly, exclusively and necessarily incurred in the performance of the duties'.[1] Surely *The Sunday Times* did not genuinely expect the designer to suffer from this rather oblique and dubious association in the long run? The article nonetheless underscores the social and even political status an Armani suit lends its wearer and the importance some have placed on acquiring such a talisman of power and success.

While the Armani suit and jacket have come to connote power and a certain type of masculinity, they have also come to embody a quiet self-assurance and unassuming authority. Wearing an Armani suit has long been seen as a deeply private affair, its wearer often not bothering to reveal or boast the label inside, an unnecessary act after all, given how the cut and fabric betray its creator. As one customer has noted '[m]ost people like buying his clothes because other people can't tell they're wearing them', while another states 'I'm particular about what I wear, but I'm more particular about people knowing about it.'[2] Despite his cultural cachet and prominence, for those who wear his Giorgio Armani collection understated elegance coupled with discretion has long been the attraction to his clothes. Clinical psychologist Oliver James has also noted how Giorgio Armani expresses a kind of new egalitarianism, in effect a sartorial challenge to the British class system, for example. Those who wear Armani, claims James, 'haven't been to public school and are in the media or music industry – one of the few areas in England where there is social mobility. Wearing these suits is a way of showing they are upwardly mobile and of expressing their newfound wealth without betraying their class origins'. For Ashley Heath, of the edgy magazine *The Face,* wearing a Giorgio Armani suit makes you look like 'you've spent a bit of money but you're saying, "Hey, I'm not trying to show off"'.[3]

In the October 2000 issue of *Harper's Bazaar* Lynn Hirschberg recounts the affect of buying her friend Christopher his first Armani suit as a birthday present just ten years earlier. The suit, she recalls, was a lightweight linen-wool blend in shades of brown and tan, a quintessential example of the type of suit he was known for at the time. Since that initial indulgence, over the years she has purchased him an additional two suits from the designer. She submits that

> [l]ike all great garments they were transforming: When Christopher wore one, he stood differently, felt different. The suits seemed to give him a sense of calm, and he liked them, but he wasn't wearing them to be fashionable. That, too, fit his idea of style. And that has always been, to me, the great secret of Giorgio Armani. He designs beautiful clothes for people who don't think they are interested in fashion.[4]

While Hirschberg's 'Giorgio on my mind' is spiked with nostalgia, the memories and transformations she describes point nonetheless to Armani's ability to translate the male body and by extension the inner core of the man himself into a sartorial proposition. While the author's suggestions of transformation might first appear superficial, we would do well to remember that since at least the nineteenth century theorists have long held that one's corporeal and material appearances expose one's inner true self and the supposed deep secrets which lurk beneath. In the case of her friend Christopher, an Armani suit provided a sort of protection without giving the semblance of armour, safety without the wearer becoming conscious of the fact; this is, we might call, the affect of nonchalance.

Mr Holiday, executive vice president of the Retail Advertising and Marketing Association in Dallas, boasts that he now has seven Giorgio Armani suits, 'one for every day of the week'. According to him with these suits: 'I get better tables at restaurants, I can drop into a liquor store and buy champagne and all I need to do it pull out a check and sign it. It's an instant credit rating.' For Holiday it facilitates 'a power look that is more cutting-edge'.[5] Here I look primarily at the jacket, given how the designer has hung his entire career on its shoulders. The goal of this chapter is to chronicle Armani's menswear by looking at the cultural meanings and aesthetic knowledge Armani's work on the suit and jacket has produced over the decades. 'It was', as he claims, 'the point of departure for everything.'[6] Early in his career Armani spoke of the desire to lend to his clothes a sense of having been lived in, an allusion to the effects of time and being-in-the-world. The early garments he created possessed the semblance of existing prior to the wearer, as if they had a history that the body could only come to know through the affects that his textiles produce. This lived-in quality, or patina, alludes to the fictions of the wear and tear of time coupled with a desire to collapse the narrative of history with the present, that is, the moment of purchase. The one constant is the body itself, that is, the fashioned body always engaged in some form of transition, transformation or translation. This relationship to the body, clothing and history (as material surface or embodied experience) is, as Michel Foucault would surely claim, the present outcome of a genealogy of meaning, knowledge, power and even pleasure. As Foucault contends:

> The body is the inscribed surface of events (traced by language and dissolved by ideas), the locus of a dissociated Self (adopting the illusions of a substantial unity), and a volume in perpetual disintegration. Genealogy, as an analysis of descent, is thus situated within the articulation of the body and history. Its task is to expose a body totally imprinted by history.[7]

The embodied, fashioned self lends the illusion and self-confidence of 'a substantial unity', one that purports to reveal its identity by way of its contours achieved through textured surfaces and the structures of silhouettes.

Milan, Armani's city, is dominated by the sartorial male gaze directed at other men, a performative and ocular act that cuts across sexual identity in a city which lives and breathes fashion. As the new postmodern capital of men's fashion, Milanese men step out in style and expect the same from others. In my experience of numerous cities in the West, no other city commands such a degree of masculine scrutiny in which the performance of fashion is of the utmost cultural, economic and corporeal importance. Armani is quick to remind us in *Made in Milan* that '[c]lothes today have become a language. We use them to communicate when we work and when we play. They're an expression of our individualism, not something that's forced on us.'[8] Elsewhere he expands his discussion of what and how clothes communicate: 'Clothes are important because they are a language through which we communicate what we are. I can tell from what a person is wearing what books that person does not read. He may want to read those books, but if he is dressed in a certain way he won't finish them'.[9] According to Armani's design ethos clothes may not make the man, but they certainly expose what lies beneath the wrinkles and folds of daily life.

Toward Nonchalance: The Suit Takes on a New Shape

> A jacket can be very sensual if it has certain characteristics. Maybe a wider shoulder, a certain length, a fitted waist, or no waist at all. But most important it's got to have a lived in look, like you just pulled it out of your closet.
>
> Giorgio Armani

48   Staples of an Armani wardrobe of the 2000s, a one-button velvet jacket coupled with a metal ball-fastened ethnic inspired shirt

Having worked for the eponymous Milanese department store La Rinascente (founded by Luigi and Ferdinando Bocconi in 1865), in 1961 Armani moved on to work for Nino Cerruti, who had inherited the family textile company at the age of 20. With a new fashion label to consider, Cerruti hired the young man to choose fabrics and design the firm's newly inaugurated Hitman menswear line. Having spent months in the firm's textile factories, Armani set out to design a collection that would become the embryo for his future success. At this early stage he sought to radically alter the cut, fabric and feel of industrially produced men's clothing. Jackets and suits were structured to lend a youthful, fluid and less stiff feel to the look. At Hitman Armani already claimed to want 'to come up with jackets that hung well rather than just covering the body' by translating tailors' techniques to industrially produced garments.[10] Previously, the tailor was a sort of alchemist for the male body, able 'to display the positive sides of a persona and hide the negative ones'. With Cerruti's manufacturing power behind the new collection, Hitman quickly became a vast operation producing 50,000 garments a year; too large a constituency to understand Armani's 'idea of nonchalance'. But these years became

> an intellectual sort of operation, a way of sounding things out, of understanding to what extent the public was prepared to cope with a new way of dressing. People who bought ready-made clothes in those days were beginning to think differently, to forget about passing clothes down to the next generation. That

was also when the idea of being able to buy luxury ready-made clothes started to make headway.

It was also at Cerruti where Armani began to challenge the gender of fabrics: 'They also thought I was crazy because I used fabrics for men's clothes that hitherto had always been thought of as woman's ones: the durability of the garment was at risk'.[11] The implication was that the fashionable suit would not last as long as the one produced by a tailor. A suit's longevity was crucial to the psychology of men's consumption patterns. As Adriano Gianelli, inaugural head of advertising for Giorgio Armani would claim: 'Men buy clothes when they need them ... [then] will wear a good-quality suit for at least three years'. To assuage, at least in part, men's trepidation within the accelerating men's fashion system, Gianelli offered five criteria to assess the quality of a suit: fabric, cut, stitching, price and appropriateness.[12]

These formative and successful years spent with Cerruti in the mills, have since become the stuff of legend. By the time Armani first met Galeotti in 1966, the latter knew Armani could strike out on his own. In 1970, with Galeotti by his side, Armani abandoned the stability and safety net of Cerruti and began to forge a profitable career as a freelance designer working for numerous textile and design firms. His arrival on the menswear scene was fortuitously enhanced through the inauguration of *L'Uomo Vogue* in 1968, a magazine that would become instrumental in the development of the Made in Italy menswear. Armani's creations were featured regularly and prominently within and on the covers of the monthly magazine. Armani quickly established himself as a serious force, designing and consulting for such houses as Ungaro and Loewe, in addition to working for Allegri, Bagutta, Bourlavaard, Hilton, Sicons, Spirito and Hitman, among other labels and manufacturers.

Armani's first collection under his own name for spring/summer 1976 featured traditional menswear fabrics transformed into softer and suppler versions. Trousers were loose while the now softer jackets took inspiration from Mao jackets and workmen's clothes, cutting across class and ethnicity. In 1977 Armani was declared 'the reigning European menswear designer' and *the* 'Italian pacesetter',[13] and within three short seasons of making its debut, the house had reached $2 million in sales. As a small and limited operation the house could no longer keep up with demand, and GFT stepped in and provided the necessary textile, manufacturing and warehouse know-how to take the business to the necessary next level. While Rivetti's industrial collaboration has already been explored in the previous chapter, it is important at this juncture to point to Rivetti's fateful timing, an historical conjuncture also precipitated by other key factors. In addition to this industrial push the designer, along with his compatriots Ferré, Krizia, Versace and Missoni, also greatly benefitted from a new generation of talented and eager young journalists like Natalia Aspesi and Adriana Mulassano, not to mention countless others, who saw this new group of Milanese fashion houses as an opportunity. Fashion journalist for Italy's *Corriere della Sera* Mulassano already wrote in 1984: 'Dozens of articles about his fashion philosophy, dozens of professional profiles, dozens of interviews, dozens of newspapers and magazines from around the world have been written about [Armani].'[14] Aspesi and Mulassano have been keen supporters and instrumental in Armani's growing importance since the 1970s, featuring him prominently in countless articles and interviews in numerous Italian magazines and newspapers.

The identity of a house and identification with a label was only in its infancy in the late 1970s, especially true within the menswear industry. While Milanese designers were inspired by and updating looks from the 1920s, 1930s and 1940s, largely inspired by Albini, Armani introduced a new silhouette characterized by broader shoulders and looser through the body, a low gorge and narrower lapel. *The New York Times* responded to this new look by claiming that men now choose clothing based on 'self-image', a radical self-reflexive move for those who had supposedly 'renounced' fashion ever since the French stormed the Bastille and opted for the sameness and emotional neutrality of black.[15] Elaine Louis of the newspaper asked what's in a lapel, to which designers like Ralph Lauren responded that it is an issue of 'identification'.[16] Emotional identification with a single designer look, aesthetic ideal or sartorial camp would become the very underpinning of

49 Spring/summer 1979. Here Armani features short shorts, garments traditionally not associated with the designer who gained a reputation for greige sobriety. He wears a glossy chintz, buttoned jacket and white cotton shorts; she wears a hot pink cotton jacket over a burgundy swimsuit

the success of Lauren and Armani who have both invested much symbolic potency in details like gorges, buttons and pockets coupled with a consistent lifestyle culture as a means not only to educate customers, but also as a way to appear as though bonding with them through this private, material form of communication.[17] In the USA, *GQ* was reporting on Armani's achievements with the blazer as early as 1978, relating to its readers that he provided men with a 'total look', one which required little effort, an outcome of his 'idea[l] of nonchalance'. According to the designer himself,

> I think my real contribution has been to allow a man who wants to look well dressed or inspire confidence – say, a doctor or lawyer – to do so without tying him up in stiffly tailored folds of fabric ... I am able to give him a softer, more comfortable look.[18]

For men who were finding their footing in this seemingly new and unchartered territory, Armani provided an easy alternative. One's mundane choices and Armani's power to facilitate the often difficult and at times onerous process of choosing one's wardrobe speaks to what is the simple, single-minded yet highly effective formula for the house's success. For some, Armani's mystique

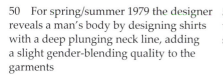

50   For spring/summer 1979 the designer reveals a man's body by designing shirts with a deep plunging neck line, adding a slight gender-blending quality to the garments

51   The model wears a tissue-thin linen jacket with lightweight cotton trousers from the spring/ summer 1979 collection

begins at the point when one gets dressed in the morning; when choosing an Armani outfit it doesn't require fuss or much decision-making.[19]

The new look Armani proposed was also a direct response to the growing desire on the part of men (and women) to nurture and sustain a healthy, fit body, advocated by the burgeoning gym and fitness culture sweeping North America, a continent Armani has always been eager to please. Clothes that were 'fluid, relaxed and clinging – that glorify the body – sexy maybe, but in a wholesome way, never blatant or vulgar,' according to the fashion editor of *The New York Times* Carrie Donovan, hit the mark in this body-conscious culture.[20] For Armani the change was an important and inevitable one. Claiming that menswear was interpreted so badly when he started to design, the designer saw that '[a] man's outfit was either like a suit of armour or he wore tight pants that showed off his sex in front and rear. Being sexy isn't showing off your sex, it's how you move.'[21] On the occasion of his well-received spring/summer 1980 collection Armani was dubbed the 'sexy tailor', a title stemming from a recipe he concocted by blending 'sex appeal and soigné tailoring'.[22] By autumn 1981, Armani was not only enhancing the male physique for those with well-toned bodies, but also began his innovative sartorial wizardry by providing a shape to those who had none through his 'knowledge of what is flattering to the male physique', a formula that has continued to keep him in good stead among male consumers throughout his career. Creating a collection which 'can only be described as muscle' for autumn the designer tightened the torso (where American jackets tend to become boxy) accentuated the waist and provided generous lapels.[23] He introduced asymmetrical closings and banded collars in bold stripes, which would become staples in his men's shirt collections. Fabrics for these suits were in bold three-dimensional woollen twills, with chalk stripes in beiges, browns, grey, forest green and blue-greys. By spring/summer 1982, however, not all were impressed with a collection the designer contended was for the narcissist. A critic from *The New York Times* referred to the leather trousers seen throughout the collection (and which appeared in heavy doses in his womenswear collections of the period) as 'outmoded' and 'skin-tight', apparently, he surmised, the cause of the models 'dour, grumpy looks'.[24] Although the critic concedes '[t]here is enough there, aside from the fashion anomalies, to keep everyone interested and to allow Giorgio Armani to barely maintain his position as premier European menswear designer'.[25] Evolving his interest in the male neck, much attention was paid to shirts and their fastenings, with Japanese-inspired asymmetrical closures, dropped shoulders and fuller sleeves, a motif which continued into his 1981 collection. In the early 1980s, after a few seasons of radical changes, Armani began to make his propositions through shirts, colour and innovations in textiles, rather than through the jacket's cut and silhouette.

For autumn/winter 1982 he moved his ideal of nonchalance into the more recognizable domain of Hollywood male glamour, a theme he initiated in the late 1970s. His sport jackets in vivid Prince of Wales checks were given shape with padding in the shoulders, and a little suppression in the waist. The resulting look was a take on what Armani conceptualized as the 'American Gangster' or 'Hollywood look'. Inspired by the 1930s and 1940s, 'instead of simply presenting a costume', Armani provided 'a direction for menswear by reintroducing classic male styling'.[26] Showing his first collection in his new and refurbished theatre located in the basement of his via Borgonuovo palazzo, Armani once again turned his attention to the masculinity of the celluloid screen, drawing inspiration from iconic male heroes such as Gary Cooper, Clark Gable and Cary Grant for his spring/summer 1984 collection which 'managed to recapture the ease and elegance of their era and pushed it forward into the 1980s with utter conviction and success'. Slouchy and supple in fabrication and featuring wide lapels, Armani continued his 'tailored clothing revolution', by developing new patterns and mixes of cottons and lightweight wools which were not only 'inspirational', but no longer available to customers.[27] Models walked the runway, hands plunged deep inside the pockets of broad, yet soft shouldered jackets featuring a high gorge and low-button placement, enhanced by very wide lapels. Spring/summer 1984 offered softly constructed jackets suggestive of the 'effortless ease of a cardigan'.[28] Armani's once famed nod to avant-garde revolutionary zeal had by 1984 moved quickly into 'a gentle evolution', with a collection inspired 'by the reality of what men in normal life' actually wear, and 'consequently what they will buy'. Wool and cotton crepes appeared washed-out or worn-in, lending a sense of nonchalance combined with patterns and fabrics that give an air of simply being thrown together. Sending his Giorgio and Emporio Armani collections down the runway together, the designer increased his interest in combining unusual and adventurous patterns together. For jackets he opted for small-scale patterned wools with comfortable and wide, large-scale patterned trousers and shorts, lending a decidedly youthful quality to the overall presentation on his 50th birthday.[29] Part of the so-called youthfulness of the collection also tapped into the exercise craze, which, while a fad in the 1970s, had become a complete and total reality by the mid-1980s. By 1983, it was reported that 38 million men were now exercising. These staggering numbers also inspired Armani for his diffusion lines such as Mani to produce jackets that emphasized a strong V shape. As Guido Petruzzi, president of New York based Giorgio Armani Fashion Corp. noted: 'A suit without shape doesn't show it off.'[30] Popular culture in the early part of the decade was replete with images of a well-toned, muscular body. Movies such as *Rocky* (1976), *Pumping Iron* (1977), *Conan the Barbarian* (1982) and of course, but in a more subtle way, *American Gigolo* (1980) displayed men's bodies openly, unabashedly presenting what was a highly active and desirable physique.

With Armani's various collections the image of the ideal fit body became a sartorial reality in the 1980s.[31]

Nonetheless, after a decade or more of developments in industrially produced menswear, by the mid-1980s it seemed for some, the industry had reached its zenith. For spring 1986 the four big names in Italian menswear – Versace, Armani, Ferré and Luciano Soprani – loaded their collections with wearable and saleable clothes. Their collective propositions were good news for retailers amidst growing fears of a troubled and faltering menswear sector, which had witnessed a period of significant growth for some time. Armani,

53   Aldo Fallai. From the spring/summer 1983 advertising campaign

however, who also introduced his underwear and sleepwear collections into Italy,[32] seemed to single-handedly give signs to the contrary with *Daily News Record* reporting that his collection was 'more brilliantly, yet quietly conceived as ever ... put[ting] the lid on any worried notions about an uneasy future for men's fashion... It is relaxed, comfortable, masculine and uncommonly sexy.'[33] Such comments from industry insiders not only reveal how for some sexy was no longer a characteristic associated with the designer's collections, but also how it was not uncommon in times of a troubled menswear sector for many to turn to Armani for directional collections to ward off fears of a slump in sales. However, the designer was quick to point out that difficult choices are part of maintaining customers' faith in the house, which might at times entail 'renouncing things you might want to do, but which are too special or avant-garde and don't fall within the framework of the company'. In the end, radical hollow gestures and '[e]very type of excess and assault you make, you pay for later', he adds. 'These excesses that have been permitted to the stores, to the clients and to the press have brought about a complete saturation of the market. And the bottom line is that the public pays for it.'[34] While Jean Paul Gaultier introduced the man-skirt in 1985 with great controversy and eventual acclaim, his initiative did little to provide any gender trouble in a substantive way beyond the confines of the runway and fashion insiders. Gilles Lipovetsky has also underscored how while Gaultier may have promoted his man-skirt on the runway, it has had little to no effect on the way men actually dress or materialize their masculinity.[35] Armani's supple and fluid fabrics, designed within a culture of machismo Italy has come to be known for, provides a more revealing and sexy version of men's muscles, resulting in a more subversive expression of everyday male fashion within the confines of serious industrial realities. In addition, the move toward soft fabrics was also a nod to the interwar period and its bohemian radical aesthetic culture. From 1926 onward, a new generation of men became obsessed with soft collars and soft fabrics.[36] His men's trousers which by 1985 no longer had creases in them, significantly added to the overall fluid effect and were a nod to a time when a gentleman's trousers did not have them, that is, when they were the result of a tailor. Armani conjures a tension between on the one hand a purported unisex material aesthetic while on the other a hard-edged muscular masculinity, a tension interestingly never resolved. It is this tension wherein lies Armani's true impact in the blurring of gendered fashion and his true subversive success. While many designers have followed suit, Armani's version of the new male trouser remained exemplary, precisely because of its tailor-inspired cut. The lack of crease requires 'a particular sort of cloth, one which never bunches up around the body but rather has the weight to pull itself down into line' made possible only by a perfect fabric combination: 'half-part the suppleness of a knit and the fortitude of a worsted'.[37] This combination allows trousers to be at once fluid, and yet skim the body effortlessly offering a flattering silhouette to the lower half of the male form, a perfect counterbalance to what his jackets offer. For spring 1986 he continued to make men feel at home with their sartorial choices, offering a collection, which was more akin 'to spending time with an old friend'. The collection also allowed a man to 'drop all pretence about fashion and just be comfortable in his clothes'.[38] To achieve this balance, clothes once again appear as if broken-in, submitting perfectly to the contours of the body, lending a sense of vintage long before it gained mass appeal.

With numerous labels within his stable, an ever-expanding empire and an aesthetic culture that revolved around the golden era of Hollywood, by 1987 the press was reporting on the similarities between Armani and his American cohort Lauren. These are two designers who maintain the most complete, complex and successful lifestyle brands that answer to every possible need of their various types of customers by adhering single-mindedly to their own aesthetic dictates. Both conjure a nostalgic old world charm through a consistent and highly identifiable visual culture. At the time, both men held complete control over their empires driven by an acute control over detail while shying away from seasonal trends. As *The Globe & Mail* reported, both 'work with loyal design teams that are adept at translating and interpreting the designer's ideas. Both exercise absolute control over every detail, every

54   October 1984, the national soccer team dressed by Armani. From left to right: Fulvio Collavati in a cashmere pullover; Antonio Cabrini in a blue wool gabardine coat; Marco Tardelli in a jacket with the new official team insignia; Giuseppe Dossena in a herringbone bomber jacket in wool

fabric and trim selection.' However, as the reporter noted, 'Armani has the edge on fabrication quality'. Armani was keenly aware of the textile advantage he and his compatriots had over their American and French competitors. 'The modern way of dressing requires lighter fabrics that drape and hang in a different way: men's fabrics for women's clothes – that is already accepted; but what about woman's fabrics for men?'[39] While most of Armani's men's clothing is industrially produced he nevertheless claims to retain 'certain artisanal procedures in his factories'.[40] By 1987, however, Armani's global reach was far more significant, propelled by the Made in Italy banner, while Lauren, though significant and highly successful in the English-speaking realm, remained mostly limited in his global impact until the new millennium when he began a more aggressive expansion fuelled by an influx of revenue when he opened up his company to public investment. Both, it is important to note, also began their careers in menswear, affecting the sartorial well-being of an entire generation of men (and by extension of women) by 'liberating them from their rigid sartorial uniforms and promoting the idea that clothes could be a form of personal expression'.[41]

By the end of the 1980s, Armani had constructed a definable visual and material culture premised on the multivalent yet recognizable Italian Look. His fashions became increasingly identified with an upwardly mobile professional type. As such, they began to stand as a sartorial signifier of the ever-increasing encroachment of American corporate culture into European business. Cesare Romiti, managing director of Fiat, decried the new breed of managers whom he described as nothing more than 'savage capitalists'. Looking back on this period,

> power, money and status became an aphrodisiac, and designer clothes become an erotic end in themselves. Wearing an Armani suit was a strong fetish item as any S&M leather or rubber accoutrement, except while the latter were usually relegated to behind the closet doors, Armani was a visible, and sexy, sign of wealth and sophistication.[42]

Aware of Romiti's concerns and the image his clothing conjured, Armani noted his own implication in this new corporate type emerging in Europe. His jackets jutted out from the shoulder as if a soldier's epaulette. As a result of what his clothes came to signify, the designer began to shy away from such a rigid silhouette toward one which fell more naturally, revealing the body more intimately. Toward this end, in the last six seasons of the 1980s Armani softened up his silhouette even more. For autumn/winter 1988 he offered a sophisticated take on bohemian chic with layers of more casual tweeds and brushed fabrics lending an illusion of a rusticated Italian tramp, a look arrived at with refined and highly researched fabrics. Trousers, still creaseless, became decidedly wider moving from a very full 24- or 25-inch knee to between 20½ and 23 inches at the bottom of the leg. This amplitude appeared more elegant and yet casual, allowing for both a greater sense of drape and ease of movement. For spring 1989 in a 'season where everyone offered interpretations of the look Armani had pioneered – the soft suit – this genuine item looked better than ever and was extensively presented in a new incarnation – the shorts suits ... which were paired with [Armani's] natural-shoulder jackets'. Fabrics included slightly iridescent silks, linen blends, washed silk, cotton and cotton/silk, wool crepes and knits in a range of colours from ecru, pale greys and blues to Indian red and tropical acids.[43] As the decade began to reach its twilight, so too did Armani's big-shouldered men begin to look toward a new culture of masculinity.

55 Campaign from the late 1980s and early 1990s for his first self-titled highly successful men's cologne. Here he takes his cue once again from the slick-haired masculinity of the interwar period

The Soft Touch: Armani's *Nuove Forme*

> A jacket should not merely cover the body. It should move with it.
>
> Giorgio Armani

The financial chaos engendered by the so-labelled Black Monday of October 1987 (the worst stock market collapse since 1929) precipitated a reassessment of the values of power and greed that in the 1980s had ostensibly been honoured and placed above all others. While the crisis was felt more acutely in North America and the UK, Europe and Asia also felt its effects. Although by decade's end recovery seemed imminent, in 1990 the economic downturn worsened fuelled by growing inflation, staggering oil prices and the first Gulf War. Faced with these bleak conditions Armani began the decade participating in two new independent initiatives of self-promotion targeted at the North American audience. The first, the short documentary film *Made in Milan*, directed by long-time friend and Armani devotee Martin Scorsese, was meant to connect with the American audience on a more personal level, a way to translate in visual terms the Armani design ethos as much as the Armani mystique. The second, an exhibition underwritten by Giorgio Armani Fashion Corp. and co-curated by Richard Martin and Harold Koda, ran from November 1990 to January 1991 at the Fashion Institute of Technology (New York). *Giorgio Armani: Images of Man* was a display of 204 photographs from the house's advertising campaigns for his Giorgio and Emporio Armani menswear collections from 1975 to 1990. In his review of the exhibition Woody Hochswender noted that '[t]o the extent that clothing performs surplus functions – conferring status, seductiveness, authority – the Armani name has great contemporary resonance. If clothing has magical functions, akin to the mystic powers of tribal vestments and jewellery, the Armani label is talismanic.'[44] I can still recall with precise detail when I received my own copy of the exhibition's coffee-table book styled catalogue. I arrived home, catalogue in hand, entered my parents' bedroom, and sat on their bed as I watched the first graphic images of the Gulf War while leafing through the pages of the glossy Rizzoli tome. Both were overwhelming, for very different reasons, but the two cohered in my mind at the point of the uncanny. The familiarity of the Armani advertisements coupled with their settings in foreign locales were set in sharp contrast to the foreignness of war and Iraq made all too familiar through the endless repetition of images inspired by a video-game aesthetic endemic to the Gulf War's reportage. Uncanny and dissonant, I watched the West attack in a desert storm as I flipped through the pages from the spring/summer 1989 collection set on location in Morocco, the spring/summer 1990 images set against a backdrop of a desert and the autumn/winter 1990 collection located on the island of Pantelleria, Armani's sun-bleached island retreat located between Italy and Tunisia. Like Armani's exotic island home, these advertising campaigns and images of war seemed located uncomfortably somewhere between West and East, here and there in a political and economic climate growing increasingly more conservative with each passing day.

56   Spring/summer 1990; the advertising campaign for the collection was set in a North African desert

Amidst grave concerns over the economy, rising wholesale prices for its garments and new competition from the USA, Germany and Canada, Italy nevertheless remained a viable choice for retailers' already robust inventories in need of trimming. The emphasis at the retail level in the early 1990s was placed on production value and quality, Italy's long-standing forte.[45] In the late 1970s Armani ushered in what for some in the menswear industry were too many changes to the silhouette of men's jackets and suits. Despite their consternation, by the early 1980s Armani had established himself as the uncontested leader in menswear, and when he moved a button, deepened a gorge or suppressed the waist of a jacket, the industry inevitably followed suit. In the slow moving sphere of menswear, buttons and lapels have the power to signify. In each decade the designer has sought to 'take into consideration the social changes that are going on by putting a different emphasis on shoulders, buttons, the lapels'.[46] Armani maintains that

> [y]ou have to realize that just moving a button an inch or two changes the feel dramatically. Move it down, and it's very relaxed and casual. Move it up, it's more dandified. The same with the lapels; narrow, high lapels recall the turn of the century, wide ones the 1940s and all that that implies.[47]

Between 1990 and 1994 Armani aggressively moved menswear into continuously new areas of exploration, by playing with the signifying potential of his buttons and lapels; their displacement connoted a new movement for the body underneath, a shifting of the menswear industry and finally a new tailored representation of masculinity. In a feature article aptly titled, 'Armani: King of the Jacket', the designer explained that '[w]ithout a jacket, one feels a bit inferior, a bit underdressed. But with one you can count on being at least equal.'[48] Armani's impact was a reinvigoration of the importance of the jacket in the daily wardrobe of men across Europe and even for the more casual-leaning North American, who since the 1950s had seemingly turned his back on the staple garment by moving toward greater informality in dress. Additionally important was the designer's assertion that the jacket provided for a social equivalency, a democratizing emblem within the realms of male bonding and aggregation. In these terms, without a jacket, then, a man is left vulnerable without the protective tailored armour provided by Italian textiles to face the new decade's ever-increasing political, social and economic challenges.

As Armani welcomed the new decade, so too did he invite an ever-increasing comfort into the classically tailored jacket and suit. His goal was to balance the seeming impossibly antagonistic spheres of the formal and informal in menswear. For the designer:

> Too formal is old-fashioned, and a bit silly. I think of my lawyer who wears his Armani suit with a crisp white shirt, elegant tie and high-polished English shoes. It's unnecessarily fussy. What people really want is to be comfortable.[49]

57   Armani's take on the Ivy League sack suit for his spring/summer 1990 collection

58   Spring/summer 1990 collection

The goal was to achieve a balance between nonchalance and formality, made possible only through a functionalist assessment of proportions. Armani's unexpected initial proposition for spring/summer 1990 set out to revive the Ivy League sack suit. Made popular in the late 1950s, the suit was characterized by flat front and cuffed trousers with a three-button natural-shouldered jacket in natural fibres. This decidedly American source of inspiration was made popular by conservative American retailers like Brooks Brothers, a once perennial favourite of the designer. Armani's version was a longer, tighter and yet much softer fit usually from a combination of wool and rayon, a blend that managed to 'convey an overall feeling that was loose as a goose'.[50] Fuller, pleated and displaying a drape reminiscent of the 1930s, the new trouser allowed men more room to breathe than did the jacket. Armani kept business suits to a minimum in a collection that eliminated the starch from tailored suits and jackets and yet at the same time provided a leaner, cleaner and more comfortable silhouette. Although Zegna and Caraceni in Florence also showed decidedly more subtle variations on the theme, Armani took the sack suit furthest, leaving some retailers concerned with the extremism of his sartorial proposition.

The broad-shouldered Wall Street look signifying greed and power and which had dominated the second half of the 1980s seemed to be just that, a thing of the past. Armani has always claimed that he's 'never been interested in dressing people to go and work in a bank – even if in America people buy [his] clothes to do just that'. Labelled 'The Natural', the new suit for 1990 was meant to provide an antidote to what Armani saw as 'the unification of taste and style', a reality he felt was up to him 'to fight against'.[51] He maintains that although he had been designing soft jackets since his debut in 1975, the new jacket entailed a novel and 'certain way of treating fabric that had previously been in the domain only of women's fashion'. In effect what he did was 'to take a traditional form and improve on it'.[52] The goal of dressing the Armani-styled man is premised on masculine comfort (not spectacle or showmanship), and perhaps more importantly a way 'to communicate an idea of [his] customer's personality'.[53] The new proposition was meant to advocate the pleasure in and the range of fashion choices once only held for women. It was also structured to fit like an old faithful cardigan, lending it a sense of familiarity and the effects of time, and hence less threatening to the male consumer. Although banal for some, others might view it, as did Armani, as 'completely avant-garde'. The new shape also coaxed a new way for men to relate to their bodies, as it neither hid any 'defects' one might have nor did it provide a slim waist or broad shoulder. Rather, he suggested a jacket that required a certain 'courage' on the part of its wearer 'to acknowledge his own defects'. Fashion that does not flatter is often thought of as the domain of avant-garde Japanese designers like Rei Kawakubo or

Yohji Yamamoto, and not that of the so-called Maestro of Milan who built an empire on ensuring comfort and control for his customer. The designer admitted that it would take time to get used to the new shape. After all, as he noted, the first time he 'did an unconstructed jacket, it sold exactly 10 pieces ... But then, after all, if what you want is a blue blazer, why come to Armani?'[54]

59   Still-life display of the spring 1991 collection

Many in the business pinned their hopes of a resuscitation of the industry on 'The Natural', and most reacted positively to it, especially in the USA where the *Daily News Record* was keen to track response to it. For Mohammed Khan of Bonwit Teller, for instance:

> Armani is the most incredibly talented person in the business today. His collection was sensational just like it has been for years. His clothing on the runway looked like someone took a machete and cut the shoulders off. It had soft padding on the shoulders and there was no exaggeration. [55]

60   Still-life display of the spring 1991 collection

61   Autumn/winter 1992

Larry Dartley of Bloomingdales liked what he saw, claiming it was both 'young and different' and would 'translate well to a fashion customer'. Ultimo of Chicago owner John Jones noted '[i]t looks peculiar to us since it is so new but we'll get used to it. Armani's rarely been wrong.' Linda Bauchamp of Saks Fifth Avenue labelled the designer a 'directionalist', suggesting that the new look would evolve rather than cause a quick and instantaneous revolution. The look would require people to 'have to train [their] eyes to see men look a new different way'.[56] While many appreciated Armani's sartorial gesture, others viewed it as a vindication of American style and taste, especially after years of American designers turning their attentive gaze to Italy. However, American designer Joseph Abboud, dubbed the poor man's Armani, was more critical asserting that 'Armani's real fashion customer might like it but it's a little too drastic for the US customer'.[57] Regardless of what retailers and manufacturers felt about the new proposition, by the end of 1990 they were all 'playing catch-up with Armani' and were only then 'finally comfortable with their modified versions of extended shoulders'.[58] In the end, the look was slightly cheaper to produce as its deconstructed structure required less fabric, underpinnings and stiffenings, keeping prices lower.

The jacket stirred emotions and ideas in many, not the least in the *Daily New Record* which chronicled in detail Armani's sartorial developments. Likely fuelled by the advent of 'The Natural', the daily newspaper commented how Armani was a

> great designer ... because of his tendency to be both a sociologist and a philosopher. He observes our changing society and, with it, our changing values, manners and attitudes. Wisely, he knows that when values, attitudes and lifestyle change, so must fashion change to express the inner man ... Armani has been really fearless in expressing the evolving relaxation of our society. It takes guts to depict a major lifestyle change seasons before most other observers are aware of its significance. When you consider the price of a suit these days, you realize just how gutsy Armani is. Now, by further softening and narrowing his shoulders for next spring, he is giving added expression to his relaxed lifestyle conviction.[59]

The value of an Armani fashion show, the newspaper noted, was to pay witness to how the designer interprets the current way of life and how he is able to translate this to the human form.

62   Peter Lindbergh. From the spring/summer 1993 advertising campaign where modernist abstraction meets desert locales

On the heels of a Christmas vacation on safari in Africa, Armani presented 'a monumental' autumn 1990 collection in four parts, which the designer 'hoped would … silence once and for all what the king of the Milan jungle scorns as nit-picking criticism'.[60] Many critics, whether they appreciated the previous introduction of 'The Natural' or not, complained the look was too young and left out men 55 and older. Armani's autumn collection, according to the *Daily News Record*: 'After a long, three-day haul of Italian men's wear that was often safe and often derivative, Armani showed a tour-de-force collection that crystallized a truly Italian modern point of view.'[61] Titled, *'Tutti Gli Uomomini Armani'* ('All the Armani types of men') he began the show with *Il tradizionalista* (The Traditionalist) in which conservative tailored single- and double-breasted suits were set in traditional menswear fabrics and masculine neutral tones. In the second section, *Il professionista* (The Professional), Armani sent out three-button jackets in camel and other equally rich fabrics with emphasized drape. Shirts were buttoned to the top, with scarves or cravats tucked in closely around the neck. This section of the collection was clearly geared to the artist or doctor, rather than bankers and corporate attorneys implicitly targeted in the previous grouping. Toward the end of the section were causal, weekend-inspired sportswear looks suitable for the modern professional who also appreciates a bit of luxury on the weekend. The third, and by far the most unique and handsome, *L'uomo all'avanguardia* (The Avant-Garde Man) highlighted clothes reminiscent of

a slightly more bohemian insouciance of the 1930s. Shall-collared double-breasted suits with incredible drape were shown without ties to lend a sense of casual luxury. Vests over tab-collared shirts featured throughout this section, whether included in the numerous three-piece suit offerings or used for sportswear were prominent as were deep-plunging, shawl-collared coats in rich, thick fabrics often topped off with a plethora of fedoras, gloves and scarves. The look was decidedly hybrid, a product of the Chicago gangster look and Parisian Left-Bank bohemianism. Of the avant-garde Armani man, the designer stated that he is a man 'who breaks the rules: he's modern, discreet, and sophisticated, but not violent in his taste. The fit, like what we introduced last summer, discovers the body.'[62]

Overall the clothing from this section was more casual in tone, but equally accomplished

63   Autumn/winter 1993

and rich and importantly it was from this section that most of the clothes featured in the advertising campaign and seasonal catalogue came. The fourth and final section focused on *L'uomo emporio* (The Emporio Armani Man and Armani/Jeans) and displayed an informal, casual interpretation of the main line, particularly of the previous two sections. Together the four sections provided for the multiple personalities or at least multiple facets of the Armani man, a strategy already in use in the 1920s by retailers to lend an identity and credibility to their costumers' choices. This emphasis on 'types', as if actors in a movie, resurfaced in menswear by the late 1970s to assist men in their at times difficult sartorial decisions, now faced with growing options. It was also a similar strategy that Hollywood studios developed for their heroes throughout the 1930s and 1940s to instil a desire for identification and increase fandom. With this extensive collection, the designer forcibly demonstrated the depth and breadth of Armani's range and capacity.

For spring 1991 Armani elected to step back from the mayhem of the runway shows, and displayed his collection of soft tailored jackets, suits and sportswear as a still-life on his then standard stick forms in his via Borgonuovo showroom. While undoubtedly a means to keep rising costs at bay, in part the move was a response to critics who felt the designer only showcased his 'latest concepts on the runway' avoiding showing his mainstay classics. For Armani the display concept was to demonstrate that although 'fashion shows have a lot of ideas ... once in the street they lose the concept. In the previous three collections, the ideas haven't been developed. It's good to stop.' Before opening his still-life exhibition, Armani revealed that he purposefully placed two double-breasted suits together, side by side, one conservative and more traditional, the other slouch and modern. The move was to emphasize the notion of choice and that both can exist side by side in a man's wardrobe. The result was 'a textile tour de force. The biggest idea was fabrics that had a crispness and a hardness but also a drape.'[63] Each mannequin was also accompanied by the original sketch as well as additional photographs to

64   Autumn/winter 1993

65   Armani's *nuova forma* from spring 1994

introduce the various processes and ideas attached to each garment.[64] In this collection Armani revived numerous long-gone corded and iridescent fabrics in neutral tones. Shirts were either shiny silks in stripes or in tie-pattern prints, linen plaids with band or rounded tab collars also featured antique stripes. The collection, it was reported, 'just made you want to reach out and touch it, which is what most of the crowd ended up doing'. The desire to touch is at the heart of Armani's clothing and textile research. In *The Substance of Style*, Virginia Postrel has also noted how '[p]eople pet Armani clothes because the fabrics feel so good. Those clothes attract us as visual, tactile creatures, not because they are "rich in meaning" but because they are rich in pleasure. The garments' utility includes the way they look and feel'.[65]

66   Peter Lindbergh. Digging for inspiration: loose silhouettes for both men and women as seen in the spring/summer 1994 advertising campaign

With this spring collection Armani moved his 'Natural' suit into a slightly more pronounced territory known as 'The Slouch', and brought it forward into the autumn 1991 collection to provide men with an 'image [of] simple, masculine style. There will be a complete redesign of the silhouette with generous and newer shapes to emphasis the body, making it more slender.'[66] The Slouch moves ever closer to the body, creating a slimmer athletic look than seen with The Natural. Jackets continued the move southward to attenuate the silhouette and were cut in a more flattering way at the hip and waist. By removing any excess fabric or drape in the chest area the new version of the jacket suggested a more fitted look while maintaining its predecessor's softness. Fabrics, tactile as always, became decidedly coarser and more textural and as a result heavier, with some treated to look 'wrinkled' in colours that ranged from brown, blue and charcoal grey to rosewood. For North America the move, not surprisingly, was too quick, and according to some, the new proposition did not allow time to educate customers.[67] Nevertheless, at least on the catwalks of Milan, Versace, Valentino and GianMarco Venturi to list only a few were all following suit and copying Armani's latest silhouette, which had itself engendered a new male uniform.[68] As Armani was shaking things up off the runway and forcing others to follow, he also set out to design another form of uniform, this time for Italy's Alitalia flight attendants and ground crew. Additionally he designed the inside of the airline's new fleet of MD-11 planes. For these interiors he worked with ten different shades of blue to delineate the various areas of the plane. The various shades of the designer's favoured colour were used to conjure a sense that the passenger was floating in the air rather than being confined to a plane.

Armani closed the autumn 1992 season as is the tradition and sent so many ideas it left the rather jaded fashion critics overwhelmed. The collection introduced three and four-button 'dandy jackets' and was meant to be more about mixing and combining elements in unusual ways rather than about a definable look to create a new fashion vocabulary for the modern man. In a collection that sent out over 300 exits the designer gave his modern man a plethora from which to choose. He closed the show by sending his nephew Andrea Camerana down the runway as the final exit wearing black tuxedo trousers and a simple black T-shirt with the A/X logo emblazoned on it. The finale was to signify the future, given that Camerana was to assume a more prominent position in the financial operations of the company as well as by showing the importance of the new label within Armani's expanding realm. The desire to provide ever-more options and looks for men took on increasingly larger proportions as the 1990s rolled on. For spring 1993 Armani assembled a collection premised on the notion that five different looks could be achieved by way of one single suit. Each variation on the theme, whether worn with a shirt and tie, a collarless shirt or scarf invariably changed the tone of the sartorial message. For the spring 1994 season he continued along

67   Peter Lindbergh. From the autumn/winter 1994 advertising campaign

the same path but infused the collection with an identifiable Moroccan twist. Here the softly constructed linen jackets were paired with ultra-wide trousers in neutrals, indigos and burgundies. The designer projected words like *primi amori* (first loves), *mastice* (putty), *naturale* and *nuova forma* (new shape) against the wall of his theatre. As with the theme of change he set in motion for spring 1990, Armani ushered in yet another silhouette, a more elegant and slightly tailored *Nuova Forma*. This new suit remained soft with fitted, deconstructed shoulders. However, now it had a suppressed chest, the waist nipped in to create a sexier hourglass shape, a silhouette more akin to the Savile Row aesthetic. Fabrics coupled with the wide trousers reinforced the ideal while stripes, plaids, linens and creamy colours emphasized the look. Also added was a Norfolk-style self-belted collarless jacket proposed with either a Nehru or mandarin collar in an array of button numbers. To show the importance of the new form and the on-going synergies between both men's and women's clothing, Armani sent women down the runway wearing their male cohort's clothes with a new age soundtrack adding to the spiritualized ethnicity that half the exits embodied. The affect of fluidity was also enhanced by buttoning only the top one or two buttons at most of a jacket which had three or more buttons, providing for greater movement when walking down the runway or street. The outcome of this effect was an inversion of the traditional V shape by making shoulders smaller, a fitted waist and a slight flair – or curve – at the hips, proportions the designer felt were more complimentary to the male form.[69]

68   Peter Lindbergh. Double-breasted suit with incredible flexibility, elasticity and movement as seen in the spring/summer 1995 campaign

The last half of the 1990s saw little in the way of design innovation on the part of the Master Tailor. Rather, he turned his attention to expanding a (Armani) man's wardrobe. For spring 1995 he sent men out in sarongs and pareos, as he had done in the past, while for autumn 1995 Armani introduced a line of skiwear (Neve) inspired by the slopes of San Moritz in the 1930s and 1940s. Its success spawned a Golf line the following season; a response to the then increasing fascination with the sport, a perfect male pastime used by corporate types to bond and relax. These capsule collections were closely followed up in 1996 with Giorgio Armani Classico as part of his main Giorgio Armani black label collection.[70] The classically inspired collection was targeted

GIORGIO ARMANI
C L A S S I C O

69   Classico for men and women, advertising campaign from late 1990s

at the professional, businessman, likely financiers or banker types whose perennial needs were for conservative interpretations of fashion classics. More traditional in cut and fabric, the range was nonetheless the same in feeling as the mainstay collection, luxurious with high-quality fabrication. In the latter half of the decade Armani sought to exhaust his growing competitors such as Prada, Gucci and to a lesser extent Dolce and Gabbana, but in the process seemed to overwhelm the press and some retailers with the sheer number of offerings. By 1996, bereft with the growing attention his minimalist cohorts were getting, Armani claimed that the fashion system was spiralling out of control: 'There is a bit of confusion in fashion today. There is space and time and energy given to something that seems more of a social happening that than style, and then the magazines and newspapers give space to that. It's a dangerous game'.[71] While Armani's statements possessed some legitimacy, it was clear he was no longer the only tailor in control of Milan, a concern that resulted in a lack of focus by the end of the decade for a designer renown for a clear vision and lifestyle aesthetic.

70   In his spring/summer 1996 collection, both men and women not only walk the runway side by side, but wear the same outfits, consisting of a v-neck ribbed jumper and wool-blend trouser with differing effects. The casual jumper-trouser combination is certainly not radical. Despite the identical shape, cut and fabric, the plunging neckline of the men's jumper exposes his chest muscles in a manner more reminiscent of womenswear

71 Spring/summer 1996

Toward a New Millennium: Looking Back, Moving Forward

Despite millennial fears of a Y2K technological apocalypse and beyond the hangovers of many, the first day of 2000 appeared no different than it had the night before. Amongst the debris of revelry and celebrations, what re-emerged was a continued interest in minimalism, deconstruction and Hamish chic, which had dominated the later half to the 1990s when fears of looking overdressed were anathema in a climate of on-going economic turmoil. German designer Jil Sander remained the reigning queen of minimalism, while the so-called Antwerp Six had taken Armani's deconstructive zeal of previous decades to new heights. Overt Gucci and quirky Prada provided the two poles of Milan fashion, particularly in womenswear, once held by feuding Armani and Versace who ignited passion around Milan fashion week. For their menswear collections Gucci, with the media-savvy eye of Tom Ford provided a sexpot hipster or hippie languid silhouette, rival Prada starched her thin-legged, geek-chic boys' collars and provided purposefully eccentric, idiosyncratic combinations of old school classics, while Dolce and Gabbana displayed their hulky, muscle-bound ideal male and wrapped him in the armour of brooding, sexed-up dark mafia suits or a low-cut tank top and groin-enhancing jeans combination. Meanwhile in Paris Hedi Slimane took over the Dior men's line in 2000 and soon caused a sensation when he sent young, ephebic men in impossibly razor sharp, thin silhouettes. So severe was his new cut that it allowed no room for bodily imperfections. Nevertheless it became so popular among the fashion pack that it compelled designer Karl Lagerfeld to shed 90 pounds in order to fit into Slimane's rigorously unforgiving pants and jackets. Dior, Gucci and Prada stood as beacons of an entirely new corporeal order and alternative masculinity, now as difficult and impossible to attain as the feminine ideal represented in fashion's many media outlets.

Their versions of what became a collective look stood in sharp contrast to the more traditionally square-jawed, dark and handsome masculinity still found on Armani's runway. While he has never shied away from putting nearly identical fabrics, cuts and shapes on both his men and women, the toned muscularity has been best set off when coupled with traditionally feminine fabrics that provided for a unique hybrid image of sensual masculinity. Given his research into alternative fabrications for men, had Armani employed the much younger and thinner male models to showcase his collections, I suggest they would have appeared resolutely feminine in a way that would have veered into the realm of camp, costume or drag. As a result they would have remained a product of runway fantasy and not a reality of the street. Throughout the 2000s the Armani male model still possessed distinctly chiselled features, muscular, though not overtly so physiques, bodies mature and yet the product of sport, their gendered identities never in denial but moved beyond traditional parameters precisely because of the fabrics and cuts Armani provided. And for those men for whom a squared jaw and sculpted physique is not a reality, Armani's trousers and jackets, it must be said, offer a way to hide defects and enhance the natural contours of the individual, leaving ample room for the wearer to breathe and feel comfortable. Even his sizing forgives male girth, with sizes as large as 42 US (58 Italian), unlike fast fashion firms like H&M and Zara which end at 36 US placing emphasis on

72 Shirt from spring 2003 with a recurring tab collar and unique curving side button fastenings lending a seductive and exotic touch to an otherwise simple men's shirt

youth and thinness. In large measure, the ideal male body in the designer's mind's eye is largely the product of the images of his childhood, best embodied in the sculptures of the Foro Italico. The sports complex in Rome was built between 1928 and 1938; at the time the complex was commonly known as the Foro Mussolini and is still today considered an inspired exemplar of fascist architecture. To this day the designer maintains '[v]ague childhood memories of the Foro Italico and Stadio dei Marmi – perhaps deriving from the black-and-white news clips shown in some cinemas in Piacenza [his native town]'. It was in the Stadio dei Marmi, a facility devoted to the training of athletes within the Foro Italico complex, where the famous 59 (of the original 60) classically inspired deco marble statues of athletes along the perimeter ominously overlook the space of the *stadio*. For Armani

> the Foro Italico has always possessed an eternal and overwhelming beauty ... each [statue] dedicated to the world of sport and expressing a virility that seems to have been conferred directly by the gods. There is something eternal and absolute about these figures, matched by an ultramodern vision of the future and a sense of individual identity, so intrinsic to our own age.[72]

Inspired by this legacy of the period, Armani continued to design with '[t]he less you add, the more you get' mantra and in 2000 created clothes that were simple and minimal.[73] By 2000, it had also become clear that Armani defiantly refused to follow any of the main trends, to the point of being labelled an 'evangelic preacher' who created his menswear 'based on an absolute refusal to compromise'.[74] It is precisely because of his single-mindedness that Armani maintains complete control and power, whether by dressing actors like Samuel L. Jackson for the mainstream film *Shaft* (2000) or 'to his clout at retail' where he and his products embody 'the best kind of [power] – staying power'.[75]

By 2002 Armani was still playing with a hybrid garment that was at once both formal and informal, asserting a healthy mix of irony and balance that provided 'the truth about how men dress'.[76] This balance attempted to conjure an elusive sense of style, an object that changes little from season to season, the true definition of what constitutes luxury for Armani. For him, luxury denotes 'something that lasts in time; fashion is something of the moment'.[77] Admittedly, his definition was a response to the events of the 11 September terrorist attacks in the USA, a period in which consumers once again prioritized their purchases and questioned the necessity of fashion. This turn to sobriety has become an important aspect of design and in turn has permitted him to foreground his celebrated research into textile development. The importance of Italian textiles and manufacturing, particularly within the burgeoning domain of menswear, also compelled foreign designers such as Lauren and Klein to present their runway collections in Milan, rather than New York. Having drawn inspiration from the wardrobe of 1950s Italian film heartthrob Vittorio de Sica, for his spring/summer 2003 collection Armani continued to

73 Spring 2004 is an excellent example of the bohemian nonchalance that has characterized much of Armani's menswear collections throughout the 2000s; a laissez-faire attitude which more often than not takes on a decidedly nostalgic flavour

develop his long-held interest in alternative versions of the traditional male shirt by pairing his linen jackets with Korean-collared shirts sensuously curved and fastened to one side. For autumn, however, Armani felt it was time for a renewal. In a season which *The New York Times* pitted porn star 'Dirk Diggler against dandy Beau Brummel', like many in Milan, Armani in an unusual turn for a man who has spent his career obsessing over shoulders and waists presented kidney-shaped jackets, which amply highlighted a man's buttocks, a part of the male body he claimed to be 'beautiful'.[78]

74   Since the 1990s skull caps have been used in numerous menswear collections to accessorize the bohemian Deauville look of the 1920s while lending an exotic ethnic touch, both endemic to Armani's design ethos

To give more comfort and renew his commitment to elegant nonchalance, Armani invented two new jackets. The first, the so-called 'Beckham', was introduced in autumn 2003 named after the iconic celebrity English footballer who was so taken by a form fitting cardigan-jacket hybrid Armani was wearing one day that the designer christened it after him. As a result of Armani's relationship with the star player, the jacket along with an entire specially designed wardrobe was provided for the national English football team between the 2004 Euro Cup and 2006 World Cup tournaments.[79] The sporty cardigan-jacket in light cashmere features a polo collar and snap closure at the neck and accentuates the waist and hips, resting snugly against the body. In an interview with British designer Stella McCartney for a special edition of *The Independent* edited by pop star and musician Bono to raise funds and awareness of his global RED campaign, Armani was direct in stating the

75   Armani's velvet revolution. On the left, a one-button velvet jacket coupled with a metal ball-fastened ethnic-inspired collar and wool crepe flat-front trousers (all c.2005): on the right, an eight-button velvet coat with red cotton scarf (2010)

sort of body he preferred to design for. 'I've enjoyed dressing soccer stars for many years ... they are the modern-day gladiators', declared the designer. 'Both on and off the field they have become icons. As a designer, it's always good to stretch yourself, and the challenge of dressing people whose bodies are fine-tuned and developed is one that I particularly enjoy'.[80] The Beckham jacket was one of a number of challenges Armani has undertaken to design clothing suitable for the physical demands in and out of the sports arena.

The second invention, coined 'The George' after its creator and inspired by the designer's own body, was sent down the runway for the autumn/winter 2004 season. For this jacket Armani padded the shoulder slightly, to provide a *soupçon* of power once again. However, this time it was combined with the softest light woollen fabric to lend a sweater-like line to the lean silhouette. The move was not only to accommodate Armani's own broad shoulders, it was more generally a response to the growing discourse and attention swirling around the metrosexual, perfectly personified once again in the figure of Beckham. 'Metrosexual is the name word coiners have invented for a man who combines macho with mild, claiming some femininity for the male sex.' For Armani it was 'a question of aesthetics, not gender'.[81] Despite Armani's ostensible apathy vis-à-vis contemporary gender debates, the supposed hybrid identity of the metrosexual was heavily debated even on the runways of Milan. In a rather condescending article on Milan men's fashion week, Guy Trebay of *The New York Times* dismissed designers' programme notes as material 'to crank up the laugh track', premised on the vain notion that 'consumers need stories before they can understand new clothing, designers tend to oblige with some pretty loopy flights of fantasy'. While Trebay is neither a fan of current fashion nor clearly has he read many contemporary artist statements, in his diatribe the critic specifically signalled out Armani, who according to him

> evinces no particular aptitude for assessing a landscape in which ideas of masculinity seem to change by the hour. Mr. Armani's showing of soft cardigan jackets, flowing trousers and high-button coats were taken by one critic as a sign of 'metrosexual style'. It happens that this discovery comes at a time when any right-thinking metrosexual seems best advised to take his inner woman over to Barney's and get her a crisply tailored suit, the better to frame all those complex masculine/feminine dualities.[82]

Despite his dismissive tone the critic highlighted the continued gender wars being waged on the soft or broad padded shoulders of men in the West. The metrosexual, as both neologism and throw back to the nineteenth century when sexual typologies were 'called into being',[83] was first defined by Mark Simpson as

> a young man with money to spend, living in or within easy reach of a metropolis – because that's where all the best shops, clubs, gyms and hairdressers are.

He might be officially gay, straight, or bisexual, but this is utterly immaterial because he has clearly taken himself as his own love object and pleasure as his sexual preference. Particular professions, such as modelling, waiting tables, media, pop music and nowadays, sport seem to attract them but, truth be told, like male vanity products and herpes, they're pretty much everywhere.[84]

76   For autumn 2006, Armani's velvet touch

Although Simpson claims a degree of sexual inclusivity, I have yet to hear a homosexual male define himself as a metrosexual. In effect, the neologism, not unlike the New Man of the 1980s is a consumer-driven strategy responding to growing male consumption and the desire on the part of manufacturers to generate ever-larger market share, all the while allowing heterosexual men to maintain respectable gender associations. The fact that a male must identify as a metrosexual, rather than simply a heterosexual who enjoys the care of the self, marks a subtle though tacit desire to distance himself from any queer associations, which might befall him. In the end, perhaps Armani's refusal to enter into a discussion of the politics of sexuality and gender speaks less to his apathy than to the knowledge that like fashion itself, the twentieth century has been all too eager to render sexualities fashionable as much as ephemeral.

77   A portrait of Gabriel D'Annunzio reproduced in a feature article on the early twentieth- century dandy in *Monsieur* (June 1921). Here the Italian dandy is stylishly draped in a cape and sporting a well-tailored one-button jacket

78   Autumn 2008 Asian-inspired collar coupled with natural shoulders and form-defining stretch wool fabric

By 2005, as with his women's collections, Armani unabashedly looked to the interwar period as a source of continued inspiration. For autumn/winter he turned to the signature tailored style of Jean Cocteau to create a collection that he himself characterized as 'Avant-garde for Armani but still wearable', with a surrealist *meli-melo* of wit and humour. Heavy on wools, prints and velvets the clothes were meant to conjure 1930s tailoring which 'made men stand tall and proud'.[85] Fashion critic Godfrey Deeny declared it to be 'his best signature men's collection' of the twenty-first century and singled out his use of velvet, 'the big comeback fabric in Italy [, as] particularly special'.[86] His velvets in deep midnight blues, burgundies and black were often combined with wool, and were laser cut for a more luxurious and unique effect. On offer were male versions of the twinsets, a matching cardigan and wool pullover combination uniquely adopted from women. Channelling his decadent French male muse, Armani closed the show with a projected image of himself, half line drawing half photograph reminiscent of Cocteau's own hybrid self-portrait of 1954. For spring Armani continued his exploration of Art Deco by infusing his 14 differently styled jackets with patterns derived from Miami Art Deco architecture. For this collection the designer also introduced a summer variation of the Beckham, featherweight with a jersey rolled collar. His tour of interwar personalities continued in autumn 2006 for which Armani drew inspiration from Gabriele D'Annunzio, who in 1918 was commissioned to divine the name for a new department store, La Rinascente, the designer's former employer. The Italian novelist, poet, journalist, fascist leaning politician and arch rival of Mussolini was, as *Monsieur*, the first men's fashion magazine in the West, declared him in 1921, an inspired dandy.[87] Inspired by D'Annunzio's sartorial panache, Armani sent out models in one-, two- and three-button jackets in a vast array of velvets with argyle and harlequin motifs in a collection aptly titled 'The Velvet Man'.

Although Armani would return to his deco-inspired sartorialism in his beautifully cut and lean collection for autumn 2010, the designer took a break from the decadence of the 1920s when he presented 'Armania' (spring 2006). So named as a word play on both the allusion to the Italian word for harmony (*armonia*) and the designer's own name, the collection and title were meant to conjure for his male customer a sense of balance, peace and harmony. For the designer, the collection provided the opportunity 'to revisit the love [he's] always had for men's wear and the ideas [he's] always had. It will represent a synthesis of the most important creative ideas that have underpinned [his] design philosophy to date'. While the jacket has shouldered Armani's career, the collection was also meant to assert his claim that he has 'done so many other things' than just the now iconic emblem. However, the numbers still speak for themselves, and according to the *Daily News Record* the designer sells 250,000 suits a year, of which 53 per cent of wholesale sales are generated by men.[88]

79   From autumn 2010, a new denim jacket coupled with velvet beret and form-fitting
stretch trousers and shirt

Taking On Savile Row

Given the impact and influence that Armani has had on the menswear industry beyond Italy and the USA, it can come as no surprise that by the early 1990s he was said to have stolen the crown from the ultimate male sartorial status symbol, London's Savile Row.[89]According to Howard Zenner, president of legendary Savile Row tailor Aquascutum, when Armani declared the three-button suit as the new male silhouette in 1990, a mere 1 per cent of the eponymous tailor's sales of suits and jackets featured three buttons. However, since Armani's sartorial move, sales of the jacket jumped to well over 15 per cent; after all, according to Zenner, '[t]here's nothing more British'.[90] As Armani repackaged the tradition of American sportswear and the celluloid glamour of Hollywood back to the USA, he also managed to do the same with his tailoring for Britain by modernizing traditions through different, Italian registers of aesthetics and design. The move toward a three-button single-breasted suit meant that by 1992 he was offering 'an elongated, softened-up Savile Row', while also returning the wrinkles that once made him both infamous and famous.[91] For spring 1993, Armani infused his Savile Row aesthetic with Oriental flare incorporating Nehru and mandarin collars to his jackets. Savile Row tailor Richard James commented that 'Armani's greatest achievement was to take the English institution of tailoring and make it Italian ... In short, Armani created a new sartorial language and made tailoring sexy.'[92] Despite the numerous, various and sometimes subtle gestures toward Savile Row, by the twenty-first century these were no longer enough for the designer to make claims to capturing the pinnacle of men's tailoring, the bespoke suit.

80   From the autumn/winter 1993 collection, a waffle textured jacket in neutral tones paired with a navy shirt as shown on the runway

In 2005 as a first gesture of true exclusivity, following the success of his foray into haute couture, Armani designed a pair of exclusive watches for women and men as part of the Giorgio Armani Privé stable of exclusive products. The Swiss made Armani/Privé Borgo 21 Orlogi he designed in co-operation with Antima, according to its small catalogue, 'exhibits a complete harmony of form, fusing restraint and functionality with beauty and originality'. The watch was originally designed to satisfy the designer's own needs and desires, a result of which was the direct response to 'the vulgarity of watches today'.[93] As with all his enterprises, morality and aesthetics are quickly collapsed in the meaning and outcome of design. As part of its mandate of exclusive 'authenticity' and 'originality' each watch is given its own 'unique serial number to certify its authenticity and track its individual history'.[94] Here history, ownership and authenticity collude to conjure the narratives of unique identity, antidotes to contemporary, vulgar design.

Armani's most concerted effort to 'bring back' bespoke to tailoring made its debut in the summer of 2006 with the arrival of *Fatto A Mano Su Misura* (Hand-

made to Measure) as part of his Giorgio Armani Borgonuovo label, gradually made available in certain key exclusive Giorgio Armani's boutiques around the world. By 2007 Ermenegildo Zegna followed suit with the refurbishment of the firm's Milan boutique, refitted with a basement 'Luxury Room' devoted to the bespoke needs of private clients. In 2007, when Tom Ford opened the doors of his plush and ultra masculine Madison Avenue boutique, made-to-measure was also a prominent feature of the store's exclusive services. In light of these various moves, '[p]ersonal tailoring' was

81   A photograph from the late 1930s displaying typical sources of influence for Armani's menswear. The period remains a consistent source of inspiration

said 'to be back' and Savile Row seemed to return to its former prominence, though with significantly fewer players.[95] For the advertising campaign Armani brought in Italian actor Raoul Bova in 2007 to serve as model while Spanish bullfighter Cayetano Rivera was also used as a testimonial for the label. Depending on the fabric selection, prices for suits begin at $2,075 and can reach a staggering $11,320. The house offers only two models with a vast array of 250 choices in fabric from which to choose including, for example, guanaco (Argentinean llama), vicuna and as always wool crepe. According to Armani, for 'a true bespoke, or handmade garment, there are certain elements you need to deliver. That is to say the suit should embody at least 10 of the recognized characteristics of made-to-measure tailoring. The Giorgio Armani Hand Made to Measure suit includes them all'.[96] In 2004, a number of prominent Savile Row tailors founded the Savile Row Bespoke Association (SBRA) as a means to preserve and systematize the criteria for assessing and authenticating a true bespoke suit. Each member tailor is required to work a minimum of 50 hours on a two-piece suit, and must adhere to 21 different criteria to address the different facets of the garment. Giorgio Armani's made-to-measure jacket includes full canvas construction, hand-stitched buttonholes, small hand-stitching on the collar, elbow, shoulders, vents and cuffs among other parts. 'The idea behind this new ... service is to provide the ultimate level of customization in a suit that is fitted to the exact body type of the wearer, but always designed with comfort and movement as the foundations of the jacket'.[97] As the publicity and exquisitely bound soft-covered booklet for the made-to-measure operation boasts, Armani 'allows a client access to the designer's studio and invites him to become part of the design process'. Here the implication is that, once again, individuality services as a prescription against contemporary vulgarity.

On the eve of Armani's introduction of his new service, reporter John Alridge, who has long covered Armani's shows, published a rather provocative article in which, as the title suggests, 'Armani attacks Savile Row'. According to Alridge Armani dismissed Savile Row as 'a bad English comedy', an apparent counterpoint to Armani's self-professed role as 'modernist' and 'innovator'. According to the journalist:

> He lampoons English tailors as men 'of limited mentality ... who make clothes for the children of lords. They have a restricted idea of how a suit is made. The suit can only be made in this shape, with these fabrics. It has to be a certain way and they don't go beyond that ... They don't research or develop something or innovate. There is no room in their head to expand into something new. They do not think of half the things that I take into consideration when I think of a hand-made to measure suit'.[98]

82   Spring/summer 1995

Accordingly, chief executive of Gieves and Hawkes Mark Henderson was astonished at Armani's apparent dismissal of the time-honoured tradition, asserting that 'Savile Row is far from history. Today it stands for exemplary standards of luxury in men's tailoring.'[99] However, tailors such as Henderson have been keen to officially structure and sanction their practice as a means to protect tradition and ward off increasing competition from Italian designers like Dolce and Gabbana, Zegna and Armani: the latter two formalized their practices following the 2004 formation of SBRA. In these equally reactive measures, nationalism and identity are clearly at play as they vie to determine a man's sartorial contours. Located under the business letters of *The Times*, Armani responded in short order to Alridge, accusing him of misrepresentation. It is, I believe, worth reproducing the letter in full here.

83   1998 Indian summer for menswear

No offence: While it might have made for a provocative cover story, John Alridge's article 'Armani attacks Savile Row' significantly misinterpreted my remarks about Savile Row.

I have the greatest respect for Savile Row, which for two centuries has been a pinnacle of excellence for men's tailoring.

My intention is to create a different kind of excellence, that reflects my personal aesthetic of bringing the traditional and the modern together, building on the best of both, while respecting the craft Savile Row has for so long made its own.

I was surprised by the way John Alridge portrayed my point of view as he has interviewed me on many occasions and knows me and my philosophy well.

First, what was said about Savile Row was provoked by Alridge himself. When I spoke of it being like a 'commedia', it was meant in a nostalgic theatrical sense in that its heritage and notoriety are linked to the past. That was my meaning. No offence intended.

I much regret that any remarks were misunderstood and presented in such a way as to make it seem that I was attacking Savile Row, which I have no wish to do. There is plenty of room for us both.[100]

With the absence of Armani's former worthy sparring mate Versace, throughout the twenty-first century Armani has sought to provoke elsewhere, whether by charging Dolce and Gabbana of plagiarism or claiming for Miuccia Prada a prominent role in the culture of ugliness in menswear which he insists is indulged by the press. Whether misrepresented or not, Armani's words nonetheless often hit a nerve, as they did in the Alridge article. This debate not only has economic implications but nationalist undertones in the context of global modernity. The race to dress the world's most fashionable men, then, is not simply a contest toward defining male fashion but points to an aspiration to impact the textured genealogy of the male body and masculinity itself on a global scale. Today that race has become even more competitive and complicated.

Notes

1   *The Sunday Times* 21 March 1993.

2   *BG* 1 October 1992.

3   *The Evening Standard* 14 February 1995.

4   Hirschberg 2000: 188.

5   *Wall Street Journal* 31 October 1990.

6   Armani in *Made in Milan* 1990.

7   Foucault 1977: 148.

8   Armani in *Made in Milan* 1990.

9   Hale 1992: 98.

10 Armani in Giacomoni 1984: 67.

11 Giacomoni 1984: 68.

12 *NYT* 30 March 1980.

13 *NYT* 18 September 1977; *NYT* 1 January 1978.

14 Mulasanno in Molho 2007: 10.

15 See Breward 1999 who refutes Fluegel's claim that men renounced the fashions of clothing.

16 Lauren in *NYT* 18 September 1977.

17 I wish simply to highlight how Ralph Lauren famously dressed Diane Keaton for her role in *Annie Hall*, while, as previously stated, Armani dressed her for the Academy Awards. These two designers are internationally recognized and successful precisely because they have created entire life-worlds, or what we might call a *Gesamtkunstwerk* (total work of art, or total lifestyle). See Potvin 2010.

18 'Armani on the Loose' 1978: 120.

19 Howell 1990: 121.

20 *NYT* 1 January 1978.

21 *People Magazine* 30 July 1979.

22 *NYT* 20 January 1980.

23 *NYT* 26 February 1981.

24 *NYT* 4 August 1981.

25 *NYT* 4 August 1981.

26 *NYT* 28 March 1982.

27 *DNR* 8 July 1983.

28 *LAT* 7 October 1983.

29 *DNR* 17 July 1984.

30 *NYT* 8 September 1985.

31 It is worth noting that Arnold Schwarzenegger was in two of these films and would later become an Armani devotee, even of his swimwear.

32 Armani licensed his lines for innerwear and sleepwear to Icap Due, which produced lines for both Giorgio Armani and Emporio Armani. This licensing agreement did not continue into the twenty-first century and today Armani only produces a line for Emporio Armani.

33 *DNR* 15 July 1985.

34 *DNR* 30 June 1986.

35 Lipovestsky 1994: 110.

36 Chenoune 1996: 148.

37 *G & M* 18 March 1986.

38 *DNR* 10 July 1986.

39 Hale 1992: 98.

40 Hale 1992: 99.

41 *G & M* 28 April 1987.

42 Buckley in 'Armani Disarmed' 1995: xv.

43   *DNR* 12 July 1988.

44   *NYT* 21 December 1990.

45   *DNR* 11 January 1990.

46   'The Power of Armani' 1993: 161.

47   *DNR* 3 April 1989.

48   *DNR* 3 April 1989.

49   *DNR* 3 April 1989.

50   *DNR* 5 July 1989.

51   *DNR* 14 July 1989.

52   *DNR* 14 July 1989.

53   *DNR* 18 July 1989.

54   *DNR* 14 July 1989.

55   *DNR* 14 July 1989.

56   *DNR* 20 July 1989.

57   *DNR* 7 August 1989.

58   *DNR* 1 November 1990.

59   *DNR* 31 July 1989.

60   *DNR* 16 January 1990.

61   *DNR* 16 January 1990.

62   *DNR* 16 January 1990.

63   *DNR* 11 July 1990.

64   *DNR* 14 June 1990.

65   Postrel 2003: 77.

66   *DNR* 7 January 1991.

67   *G & M* 7 March 1991.

68   *DNR* 3 July 1991.

69   Howarth 1994: 9.

70   The Neve and Golf lines have since dissolved while the Classico line has been absorbed into
      the black label collection with no distinction made in the labelling. Always ahead of the game,
      as a way to adapt to the current economic crisis, for the spring/summer 2010 season Armani
      introduced a capsule white label collection (not to be confused with the 'white-label' he began in
      1978), as part of his Giorgio Armani main-line collection. The new endeavour was to replace and
      reintroduce the principles behind the Classico sub-line he began in 1996 while providing a more
      rigorous and tailored suit, more suppressed in the waist and an overall leaner cut at an entry price
      point of about 20 per cent less than the rest of the collection.

71   'Twist and Shoot' 1996: 191.

72   Armani 2002: 40–4. Inspired by the statues of the Foro Italica, for his spring 1985 Emporio Armani
      campaign shot by Aldo Fallai the designer used a sculptural motif in which stone statue merges
      with human flesh and clothing, leaving the viewer unclear where the human begins and the
      sculptural ends. Armani also wrote the introduction to George Mott's photograph-based book *Foro
      Italico*, 2003.

73   *LAT* 14 January 2000.

74   *Sunday Times Style Magazine* 14 May 2000.

75   Foley 2000: 382.

76   *DNR* 2 July 2001.

77   *Sunday Times* 30 June 2002.

78   *NYT* 19 January 2003.

79   Armani has long maintained an intense relationship with the arena of sports by having numerous male sports figures pose in advertisements, through team sponsorship or technological innovation in design. This relationship deserves a separate study beyond the scope of this book. To attend to it in cursory fashion would only prove to be a disservice.

80   *The Independent* 16 May 2006.

81   Associated *Press* 15 January 2004.

82   *NYT* 18 Jan 2004.

83   See Foucault 1990a.

84   See 'Meet the Metrosexual' 22 July 2002 www.salom.com.

85   *The Independent* 21 January 2005.

86   *Fashion Wire Daily* 21 January 2005.

87   'Sur un portrait de Gabriel d'Annunzio Dandy' 1921.

88   *DNR* 20 June 2005.

89   Hale 1992: 97.

90   *DNR* 29 March 1990.

91   *DNR* 3 July 1992.

92   *IHT* 17 March 1997.

93   *Financial Times* 30 March 2006.

94   Borgo 21 catalogue.

95   *NYT* 15 January 2007.

96   *DNR* 19 June 2006.

97   Armani in *DNR* 19 June 2006.

98   *The Sunday Times* 9 July 2006.

99   *The Sunday Times* 9 July 2006.

100   *The Times* 16 July 2006.

5

Armani/Womenswear: Hybrid Modernity

> There's the Versace woman who dresses for men, sans doute. Versace girls make a career of sex; they don't have girlfriends, they're too much competition. The Armani woman dresses for herself.
>
> Jasper Conran

> I'm not worried whether they're sexy, or beautiful, or tall. I want the women who wear my clothes to be intelligent. I don't dress the woman just to attract a man at the end of the evening.
>
> Giorgio Armani

Over his career Armani has drawn consistently from the same sources of inspiration when he dresses men and women, generally opting for reality over whimsy. His insistence on functionalism, fundamentally simple clothes embellished with refined and detailed textiles, has meant that his fashion has not always been easily photographed. Not unlike her male cohort, the Armani woman is intelligent, thoughtful, involved in the world, self-possessed and works hard for her achievements. Irony, tenderness and femininity are matched with a heavy dose of charm and sobriety. Armani's design praxis for womenswear began when his sister Rosanna (once a model and who appeared in his spring/summer 1979 campaign), and her friends began wearing his men's jackets. The result was a continuation and improvement on the tradition most credit Yves Saint Laurent as starting, and who, by the 1980s had already become moribund according to an unforgiving fashion press. By borrowing a sartorial vocabulary from menswear, Armani also suggested a new erogenous zone for women. In his pantsuits, usually displayed on flat chested models, emphasis was no longer on the breasts, which had long captivated men, but rather on the hip and buttocks, traditionally so-called trouble areas for many women. By the late 1980s, however, he softened the contours of his ideal woman, and while the jacket would remain the centrepiece of the quintessential Armani wardrobe for both men and women, for the latter he provided a new playfulness, fantasy and femininity. The Giorgio Armani ethos is constant and steadfast, unaffected by the vagaries of the world outside the walls of his palazzo. Through the ebbs and flows of fashion's many lives, Armani's designs have remained focused at the nexus between: cross-gender material performances; a nostalgic modernist zeal (his debt to the 1920s, 1930s and 1940s); and Orientalist inspiration (Asia, India and North Africa). These central themes inform this chapter and its sections. By exploring the genealogy of Armani's womenswear and his more recent foray into furniture design with Armani/ Casa, this chapter seizes on the key developments and motifs previously mentioned and concludes by addressing his eveningwear, arguing it marks *the* site of tension where the designer has sought to claim his position within the history of fashion and safeguard his cultural patrimony.

84   Spring/summer 1989

Toward A New Masculine Femininity

In 2004 Armani placed an advertisement for his Armani Junior line in various magazines around the world. In the UK, however, the Advertising Standards Authority requested the designer and his UK licensee for the line, Orthet, withdraw one particular image. The questionable advertisement displayed a shirtless, longhaired boy wearing baggy jeans and a necklace. Seventy-four complaints were registered arguing that the image, while not sexually suggestive, was nevertheless sexualized because the model's gender was ambiguous, consequently drawing attention to the child's sexuality. Although in this instance it was a child who caused discomfort, issue VII of *Dossier* (May 2011) featured the highly androgynous, and equally contentious model Andrei Pejic shirtless, sporting large golden locks. American booksellers Borders and Barnes and Noble refused to carry the magazine in their stores as a result. Although these large-scale booksellers carry *GQ* and numerous men's fitness magazines on their shelves, on whose covers semi-naked women and shirtless muscle-endowed male models appear, the androgyny is what left these retailers feeling out of sorts. What these two incidences indicate is that, at least in the English-speaking West, Butler's troubling of gender has had little impact in the cultural wars in an ever-increasing conservative climate in which gender, sex and sexuality are quickly collapsed. Indeed, there is a double standard in regards to androgyny in our culture. Women have longed embraced, mostly out of necessity, a sartorial armour to help 'pass' in a male-dominated world, while men must ensure a proper and clear representation of masculinity in line with a preferred male ideal.[1]

Since the late 1970s women in the West have gained considerable success and access to power, emblematized through their sartorial choices, by 'playing the part' making them look, as some critics of the period claimed, like an 'imitation man'.[2] In his influential book from 1977, *The Woman's Dress for Success*, John T. Molloy matter-of-factly outlined the sartorial elements women must steer clear of to escape the 'Imitation Man Look'. A man's fedora, shirt and tie as well as pinstripes are prohibited by Molloy, as these only serve to diminish a woman's access to authority. Molloy asserts that

> [t]he 'imitation man look' does not refer to looking tough or masculine … When a woman wears certain clothes with male colors or patterns, her femaleness is accentuated. She frequently looks diminutive. And this reduces her authority … Obviously those fashion designers who turn out 'imitation man' clothes and call them career apparel are advancing only their own careers.[3]

Instead Molloy insists on brightly coloured, contrasting vests and pants, declaring these to be 'ultra sexy'.[4] What came of these developments in womenswear in the late 1970s and 1980s was a power dressing that according to Joanne Entwistle was not about expressing individuality in dress. 'Power dressing' did not set out to rock any boats, its main aim was to enable women to steer a steady course through male-dominated professions, and it therefore sought to work with existing codes of dress. In this respect 'power dressing' was inherently conservative, recommending women to wear the female equivalent of the male suit, and to avoid trousers in the boardroom at all costs since these are supposedly threatening to male power.[5]

The goal of the Armani woman has never been to identify as or with a man, but rather to blur the boundaries and the limits of a gendered self-presentation. Among the numerous changes the designer made to a woman's wardrobe were form-fitting silk or wool t-shirts, shoulder pads and colours traditionally exclusive to menswear. Men's worsteds, checks and patterns, and men's formal and linen shirts also became staples. He also took the pantsuit, double-breasted jackets and the cardigan and applied them to womenswear. *Esquire* described the look of the late 1970s with its attention to '[c]loth caps as worn by English proletariat. Tweeds in dun and brown and beige. The lesbian touch, but dinkily done, nothing too butch.' However as Armani qualifies, 'I always left them with a beautiful soft, silky shirt underneath.'[6] A number of years later; when he began to move away from a more purportedly severe look and shape for women, he reminisced about his influence and what became identified as the Armani look at a particularly important juncture in women's recent history. Armani has himself shied away from labelling his clothing unisex, stating frankly: 'My fashion is not unisex, but it does insist upon more gentleness for men, and more strength for women ... far from the extremist stereotypes of the macho man and of the woman imprisoned in the squalid part of the doll-whore'.[7] Armani's first men's collection featured women's looks with a slight matronly quality to them, reminiscent of his contemporary Walter Albini. This first attempt at womenswear was soon replaced, or in the least reworked, in January when Armani presented his first official 30-piece women's collection (spring 1976) in a small but established restaurant, Carminati, in Piazza del Duomo in Milan. His soon to become iconic women's masculine-inspired jackets were the stars of that inaugural collection. Labelled 'a superb show' by *Women's Wear Daily*, the collection drew inspiration from India and presented what was considered by some as the 'youngest' and 'most innovative' collection of the season.[8] The garments, especially the jackets with their traditional menswear fabrics, appeared to be poor, as if already lived-in with a distinctly vintage feel, a popular aesthetic amongst artists and young hip professionals of the day. Here too, male models walked alongside (also featuring 30 pieces) in oddly coloured terry-clothed suits. In these inaugural collections Armani not only established himself, despite near non-existent sales, but importantly also featured two vital elements of his design ethos: the influence of the so-called Orient, and the cross-pollination and mixing of sexes. A few years later Armani recalled: 'When I made the first jacket for a woman, copied from the man's', he submits, 'they told me, "It's too hard, too masculine. Women won't accept it". They were wrong.'[9] Women understood right away that a man's jacket coaxes her personality out and reveals itself in a wholly new way. Armani and Galeotti soon moved their collection presentations to the hall of the Palace Hotel where the other designers were showing and for the autumn 1976 collection Armani's models wore jackets in tweeds similar in cut to those of his menswear, yet had the lightness and fluidity of a dress. For the end of the show, the designer sent his 12 models down the runway, while Galeotti played a random record of the then popular Inti-illimani while the models spontaneously began to dance and move to the music. The event was a success and importantly marked Armani's sanctioned arrival on the fashion circuit.

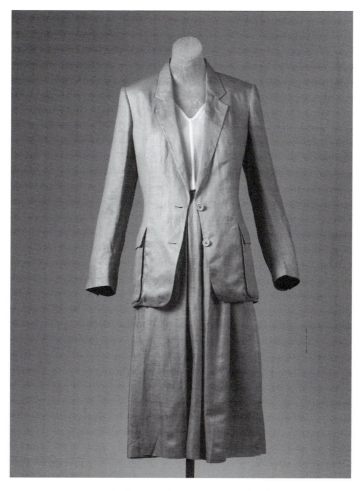

85   A c.1979 suit once worn by Lauren Bacall and gifted by the actress to the Costume Institute, New York

Having been declared the number one menswear designer by *The New York Times*[10] and numerous others by 1978, Armani translated his desire to improve his women's jackets by broadening and padding the shoulders. Displayed in his newly acquired Palazzo Durini, his jackets for autumn 1978, an about-face from the fluid and loose silhouettes he had revolutionized in the previous seasons, were inspired by 1940s Prince of Wales suitings and military shouldered jackets reminiscent of Second World War doughboys' uniforms. These jackets were paired with trousers, culottes and skirts. The military precision and structured silhouette was softened by way of smocking at the yoke of jackets, ruffled scarves and fur boas, ubiquitous to a fault. For the season he also designed a rare, but luxurious line of fur coats in beaver and mink, often in the same pelts as the scarves and boas. As a whole, the collection 'considered by most to be the best in Milan' was not only well received by buyers and the press, but bravos and cheers 'rang the rafters'.[11]

For spring 1980, which marked a turning point for his womenswear, the designer not only received a standing ovation for his presentation, but the fashion press unanimously anointed him 'The King', a title which would endure throughout the 1980s and 1990s. For what was a more 'contemporary' and 'easier and less contrived' proposition,[12] menswear once again proved to be the definite source of inspiration for a collection which featured the innovation of a 'shoulderless' suit, or as W christened it, the 'jacket-minus'.[13] The suit was simply a tailored skirt and a matching strapless top with the bodice fitted tightly through the hips, providing a wrapping for the body. Underneath his classically tailored suits with strong shoulders, Armani placed sheer or in some cases transparent men's linen shirts, 'sure to be worn by both sexes'.[14] *Women's Wear Daily* characterized the collection as both 'modern chic' and 'charming, precise, neat and even humorous'.[15] Classic tailoring, from which the designer has never veered, was an early source of inspiration and innovation, 'building a big business and reputation on classicism with a twist'.[16] It is precisely this hybrid character of his clothes, tailored yet relaxed, classic yet modern, that bears the mark of his personality and aesthetic since these early collections

86   Autumn/winter 1981. The jacket, in heavy and textured tweed coupled with a narrow lapel in leather, is reminiscent of a kimono. Many jackets, like this one, were also minimally embellished with double-track ridges from shoulder to sleeve, here cuffed in leather like the collar. The jacket is paired with pleated culottes in the same fabric

and *W* dubbed as 'neither loud nor quiet, classic nor antiestablishment'.[17] His success already noted and celebrated with a prestigious Neiman Marcus Award in 1979, Armani was all too aware that his creations were being copied by others, a reality to which he responded: 'I love to see myself copied. I have a certain "tenderness" for those who copy me. Sergio, on the other hand, goes out of his mind when he sees a copy. He is infuriated. I guess that's normal'.[18] Despite this purported 'tenderness' for those copying his designs, as we have already seen in Chapter 2, the house in collaboration with GFT initiated a secondary, diffusion line destined for the North American market where much of the copying was taking place. By 1980, Milan as the new centre for Italian fashion had definitively shown itself to be a capital force to be reckoned with in the industry and further afield, boasting a 50 per cent increase in exports and an influx of international designers like Issey Miyake and Geoffrey Beene, who opted to showcase their collections in the industrial epicentre. With production and travelling costs rising by as much as 19 per cent within the short period of one season, retailers were forced to make tough decisions in their purchases for the autumn 1980 collections, compelling designers to focus on more classical, less risky design choices. Armani continued to earn his title of King of the blazer, providing retailers with functional, yet elongated jackets for women paired with cuffed trouser-skirts, a combination of skirt in the back and trouser in front; the hybrid garment would return throughout his career in various permutations. Shoes lent an air of masculine solidity with the designer completing the looks with one-inch suede pumps and Oxfords. Armani's timely emphasis on man-tailored garments was well received in a period marked by an increased incursion of women in the corporate workforce.

Along with Albini, Armani opted to show his spring/summer 1981 collection away from the then customary Fiera exhibition halls, and presented his collection over three days in his via Durini headquarters. The move was to provide a more intimate setting and experience for the 20 to 30 buyers and members of the press invited for each showing. The designer showcased a feminine and light collection introducing 'wacky pants' though not as wacky as those by his competitor Versace,[20] who made his debut on the Milan catwalk under his own label in 1978 after numerous years of successful freelance designing and consulting. Skirts were altogether absent, with myriad-shaped, textured and coloured trousers filling the void. Often in bright colours and bold combinations, textiles for the collection betrayed Armani's technical process and steadfast research into fabric innovation; by this point he was designing upwards of 90 per cent of the textiles used in his collections. By choosing to display the collection in a more intimate setting, at this early stage of his career Armani emphasized the significance of textiles over cut and image, and playfully drew attention to the importance they held in the creation of haptic visuality. At first glance fabrics appeared as if moiré taffeta, for instance, while in effect these were mimicked through cotton printed moiré patterns, an innovation bridging high with low. Jackets took inspiration from the traditional Japanese kimono, while others with Nehru cuts and details were belted with an obi sash; both propositions allowed ample room, softness and fluidity for their wearer. Marking the designer's first substantive foray along the Silk Road to the so-called Orient (a term still used today in Italian to designate the Far East), Armani had his models swing Chinese baskets over their shoulders in lieu of handbags while some held lacquered fans. Proving his ability to adopt a menswear formula to women's fashion by mixing it with subtly evolving influences from the East, the collection marked a clear objective to conjure a new contour of femininity. According to Armani:

> I tried to envision a more flexible woman, one who is receptive to innovation, who enjoys being female but doesn't need all the banal and boring traditional trappings of femininity. I believe that we are ready for a new kind of femininity, one that needs no fussy, frilly, overdone clothing or bon-bon colors to assert itself. It's much more direct and straightforward. I've always believed that a woman – especially a confident and self-aware woman, is beautifully showcased in precision cut, clean-lined men's wear styling. Nothing sets her off to better advantage, and if she takes genuine pleasure in being female, she never needs to exaggerate that femininity. That's why I don't do frou-frou.[21]

With his message for daywear now firmly in place, his propositions for eveningwear had until then, by his own admission, been lacking and unexplored; these were usually the product of translating evening fabrics to his near replicas of his daywear silhouettes. The so-labelled frou-frou, anathema within the Armani design lexicon, is a decided counterpoint to his early modernist functionalism, an impulse premised on the elimination of 'the superfluous in life – whether at work, home, even in [his] social life'.[22] Within the modernist paradigm of form must follow function, textiles and form cohere to bring about a harmony premised on 'quality, elegance and practicality', ideals the designer believes to be the very underpinning of modernity and luxury itself. In the first decade of Armani's men's and particularly so of his women's collections, the modernity of his clothes resided in the idea that they were directly relevant to a global place and contemporary time; after all, the word modern derives its root from the Latin word *modo* meaning just now, a consistent, verging on obsessive, term used by the fashion industry more broadly. According to Armani: 'For me, realism and modernism should never be far removed from creativity.'[23] Armani further maintained that his clothes rejected historical references to a previous designer culture, specifically referring to the classic combination of 'a crepe-de-chine blouse with a bow, a coordinated ensemble where everything matched – the shoes, the gloves' that had become the Chanel paradigm.[24] The so-called modernity or newness of his design begins with the creative process itself, often derived from the movies, walks in the city, picture books or conversations with staff. Inspired in this way, Armani always starts with a blank page in an unadorned, untroubled room. Once imagined, the sketch is only truly ever called into being when the fabric swatches are pinned to it, lending a haptic affect to the ideal made visual. Regardless of the source of inspiration, all design begins with fabric, the result of his early training at Cerruti.

By 1981, Giorgio Armani had already become a $120 million empire. This early success coupled with his role as head designer for Erreuno and Mario Valentino meant his aesthetic and name were becoming increasing widely distributed. One solitary muse has never fuelled his creativity, for as he once stated of Lee Radziwill who by then had become a loyal client, 'if she looks wonderful in one of my Japanese kimono jackets, it's a great pleasure for me, but I do not design with her in mind. I cannot afford the luxury of thinking of one woman.'[25] Already by the early 1980s the finance of fashion was a significant preoccupation, as was the burden of fathering such a large-scale enterprise. As Armani powered his way through the early 1980s, so too did his women continue to sport broad shoulders. For autumn/winter 1982, for example, his highly tailored and commercial collection centred on the oversize jacket, rendering it as effortless as women pilfering through their father's closets to locate those comfortable yet strong, structured though lived in blazers. These were paired with loose trousers that came to just below the knee, reminiscent of Argentinean gaucho pants, while the few skirts that made it into the collection took inspiration from Japanese field workers paired with crepe-de-chine, collarless blouses. The same motifs and ideas were translated for the wildly received Mario Valentino collection, which focused on leathers and suedes . Leather became a perennial material in his collections throughout the period and according to the designer '[w]omen feel good in leather ... It is such a sumptuous material.'[26] Having incorporated leathers into his womenswear since 1976, Armani asserts that the skin 'has sex appeal' and unlike fur, 'leather falls and folds on the body to become a second skin'.[27] For Mario Valentino, whose relationship to and transformation of leatherwear was akin to what Fendi did for fur, Armani also showed gaucho trousers in Guatemalan cottons and tapestry effects.

The spring 1984 collection continued the gender-crossing thread he had set in motion in his first collection. This along with his creations for both Erreuno and Mario Valentino combined Italian fabrication with American sportswear to offer accessible and yet innovative clothes for the well-heeled working woman. While the collections were received with mixed reviews, his namesake collection was deemed 'triumphal'. Armani's 'studied simplicity' made more 'conventionally designed women's clothes look overdone', noted *The New York Times*. The looks were a result of a combination of men's slouchy suits coupled with men's shoes and ties, lending an androgynous

GIORGIO ARMANI
24 South Molton Street
London W1Y

87   Gian Paolo Barbieri. From the autumn/winter 1983 advertising campaign

look to the tall, languid models who professed to have 'felt wonderful in their slightly androgynous clothes'.[28] In a highly reported on collection, the designer suggested two core propositions for jackets. The first was man-inspired with a draping lapel to give a feminine touch and buttoned at the waist, enhancing the stomach area of the wearer's body. The second was a simple yet inventive wrap-around collarless hip jacket. Armani continued to belt his outfits with the obi sash he had introduced several seasons before. Having eschewed the circus of the runway circuit, Armani's return was met with vigorous applause and shouts of bravo! Importantly in the audience of 450 was Anna Craxi, wife of the socialist prime minister of Italy, who along with the other guests feasted on fresh oysters and champagne before being led to his plush carpeted downstairs theatre.

For the 1984 seasons, after years of presenting mannish clothes for women, *Women's Wear Daily* declared

88   Spring/summer 1985

> Giorgio Armani wins the battle of the sexes hands down. While the debate over masculine versus feminine dressing has waxed furious throughout the ready-to-wear collections here this week, it took Armani to make a woman look like a woman in man's clothes – and a very sexy woman at that. It's a very sophisticated balancing act, and it wins Armani four stars for what was not only the best collection of the season, but one of the best Armani collections ever.[29]

Despite a steadfast approach to each season, Armani once again won over the press, retailers and consumers through his research into fabrics. In a collection featuring an impressive 350 different fabrics, for autumn Armani combined corduroy for shirts with wools that pass for silk in colours that ranged from purple and red to charcoal and wood. One reporter noted the limitations of traditional runway presentations when he claimed how '[y]ou had to look closely and carefully to appreciate the subtle plays on color and texture, the unusual juxtapositions of rich, sombre color, plays on pattern and contrasts of surface texture'.[30] To add a sense of humour to his otherwise serious menswear inspired jackets he pinned bowties to the pockets.

This, as with his previous collections, was aimed at a more mature and well-heeled woman who might be in need of some textured armour. For the designer too much of contemporary fashion was aimed at the 'teenager', neglecting in its wake the real woman who can afford high-end fashion. Armani conceded a degree of naturalism vis-à-vis age in fashion; for him, 'the idea of women trying to look like children, trying to be a baby doll' is 'unnatural'.[31] In what was a very well received autumn 1984 collection Armani also shook things up by creating what was ostensibly the first backless shirt, which he coupled with

89　A look from autumn 1986 featuring power shoulders met with feminine pink fabric and unusual styling

fluid cuffed trousers, a look directly referencing menswear of the 1930s when cuffs on trousers were de rigeur, garments that the *Los Angeles Times* called 'true gender-benders'.[32] The same gender-bending zeal continued into the spring 1985 collection for which he received another standing ovation, and whose overall affect lead the 'totally enthralled' audience members to claim to be 'transported into another world by an exhilarating theatrical experience'.[33] For autumn, according to Natalia Aspesi, who characterized the collection as a true spectacle beyond the numerous professionals and celebrities filling the

90   Aldo Fallai. From the autumn/winter 1986 advertising campaign, shot in the designer's via Borgonuovo palazzo before it was remodelled by Peter Marino

front row of his theatre, 'Armani taught us once again that the man's jacket is a woman's best friend, bent on proposing dozens of versions, always with the shoulder and sustained without a collar'.[34] Although Armani continued his man-tailoring into 1986, he complained of feeling endlessly copied by his competitors, which suggested no way out from within the Giorgio Armani aesthetic for the designer himself. He often lamented that he felt sacrificed by the pressures of financial success and the rigours of an Italian fashion system that does not allow him to be as free as designer like Thierry Mugler and Claude Montana in Paris. By 1987 time had come, however, to redefine the Armani woman and search out a new femininity and a new approach.

The Time of Gender: Left Bank Chic and the Return to Deco

> It's OK to be inspired by history and to use it as a starting point in design, but not to re-create it.

> Giorgio Armani in 1981

In the 2010 'Frames for Life' campaign for Giorgio Armani Occhiali (eyewear) two unique short films were commissioned to stylishly insert eyewear into the continuing narratives of the Armani man and woman. Inspired by eyewear from the 1920s and 1940s, the film for the men's campaign took place in the designer's city, while for the women's campaign he opted to film in Paris, the centre of all things fashionable and feminine since at least the nineteenth century. At the time of the much celebrated 1925 Exposition des Arts Décoratifs et Industriels Moderns in Paris, it was concluded that: 'Whereas men go to London for suits & shirts, women all dream of being dressed in Paris.'[35] Parallel with the challenges he had levelled at Savile Row, through this particular campaign Armani echoes the geo-cultural and design ethos of 1925, with Milan importantly replacing London as the international capital of menswear. With the rise of haute couture in Paris, the City of Lights has long held sway as the capital of fashion and all things chic. As a centre of both colonialism and avant-garde aesthetics, Paris's rise to cultural hegemony also allowed for a fashion industry to take on a widely advertised and disseminated international importance. Paris, then, was best personified by the young, beautiful and highly fashionable Parisienne, a woman of international distinction and *savoir faire*.

Armani's consistent – verging on obsessive – fetish for both Asia and the glory days of the interwar period (1920s and 1930s) service as archival sites for subtle gender trouble and aesthetic avant-gardism. Art historians like Thomas Crow have vehemently argued that fashion and commerce are antithetical and antagonistic forces to avant-garde and modernist art.[36] However, as Lisa

91   Spring/summer 1987: a softened version of the traditional man's tailored suit, made light and fluid for the summer months in Capri and Deauville

Tickner exposes, the Baudelairian notions of the fleeting, contingent and the ephemeral, the one half of 'modernité' were associated with mass consumption and important developments in technology by the turn of the century.[37] Don Slater has shown how, unlike in the nineteenth century, the 1920s was the first period in which modernity was not simply the prerogative of a select avant-garde coterie, but rather had 'arrived' for the population at large. It is precisely within this populist and consumerist expression of modernity that Walter Benjamin explored the world of Baudelaire and it is to him that we owe much of our perceptions of the nineteenth-century poet and critic. The period created a commodity out of modernity itself; public experiences were transformed into spectacle, domesticated comfort ruled the world of design, exotic costumes were the result of greater knowledge and the commodity was itself the ultimate goal of modernity.[38]

92   Aldo Fallai. From the spring/summer 1987 advertising campaign

In the acknowledgements for this book, I fondly recall the first Giorgio Armani advertising campaign I ever saw. For the spring 1987 collection, magazines were provided with the largest number of images he had ever published, taking up as many as 39 pages in *Vogue Italia*, for example, of advertising space. Cinematic in tone, the sepia-infused images were inspired by a series of photographs of Curzio Malaparte in Capri. The photographs, taken by perennial favourite Aldo Fallai, were not shot on location in Capri but rather in a studio aided by props, lighting and painted backgrounds in order to 'create the necessary magical detachment of the images which had inspired [him] in the first place'.[39] For every image, a moody explanatory text poetically summarizing the inspiration or hinting at the atmosphere were provided on each facing page. This doubling of pages not only enhanced the affect of the image through each short text, but also added to an overall sense of luxury (and cost). The effect was described as 'outfits that sometimes look created for a dream sequence in a Fellini film'.[40] Inspired by the universalizing ideal of 'style' which portends to place experiences and garments outside of history, the epigraph for the collection of advertising images read: '*Un modo di essere oltre il tempo*' (A way of being beyond time). This discursive strategy lends itself perfectly to two imbricated notions long held important by the designer: first, there are no identifiable sources in his designs, and secondly, that what he produces will live beyond the season of its origin. The result is that his work resides uncomfortably somewhere outside of the fashionable and fashion itself. With this campaign the designer was proposing a state of being, a state of mind, rather than seasonal propositions. According to him, both 'men's and women's collections that year were aimed at stimulating the fashion scene, which had become rather vulgar, into rediscovering the cultural chic of the years between the wars'.[41] The various epigraphs throughout helped to conjure the interwar period, suggesting his characters were part of the glamorous and chic enclaves that formed in Deauville, Capri or Forte dei Marmi. Three male, one female and one child model (the latter recalling the character Tadzio from *Death in Venice*, an apt allusion) were set against backdrops of rocky beaches, rippling water and country homes. While the handsome male models, with their jet black slicked-back hair, appeared European yet worldly, their female companion Gina di Bernardo, who served as the designer's house model for over five years, appeared as an elusive, captivating and impossibly elegant beauty.[42]

Beginning in 1987, Armani significantly softened up his masculine-inspired womenswear, striking more of a balance between the feminine and the masculine than he had throughout the previous decade. His collection for spring represented a major shift away from the broad-shouldered boardroom aesthetic, which made him one of a few designers of choice for the career-minded cosmopolitan woman. When he presented the collection Armani declared: 'Men's wear for women is dead'.[43] The supple and ultra lightweight collection revolved around feminine shapes and fabrics such as chiffon and silk crepe and 'created a ground-breaking femininity' providing a look that *Women's Wear Daily* referred to as 'modern, and never lapses into nostalgia'.[44] The collection was not only a marked move away from his menswear-inspired cuts and fabrics, but also launched a new and significant phase in his design aesthetic which refocused attention on a interwar Parisian bohemianism, adapted for an equally independent and upwardly mobile woman of the late 1980s. However, according to the designer, the clothes were not suitable for everyone. Rather, they 'belong to a really sure, elegant, sophisticated woman'.[45] *The New York Times* declared the show to be 'wonderful', remarking that nothing remained legible from his first showing from 1975.[46] Armani described this shift from 1987 years later in 'Armani Disarmed':

> I know that many were disconcerted when I came out with short chiffon skirts, shirt-jackets and other apparently strange ideas. But I felt that there was a need for levity, a need to bring back lightness and ease in postures and gestures for which I myself had often been partially responsible, when I gave form to that Armani woman who was no longer man's better half, but more like his antagonist. A woman willing to reclaim for herself, from her rival, significant portions of the will to dominate. I wanted to go beyond that, to progress toward a new separation of the figures, to redefine their images, to declare the definitive obsolescence of any complexes regarding the role of the woman, any doubts about competition or subordination. For me this is a feminine image which confirms a style, a precise quality of design, beyond custom, or the costumes, of the time.[47]

Here, interestingly, Armani provides his definition of woman in relation to man, and creates a binary relationship in which the sexes are meant to be distinct from each other, rather than come closer together. The turn in the late 1980s to a seemingly more neutral femininity was also largely fuelled by Armani's desire to provide an antidote to the vulgarity of design and culture of aggression he felt represented his times.[48] As if channelling R. Loewy's famous dictum from the early twentieth century, 'Ugliness doesn't sell',[49] the point of the collection was to give women a design proposition that best represented the new intelligence and realities of women. As the programme notes asserted, the goal of the collection was to achieve a 'perfect balance between mellowness and assurance'. The move toward a new femininity did not dethrone Armani from his seat as King of Italian fashion, rather for many he remained unchallenged 'as Italy's most distinctive designer'. With this new direction, he also continued to offer a style that was emulated in both Italy and the USA. Compatriot Franco Moschino, for example, known for his outlandish and highly witty and whimsical outfits for women, reputedly admitted to striving to recreate the perfect cut of an Armani jacket. Moschino was one of several designers seen to be attempting to reproduce the Armani affect, a phenomenon that some noted resulted in a rather repetitive Milanese season.[50] Although the collection was generally well-received, some also sensed feelings of loneliness and even melancholy while watching the collection, the result of Galeotti's death in August 1985, which continued to spike the overall mood and emotional intensity of subsequent shows.

93   Peasant-inspired and simplified glamour for spring 1988

For autumn the Milanese tailor continued to provide gentility to his collection by beginning to eliminate all of the elements he did not want, a direct 'rejection of vulgarity, of anything "not pleasing to the eye. Clothes like those do not take into consideration that a woman needs to be treated with gentleness, so does a man"'. Women of the 1970s and early 1980s needed clothes to help conjure assurance. By the late 1980s, however, at

94   Aldo Fallai. From the spring/summer 1988 advertising campaign

least for the woman Armani envisioned, she had achieved much and could now portray a hint of vulnerability and gentleness, while maintaining her intelligence and independence.[51] And while shoulder pads did not disappear from his jackets, they were nevertheless more rounded and subtle, hugging the shoulders in a more intimately natural way. The clothes were a continuation and not an entirely new proposition and as with his

95   Bohemian chic from autumn/winter 1988

entire career to date, Armani held that while 'the woman [he] design[s] for changes and moves ahead' she 'continue[s] to talk the same language'.[52] New ideas and propositions needed to be translated into a recognizable and familiar idiom, one which has created an intensely loyal following among his international clientele. For spring 1988 Armani continued to hear bravos as a response to a collection once again inspired by featherweight fabrics for jackets and sheer chiffons for cocktail dresses. The theme revolved around 'sophisticated peasants',[53] who were clothed in sarong dresses and headscarves, creating a hybrid image of metropolitan glamour mixed with exotic details that included Chinese porcelain and floral prints for skirts and dresses. As with those from his first collections, a hint of patina lent to the garments the impression of something 'a little used, not absolutely prefect'.[54]

The notion of patina, the powdering and blurring material effects of time, use and history is vital to understanding the collections that followed from autumn 1988 and into 1990, extensive collections targeting Armani's efforts on recreating an aesthetic entirely premised on the exoticism of the East coupled with the bohemian haughtiness and indifference of Parisian Left Bank female dandies of the interwar years. In a protracted recessionary period in which most consumers were spending less on clothing, Armani took inspiration from the 1930s and 1940s and, as Chanel had done before,

96   Autumn/winter 1988

premised his collections on separates, garments easily interchangeable in a wardrobe. For autumn sportswear looks were accompanied with a fedora and men's shoes, but according to the designer his ideal women never appear as though cross-dressing. According to Judith Thurman, the best looks of this and other collections have always possessed 'an attitude of defiance toward the mainstream of Italian design – and contemporary fashion – which is still flagrantly romantic'.[55] By the late 1990s this apparent lack of rapport with the world outside became the source of negative critical attention.

97   Spring 1989 formed part of a period of fluid femininity which had not characterized his designs prior to 1987

For spring 1989 Armani extended his mantra of fluidity and softness to create a collection in which chiffon, georgettes and silks were the heaviest fabrics in use; even fingerless gloves in the most transparent and diaphanous fabrics were used as accessories to reinforce his rarefied ideal. As a master of textile deception, one fabric used, for example, appeared as faux granite and yet fell away from the body with the lightest of ease; here visual appearance belies materiality, a common motif in his innovative use of textiles. The collection was inspired by the work of Leon Bakst, particularly one outfit he designed for Gertrude Vanderbilt Whitney which Armani replicated for one of his evening outfits in addition to using the black flora motif as decoration for the walls of his theatre. Set to a soundtrack of hypnotic electronic music, the models were decidedly androgynous, gamine-like and flat-chested with their hair either styled in a tight chignon or slicked back entirely. Each outfit was complimented with flat sling-back loafers enabling the models to glide effortlessly down the runway. Jewellery, as always, was kept to a minimum with only Bakelite and resin earrings in either organic leaf or simple geometric shapes used as embellishments to what were ethereal outfits.

98   Autumn/winter 1989

In autumn 1989, the house produced its first catalogue in which respected journalist and writer Oreste del Buono proposed that the numerous pictures of models Ben Shaul and Gina di Bernardo possessed a glimmer of the 1920s rather than the late 1980s. In an introduction to these faintly nostalgic images, del Buono listed as connections with the past period: 'The years of Proust's *La Recherche* and of that generation lost in Gertrude Stein's Paris salon, of the first dada exhibition in Berlin, of [Erich von] Stroheim's *Femme follie*, of Erté's applied arts and [Thomas] Mann's *The Enchanted Mountain*, or Poiret's clothing designs'. To help capture the mood and atmosphere the images cast he also included among his list Sonia Delaunay, Greta Garbo, Jean Cocteau and Walter Gropius, equally significant cultural forces in the development of modernism. Undoubtedly one of Giorgio Armani's most comprehensive and beautiful shows, the autumn collection presented a rainbow of colours for jackets that ranged in shapes so diverse, they were only outnumbered by the number of models he employed for the show. Rusted oranges, moss greens, royal purples, grey tones, beiges, reds, deep mauves and myriad subtle and even bold prints were used for jackets that were paired with short skirts reaching the longer jackets' edge and fluid man-inspired trousers. Collarless, tulip-shaped and Nehru jackets at various lengths were fastened tightly to one side, double-breasted, buttoned deep or even below the waist. Coats were long and full, often at shoe level, and their billowing movements were reminiscent of flower petals. The coats billowed so intensely they seemed to take flight as the models spun around like Dervishes, a spectacle through which to enjoy the lightweight winter fabrics. Soft, lush and protective, the Armani woman of 1989 was well covered for the elements in any European, North American or Asian city. The to-the-ground gowns, mostly monochromatic sheaths, skimmed and caressed the model's bodies without hampering movement or revealing too much underneath. As seen in his previous spring collection, accessories were limited to Bakelite earrings and bracelets for evening, while hats and scarves featured heavily in the daywear segments. As with his collections of the 1980s, gloves were also used throughout for both day and eveningwear, lending both grace and glamour to the looks. Hair was pulled back tightly in an elegant chignon. From the pared-down to the most intricately elaborate fabrics and pairings, the designer constructed a sophisticated and convincing tension between masculine and feminine with cuffed trousers, for example, swishing back and forth with an insouciance reminiscent of Katherine Hepburn in her man-tailored clothing. Fabrics in the collection, following from the new ethos established in 1987, moved with an energy and dynamism that gave them a life all their own, all the while avoiding overpowering its wearer. Long puffed balloon skirts were paired with colourful bustiers and fedoras to reinforce the masculine-feminine theme played out for daywear. Here too the colours ranged from gold, fuchsia and deep purple to champagne, beige and black. The show ended on an operatic high note, with a male model escorting the last model to a then signature quilted fabric chair in the middle of the runway. When the lights were turned on one final time models paraded the eveningwear along the runway's mirrored entrance to the theme song from the *Phantom of the Opera* while Armani took his bow. Indeed these clothes were theatrical and worthy of any night at the opera. Was Armani the phantom lurking in the recesses of his via Borgonuovo theatre, the man all too often described as the hermit in the cell? Like the seduction of the Andrew Lloyd Webber production, Armani seduced his audience with exceptional fabrics and mystifying silhouettes, and as he explained to *Corriere della Sera*, the collection was an attempt to 'fight against vulgarity, excess, useless display'.[56]

Seemingly freer from his own past, Armani acknowledged in British *Vogue* that '[f]ashion recently has not been speaking [his] language'. As a result he opted not to make any concessions or 'comparisons to the outside world'.[57]

99   Spring/summer 1990

100   Evening for spring 1990 inspired by Poiret and Nijinsky

101   Evening looks from spring 1990 that seem as if a woman threw on a piece of fabric over herself and draped it according to the natural contours of her body

For spring 1990, undoubtedly one of the house's most refined showings drew from the sands of North Africa and the exoticism of an imaginary East filtered through the early-century lens of Poiret. Given that many of his compatriots were defecting to show their collections in Paris, Armani decided on a larger and grander show, leaving behind the intimacy of his via Borgonuovo theatre and opting to show his collection in the historic Palazzo del Senato a few blocks away. Shown over two evenings to four different audiences, the collection sent out men alongside women and proposed the identical 'Slouch chic' for daywear he had introduced for men in a show that left its audience 'in stunned silence for a few moments after his show', which quickly segued into thunderous applauses, forcing the designer back for a second bow. Presented to a soundtrack of sitar music, the rather simple aim of the collection was to present clothes 'as if a woman took a piece of fabric and threw it over her body in a natural gesture ... to give emphasis on the line'.[58] For this and his menswear collection, Armani shot the campaign in the deserts of North Africa, winds blowing the fabrics to emphasize the fluidity and colour palette they offered, blending in perfectly with the natural surroundings of the sandy exotic locale. The sleeves of the women's filmy silk blouses were loose and long, hitting the knuckles with the hems resting at the jacket's edge. Jackets were loose, either opened and oversized menswear 'Slouch jackets', or buttoned with slits cut along the sides from the hip to allow the blouse underneath to billow out. These were paired with loose fitting cuffed trousers or short skirts. Eveningwear was inspired by Nijinsky and Poiret, which made for rich and exotic looks that included haute couture-quality techniques. One of the most striking examples from the collection remains a spider-web gown with an overlay of webbing outlined with pearls and beading.

Divided into three discreet sections, the autumn 1990 collection marked the climax of Armani's move toward interwar bohemian glamour and blatant Orientalism. In the collection, models wore Basque berets and various hats inspired by the East and were devoid entirely of jewellery. The collection featured three unique sections. The first, a Left-Bank (fluid though mannish) lesbian chic that toyed with the visual culture of an unidentified contemporary Cuban artist whose work of bohemian men was projected on the wall of the runway. This first section featured numerous slouch suits in exquisitely rich and sumptuous fabrics. The second section, following off from the first's use of neutrals borrowed traditional shapes and fabrics from Mongolian menswear and translated them into Western womenswear. The final section travelled across both time and space to rediscover the imperial glory of China. Scholar Annette Kuhn has posited that cross-dressing is a 'mode of performance in which – through play on the disjunction between clothes and body – the socially constructed nature of sexual difference is foregrounded and even subjected to comment: what appears natural, then, reveals itself as artifice'.[59] The cross-dressing in Armani's designs for women in particular has been systematic and consistent and comes from a period, which significantly parallels the timeline of his success from the late 1980s to the early 1990s. The interwar period is one characterized by women's increased emancipation, but also more specifically a group of radical (often lesbian) women who regularly and subversively donned men's clothing. In the 1920s there was much debate swirling around as to the nature of feminine and female identity, which seemingly culminated in the 1929 psychoanalytic essay by Joan Riviere, 'Womanliness as Masquerade'. In the essay Riviere posits a distinction between on the one hand the masculinity of the mannish professional woman which is suppressed in favour of a, on the other hand, more feminine performance and ultra feminine attire while performing in front of male colleagues. Riviere saw this purposeful masquerade as a means to assuage male fears (of castration fundamentally) and avert any retribution or retaliation.[60] As numerous artists, writers, theorists and scholars have demonstrated over the years, sexual and gender identity is a performance, conscious or otherwise, which must often reconcile the gender poles. Armani's collections created for his women from this period tacitly resonate this truth.

What makes Armani's repeated referencing of the radical chic of the 1920s and 1930s compelling

102   Interwar chic inspired this lush and full velvet coat, collarless silk man's shirt and beret for the autumn 1990 collection

is his own incorporation of forms and techniques of masquerading. Armani at once references a period when women donned masculine attire, while at the same time he incorporates more fluid fabrics still inspired by traditional men's textile patterns and tailoring. Here the designer does not reference the flapper with her cropped *garçonne*, the iconic feminine heroine of the 1920s French metropolis, but the radical and subversive figure of the Left-Bank lesbian dandy, a figure neglected by history. Although the critics and cultural commentators who suggest Armani's sources of inspiration are numerous and diffuse: 'the original garments are never quite identifiable',[61] I wish to posit otherwise. For, as we have seen since 1987, while the designer clearly projects through his mind's eye an ideal woman for the late 1980s, there can be no doubt as to the interwar references and the impulse toward North African and Asian aesthetic precedents. A certain female muse of history coheres with actual women from the 1980s, both periods marked by women's renegotiation of gender codes and boundaries, coupled with new emancipation and challenges. Like the 1920s which witnessed an acceleration and expansion of modern consumption, the '1980s saw one of the most powerful rediscoveries of consumerism'.[62] The late 1980s also saw Armani's first proliferation of boutiques in certain key cities around the world through which to precipitate and contain this consumer culture. The conflation of the 1980s with a 1920s-inspired aesthetic was not entirely uncommon, given the commonalities the two periods shared. Alexis Carrington Colby Dexter of late-night television hit *Dynasty*, for example, wielded her menacing authority while wearing the iconic power suits of the era with dresses and affected poses reminiscent of the celluloid goddesses of the deco period. The relationship is largely, and significantly, an issue of access to consumption and the social and cultural prestige accrued in buying power and the cultural associations of the objects one has elected to identify and surround oneself with. Slater has claimed '[c]onsumer culture is about continuous self-creation through the accessibility of things'.[63] Since the 1920s, global modernity had decidedly become bourgeois and middle class, driven by consumer culture; consumerism effectively has become the 'path to modernity' itself.[64]

In 1995 Armani was invited to participate in an exhibition devoted to cinema by contributing both garments and his thoughts on film star Marlene Dietrich, whose iconic mannish style and radical sartorial gestures had been tacitly visible in his collections. Despite his self-proclaimed obsession with cinema and obvious parallels between his imagery and that of Dietrich and Greta Garbo, in his catalogue essay on the German star he admitted that at the time he 'wasn't yet really conscious whether in [his] collections, in [his] creations as a fashion designer, something would reveal itself that would connect [his] style direction with Dietrich's'. It was only when he went back over his own catalogues from the late 1980s and early 1990s that he 'saw

103   Marlene Dietrich arriving at Gare St Lazare, Paris, bound for a three-month holiday in France, 'chooses to continue her disguise of men's clothes and brown sun-spectacles'. She wears a deep reddish-brown polo coat, matching her beret with a twill suit with cuffed trousers, popular in the 1930s (19 May 1933)

how many overlaps there were in the style of fashions she wore and with his collections', concluding that '[m]any of Marlene clothes might as well have been clothes by Giorgio Armani'.[65] A classic example of the parallels he notes is 'Dietrich's predilection for veils not only as a symbol of chastity, but also as an intriguing and mysterious means of refined seduction'; veils have appeared in myriad guises in a number of his collections. Both Armani's and Dietrich's styles often deployed long flowing gowns and dresses that only hinted at the body underneath, avoiding even the slightest hint of vulgarity. Armani concludes that their similarities are especially hinged on 'the tendency for the androgynous – an interpretation of androgyny that is far removed from travesty. In this form of public appearance Marlene was a pioneer in life, just as I am in fashion, by translating many elements of the masculine style into female style'.[66] Armani's role within the special exhibition was not simply celebrity affiliation, endorsement or self-aggrandizement, but rather importantly he contributed to the restoration of the costumes on display in the one room devoted entirely to her personal and filmic life. Dietrich for the designer has meant 'magic and magnetism. A star you want to touch.' In this conceptualization of her iconic stature, the haptic and the visual are brought closer together precisely because of her ambivalent sartorial image on and off the screen's surface. The exhibition's costumes were displayed in glass boxes half a metre off the ground, suspended, as if frozen in space and seemingly as dematerialized as her persona. In front of these vitrines were placed mannequins displaying complementary Armani garments, 'each an echo, a distant sound, but never a reprise'.[67]

104   Diaphanous veils are often used by Armani, as seen in this example from autumn 1993, reminiscent of Dietrich's own unique use

105   Autumn/winter 1997

Fashion, Furniture and the Nostalgic Turn

The spring 2001 womenswear collection based on the elusive image of the 1920s gamine beautifully personified by the regal, blue-blooded model Erin O'Connor, demonstrated again how as a designer Armani makes few 'concessions to current trends'. Drawing inspiration anew from nautical motifs and emblems of 1930s Deauville culture 'with a bit of lesbian chic thrown in',[68] the collection harmoniously coincided with the debut of his furniture line, Armani/Casa. The line's inaugural collection took inspiration from his own minimalist Milanese palazzo, replete with furniture by French Art Deco designer Jean Michel Frank (1895–1941). The underlining design ethos for both his furniture and fashion is marked by the ideal that an individual's personality is best expressed through a paring down to a sort of luxurious and tactile essential rigour. Armani has long held that he does not over-decorate his homes or place pictures on his walls; rather, he prefers people to animate the spaces.[69] Almost two decades and many homes later, the designer understands that '[p]eople's homes tend to be reflections of themselves' and in this way Armani/Casa is 'a natural extension of [his] fashion collections. Each year the Armani/Casa collection is enhanced with new colours, new finishes, accessories or simple details that in many ways reflect [his] most recent fashion collection'.[70]

Armani's interior design programme ostensibly functions as a natural progression in his career toward both greater market share and global aesthetic expansion, continuing to affect people on an equally personal, private and intimate level to his clothing designs. The move highlights a significant turning point in the designer's overall focus, moving from fashion to interior design, from the public to the private. Although numerous are the examples which reveal the overt and subtle relationships between the two disciplines, the cross-dressing between fashion and furniture in the autumn 2005 women's collection sees the fabric used for shorts and wraps transformed into throws for living spaces for the home. As a spatial and visual backdrop, the home collection provides a complete atmosphere for almost every type of Armani customer to aspire to, while at the same time hinting at upward mobility within the ranks of his various labels. As Gilles Lipovetsky has observed:

> Unlike 'fashion', characterized by perpetual stylistic reversals, design is homogenous; [design] restructures the environment in a consistent spirit of simplification, geometry, and logic … In its reaction against irrational sentimentality of objects, in its use of raw materials, in its consecration of orthogonal streamlining and aerodynamics, design does not leave the order of seduction behind; instead, it invents a new morality for this order. Staging and artificiality have not disappeared; they have become accessible via the unprecedented pathway of minimalization, letting 'truth' of objects speak for itself, with the discreet charm of simplification, economy of means, and transparency.[71]

Like many designers, Armani has recognized that in order to remain financially viable, competitive and affect millions of customers, every facet of their lives must in some way work toward a complete look, lifestyle or atmosphere, in other words a postmodern *Gesamtkunstwerk*. The private domestic realm marks out new territory in global designer expansion aspirations. As one has come to expect, the aesthetic principles for the collection, made particularly

106 Spring 2001 channels Left-Bank chic and its female homosocial culture of the 1920s

acute in the inaugural annual collections between 2000 and 2003 and as stated by the designer himself, are defined by a 'combination of comfort, and sophistication, functionality and elegance. The Armani/Casa atmosphere mirrors the Armani fashion philosophy: rigorous shapes – which make people feel comfortable – enriched with precious materials, creating a unique, luxurious atmosphere'.[72] With an ever-expanding colour palette ranging from tobacco, grey and beige to silver, opal and champagne (the perennial use of neutral colours that seem to transcend the fickle whims of fashion) as well as through a relentless research into textiles, the development of the home collection has paralleled the designer's initial and earlier entry into the world of fashion. Scholar Patrizia C. McBride argues that modernist architect Adolf Loos' 'immanent self-positioning enabled him to pass up all avant-garde dreams of a *tabula rasa* and radical new beginnings to ponder the question of how one can best make the present world a more desirable, homey place', an ideal she sees as 'more appealing in retrospect than the intransigent gesture of erasure that characterized much avant-garde discourse'.[73] Seven years after his initial collection, Armani's reductionist, modernist gestures remain intact when he states that '[m]uted colors are not distracting and create a pristine and perfect environment'.[74] Noting that his more colourful pieces underperformed when compared to the more natural tones traditionally associated with the designer, Armani claimed that '[p]eople are looking for noncolor'.[75] Neutral non-colour operates for the designer to distance his design from conspicuous consumption and the indefatigable cycles of fashion, akin in spirit to Loos's modernist ideal.

'Consummate fashion lives on paradox',[76] particularly its relationship to temporality. At once it must be of the moment, yet it possesses an inherent morbidity for as soon as the lights come on after the runway show it ceases to be new. After all, in a nod to the realities of postmodernism, Armani has himself claimed that '[i]n fashion, everything has been done … It's the way they mix', which marks it as new.[77] The maxim 'the more things change, the more they become the same' allows us to rethink Armani's eternal returns to the 1920 and 1930s. By rarely abandoning the comfort and control of the interwar period as his siren of history, Armani defers to and yet conjures the present, for as Maxime du Camp noted: 'History is like Janus; it has two faces. Whether it looks at the past or the present, it sees that same thing.'[78] In the Armani/Casa line names are given to each piece of furniture or decorative object that conjure the great leaders of and contributors to the development and progress of modernity: The 'Dandy' embodied in a plush yet minimalist bed; a 'Bon Ton' screen meant to conjure the *Gazette*'s curvilinear deco style; the Camus writing desk to inspire great, solitary prose writing; luxury and comfort embodied in the Benjamin bed perfect for the haute bourgeois home he once described; and finally the Baudelaire chest to store objects, fashions and memories of the modern flâneur. Here Armani self-reflexively materializes his modernity and its unabashed provenance; a way to fashion

himself as historically tied in with this larger timeline of modernism, and therefore marking the work as historically significant and intellectually grounded.[79]

At the same time, never satiated fashion crooks its neck to glance back, even if only partially, to the past as an endless source of inspiration; what was new yesterday can become new again tomorrow, though in the present it always appears to be old news. Nadia Seremetakis makes a crucial claim of the different cultural associations between the English and Greek uses of nostalgia, pointing out that for the former the associations are reduced to pejorative connotations. In Greek, on the other hand, *Nostalghó* is composed of *nostó* and *alghó*:

> *Nostó* means I return, I travel … *Alghó* means I feel pain, I ache for, and the noun *álghos* characterizes one's pain in soul and body, burning pain (*kaimós*). Thus *nostalghiá* is the desire or longing with burning pain to journey. It evokes a sensory dimension of memory in exile and estrangement.[80]

The Armani/Casa line has been labelled a sort of 'proto-modernism as nostalgia … a world of space, luxury, sensuality, discretion, subdued light', in other words an atmosphere premised on an otherness, a difference from the present condition and location.[81] Nostalgia is marked by 'a yearning for a different time – the time of our childhood, the slower rhythms of our dreams. In a broader sense, nostalgia is a rebellion against the modern idea of time, the time of history and progress.'[82] In this manner nostalgia is itself a crucial facet of our postmodern condition which continuously attempts, through great pain, to defy the logic of diachronic time, inviting us to pilfer from the past as a way to revitalize what may be perceived as a barren present in the hopes of re-imaging the future. In the case of Armani's design there is always an underlying sense of moral implication to this nostalgic impulse. When asked if he felt there was much 'vulgarity around and that woman lack style today' the designer responded: 'Bad taste bothers me, but it isn't necessarily the shopper's fault. She might not have enough critical sense, and may be easily convinced by the latest designer brand hailed by the press. I believe my clothes respect women and that my aesthetic sense has set an example'.[83]

Out of step with his contemporaries, both in terms of fashion and furniture, the year of his birth (1934) is more suggestive of the significance he attributes to the interwar period and clearly informs his nostalgic turn: 'The years from 1930 to 1940 were years of great invention and creativity', he concludes. 'I have always referred to them, both in my fashion and my furniture.'[84] We would do well to recall how Art Deco, the single most important locus of inspiration for Armani, as a broad design programme was ultimately anti-Victorian in its impulse and hence vehemently contra the excess that culminated at the end of that earlier period. Warren Susman suggests that 'myth, memory and history mark three alternative ways to capture an account for an allusive past, each with its own persuasive claim', and perhaps each, in their own way appear in Armani's various collections.[85] However modernism, with its patrilineal dependence on masculine values, was tacitly forced into a difficult and unholy alliance with the supposed feminine realm of mass consumer culture. In the male dominated fields of design and architecture, for example, designers were compelled to respond by either adapting styles or become increasingly staunch moralizing social forces.[86] As design historian Penny Sparke importantly notes, Art Deco, at this important historical juncture, played a formidable role in the democratization of luxury, and the ideals of internationalism (today re-calibrated as globalization) and democratization became its guiding ethos.[87] In the USA, for instance, Art Deco was seen as a style more open to all. In an article in *The New York Times* from 1929, 'Luxury is Democratized', the author claims that now, with the new French style, beauty can be obtained by 'all the classes'.[88] The new style was also legibly associated with the New Women of the period. For Armani I suggest the interwar period and the moderne – or Art Deco – aesthetic services as an antidote to the excesses he saw in 1960s and 1970s as well as the 'vulgarity' of contemporary design. The period is also akin to his use of Japanese, Chinese and North African motifs and sources of inspiration, and like the primitivists of modern art, Armani productively seeks to draw attention back on the West, its lack of inspiration and its irrational excesses, leaving these sources and therefore his own products to register as counterpoints of simplicity, calm and tranquillity. After all: 'Good design makes for good business'.[89]

By autumn 2002, however, critics were calling for Armani to 'freshen up – and lighten up – his act'. Inspired again by the amazons of the Deco period many critics bemoaned his use of wide-legged bloomers and harem pants complete with stirrup ankle cuffs topped off with leather aviator hats reminiscent of Amelia Earhart. It might be worth pointing out that by the summer of 2007 harem pants were so prevalent throughout Paris, for example, they were being sold by street vendors on every other corner. Frustrated by the growing antipathy toward his womenswear collections, Armani rebuked by claiming:

> If people don't like the [aviator] hats, the skirts, the pants, I don't care. You always have to do something more, and when you're creative, you risk a bit. Galliano, McQueen, Gaultier, my colleagues have fun. This is my fun ... This is my couture.[90]

The catalogue for the collection not only featured separate folders for menswear and womenswear, but also one for Armani/Casa (the first and only time the house did so). In the catalogue the designer wrote of being motivated by the painted Amazons of Russian-born Tamara de Lempicka whose work epitomized the new independence and sexual freedom of Paris in the 1920s. His concept of elegance resided somewhere between sports and military, referring to the women of his collection as 'style pilots', with their leather flyer

108   Autumn/winter 2002. Leather aviator hat, long leather jacket and glasses
reminiscent of Amelia Earhart

caps. As the catalogue continued: 'In the world of Giorgio Armani fashion becomes portraiture. A statement, a uniform, an immediately perceptible way of being.' The metaphor of painting renewed the relationship between the jacket and the body, where the former was now simply and eloquently 'brushstroked' onto the latter to provide a symbiosis 'of signs and inimitable patterns'. These so-called portraits take on, not surprisingly, a cinematic and

109   Peter Lindbergh. Placing women in the director's chair. From the autumn/winter 2001 advertising campaign

narratological initiative for the designer to help create a clear and unblemished 'atmosphere' endemic to his overall strategy of repetitive imagery and devices. As the generally acerbic critic Robin Givhan once asserted:

> The quiet complaint about Armani's work is that it has failed to evolve. The reality is that Armani's style has never been about change. The strength of his vision has always been its consistency, the manner in which it can reassure the wearer that no matter the situation she will be appropriately, elegantly dressed. There's not much theatre in a beautifully cut suit – it is neither dynamic nor romantic – but there is always a need.[91]

Givhan's comments ironically enough coincided with growing complaints among analysts who note the increasing gap between the runway and the real world by designers in general.[92] Despite the myriad complaints of Armani meandering toward the moribund side of creativity, he remains for women an emblem of power, elegance and glamour. As Givhan herself commented at length in a feature article on Nancy Pelossi (then Speaker of the USA House of Representatives), she looks 'polished and tasteful' in her Armani suits. With the hard broad shoulders of the 1970s and early 1980s long gone, Armani still 'stands as a kind of professional armour. It is protective but soft. Tailored but draped ... An Armani suit, for a woman, is a tool for playing with the boys without pretending to be one.'[93] Women around the world fetishistically cling to their Armanis, enjoying the power they enable, comfortably balancing the performances of gender.

Hybridity and the Dialogics of Orientalism

The rich aesthetic traditions of Japan specifically and Asia more broadly have long held sway in the work of Armani, and no collection better embodies his Orientalist penchant than the one he created for the autumn 1981 season. Inspired by Japanese director Akira Kuwasawa's iconic film *Kagamusha* (*The Shadow Warrior*) from 1980, the collection featured culottes in Japanese tobacco coupled with silk samurai-inspired jackets. *W* coined the collection 'modern Italian chic – minimal in look, maximum in quality' while its sister publication *Women's Wear Daily* dubbed him 'Italy's shogun'.[94] Such a strong and powerful fashion statement required an environment and atmosphere worthy of its calibre. Presented to Italians and Americans separately, the offices in via Durini were lined with Japanese screens and transformed into a dimly lit teahouse. Japanese music played as each outfit was displayed on three different models that stood on three black lacquered platforms facilitating utmost visibility. With a nod to the past, Armani presented samurai-inspired garbs fused with ceremonial robes, creating an elliptical silhouette. New were his first dresses, in soft fabrics like wool jersey and crepe de chine, shown under Armani's celebrated jackets. Lapels, reminiscent of the kimono, stopped halfway down. Jackets were often cut with slits on either side at the hems to accommodate the full skirts. Some jackets appeared in black or brown leather with bodices intricately worked and finished off with tubular belts. With over 100 different fabrics used for this collection, the designer chose to include numerous and differing types of velvets, especially for jackets, which were also done in wide-ribbed corduroy, jacquard tweeds, satinized and worsted wools and *trompe l'oeil* prints. Hats were dark, stiffly-shaped, most with a wider back brim that served to enhance the samurai look. According to the *Toronto Star* 'it was the structured shapes which are Armani's great strengths that provided the signature looks for fall. The key to almost every ensemble was provided by the jackets, which were quite simply remarkable in cut and detail.'[95] A number of the heavier tweed jackets had a double-track ridge moving down the shoulders along the sleeves. Armani's unique talent for colour combinations had editors and well-dressed women gasping in delight. However, it was his eveningwear that had the audience fascinated and mesmerized. The show's significance rested on the fact it was the first time he showed dresses and a clear eveningwear collection. What he achieved according to some was to:

> re-invent eveningwear, producing looks that are so unlike what other designers have ever done, and so completely distinctive in shape and concept, that all of us could only watch in complete fascination as the models presented their samurai-like short and long evening separates and dresses ... which played texture against shine, matte against glitter, and glowing satins in never-before colors against black.[96]

110   'Italy's shōgun' seen here in a navy blue pullover and brown leather trousers surrounded by models displaying his autumn 1981 collection

111 'Samurai armour'. Ensemble: fitted peplum jacket in taupe silk satin with overall parallel trapunto, stylized kimono sleeves with contrast black velvet side and sleeve gusset; black silk satin culottes with black sequins inside the side pockets

Glamorous evening outfits were nevertheless available with silk golden/ beige samurai jackets and silk black culottes covertly embellished with black paillettes in the pockets, a tactile and luxurious detail made accessible only to the wearer, lending a sense of privacy to the luxury he provides.

Hailed as the 'new Saint Laurent', in the early 1980s Milan was attempting to 'produce a hero to rival Paris designers', seen to be embodied in Armani.[97] The connection to Saint Laurent is an important one, for not only was Armani taking on the mantle of dressing the new career woman with perfectly tailored suits and daywear, apart from his French rival no other designer has consistently turned to the East and North Africa as sources of continued inspiration. While Saint Laurent depended on the rich, exuberant and fantastic jewel-toned hues of Russia, Morocco and China, Armani enlists the neutral hues and textured irregularity of nomadic peoples, the sandy – *greige* – tones of Italy and North Africa and the shapes and silhouettes of Asia to create a hybrid garment for the modern wardrobe. In his interrogation of the dynamics of globalization as it cuts across the discourses and realities of modernity, Arjun Appadurai emphasizes how through the migration of both persons and signs, cosmopolitan human experiences enact a form of translation whereby individuals 'seek to annex the global into their own practices of the modern'.[98] By bringing the global into their work, designers like Saint Laurent and Armani also share in common the impossibility of locating any other designer's work in their creations, unnecessary for men stirred by the locations of exotic difference. Clothing, like a text, can be taken in and absorbed, translated into one's own cultural language, devoid of any real knowledge of the source of origin. In the performance of translation, the agent of this act can never escape the burdens and possibilities of his mother tongue.

Referring to Italian houses and manufacturers *The New York Times* noted how in the 1970s, 'they fought to win acceptance for their own designs. Today they are ready to change the world. One of their major weapons is their closeness to the world's best fabric mills. Even Paris designers shop here. Another weapon is the Italian sense of style'.[99] With 37 houses presenting their collections for the autumn 1981 season it seemed as though all of Milan was hit with the Asian bug. However, journalists claimed that '[a]fter Armani, other early collections rather paled by comparison and seemed rather drab'.[100] According to then editor-in-chief of French *Vogue*, Francine Crescent, the collection was: 'Superb, superb! I want to dress like that! And most important: it's very sexy.'[101] *Women's Wear Daily* praised it 'as strong as the samurais that inspired him and as beautiful as a Japanese floral arrangement' proving the designer to be much more than a master tailor. 'He has the versatility of all great designers.'[102] Despite the numerous accolades that followed the show, the collection remained a source of some doubt and tension for the designer. While on tour in Japan in 2007 for the

112   Mannequins from the Guggenheim exhibition displaying outfits from the
controversial autumn 1981 collection

inauguration of his behemoth Armani/Ginza Tower, the designer claimed it
'was heavily corseted and not really wearable at the time. The press raved
about it, but it didn't sell well. I learned that I'd rather sell a collection than
have the press talk about it.'[103] His comments in 2007 must also be read in
contrast to his statements from only a few years earlier, when he claimed
that the press ignored the Japanese-inspired collection though it remained
one of his favourites.[104] Armani's drive to balance finance with fashion is at
the core of his global success and tacit desire to create what is ultimately
a hybrid garment more amenable to a global clientele. Nostalgia is 'also a
romance, with one's own fantasy. Nostalgic love can only survive in a long-
distance relationship'.[105] Armani's love affair with the interwar period and
the exoticism of the East also serves as a nostalgic turn to an erotics of the
'other' wherein cut and textile assist touch and sensuality while reinforcing
steadfast Western tropes of long-held cultural fantasies. Defined by Edward
Said, Orientalism is

a way of coming to terms with the Orient that is based on the Orient's special place in European Western Experience ... In addition, the Orient has helped to define Europe (or the West) as its contrasting image, idea, personality, experience. Yet none of this Orient is merely imaginative. The Orient is an integral part of European material civilization and culture. Orientalism expresses and represents that part culturally and even ideologically as a mode of discourse with supporting institutions, vocabulary, scholarship, imagery, doctrines, even colonial bureaucracies and colonial styles.[106]

We might also importantly add to Said's list, adopted sartorial styles. At the inauguration of Armani/Ginza Tower, the designer was asked about his interest in and influences from the Orient and whether he had time to visit Asia on his trip. He responded by suggesting that '[w]hat better inspiration than to dream of a country that you don't know? Reality can be disappointing. I'd rather nurture an idea, a romantic image that I have kept in me with all my strength.'[107] For Armani, inspiration taken from the East is not unlike his inability to travel back in time to the interwar period and occurs through the illusory, the creative and the translation of an aesthetic language .

Regardless of the ambivalence of Armani's perception of his collection from 1981 it nevertheless charted a course for the designer who had always sought to wed fashion and finance, significantly here at this juncture of Asian-inspired aesthetics. I suggest this has led to a visual and material economy premised on a double act of translation in which Armani does not simply derive inspiration from other cultures and locations, but does so through the aesthetic lens of early twentieth-century modernism. Take for example his Tahitian-inspired collection for spring 1993, in which models were adorned with silk lei around their necks and on their heads to lend a Polynesian flavour. To further layer and complicate the references to other sources, Armani included pastel coats over Indian djellabas and narrow cotton trousers. On the dresses and even swimwear, Armani chose Gauguin-inspired seated Polynesian female figures reminiscent of the artist's time in the region. Gauguin, however, had a rather dubious relationship with the communities he settled in, ignoring local customs and even dishonouring contracts he entered into. Nevertheless, his modernism was premised on the abandonment of bourgeois existence and all that it signified in order to fulfil yet another predominantly Western white male's 'quest for an elusive object whose very condition of desirability resides in some form of distance and difference, whether temporal or geographical'.[108] As Armani moved into new territory, dragging along the familiar Armani aesthetic, one has to wonder what was at the root of his visual play. It would be facile to simply read the use of such imagery as a form of postmodern play, especially when one looks at the closing image of the runway show with Armani standing over his harem of Polynesian beauties. One is quickly reminded of Gauguin's dubious legacy, his importance to the lineage and history of modernism and how the notion of male genius has serviced meaning and the power structure of art itself. Modern artists like Gauguin used the female body as an inscriptive surface through which to work through myriad social, aesthetic and political challenges, for better or for worse. Armani's reference of Gauguin leads one to ponder his relationship to the body within the political economy of modern fashion. Is he hinting at creating a language away from the contemporary

113   Aldo Fallai. Inspired by rustic Mongolian herdsmen. From the autumn/winter 1990 advertising campaign

shackles of Western bourgeois mores, here understood as the fashion system he so vehemently rails against again and again? Armani uses Oriental motifs, themes, silhouettes and ideals as a means to conjure the new society of the 1990s he characterized as 'more intimate, individualistic choices that are less categorical and more considered', a utopian vision not too far away from Gauguin's.[109] As Richard Martin and Harold Koda have ventured to assert in the catalogue for their exhibition *Orientalism: Visions of the East in Western Dress*: 'Orientalism always challenges the Western mind: it is Orientalism that makes Western culture incomplete and that the West uses to see itself as whole ... The power of costume is in its capacity to be absorbed. Nonverbal, the rich textiles and traditions of dress of the East transcend language barriers'.[110] While transcendence is itself a modernist idiom, Orientalism services as a vital and dynamic moral antidote to the vulgarity Armani sees in contemporary culture and design.

Referring to Armani's spring/summer 1993 collection, *Harper's Bazaar* reported that what Armani 'showed encompassed influences from faraway places: Indian gauzes glistening under embroidery, silken paisleys, translucent Polynesian prints, simple shapes and fastenings that contain an echo of ethnic dress'.[111] As Armani explained: 'The whole collection followed the idea of the mix between Western and Oriental.' He asserts that what he

114   A trip to Polynesia was the inspiration for the spring 1993 collection

115   The designer grafted layers of meaning onto his fluid dresses for spring 1993 by displaying Paul Gauguin's iconic seated Tahitian women

is trying to achieve 'is to make those influences wearable for a Western woman. The point is to make clothes that you can move in easily, that have a natural, relaxed feeling.'[112] It would seem that his ability as a translator was so successful that *Harper's Bazaar* reported a 40 per cent increase in sales for this collection. Often Armani's textile sources are peasant and nomadic, possessing deeply tactile qualities, ideally suitable to his modern aesthetic. If as Judy Attfield argues, textile 'materialises the connection between the body and the outer world', what, then, do we make of the social relations between those who consume Giorgio Armani and those who originally inspired the material objects themselves?[113] Does the woman who consumes these frocks support a colonial past, which artists like Gauguin perpetuated through paint and canvas? And what do we make of the many examples in which traditional quotidian men's trousers (seen in many parts of the Islamic world) have been transformed into elegant, fluid and luxurious trousers for women?

The hybrid object is at once a product of time across space, and is produced by blurring the boundaries between dressmaking and tailoring. The Orient lends Armani the material language in which to create lighter clothes for men and women. For the autumn/winter 1988 collection, for example, India and China were said to conjure a synaesthesic response for the audience, in which 'spice of incense and the tinkle of temple bells came through in fabrics ranging from rich embroideries and dark gold-mesh lace to lustrous damasks, and patterns including elegantly intricate batiks, soft floral and muted paisleys, their shapes often traced in gold thread or glazed with clear sequins'.[114]As highlighted briefly in the previous section, for the autumn 1990 collection

116   Rough nomadic textures for menswear transformed into luxurious cashmere garments for women as seen in the autumn 1994 collection

Armani dipped into nomadic Mongolia and the luxury of Imperial China to create clothes inspired by rugged fabrics used by herdsmen as well as delicate porcelain prints of floral and pearl appliqué to conjure the timeless elegance of a Ming dynasty vase. The silhouette of jackets and even dresses was long and lean, often given a belted cord similar to a Chinese robe. For the premier of Scorsese's *Made in Milan* at the Venice film festival in October 1990, Armani threw a lavish Moorish garden party at Giovanni Volpi's Giudecca villa, with 170 A-list guests, many of which were from Hollywood, including Michelle Pfeiffer. 'I wanted it to be elegant but relaxed', claimed Armani. As for the Arab theme, the designer stated that 'Venice is a Moorish city'.[115] The villa's garden was canopied by an off-white chiffon tent with several wings and decorated with lanterns brought in from Tangier. Jasmine buds covered with carnations from Tunisia created the necessary scents while Armani outfitted his local, attractive waiters as Moorish sentries. The autumn 1990 collection with its three independent sections is the same collection featured in the documentary film. As Scorsese noted of the documentary: 'Clothes are characters ... Giorgio is sensual and the film is about the beauty of his work.'[116]

A few years later, in early 1993, Armani launched his new women's fragrance Giò, which was to replace Armani's original self-titled fragrance that debuted in 1982. For the $20 million print and video advertising campaign for Giò Armani hired model Lara Harris who, according to the designer, possesses the 'charm, beauty and risks' he believes the fragrance represents.[117] Taken from notes of hyacinth, orange blossom and tuberose, the fragrance made history when it made its appearance. In New York where Giorgio Armani has a significant presence, each department store featured a large campaign.

117   Gina di Bernardo posing as the face of the first Armani self-titled fragrance which made its debut in 1982

Saks Fifth Avenue, for example, created a two-week campaign titled 'Giorgio Armani: Portrait of a Designer', a strategy which paid dividends as it was that company's largest fragrance launch in its illustrious history, eclipsing those of Calvin Klein's Eternity, Bijan and Givenchy's Amarige. On every floor of Saks Armani products were sold,[118] while in their store front window displays two large screen televisions replayed the perfume's commercial followed by excerpts from *Made in Milan*.[119] Armani also chose the American city to celebrate the perfume's launch with a Matisse-inspired Moroccan gala in benefit of Women in Need, a New York social-services organization. With a reported $2 million price tag, the 500 guests, which included Cher, Lee Radziwill, Whoopi Goldberg, Isabella Rossellini, Robert De Niro, Gregory Hines and Ian Schrager, feasted on lamb and chicken couscous in a purposefully remodelled space in the Solow building at 57th Street. Here cork floors were brought in and painted to resemble Moroccan tiles in addition to brass dinnerwear, while sisal-like tablecloths and a tented ceiling were also meant to authenticate the space and atmosphere. Guests were not only treated to a presentation of the recent spring collections, but were also entertained by belly dancers while reclining North African-style on throw pillow banquettes.[120] In an evening that recalled Poiret's 1911 launch of his Parfum de Rosine for which he staged an elaborate costume party, 'la mille et deuxième nuit', Armani himself was transformed for the night's festivities into the Sultan of the Senses.

118   Autumn/winter 1994

In the 1990s Armani's inspiration came from 'a vague Islamic Orient ... for the expression of an idea of simplicity and interior, spiritual wealth ... [it] alludes to a man who knows how to be gentle, and to a woman who knows her own mind'. Armani states that his 'interest in the Orient is not a stylistic whim'. Rather, 'it is based on a certain spiritual affinity for the East and its cultures'.[121] However, as Amy de la Haye has argued in her discussion of ethnic minimalism in the work of Shirin Guild, '[i]n times of economic and social fragmentation "advanced" industrialized societies often romanticize and make fashionable' aspects of cultures deemed 'undeveloped'. De la Haye notes that certain decades in the twentieth century, like the 1990s, placed greater 'emphasis upon the cut of non-Western clothing and hand-crafted textiles'.[122] While it is important to remember that since Armani's earliest collections in the late 1970s, the designer has consistently gathered inspiration from various Eastern cultures, in the 1990s he derived it from a vague pan-Islamic North African and Near Eastern aesthetic, a region of the world his primary international market knew only through constant (and distorted) media reports. In this context, it would seem that a minimalist aesthetic became a necessary mode to translate the exoticism of a location violently under attack for a Western constituency that is politically detached, geographically removed and psychically distanced.

Turning our attention back again to the interwar period in particular as the primary source of inspiration in the work of the designer, we note how at the time Orientalism was not simply an aesthetic strategy but a rhetorical device deployed by artists and designers to address the social transformation they were experiencing at the time, including how they understood and articulated bodily realities.[123] According to Peter Wollen, 'Poiret and Matisse were the last Orientalists (in art) and the first modernists. They broke with the official art by which they were formed, but without embracing functionalism or rejecting the body and the decorative.'[124] For autumn 1993 Armani moved his audience through both space and time, as he turned to Matisse's Tangier period at once modernist and exotic; pyjama trousers, vests over bare chests with floral patterns and often in bright Fauvist colours. Fringed shawls and dresses were paired with exotic bold beaded necklaces, with models' hair done in rosette curls. After the show, his guests were again treated to a party located under an Oriental tent to attenuate the ideals and atmosphere the clothing was meant to conjure.

With the inauguration of his Armani/Casa line, the imposing references to the Deco period were also given a heavy dose of Asian motifs, again to fashion a multi-layered hybrid product; East meets West through the historicizing lens of the interwar period. As with the 2003/04 collection, ambivalence and ambiguity purposefully marked the 2004–05 collection which was summarized as at once '[e]thnic [and] distinctly art deco but never merely exotic ... a new level of harmony between pure form and sophistication'.[125] Equally relevant

119   Spring/summer 1995: East meets West, masculine meets feminine

to fashion as to domestic design, Carla Jones and Ann Marie Leshkowich have argued that 'Asian styles may be reorienting global fashion, but the very same globalization processes that have garnered international attention for Asian dress are re-Orientalising Asia and Asians.'[126] The products, spaces and domesticated lifestyle Armani/Casa has been proposing is influenced by a nostalgic China before the rise of totalitarianism and communism, and yet decidedly post-Imperial; in other words, a vague hybrid Orientalist vision, as seen through the eyes of a European armchair traveller repackaged for the comfort of bodies within homes around the world at a moment paying witness to the ascendancy of China on the economic and cultural maps. Truly fraught and ambivalent, the interwar period in China is here celebrated for its aesthetic accomplishments and inspiration. Subtly yet tacitly, Armani invokes a period of luxury, excess and even trouble, and perhaps more significantly yet, a period of transition, of liminality, not unlike the China of today. By referencing this particular moment in Chinese history, Armani suggests that the China of today must return to this era of glamour and adopt it as a consumerist ethos for tomorrow. Shanghai, as a vital epicentre of design in the 1920s and 1930s and in particular Art Deco, neatly adheres to the glorious heyday of *Gai Paris*. I wish to highlight the importance of Shanghai in particular because the city marks a turning point in Armani's more recent expansionism and incursion into China. In 2004 the designer toured China to celebrate the opening of his first boutique in that city. Built in the 1920s, the buildings along the Bund strip stand as emblematic of the city's Art Deco glory days, Shanghai before the communists discontinued the production of Art Deco furniture in 1949. Shanghai in the 1920s, at the height of its modernity, was a city whose urban topography was mapped out according to international enclaves that facilitated its cosmopolitan reputation on par with Western European cities like Berlin and Paris. Like the 1932 film *Shanghai Express* featuring the iconic Marlene Dietrich, The Pearl of the Orient, as the city was known, is repackaged in a highly glamorous Westernized version devoid of dubious associations. However, the influence is more significant than mere appropriation or inspiration, but obliquely refers back to the designer's imperial aspirations within Asia, at the exact time when he draws inspiration from the region. For spring 2005, Armani combined the interwar and Old Shanghai in a women's collection he titled 'Shocking', inspired by Elsa Schiaparelli. The Surrealists railed against Western norms and infused in their work a radical *soupçon* of the Orient to push against European binary logic.[127] Armani in the mid-2000s began to turn directly and unabashedly to Surrealist figures and ideas at a time when the USA failed to set the tone of his empirical aspirations. Interwar Surrealism and Armani's own global modernity provide an antidote, even if superficial, to those critics who desire a more pared-down, simplified, rationalist aesthetic from the designer.

In the early twentieth century a strong mechanistic current affected the cultural production of the period, resulting in an intensification of a functionalist though disembodied approach to design, art and culture. Writing in *Luxury and Capitalism* (1913) Werner Sombart insisted that

> [a]ll personal luxury springs from purely sensuous pleasure. Anything that charms the eye, the ear, the palate, or the touch, tends to find an ever more perfect expression in objects of daily use. And it is precisely this outlay for such objects that constitutes luxury ... for sensuous pleasure and erotic pleasure are essentially the same.[128]

Interesting is how emphasis is placed on the everyday not as objects of difference, but as basic as those which constitute a sensuous and erotic essence. Luxury then is not removed or distant. Lynn Garafola has labelled the developments in the post-Second World War period as a sort of 'lifestyle modernism', a period in which Orientalism was being replaced gradually by the onslaught of masculine modernism.[129] Perhaps, once again, this might be understood as a fluid and hybrid moment in the history of gendered ideals and cultural production. However, like all cultural phenomena there are two sides and we would also do well to remember that part of the Orientalist project is to render the East as a static image, where history has no place or affect. Homi Bhabha notes how 'cultural difference' challenges the fraught relationship between present and past in what ultimately becomes an arbitrary division between the two seemingly distinct states of time. What he suggests is that the one who possesses authority over translation of cultural memories cannot act with pure faithfulness to what is understood as tradition or even perceived as cultural memory itself.[130] In this manner differences are products of repetition under the guise of accurate representations. Within

120   Spring 2005: Model Erin O'Connor transformed into an Orientalist siren, inspired as always by interwar notions of the region

the context of fashion, which already has an equivocal relationship to time and history, the so-labelled Orient becomes a cultural trope through which to transcend *fashion* and elevate creative output to the more iconic and long-lasting status of *style*, the embodiment of global modernity where time and space cohere. The eternal return back into history is similar and important to the endless mythical travels to the East for Armani, as both function to escape from and yet call attention to the deficiencies of contemporary time and place. As Armani himself once commented: 'I have long adored the Orient and used it as a source for my design ... because they have great respect for the past, and they maintain a lifestyle that is extremely rational and sane.'[131] The constant referring back to the interwar period as to the Orient served as an important and much-needed antidote, for example, to grunge and the heroin chic of the 1990s. Armani is focused on controlling the future by remaining in the historical past, and by defiantly denying what his colleagues are doing in the present.

Armani's Orientalism then is not a strategy of appropriation and domination; rather, it is a premise by which to fashion a productive site of difference even if also a space of tension. The so-called Orient marks *the* site of modernity itself, an emblem of global modernity in which feminine and masculine cohere, a way to update, through the past, the West's seemingly tired sartorial and visual lexicon. Orientalism is not a sign of spectacle or the spectacular as it was once for Saint Laurent, rather it is merged in the experience of modernity as an expression of everydayness. In this way, rather than simply falling into the trap of viewing influence as an act of mere appropriation or hijacking, I wish to follow on from Mikhail Bakhtin's notion of 'dialogics' and the dialogical to insist on the exploration of ways seemingly opposing concepts, ideals, motifs, aesthetics, cultures and processes might enter into a dialogue – or symbiosis – toward a creative end, rather than simply viewed as antagonistic elements resulting in nothing substantive at all. Bakhtin was clearly invested in the integration of the networks of meaning and culture of languages. He concluded that every language is in actuality the product of dialogics, a comingling and aggregation of meanings and sources, whose provenance is not always clearly identifiable. What is suggested is how language is a process of responses to what has been 'said' before, as nothing exists in a vacuum. Language – or for us fashion – is a relational and dynamic synergy, whose activity is in a constant state of transition, transformation and translation toward the continual renewal of relevance and meaningfulness.[132]

For his women's spring/summer 2011 collection titled '*La Femme Bleue*' the designer took inspiration from the Touareg tribes, affectionately named the Blue People of the Berber tribe of Saharan Africa, but also I posit an allusion once again to Matisse and his *Blue Nude* of 1907. For the campaign and catalogue Armani wrote: 'An image, possibly a photograph or a still from a movie, the Tuareg, blu [sic] nomads of the desert. A journey that transforms this concept

121   Dreadlocks and kimono sleeves: autumn/winter 1998

into an inspirational idea, but with a feminine interpretation.'[133] Here again the crossing occurs between men and women, as well as between cultures. For the campaign Armani also hired British photographer Nick Knight to capture models Elisa Sednaoui and Ben Hill in an exotic and seductive one-minute film replete with an updated ambient North African soundtrack. For the women's collection, which overshadowed his menswear for the season, Armani offered over 40 shades of deep blue, including midnight, cobalt and cerulean. 'There's a certain nobility about the Bedouin life I've always admired', claimed the designer. 'It's simple but elegant and in sync with Giorgio Armani ... There's a grace about the desert veil that seems right for today and this collection.'[134] Although Armani avoided making any social or political comment on the fact that days before his show France had banned the public use of the burqa while it was debating and imposing the extradition of its Roma population, he was clear to claim in 2004 after controversy erupted over the garment in light of terrorist attacks in Western Europe that: 'It's a matter of respect for beliefs, cultures and ideas of others. And you have to live these ideas, we must learn to do it.'[135]

Here, perhaps, the work of theorist Bhabha is more productive to view Armani's design beyond the by now trite postmodern cliché of pastiche. If the 'act of cultural translation (both as representation and reproduction) denies the essentialism of a prior given original or original culture, then we see that all forms of culture are continually in a process of hybridity'. Marking out a 'third space', hybridity provides for 'new positions to emerge. The third space displaces the histories that constitute it'.[136] While Bhabha's preoccupation is definitively political in its aspirations and cultural in its outcome, it is equally useful to engage with in discussions of aesthetics in general, and the work of Armani more specifically. First, critics make repeated mention of how the original source of inspiration and specifics of the borrowed original are nearly impossible to pin down in Armani's work. The result is a hybrid object which is always rooted in Eastern sources while filtered through a Western idiom. As Franca Sozzani narrates:

> Indian gurus' jackets are transformed into embroidered golden vests worn over flowing pants, or become overcoats cut like frock coats, opening over wide, ruched skirts. The 'guru' collar then moves to China, and the body of the jacket becomes wider. On to Japan, and the sleeves deepen to form a kimono, with old pottery patterns serving as decorative motifs printed on silk or taffeta.[137]

Second, Armani separates himself by two degrees in his historical object/ moment of references. By this I mean to suggest that he does not simply reference an historical moment, but an historical moment itself understood then and now as a product of hybridity, translation and transition.

In a late capitalist (or post-industrial) West, Orientalism has lost its edge, its subversive *soupçon*. In the nineteenth and the beginning of the twentieth century, the Orient functioned as a utopian antidote to the rationalist severity of Western capitalism and modernism. The implication is that surface and pastiche are without substance and point to that which is tasteless, vulgarity itself. However, Armani's voracious adaptations are not random, but specific and consistent. Following from Seremetakis' beautiful evocation of the Greek definition of nostalgia, Elia Petridou makes claims for the importance of taste, whose moral implications are significant: 'Tasteless … is an equivalent of meaningless. As stated in the Greek dictionary, *anostiá* (lack of taste, tastelessness) also bears meaning of *anousiótis* (lack of substance, lack of meaning).'[138] Taste is fundamental to the elucidation of a lifestyle concept and to the notions of exclusivity and luxury to which the Armani/Casa and Giorgio Armani collections makes clear claims through an on-going translation of an elusive and so-called Orient.

Legacy: Eveningwear and Haute Couture

By way of conclusion, I wish to single out Armani's eveningwear as the ultimate site of tension in the designer's drive to safeguard his cultural patrimony and his posthumous legacy. While there can be no doubt of his contribution to the modern wardrobe, since his earliest collections he has also attempted to achieve what has been a somewhat elusory status as iconic dressmaker. Dressmaking is considered the ultimate in creative expression,

122   Peter Lindbergh and Paolo Roversi. For the spring/summer 1997 advertising campaign

a practice which uncomfortably rubs up against the status of high art. While Armani has made jackets and suits such an important part of his image, in their ubiquity, despite their mastery, they are easily taken for granted. It is no wonder then that he continues to obsess in his exhibitions over the work he has done for eveningwear, after all the man is single-handedly responsible for bringing back glamour to the Hollywood red carpet. As early as 1986, Armani was claiming that he wanted to leave behind a legacy, noting that: 'I feel there has been a total erosion of values, and I have very little hope they will return.'[139] Here, just over one year after the death of his former lover and business partner, Armani mixes nostalgia, morality and legacy in a tonic for the future, one which increasingly began to dominate his aesthetic decisions and cultural initiatives. The Third Earl of Shaftesbury writing in 1711 contended that our 'moral sense' was at once the ethical when pertaining to actions and dispositions and the 'aesthetic' when applied to nature and art;[140] the two sides of the same coin of taste and the critique of cultural life. For David Hume objects possess nothing inherent that makes them aesthetically pleasing or displeasing, but rather point to our own psychological responses to them. There is an important distinction – apparently – to be made between the desire for possession on the one hand and on the other distanced and detached aesthetic contemplation. One is valued over the other, both are distinctly and oppositionally gendered and refer back to our cultural assumptions that collecting has traditionally been understood to reside within a distinctly male purview while consumption remains in the domain of the feminine which, coupled with its ephemerality, is deemed unworthy as cultural patrimony.

Armani's first attempts at eveningwear did not occur in the initial years of his career. This cannot be entirely surprising for a designer who began in a menswear studio and textile factory. His first recorded foray began with his controversial samurai collection in 1981, in which he simply took the same ideas, shapes and garments and translated them into eveningwear by way of more luxurious fabrics. From 1981 to 1985, Armani continued to try his hand at eveningwear, usually creating glimmering, shining and bedazzling yet simple dresses. For autumn/winter 1984, for example, he created long floor-length shift dresses entirely out of diamonds. However, perhaps for the first time in his career, his eveningwear creations for his autumn 1985 creations were as well received and as impressive as his daywear for his autumn 1985 collection. Importantly the expanded eveningwear segment for this collection marked a new strategy the house had begun the previous season. Gabriella Forte emphasized that the garments were couture in both attitude and craftsmanship with 'special fabrics ... created in an atelier'.[141] This was already distinct from Ferré and Versace who at the time only produced a semi-separate evening collection once a year for the autumn season; a practice the houses have since altered. The autumn showing of his eveningwear was also a paean to Galeotti, as it was the last decision the two had made together before his death. As was the case with a number of initiatives, such as leaving the security of Cerruti to strike out on his own, Galeotti 'pushed' the designer to undertake new challenges.[142] Having come to eveningwear later in the game, the decision was less about inability than a calculated economic decision on his part. 'You really had to invest, and we weren't ready to do it,' recalls Armani. 'So when we decided we could afford this step, I had to face

123   Seeing double: repetition and the modern art of Armani from autumn 1988. Armani customarily gave buyers options for each garment with three to four different colours and/or fabrics, highlighting the modernist fetish for repetition, but also lengthening his runway presentations considerably

the challenge that it presented to me and my style ... I tried to use surprising fabrics, lace, and embroideries. I played with light and shadow', the tools often ascribed to painters.[143]

In 1992, Armani was the subject of a 100-piece installation curated by friend and architect Gae Aulenti as part of the fortieth anniversary of the Sala Bianca, the Florentine event that launched the Made in Italy movement on the heels of

124 Autumn/winter 1988

the Second World War. On the occasion of the event, Armani insisted that his label still held importance, especially in an increasingly global marketplace. In the process of reinforcing his own position within the Made in Italy phenomenon, he publically slammed the vulgarity of contemporary clothing that displayed, according to him, 'the image of a woman as a receptacle for men, the incarnation of low-level sexual fantasies, the nightclub where

125   Eveningwear from his spring/summer 1989 collection

stripteases are done for provincial wolves'.[144] While the designer made himself heard in terms of the sort of women he designs for, he also importantly began the process of creating his self-styled legacy. Of the 100 garments presented in the exhibition, the vast majority were not only womenswear, but also more significantly eveningwear, relegating the very few examples of menswear and women's sportswear to the background (both spatially and conceptually), giving them a secondary status. Armani and those around him, as we have seen, has been single-minded in their attempts to safeguard the image of the house, however, this particular move was a conscious effort to begin to think about the house's life after Armani. While the designer has been credited with reinventing and reinvesting significance in the jacket for both men and women, the press has often held ambivalent opinions in their reviews of his eveningwear. Criticism was targeted at the exhibition's focus on his eveningwear, rather than on his sportswear and jackets said to be the source of his success under the Made in Italy imprimatur. When asked why his menswear was restricted to only a few examples while his women's evening frocks were given more space, the designer responded: 'Women change – that fashion is for the moment. For me, the ideal man never changes. It is more *esprit de la mode* and of emotion.'[145] In 2000, when the Guggenheim Museum hosted its retrospective a nearly identical charge was levelled at the show's organizers, leaving many to feel as though history was being rewritten.[146]

In 1989, definitely Milanese in his allegiances, Armani declined an offer by Maryll Lanvin to head the atelier for her family's venerable house. However in 2005, he would change his mind and inaugurate his own haute couture label, Giorgio Armani Privé to be included in the regular Parisian couture calendar.

For his inaugural collection only 35 evening gowns in Ottoman silk, tulle, lace, satin organza, with elaborate beadwork and enamel appliqué were shown to the elite crowd in attendance. Haute couture was established in 1868 and over time would develop into a system with very specific and exacting guidelines. According to these, Armani's first showing did not conform to the rules systematized in 1945, which established that day and eveningwear are equally to be shown. The designer did, however, as per the regulations

126   Evening ensemble from spring 1991. Grid-like structure over a feminine and fluid fabric. Eveningwear which plays with concealing and revealing: Armani is adept at giving the appearance of transparency, nudity and revealing skin in various though not offensive ways. Here it is done through a zipper, a unique choice for an evening garment

of the *Chambre Syndicale de la Haute Couture*, open an official atelier devoted exclusively to this new enterprise. Located at 11 and 21 via Borgonuovo (the former he purchased in 1993), the atelier comprises 20 *petit-mains*, many of which were hired from the Versace Atelier studio when it temporarily closed due to a significant downturn in the house's fortunes following the death of its

127   Embroidered dress from autumn/winter 1994

founding designer. The goal for the highly specialized couture collection was not to sell perfume, according Armani, but rather to sell one of a kind, custom-made garments which he had previously been showing as part of his Giorgio Armani Borgonuovo collection. The rather practical impetus for the venture was that numerous gowns were left unsold in his boutiques around the world because these did not perfectly fit the select few women wealthy enough to afford the creations. In this way, dresses which already had near-couture price tags and techniques could now be properly fitted to the contours of each individual client; a rationale which made perfect financial sense. As Robert Triefus made clear: 'Mr. Armani never does anything without a practical business reason.'[147] However, the move was also to assert his position in the realm of dressmaking and mark his presence in the international capital of womenswear. Concerning the then current state of haute couture, Armani defiantly claimed that

> [h]aute couture is not theatre. All women do not want to be regarded as idiots ... I adore Galliano, but they [Dior] gave him the possibility to do whatever he chooses to have maximum coverage by the international press, and in the back sell their bags and cosmetics ... They have killed haute couture. I simply wish, without any pretention, to prove the point, to show women they can dress in haute couture without being ridiculous.[148]

As British fashion journalist Lisa Armstrong noted, 'Armani's first foray into French fashion territory shows he's not finished yet.'[149] In tandem with his foray into the privileged sphere of couture, Armani also inaugurated a limited Privé jewellery collection. Consisting of only 40 pieces (of which 8 were for men), the collection has become a personal 'private laboratory' for the designer.[150] In addition, he also included an exclusively distributed quartet (which has since expanded to six) of unisex scents under the label. These were designed with the idea of conjuring special associations and one in particular, Armani/Privé Bois d'Encens, was created out of a desire to relive childhood memories. For Armani, who had carried around a flask of the scent years before it was ever put into production, Bois d'Encens was a reminder of his youth when he would go to church with his family. The scent of 'incense would make the situation bearable', he recalled.[151]

For the final destination of the itinerant *Giorgio Armani: Retrospective*, which began in a whirlwind of controversy in New York, Armani upped the controversial ante in a highly symbolic and telling move. On 19 February 2007 he presented his autumn 2007 women's collection. The final exit was an impressive – and the only – floor-length Giorgio Armani Privé dress, embroidered with new Swarovski crystals cut to his specifications displayed to glittering effect. Immediately following the runway show the dress was transported to the Milano Trieannale, where the exhibition, sponsored by Swarovski,[152] was set to open that evening and where it would remain as part

128   Final exit from the autumn 2007 collection which made its way directly into the
final stop of the itinerate Giorgio Armani exhibition at the Trieannale in Milan. Fitted
Giorgio Armani Privé evening gown with flared skirt embellished all over in horizontal
rows of faceted Swarovski crystal beads in graduated sizes from neckline to hem and
smaller crystal rhinestones. Sleeveless with scoop neckline, sculpted décolletage at back
and tank top straps. Apart from Christian Dior, Armani is the only designer to have a
specially designed crystal for his exclusive use, the 'Diamond Leaf' seen here in this
floor-length dress

of the exhibition's ever-expanding collection of by then 600 garments. Critics of the show have maintained, once again, that Armani's daywear, his suits which revolutionized men's and women's clothing, seemed to play second fiddle to his glamorous red-carpet worthy dresses. In one evening the designer penned the final chapter on the story of his cultural aspirations. It would be easy to claim that this was simply an attempt to sell more clothes. In a world where celebrities pen their own autobiographies in their early twenties, fashion has become a serious and tenable academic discipline, publishers clamour to produce innumerable glossy coffee table books celebrating the past and present achievements of designers and museums cash in on the cultural cachet of fashion, designers have become all too aware of their own role in the culture wars of legacy, which enhance their economic and more importantly historical and long-standing credibility. For any designer once the runway show has been presented, the creative process has ended, all that remains is the press reviews and the hard business of selling. In other words, in the realm of aesthetics it has already become old news, perhaps even part of history itself. If you have conquered every facet of contemporary life, as Armani clearly has, what is there left to achieve, other than to make a claim to history, which the space of the museum portends? At the Trieannale exhibition history was oddly represented and definitively skewed, with no dates given to any of the displays. I suggest that this is a need on the part of the designer to make the slogan, 'style is timeless' living and real. The desire on the part of Armani to render his fashions from past collections indistinct from the present, make the garments from the 1970s or 1980s decidedly contemporary, and therefore ironically remove any historicizing limit. This exhibition embodies what we might label the time of fashion, a temporal reality removed from linearity and a teleological impulse and yet at the same time have one's garments embedded in the future recording of history. The exhibiting spaces of the Trieannale, which opened its doors in 1933, have become a crucial institution providing a venue to create and perpetuate a real interest in contemporary design.[153] The reconstruction of the city, the development and construction boom and a growing interest in design through various media outlets helped to foster and perpetuate Milan as the centre of design as well as a definitive (if unclear) Italian Look. The fact that this was the last stop along the exhibition's route tacitly reinforces Armani's mark on Milanese fashion and the city itself.

In 2008 the Costume Institute's annual blockbuster exhibition and gala featured *Superheroes: Fashion and Fantasy* and was co-hosted by Armani. The gala is touted as the most important night in the social calendar, but is also a vital component to the health and well-being of the Institute because as a fund-raiser (which in the past has raised over $45,000,000) it provides the necessary operating budget of the quasi-independent department. This gala was no exception, with every A-list celebrity in attendance. Among them, the designer's own legion of supporters: David and Victoria Beckham and Tom

129   Left: 1993 worn by Katie Holmes; Right: 1995 worn by Victoria Beckham at the 2008 Metropolitan Museum's Costume Institute Annual Gala

130   Dress in the immediate right-hand foreground seen here in the Guggenheim exhibition and taken out of the Armani archive to be worn by Katie Holmes at the 2008 Met Gala

Cruise and Katie Holmes. I wish to signal Beckham's and Holmes's choices of dress, orchestrated by Armani himself. Both celebrities wore vintage selections featured in the itinerant exhibition, which made their debut anew as both and at once vintage and living museum pieces. Here the designer reasserted his own history by speaking to the ever-increasing interest in vintage and challenging the fraught relationship between museum and living design by translating – through space – the fashioned object from runway to street to museum to red carpet. The day after the MET gala, the Fashion Institute of Technology (FIT) presented Giorgio Armani with the first Couture Council Award for Global Fashion Leadership. The *Harper's Bazaar* and Swarovski-sponsored luncheon was held at the Hearst Tower where editor-in-chief Glenda Bailey and Armani-clad actress Glenn Close bestowed the accolade on the designer. For our purposes, what is important to note is that Armani's celebrated full-length Swarovski crystal-encrusted dress from his autumn 2007 collection and featured in the Trieannale exhibition was donated to the FIT museum on this occasion.

Art historian Griselda Pollock asserts that canons are 'the retrospectively legitimating backbone of a cultural and political identity, a consolidated narrative of origin, conferring authority on the texts selected to naturalise this function'.[154] Canons establish transcultural, transhistorical and even transnational systems of valuation. In the case of Giorgio Armani the desire is to control the house's cultural patrimony. The ethics of legacy might simply be a question of vested interest, an assurance in the ideal and preferred interpretations of a creator's work, in defiance of third-party gatekeepers' interpretations, but more interestingly it might also be a question of deeply dysfunctional notions of what the marriage between art museums and fashion currently exposes. One has to ask, however, are Armani's vested interests in the Guggenheim exhibition really any different than the creation and curatorial practices of the Fondation Pierre Bergé-Yves Saint Laurent, inaugurated to house an archive and erect various fashion (mostly YSL) exhibitions around the world, directly and palpably influenced by Bergé himself? Since the death of the French designer, his former partner has worked tirelessly to ensure the house's cultural heritage and claim its canonical status, a response, undoubtedly, to the mediocre if not hostile press Saint Laurent received toward the end of his illustrious career. Should the press really operate as arbiter of history and legacy, especially given how they are invested in the here and now, a position unabashedly spiked with a strong dose of ageism and commercial interest not unlike the annual Met gala?

I wish to conclude by briefly exploring the display style for the 2008 Armani/Casa line at both the annual Salone de Mobile in Milan and London Design Festival, which included mannequins sporting vintage Giorgio Armani garments from previous collections. These garments formed part of the *Giorgio Armani: Retrospective*, and are planned to be housed in the archive of the house's museum in Milan, initially scheduled to open in 2010. Here Armani forecloses on the possibilities of the polyvalence of clothing. In the act of self-translation and interpretation, he controls the orbit of meaning by not having his clothes interpreted by the museum, curator or press, avoiding the transformation of his intent. Here he consolidates and substantiates his own

131   Peter Lindbergh. From the spring/summer 2002 advertising campaign

historical and material worth, longevity, legacy and gravitas. It also marks, I wish to submit, a dialogical relationship with the present moment and Armani's continued dissatisfaction with the contemporary fashion system, controlled in large measure by gatekeepers such as editors rather than simply creative designers. The press release for the collection asserted that '[t]his combination of furniture and furnishings, and fashion, clearly emphasizes how Armani/Casa represents a harmonious extension [of a] common philosophy and unity of style'.[155] With this collection Armani deploys his own history through past collections to lend cogency to the symbiosis between interiors and fashion, past and present, to summon the timelessness of his designs. However, the fashions he pulls from the archives are themselves inspired by the interwar period, the influence legible in this Armani/Casa collection. The designer cogently historicizes his own work, a nostalgic nod to his own past as he embarks on a programme of archiving his life's work. In this way Armani places his work – and himself – within history itself, reinforcing the idea that his historical citations always possess two degrees of separation. Benjamin deployed the concept of *Tigersprung* to highlight how fashion leaps to the past to conjure a constantly renewing ever-changing present. To take from here, to borrow from there resides at the heart of any designer's collection, but here Armani springs back to his own legacy to reinforce his potency as a brand, label and house. The tacit goal is to conjure iconic pieces that resurface from time to time, to lend the credibility of time and timelessness simultaneously. As we have already come to see, Armani regularly leaps back; but more often

132   Mert Alas and Marcus Piggot. From the autumn/winter 2004 advertising campaign

than not he stays, dwelling in the chora of nostalgia. For the presentation of his 2008 Armani/Casa collection he sprung back into imbricated histories, for here he traces his own past within the present, as well as the cultural product of the historical past as part of the creation of empire and its legacy, both of which operate in the service of each other. For Benjamin the leaping backward through time (and we might add, importantly, space), is a way to map out, or trace the past through the present, rather than simply seeing the present as a consequence of a forward moving momentum. History is 'blasted' from its roots, a destabilization of continuity, a translation in which meaning travels through time and space, appropriated toward new and dynamic ends. Here sensuous matter holds the truth of history itself. Returning to Seremetakis, '[n]ostalghiá speaks to the sensory reception of history. In Greek there is a semantic circuit that weds the sensorial to agency, memory, finitude, and therefore history – all of which are contained within the etymological strata of the senses.'[156] She contends that this circuit of sensorial meanings and emotions can 'provoke important cross-cultural methodological consequences'.[157] Dress crossed between womenswear and menswear, dress crossed from fashion to furniture, dress crossed from past to present and dress crossed from Oriental to Occidental foreground strategies by which Armani evokes the hybrid nature of the body's sensual and cultural life, the attempts of the designer to conjure a lasting identity for his house. When one turns to his eveningwear one sees the dilemma he has found himself in, a desire to be known for challenging gender sartorial codes through textiles and the jacket, while simultaneously driven by a need to be known for creating beautiful red carpet moments whose memories last beyond time ... until, of course, the next red carpet is rolled out.

Notes

1   For an important and more complete theoretical discussions of gender, clothing and cross-dressing see Garber 1997; Butler 1990.

2   Garber 1997: 42.

3   Molloy in Garber 1997: 41–2.

4   Molloy in Garber 1997: 42.

5   Entwistle 2007: 216.

6   *Esquire* 22 May 1979.

7   'Armani Disarmed' 1995: vi.

8   *WWD* 11 May 1975.

9   *Time* 6 April 1981.

10   *NYT* 26 March 1978.

11   *WWD* 4 May 1978; *NYT* 4 April 1978.

12   *NYT* 6 October 1979.

13   *W* 26 October–2 November 1979.

14   *NYT* 30 September 1979.

15   *WWD* 9 October 1979.

16   *W* 26 October–2 November 1979; in the twentieth-first century the same expression would resurface as 'Classicism con twist' to designate his approach to his tailoring.

17   *W* 26 October–2 November 1979.

18   *W* 26 October–2 November 1979. However, by 2010 Armani had chastised Dolce and Gabbana of plagiarizing a pair of trousers for men he claims he sent down the runway the previous season.

19   *TS* estimates that the wholesale prices for Italian fashion increased between 20 and 30 per cent between spring/summer 1980 and autumn/winter 1980, 21 March 1980.

20   *NYT* 5 October 1980.

21   *TS* 28 November 1980.

22   Armani in *W* 28 August–4 September 1981.

23   *Elle* (France) 3 August 1982: n.p.

24   Armani in *W* 28 August–4 September 1981.

25   *LAT* 2 October 1981.

26   Armani in *Newsweek* 19 October 1981.

27   *Time* 1 February 1982.

28   *NYT* 7 October 1983.

29   *WWD* 14 March 1984.

30   *TS* 22 March 1984.

31   Polan 1983: 154.

32   *LAT* 19 March 1984.

33   *NYT* 11 October 1984.

34   *La Repubblica* 15 March 1985.

35   Quoted in Gronberg 1998: 22.

36   Crow 1996: 4.

37   Tickner 2000: 190.

38   See Slater 1997: 13–14.

39   Bocca 1990: n.p.

40   *LAT* 10 October 1986.

41   Bocca 1990: n.p.

42   Gina not only appeared in his runway shows, but also in Giorgio Armani campaigns from 1987 to 1990 as well as editorial content for numerous magazines in North America and Europe.

43   *WWD* 9 October 1986.

44   *WWD* 9 October 1986.

45   *WWD* 8 October 1986.

46   *NYT* 10 October 1986.

47   'Armani Disarmed' 1995: vi.

48   *The Times* 6 October 1987.

49   Loewy in Lipovetsky 1994: 138.

50   *G & M* 14 Oct 1986.

51   *G & M* 10 March 1987.

52   *G & M* 17 March 1987.

53   *NYT* 8 October 1987.

54   *Rolling Stone* 21 April 1988: 60.

55   Thurman 1988: 92.

56   *Corriere* 9 January 1989.

57   Mower 1989: 342.

58   *NYT* 13 October 1989.

59   Kuhn 1985: 52.

60   See Riviere 1986.

61   *Giorgio Armani* 2000: 163.

62   Slater 1997: 10.

63   Slater 1997: 10.

64   Slater 1997: 13.

65   Armani 1995: 103.

66   Armani 1995: 110.

67   *Die Zeit* 14 April 1995.

68   *The Times* 5 October 2000.

69   *Time* 5 April 1982.

70   Armani in *The Times* 22 September 2006.

71   Lipovetsky 1994: 141.

72   Armani in *The Times* 22 September 2006.

73   McBride 2004: 762.

74   *BG* 13 September 2007.

75   *WWD* 25 April 2008.

76   Lipovetsky 1994: 12.

77   'The Armani Edge' 1992: 320.

78   du Camp in Benjamin 1999a: 14.

79   For a thorough discussion of Benjamin's notion of *Tiguresprung,* or fashion's leap back through the past, see Lehmann 2000.

80   Seremetakis 2001: 4.

81   *The Independent* 12 April 2008.

82   Boym 2001: xv.

83   *WWD* 11 June 2007.

84   Armani in the *Independent* 12 April 2008.

85   Susman in Fischer 2003: 151.

86   Sparke 1995: 120.

87   See Sparke 1995: 124–5.

88   *NYT 26* February 1926.

89   Lipovetsky 1994: 138.

90   *WWD* 5 March 2002.

91   *The Washington Post* 3 October 2003.

92   *Sunday Times* 26 October 2003.

93   *The Washington Post* 11 November 2006.

94   *W* 27 March–3 April 1981; *WWD* 25 March 1981.

95   *TS* 23 March 1981.

96   *TS* 23 March 1981.

97   *NYT* 28 March 1981.

98   Appadurai 1996: 4.

99   *NYT* 31 March 1981.

100   *TS* 23 March 1981.

101   Crescent in *Time* 6 April 1981.

102   *WWD* 23 March 1981.

103   *WWD* 6 November 2007.

104   *US Weekly* 23 October 2000.

105   Boym 2001: xviii.

106   Said 1979: 1.

107   *WWD* 11 June 2007.

108   Solomon-Godeau 1989: 314.

109   *Sunday Times* 9 January 1994.

110   Martin and Koda 1994: 9.

111   Mower 1993: 143.

112   Armani in Mower 1993: 143.

113   Attfield 2000: 124.

114   *Chicago Tribune* 13 March 1988.

115   *W* 15 October 1990.

116   *W* 15 October 1990.

117   *New York Magazine* 25 January 1993.

118   In the two-week period Saks sold $1 million in Armani products.

119   *WWD* 5 February 1993.

120   *DNR* 8 February 1993.

121   'Armani Disarmed' 1995: vii.

122   de la Haye 2000: 64.

123   Wollen 1993: 30.

124   Wollen 1993: 17–18.

125   2004–05 Armani/Casa catalogue.

126   Jones and Leshkowich 2003: 5.

127   Wollen 1993: 24.

128   In Wollen 1993: 19.

129   See Garafola 1989.

130   Bhabha 2004: 51–2.

131   Armani in *Newsweek* 27 October 2003.

132   See Bakhtin 1981.

133   Spring/summer 2011 Giorgio Armani catalogue.

134   Armani in *FWD* 28 September 2010.

135   Corriere 28 September 2004.

136   Bhabha 1990: 211.

137   Sozzani in *Giorgio Armani* 2000: 79.

138   Petridou 2001: 89.

139   'Giorgio Armani' 1986: 107.

140   Miller 2007: 33.

141   *WWD* 19 September 1985.

142   Mower 1989: 342.

143   Armani in Molho 2007: 162.

144   *WWD* 25 June 1992.

145   *DNR* 25 June 1992.

146   See Potvin 2012a.

147   *NYT Magazine* 6 February 2005. Accordingly, the debut collection sold two-thirds of the 35 exits, while 90 per cent of the follow-up collection which featured 60 exists was sold (*WWD* 5 October 2005). Armani made fashion history with the first ever, live streaming of a haute couture show on 24 January 2007 via MSN and on Cingular cellular phones.

148   Armani in *Paris Match* 7–13 July 2004.

149   *The Times* 24 January 2005.

150   *The Times* 19 March 2005.

151   Colavita 2004: 144.

152   Armani's relationship with Sworvski is long-standing and he is the only designer apart from Christian Dior to have a specially designed and unique crystal for his exclusive use, the 'Diamond Leaf' seen in the final exit of his autumn/winter 2007 collection.

153   Foot 2001: 110.

154   Pollock 1990: 3.

155   Armani press release 17–23 September 2008.

156   Seremetakis 2001: 4.

157   Seremetakis 2001: 5.

6

Armani/Space: Boutique Cultures

Armani's clothes have repeatedly enjoyed the film camera's spotlight, at times obscuring an actor's performance, so too have his boutiques served as locations vital to a character's transformation and development. In *Joe Versus the Volcano* (1990), in what is surely a silly plot, Tom Hanks' out of work protagonist Joe is given four gold credit cards to use at his discretion in exchange for throwing himself into a volcano. Equipped with his plastic power and with his impending doom on his mind, Joe is driven around New York by a chauffeur who helpfully instructs the unfashionable Joe where the best suits and tuxedoes are to be bought. Armani's powerful impact is suggested to have filtered down even to the service classes when the chauffeur drives Joe directly to the designer's Manhattan store. For the film the Beverly Hills boutique stands in for the Upper East Side store where Joe not only buys himself a tailored tuxedo but also one for his instructive chauffeur. In the thriller *Double Jeopardy* (1999) the lead protagonist played by Ashley Judd recounts the story of Elizabeth Parsons, just released from prison after serving a sentence for the murder of her husband Nick Parsons (Bruce Greenwood). Elizabeth, however, is falsely accused and framed by her still-living husband and is in hot pursuit of revenge. In her quest for justice, she arrives at a luxurious hotel where her husband is staying with his new love interest. To blend in with the wealthy hotel clientele she goes to one of the hotel's exclusive boutiques, itself a makeshift fictitious Giorgio Armani store, obvious only to the Armani connoisseur given that the store is not labelled in any obvious way. Finally, in Steve Martin's highly acclaimed short story adapted for the big screen, *Shop Girl* (2005), the Beverly Hills Giorgio Armani flagship boutique once again services as a backdrop for the transformation of the story's central character Mirabelle Buttersfield (Claire Daines). Here she is bought a made to measure floor-length evening dress by one of her love interests (Steven Martin). Featuring designer boutiques in films is not unique to Armani, neither is it new. However, in these instances they separately mark important transitional moments in the narratological development of each of the films' central characters. Apparent from the specific use of the Beverly Hills store (*Joe Versus the Volcano* and *Shop Girl*) or a replica (*Double Jeopardy*), the three films share a common metaphor of transformation made possible in and through the space of the boutique. The idea that Armani boutiques are sites of transformation is not strictly confined to the cinema. In real life we witness the transformation of celebrity figures such as 50 Cent, rappers who shed their urban street clothes for slick and sophisticated dark tailored Armani suits to designate that they too have 'arrived' on the cultural map, itself a spatial metaphor to designate success. Transformations such as these are achieved through socially sanctioned, often exclusive, rituals and specialized spaces. Armani's spatial regime is an important means to connect with his consumers in a tangible and material way while also offering a luxurious space for the direct and controlled translation of his design and aesthetic ethos, unobstructed by third-party gatekeepers whose investments and priorities are not necessarily those of the designer's.

Over the past 35 years, Armani has collaborated with more than ten design firms, which have included Giancarlo Ortelli, the late Naomi Leff, London restaurateur Michael Chow, Peter Marino, Tadao Ando, Claudio Silvestrin and Massimiliano and Doriana Fuksas to create some of the most beautiful, calming and sophisticated retail environments in the world. Since the inauguration of his first store in Milan in 1981 Armani has been slow to change or alter his boutiques, unusual for most high-end retail establishments which refit or refurbish boutiques every five or so years. Since 2000, however, Armani seems increasingly eager to redesign and set new standards in interior architecture, creating more unique and distinguished spaces rather than adhering to a specified and repeated blueprint. In this chapter Armani's extensive global retail network and designs have been purposefully reduced and restricted to three large geographic regions, each introduced chronologically based on the first boutique opening to proffer a more holistic purview of the designer's global retail strategy. Each region explored here reveals overlapping yet unique spatial translations and the cultural challenges associated with Armani's expanding empire. The first region, where the designer introduced his first wholly owned retail boutique, focuses attention therefore on Europe. Interestingly, both Milan and Paris vie for exclusive status as the preferred location to inaugurate a new retail design. The second, North America, which through the years has varyingly comprised roughly between 25 and 33 per cent of the designer's retail and wholesale figures, is not only his most important market outside of Italy, but has also featured unique or idiosyncratic retail spaces not copied elsewhere. Like the other two, the third and final region, Asia, has been the focus of considerable collaboration and effort on the part of the designer and has offered exceptional potential for expansion in the late 1980s and early 1990s in Japan in particular, and in China more recently.[1]

The 'symbolic magic' of a fashion designer's label possesses the auratic potency to conjure the mystique of distinction, authenticity and exclusivity, in turn engendering a fervent dedication (verging on the religious) on the part of faithful costumers. The aura surrounding the name of the designer transforms objects of no real value to objects of luxury, preciousness and desire. However, the label itself is not enough; it must be housed in spaces equally endowed with the potential to elicit reverence and pleasure, a coveted destination wherein the embodied consumer is interpolated into the narrative force of the brand. 'Through processes of mimesis and identification the consumer enacts a performance that is at once somatic and embodied.'[2] Boutiques attenuate the designer's aura through the preferred pathways of engagement with the space and merchandise. In his discussion of retail design Otto Riewoldt contends that

> [w]ith the same care and professionalism as in the theatre, the sequence of events [of shopping] must be worked out in detail, including everything from props to stage directions, in order to transform the sale of merchandise into an experience-intensive act – one in which the potential customers are actors rather than passive spectators.[3]

To best achieve this, a designer must create spaces that communicate the brand as distinct from all other designer and public spaces. As Armani attempts to make his mark, therefore, so too must he employ an architect whose own unmistakable material signature will assist in the proposition and perpetuation of a so-called authentic material and visual identity. The boutique must retain the same visual effectiveness and material aura as the discreet label sewn into an Armani garment. Through space, the brand must not only articulate a 'distinctive message' but also an 'emotional identity'.[4] Robert Triefus, executive vice-president of worldwide communications for Armani in Milan, makes a similar claim when he states that '[s]tores are the face of a brand ... It is the entire image as we want it to be seen. Architecture is a very important part of brand communication. When you arrive [at a store] it should conform to your expectations of the brand'.[5] The mystique surrounding Armani is made palpable in the rarefied minimalist spaces of his boutiques around the world. His auratic presence is made tangible through a rarity of objects rather than through a saturation or overabundance, a subtle reminder of control and power over his imperial domain.

Michel Foucault's notion of the heterotopia is useful to think through the significance of the aura of a boutique's space. While Foucault outlined numerous definitions for the term, most useful is how a heterotopia marks itself out a space of difference, and through the rituals associated with that space occupies a position 'outside of all [other ordinary] places'.[6] Boutiques can also be viewed at once as 'mythic and real, imbued with elements of fictional space and material space ... Heterotopias do not exist in isolation, but become visible through their differences with other sites as they upset spatial relations or provide alternative representations of them.'[7] As a space of luxury and exclusivity, high-end designer boutiques and more recent mega-stores operate as cultural destinations on an expanding tourist circuit. Armani offers spaces of calm and beauty while providing counter-sites to what he has argued is the aggression of most design in the world at large. In this way, the aura of the boutique and hence the label itself is maintained by way of its separateness from the quotidian, and in the case of Armani a moralized antidote to his competitors. The footprint of the boutique and its marked difference from the streets' culture outside force complete immersion and transformation. Through the rituals of consumption structured by progressive and marked stages in a temple-like space, what occurs is a sort of transubstantiation whereby the visual image of fashion object (seen through the spectacle of advertising and runway presentations) is mythically and materially transformed into reality through the embodied fashioned subject. The final touch which adds to the aura is how, within the dynamic interplay between absences and presences, the boutique accommodates and spatially translates 'the magical timeless quality of an Armani collection with the equally timeless quality of a distinguished . . . building'.[8] The simplicity and unadorned 'timeless' architecture Armani always commissions acts as antidote to and defiant critique of the fashion system and its endless, fast-paced cycles of change.

Europe: Setting Up Shop

Since Charles Frederick Worth established his *maison de haute couture* in 1858 in Paris, forces have been at work to seal that city's position as pre-eminent centre of modern fashion and modernity. By the mid-nineteenth century the City of Lights was itself marketed and packaged as an object of fashion.[9] Paris's position remained mostly unchallenged until after the Second World War when both New York and Milan vied equally to be recognized as serious capitals of fashion, merchandizing and retailing. Although for some the French capital continues to be the undisputed centre of high fashion, New York and Milan have successfully forged themselves as unquestioned specialists of prêt-à-porter. At least in terms of textile production and the successful wedding of commerce and creativity, Milan however has edged out New York and Paris through their unique, winning formula. As a centre for all things designed, Milan in 1981 was pronounced to be 'a city of the future rather than of the past. Milanese attention to visual detail and beauty is part of a living, developing style'.[10] The relationship between Paris and Milan has been a rather fraught one, with competition at times reaching operatic heights. However, despite the Italian city's clear influence on Armani and his creative output (the soberness of his colour palette iterating the bleak, grey façades of Milan's architecture), the designer has also maintained an unexplored and unquestioned relationship with Paris, specifically as it pertains to his retail outlets. In this section devoted to select European retail spaces, I wish to narrate the tale of two cities, Milan and Paris, as a means to expose the on-going challenges of defining spatial integrity and brand image on a global terrain.

Seven years after inaugurating his namesake label, Giorgio Armani finally set up its first wholly-owned, free-standing boutique at number 9 in the quiet and assuming street of Sant'Andrea, Milan in the fall of 1983. Designed by architect and former La Rinascente colleague Giancarlo Ortelli, like many of the stores in the city in the early 1980s, from the outside the Giorgio Armani boutique was not overtly glamorous, its stone façade avoiding to call attention to itself. Rather it presented itself as though tucked away, a slightly concealed private destination for a select few in the know. Adhering to the Milanese ideals of restraint, sobriety, decorum and quiet elegance, *The New York Times* declared that '[n]othing in all Milan, however, is quite like the Armani boutique'.[11] The softness of the textured rubber matting used for the flooring was juxtaposed with the steel girders and translucent acrylic sheets that comprised the walls. Track lighting in the ceiling ensured a perfect showcasing of each garment while also allowing for a darker, more mysterious atmosphere.

In the second half of the 1980s, Armani began closing, moving and reopening boutiques to consolidate and take greater ownership of his retail network. Exemplary of this initiative was the 1987 inauguration of the Paris boutique in 6 Place Vendôme in which Armani honed and perfected the design he had initiated with his Sant'Andrea boutique. The store replaced a previous franchised store located on the Left Bank. The former boutique, according to Armani, was too small and 'didn't project the necessary image'.[12] The decision was more emotional and intuitive than financial, given that the global recession began that year. However, despite the gloom and doom hanging over the retail sector, first-day sales for the 371 square metre (4,000 square foot) store reached an impressive $40,000. As Armani himself noted, the economic downturn would pass, claiming that the 'store has been a dream for me. It's for me. It's a question of my image more than my business.'[13] The opening of this Paris location is significant for two important reasons. First, with this Place Vendôme store, Paris, and not Milan, served as the perfected conceptual blueprint for every subsequent retail or renovation project around the world for nearly a decade. Second, and perhaps more significantly, in times of serious economic downturn Armani has often gone against conventional retail wisdom by opening boutiques that were either completely redesigned, larger or strategically better located, often with steeper rents. In every instance, each choice has proven to be shrewd marketing and retail investments for the future of the house.

133 Outside shot of the stately façade of the Place Vendôme location

With its central column crafted after Trajan's column to commemorate Napoleon's victory of Austerlitz, Place Vendôme in the twentieth century has come to personify glamour and luxury, the column itself marking the epicentre of fashionable Paris. For the location of his boutique Armani purposefully removed it slightly from the fashionable core of Faubourg Saint-Honoré. Place Vendôme, according to Armani, defied the logic of the fashion system. Referring to the streets made famous for their high-end designer boutiques, Armani claimed that '[t]hose areas are like fashion. They're always changing. Place Vendôme will always be Place Vendôme.'[14] By locating his boutique in this time-honoured square, the move not only implied a spatial removal from the quotidian or typical, but also and perhaps more suggestively denoted a desire on his part to deploy the historically rich and architecturally significant neighbourhood to make his own claims for longevity, a classic and elevated style at once outside of and removed from the relentless system of fashion itself. For this boutique, Armani wanted something 'elegant, luxurious that work[ed] with the surrounding environment' and yet at the same time something that was undeniably his style to mark his presence.[15]

Formerly the British Tourist office, the Paris boutique was designed by Ortelli and run by French socialite Dreda Mele, who also served as an important cultural and social liaison between the two countries. Trimmed in red-briarwood, with pale grey used for the walls and small leather chairs, the look of the store was significantly 'more refined' than the Milan boutique which inspired it. Sparing no expense for this store, Armani stated: 'I wanted my colors ... my look.'[16] For the job, Armani sent 21 Italian construction workers to France, accommodating them for nearly three months. The boutique adhered to the designer's fascination with the 1920s and 1930s, offering customers segmented salons for the womenswear on the ground floor. To help outline smaller independent intimate spaces within the larger space of the boutique, he created interchangeable two-sided briarwood backed chairs and display cases which illuminated accessories and garments from below. In addition, these segmented spaces which showcased different clothing themes (daywear, sportswear, eveningwear) were also demarcated by way of mirrored columns and carpeting. A special fitting room was built a few steps up from the ground floor, to provide a select clientele more privacy. The first floor, which housed the menswear, continued the geometric patterning of the space and displayed the garments along the squared U-shaped circumference which provided an unabashed panoptic purview of the comings and goings on the ground level at whose centre was a staircase connecting the two floors. Here, on the first floor, the small dressing rooms were also located one short step above along a runway-like corridor.

Looking toward the new millennium, Armani commissioned London-based architect Claudio Silvestrin in 1999 to create a new design concept for the renovation of his Giorgio Armani boutiques. Notably, the first to be refitted was not his Milan flagship, but rather the boutique in the French capital. Over the course of six years, Silvestrin would renovate more than 20 boutiques around the world in cities such as Tokyo, Düsseldorf, Atlanta, Moscow, São Paulo, Costa Mesa and London. These many boutiques share in common an absolute and uncompromisingly similar use of materials, design, space and textures. Silvestrin's redesign of the Place Vendôme boutique renewed and improved upon Armani's emphasis on the luxury of space, largely by controlling the manner through which visitors immersed themselves into the boutique, contriving a gradual and segmented approach to the inner sanctum. According to the architect, 'the entrance becomes a poetic pause between the exterior and the display area'.[17] Once inside the entrance, a limestone wall obstructs a complete gaze into the interior of the boutique. A second, smaller area of transition attenuates the effect of slowing down the time of consumption and offering the possibility of contemplation. This space contains only a large stone vase in material identical to the walls and floors. While water is not a feature of the vase, it nonetheless conjures the baptismal fonts displayed prominently in the entrance of Roman Catholic churches.

134   View of the menswear floor of the London boutique designed by Claudio Silvestrin

Mirrors throughout the spaces of display not only operate in a typical way, extending and expanding the sensation of space, but also mark transitional points as the customer moves through the boutique. The lighting also helps to articulate and define the space. As has always been the tradition in a Giorgio Armani boutique, special, soft lighting hidden in the ceiling and embedded in the walls adds a calming and luxurious tone, focusing solely on the garments displayed at exact intervals, an effect translated from the runway in his Milan theatre in via Borgonuovo.

Referring specifically to the new prototype created by Silvestrin, Armani stated: 'I'm always looking to create an environment where the store architecture supports the presentation of the collections in a way that is modern and accessible for our customers.'[18] While each store features a special distinctive and often soothing element such as a water fountain (London) or even a glass waterfall (Milan), Paris importantly served as the initial prototype for the global retail face of Armani. Like numerous high-end designer boutiques, the materials and spaces conjured are consistent with a singularly defined global image so that no matter where the modern customer may find themself, there is comfort in knowing what can be expected in a Giorgio Armani retail space. The exquisitely rare and precious St Maximin, a soft compact cream-coloured stone, is featured throughout the boutiques both for the walls and flooring and is contrasted with the deep Macassar ebony and oxidized brass selected for the furniture and the fixtures designed by Silvestrin. The exclusive and limited use of one type of stone and one type of wood removes any complications or distractions; here architecture is stripped bare of itself, only to reveal the essential of Armani, his textiles hanging on the walls or folded on the display cabinets. For the new Silvestrin design template,

135   Mannequins reminiscent of the silent beauties of the 1920s as conceived by Siégel, though in Armani's case the mannequins are unisex. Square lighting receded in the wall recreates a structuralist and repetitive grid patterning

mannequins were also changed to white unisex forms nearly identical to those advertised by Siégel in Paris in the late 1920s, which announced its mannequins as 'adapted modernism à la mode'.[19]

Modern, pure, timeless and sleek are fitting adjectives to describe this new boutique design more often than not likened to a temple. Referring to Silvestrin's redesign, critic Arian Mostadi claims that '[o]ne could say that time stood still at the precise moment when Place Vendôme was created'.[20] The Paris boutique formed a natural continuity with its outside environment as it extended the stone façades of Place Vendôme and the solemnity of the square, which is also said to have once housed a monastery. Silvestrin has interpreted Armani's classical and modern ethos to create a minimalist space without a hard edge. According to the architect, minimalism should be at once '[s]trong but not intimidating', '[e]legant but not ostentatious',[21] and he speaks of architecture in terms of the 'thickness of space and depth of the world'.[22]

Significantly larger than the Paris boutique, the London location with its complex of rooms was opened up by Silvestrin to create an expansive, ethereal experience. Located on three floors, the new boutique was designed somewhat as a maze, given that it was wrapped around the first two floors of a pre-existing apartment block. In the architect's re-visioning of the space, a labyrinthine series of connecting corridors and staircases connect the various areas of display and consumption. Fitted within the wall of this corridor are square recesses showcasing the holy relics of the fashion industry, that is, women's accessories. Through the expansiveness of space, a luxury in itself, all three floors are connected through various open staircases, lending a panoptic view of the menswear floor in the lower ground level. Light pours in from a special skylight all the way down to this men's area, as if illuminated from a divine source in which adherents are bathed in the illuminated grace of

136   London boutique, view of women's section

137   Menswear floor of the Paris boutique

138   A panoptic view of the menswear floor in the London, Sloane Street boutique

good design. In the menswear sections of this boutique an elongated series of small square recessed glowing spotlights draw attention to the parallel series of men's shirts resting on the Macassar wood drawers, a modernist paean to repetition.

In a world of increasing fast fashion, where customers are called upon more and more to serve themselves (and even rehang garments), minimalist designer boutiques stand out more as spaces of exclusivity marked by reverential service rituals. These spaces are prescriptive antidotes to the rapidity by which we conceive of the world changing around us. Speaking of the sense of the sacred with which Silvestrin imbues his spaces, critic Massimo Vignelli states that

[m]inimalism is not a style, it is an attitude. It is a fundamental reaction against noise, visual noise, disorder, vulgarity. Minimalism is the pursuit of the essence, not the appearance. It is the persistent search for purity, as an expression of unconditional being, the search for serenity, for silence as a presence, for the thickness of spaces, for space as immensity. Minimalism is beyond time – it is timeless, it is noble and simple materials, it is the stillness of perfection, it has to be the being itself.[23]

For Armani's flagship in Milan in Sant'Andrea, Silvestrin emphasized an abundance of empty and ultimately commercially inactive space. The extreme linearity of the Milan store, enhanced by its narrow elongated space on both levels, allowed the architect to create a series of more intimate, individual mini-boutiques, breaking up the space further. For this store, Silvestrin cut into the 1940s façade, receding the entrance away from the pavement to conjure the semblance of an arcade. The entrance boasting a subtle, stone waterfall seamlessly blending into the overall architectural space functions like the vase in the entrance of the Paris boutique, as a sort of poetic and calming pause. Elements like these, despite the commercial aspect of the space, refer back to Silvestrin's deeply philosophical position vis-à-vis the construction of space. For the architect there is no fundamental difference between a retail space and that of a home, after all, '[i]n both you need a place to put your socks'.[24]

Minimalism, according to art historian James Meyer, 'removes any trace of emotion or intuitive decision-making ... Minimal does not allude to anything beyond its literal presence, or its existence in the physical world.'[25] Minimalist painting, and design more broadly, denies illusionist space, its non-representational ethos occludes the body within the visual field of painting, but also denies haptic possibilities. Armani's garments, however, are the agents or conduits for emotional engagement and sensorial responses. Hung

139   Recessed alcoves devoted to the holy relics of contemporary fashion, women's accessories

140   Verticality punctuates the overarching expression and at times overwhelming
experience of space in the London boutique

along the walls the textiles of each specially combined suggested outfit make their presence felt (literally), and conjure the layers of embodied haptic space. Armani has always maintained that a customer 'must feel able to touch the clothes, feel the textures and forget the architectural scale and design'.[26] The large glass window of the Milan boutique allows the customer to see into the entrance on the left, while on the right-hand side one can peer down into the cavernous space which houses a long stone ramp and facing staircase leading into the lower-level menswear floor. On the ground level, the exaggeration of the space's linearity is made tangible by a 40-foot shelf lining the outside of the chasm wall beginning from the entrance and ending at the staircase leading downstairs. Armani's use of Silvestrin as his architect of choice for seven years is significant and speaks to the phenomenological investments Armani places in both his fashion and spatial designs. The writings of the French phenomenologist Maurice Merleau-Ponty have resonated strongly with Silvestrin in the way the philosopher 'attributed more importance to perception'.[27] 'Space', 'orientation' and 'depth', vital to his architectural praxis, were quickly redeveloped to think about meaning through perception and the subjective interaction with objects.[28] For Silvestrin, working through Merleau-Ponty and influenced by Italian minimalist architects like A. G. Fronzoni, perception through feeling supersedes thinking which is ideally suited to the experience of consumption.

Although Milan remains the epicentre of Armani's inspiration and influence, Paris has tacitly informed his approach to the culture of retail. It is here, as we have come to see, that Armani attempts to position himself vis-à-vis the fashion system, and stake a claim for his importance. It is with his Paris boutique where the spatial metaphor that he has 'arrived' on the map takes shape. The move to relocate his store from Place Vendôme to the illustrious Avenue Montaigne in 2006 best embodies my claim. The new Paris boutique

141   View of the men's accessories in the London boutique

is located in the prestigious street known for housing the fashion capital's haute couture salons. With the inauguration of his own haute couture atelier, Giorgio Armani Privé (2005), whose showroom is located at 2 Avenue Montaigne, and by moving his boutique from Place Vendôme to a few feet away from his atelier, Armani definitively marked his claim to the highest order of fashion and made his presence felt on the cultural map of fashion's elite global clientele who descend on Paris twice a year for the collections' showings. Covering slightly more than 400 square metres (4,305 square feet) on two floors the new concept was designed by Armani with a team of in-house architects in collaboration with Silvestrin.

Recognizing the ebb and flow of a city's fashionable places of consumption and display, the designer opted to open on Avenue Montaigne because of

> its place among the world's most prestigious high fashion retail destinations. The street also represents a great symbol of historic European architecture which creates an atmosphere of classic sophistication and elegance. In the design solution for my new boutique I therefore wanted to provide a modern rendition of what is now a by-gone era with the sense of a personal and intimate space where the collections are presented in wardrobes and trunks. The result is intimate and luxurious, a truly personalised experience that perfectly matches the history and grandeur of this world renowned avenue.[29]

In 2003 he inaugurated the Armani/Casa Interior Design Service as a logical extension of his line of home furniture and furnishings. As a result, with this boutique Armani began to increasingly turn to his in-house team of architects and designers not only to create but also furnish his retail interiors. With a slight Oriental flair, while retaining the classic minimalist Armani aesthetic, the Armani/Casa furniture replaced Silvestrin's specially designed chairs and display cabinets made in Macassar wood. The boutique is at once atmospheric, dark and intimate in an attempt to carve out personal space within the very public realm of consumption. On the first floor, where the women's collection is showcased, Armani controls the light completely, obstructing any natural light to pour into the space and alter the effect of the spotlights directed on each garment. As with his specially designed luminescent runway, in this store Armani wants to display the colours in their purest, unadulterated form. Wardrobes and trunks showcase the collections. For the walls, two luxurious and distinctive materials play off each other. Continuity between the two levels of retail space is achieved through the onyx flooring and the furniture. Devoted to menswear, on the ground level the walls are covered with grey horizontally pleated brushed silk, reiterated in the tops of the black lacquered display tables, which creates a sensually smooth yet variegated feel and look. Like on the first floor, the sense of luxury displayed on the ground level is also matched by way of the folding luminescent onyx walls.

142   Façade of 2 Avenue Montaigne, Paris, where the Giorgio Armani Privé salon is located on the second floor

143   View of the first floor womenswear section of the Avenue Montaigne boutique, Paris

On the top level, clearly marked as the inner sanctum of the boutique, the room furthest away from the store's main point of access and staircase showcases women's eveningwear. Seen all over the world at red carpet events, the glamorous eveningwear is presented in a dark and intimate salon. The space of the first floor closes in on itself, and contains the ideals of the Armani world, where even natural light, space and the realm of shadows are controlled. Armani's illuminated ideals are activated by the translucent resin mannequins, which give warmth and an inner glow to the garments. Here the walls are once again pleated brushed silk, but in a black sheen, lending a distinctly glamorous and night-time atmosphere to the room, ideally suited for ball gowns and cocktail dresses. In 2008, inspired by the Avenue Montaigne boutique, Armani moved his Milan flagship from Sant'Andrea to 2 via Montenapoleone, making it the largest free-standing Giorgio Armani boutique in the world. Situated within the historically rich sixteenth-century Palazzo Taverna, the space was once occupied by one of Milan's most important poets, Carlo Porta (1775–1821). Comprising three floors over 2,000 square metres (21,528 square feet), the store was designed by Armani's in-house architects. As if an extension of his own home, in this store interior design and fashion harmonize more intimately and completely, enhanced further on the ground floor where accessories from the Armani/Casa furnishings collection are displayed side-by-side with accessories for men and women, reminding his clients of the seamlessness of his complete lifestyle proposition.

144   View of the first floor womenswear section of the Avenue Montaigne boutique, Paris

The designer life-world Armani creates is akin to Benjamin's notion of phantasmagoria. In his *Arcades Project* Benjamin defines phantasmagoria explicitly through Adorno verbatim, which he himself defined against the background of Marx's notion of the commodity fetish. According to Benjamin, then, phantasmagoria is defined

> as a consumer item in which there is no longer anything that is supposed to remind us how it came into being. It becomes a magical object, insofar as the labor stored up in it comes to seem supernatural and sacred at the very moment when it can no longer be recognized as labor.[30]

In a post-industrial culture and specifically within a Giorgio Armani boutique, the cash registers and the monetary transaction of consumption, which point to economic realities and financial networks, are eliminated from plain view and occur in a small back room on the ground level where, usually, the garments are wrapped in specially printed tissue paper, boxed if necessary and placed in carrier bags. As part of this sensory experience one becomes captivated by the commodity, luring us further into the quiet, assuming spectacle, the phantasmagoria.[31] This captivation is elicited in phenomenological architecture which honours a 'pronounced intensification of presence' marked out by a potential to be at once 'mysterious' and 'enlivening'.[32] The introduction of phantasmagoria at this juncture is not simply to think about the way consumers are lured into a false sense of reality through consumption within the capitalist system, stripping any degree of agency and free will, but more specifically to illuminate the way the designer manipulates light and shadow to evoke sensory experiences. Phantasmagoria elicits, entices, a play with the senses. Referring back to the definition of the Aesthetic, we recall how it is defined as the apprehension of beauty through the senses. Armani's orchestration of space itself conjures perfectly the corporeal and sensorial apprehension of Armani's moral aesthetic code. With every store the designer creates, the spatial and visual configuration continues to reinforce a desired aesthetic experience and his imperial control.

145   Outside façade of the most recent Giorgio Armani boutique in Milan in via Montenapoleone

North America: Conquering the New World

In an interview with journalist Daniela Morera in 1977, Armani summarized what would become his retail and distribution philosophy:

> we have a small, very exclusive production for the moment. Even in Italy, Germany and England, where we are very famous, we sell to just one boutique in each town. So, who is able to buy an Armani suit is a privilege. We have so many demands, we are going bananas.[33]

His almost instant success was initially tempered by the company's inadequate industrial network for production and distribution. However, Galeotti and Armani were quick to harness over-distribution of their products, fearing too rapid growth, oversaturation of key markets and loss of control of the company's image. Galeotti's zealous control of the retail distribution of the Giorgio Armani collection began in earnest in the North American market, parallel with the inauguration of the company's first wholly-owned free-standing boutique in New York in spring 1984.

By the time Armani opened his boutique at 815 Madison Avenue, near 68th Street in February 1984, Versace had already opened a 260 square metre (2,800 square foot) boutique across the street and Missoni was about to follow suit down the block. The area between 60th and 80th Street along Madison Avenue had been an upscale retail district for decades. By the mid-1980s the street's identity was shifting to contain increasingly more high-end European designer boutiques and by 1986 the overwhelming European, particularly Italian, presence on the prestigious avenue was recognized as part of the continued success of the Italian fashion industry as well as the trend toward a more pronounced global presence in key markets. 'We located here because we wanted to keep a European flavour, and Madison is the most European street in New York', said Pierfilippo Pieri, a spokesman for Giorgio Armani. 'Physically the buildings are lower, there aren't any skyscrapers.' Unlike Fifth Avenue, the pace and tempo of Madison Avenue was slower, more conducive to gazing, window shopping and in effect the lifestyle shopping the designers were now interested in cultivating.[34]

Many viewed it as an exercise in image building. *The New York Times* reported that '[i]t is popularly believed that many European merchants are on Madison Avenue to create a prestige presence for themselves and to build business for their wholesale divisions rather than to make profits on their retail operations there'.[35] Madison Avenue's shift in identity marked a significant initial stage in the global expansion of designer culture. Given that the rent for the five-storey, 929 square metre (10,000 square foot) Georgian brownstone that Giorgio Armani rented had doubled in the span of five years from $150 to a then staggering $300 per square foot, a spokesperson for the designer was quick to stress that the move was 'not a public relations venture, it's a business'.[36] Gabriella Forte adamantly dismissed the promotion-rather-than-profits idea. 'The Europeans are like Americans', she claimed. 'They don't do anything unless they make money. Would you move into a space just for the fun of it? Who is saying this? American retailers? They are nuts.'[37] In fact, projected sales for the new store were $3,500,000 for the first year alone.[38] Leased by antiques dealer Ginsburg and Levy to Giorgio Armani for $660,000 a year,[39] the store was a replica of the Milan boutique and not nearly as sophisticated and luxurious as the yet to be opened Paris location. The first three floors carried the Giorgio Armani, Emporio Armani and children's lines, while the top two floors housed showrooms and offices.

146   Façade of the first New York store at 815 Madison Avenue

Controversy surrounding the house's desire to enhance the new New York boutique's retail presence and image began during Milan's autumn 1984 fashion week, when Armani's women's collection was overshadowed by the company's move to pull its line from a number of smaller retailers in both Canada and the USA. The controversy was fuelled by the brewing feud between *International Herald Tribune* columnist Hebe Dorsey who was engaged in a war of words with Bepe Modenese, claiming that the Italians are only interested in money. Dorsey immediately singled out Giorgio Armani for its closure of an account with a retailer which hadn't sold enough of its products for the previous two seasons. Things worsened when the bouncers at Armani's Erreuno runway presentation roughed up Dorsey's accompanying photographer, who happened to be her son. In a dismissive swipe of her pen, Dorsey simply wrote of Armani's significant collection: 'Their attitude has to change.'[40] The situation was exacerbated further at the spring/summer 1985 collections when retailers gathered in Milan preoccupied less about the shows themselves than about whether they would be allowed to continue to sell the Giorgio Armani line. Rumours were circulating among North American buyers that Armani had designs on cancelling contracts with all but two of his New York retailers. While this did not materialize, Galeotti did cancel all stores with consistently low budgets for the line, which amounted to $20,000 or less per season. In the end, seven doors in both Canada and USA were closed to the designer's collection. 'As a company, we do not impose minimum dollar amounts on our clients', claimed Galeotti. 'But if a small amount is spread through deliveries, it's no good for the image of Armani or for the store, because it doesn't keep enough merchandise in stock to develop an Armani customer.'[41] Armani's move in New York and the region was not unusual, nor was it a one-time initiative. In Germany, for example, when the house opened its own freestanding boutiques, the designer pulled the Emporio Armani label from 150 clients and from 10 others, the Giorgio Armani collection. The move was meant to give the lines more cachet and the allure of exclusivity, which in turn served to enhance the identity of its wearers who were considered to be in the know. Throughout the 1980s and into the 1990s, Armani boutiques were never listed in local telephone directories; his boutiques were sought out, and clients had to know where to go. Image for the house was endemic to its success from the beginning, and Armani has always maintained that his boutiques and outlets carrying his Giorgio Armani black label collection needed to clearly articulate the correct and consistent image he wanted to project to the customers for whom he designed. Even in these early years of the house's history, he recognized the need for a clarity and consistency of vision toward educating retailers and customers. He himself later claimed that, '[i]t's fundamental to know retailing because you know your customer. You can control and improve the product and also educate the public – the maximum way to function as a designer.'[42] In these seemingly ruthless manoeuvres we can clearly identify the embryo of lifestyle branding before the concept was thrown around by corporate global retail giants who have since taken over the fashion industry. Image, to the house's success, was fiercely maintained by Galeotti who also threatened to discontinue the line from stores poorly displaying the clothes.

Meanwhile in Toronto, retailers were also lamenting the city's and the country's loss of the Giorgio Armani label. Since the late 1970s, Torontonian women and men had enjoyed their own Giorgio Armani boutique in Hazelton Lanes, an exclusive upscale mall in downtown Toronto. As Krystyne Griffin, president of DWS Retail, which owned the Armani boutique, explained: 'Armani is a cult, a mentality, it's esoteric ... It's not for every day, though you can look infinitely original in Armani.' According to Griffin, the 50 or so women who were regular devotees spent between $10,000 and $25,000 a year in the store, with average sales of $2,000 to $3,000 per visit. She also advocated

the early cult-like status associated with Armani, present almost from the outset, aided greatly from the initial and purposefully limited accessibility to the label. Armani, she claimed, is 'a discipline, it's a bit of tyranny really. And it's very hard to teach people who are timid about themselves.'[43] Self-assurance and a *soupçon* of fashion forwardness have always been endemic to Armani's collections, and perhaps for this reason Canadian men have never been privy to their own Giorgio Armani black label boutique experience since the Hazelton Lanes boutique closed in 1982. In a number of discussions with various sales associates and managers, the conclusion was resoundingly clear: Giorgio Armani's main collection for men is considered too 'fashiony' for an overwhelmingly conservative Canadian male clientele who often wish to blend in rather than outshine peers. As Griffin stated of Armani's uniqueness: 'His originality is undisputed, he's better than anybody, but he's for a leader in fashion, for a woman [and a man] who never wants to run into herself[/himself].'[44]

With the closure of the Hazelton Lanes store, Chez Catherine remained the only retailer to carry a small portion of the collection. However, by 1985 it too was under threat. Declaring Armani as 'the single most important designer at work in the world today', *The Globe and Mail* reported on the continuing challenges experienced by stores such as Chez Catherine, which was being forced to buy the diffusion (white label) line in addition to the black label collection.[45] The problem, according to the Toronto retailer, was that deliveries for the main line were not keeping pace with the North American retail season, invariably arriving long after most women had already made their major purchases for the season. This was a common complaint heard throughout the industry. In addition the store was not interested in purchasing the GFT produced diffusion line, but only and exclusively the black label collection. According to Stephanie Hill of Chez Catherine '[t]he fashion image is the couture line and their capacity [to produce it] is full until they get re-organized. But it's like a love-affair, when it's the top, you keep going back.'[46] However, consolidating the house's retail network and image did not seem to translate into better and more consistent delivery patterns. As late as 1989 retailers remained unimpressed with the shipping and delivery times for the men's black label and GFT collections, often claiming their shipments were at times incomplete, at least for independent retailers.[47]

The concept of a pre-season capsule collection developed around 1982 and by 1988 included 50 to 100 pieces that gradually, through the season, folded into a main collection, with no distinction in style, label or theme. The difference between pre-season and mainline collections is that buyers usually spend at least 50 per cent of their budgets for a given designer on these pre-season offerings, mostly to ensure swift and timely delivery and guarantee the best options for regular clients. With most factories closed in August in Italy and France, North American women have usually already made their purchases for the fall season before September. These pre-fall clothes make their way to the stores by June or July at the latest. They do not want to lose out on those important 'must-have' items, which often sell out early in the season. However, the growing pains to which Hill and other retailers refer in terms of both production and distribution were also intimately connected with the house's desire to maintain the integrity of its image. As Forte made clear:

> It is not up to us to tell stores what they should buy, but we are not interested in just selling more. The impact of Armani is very cohesive ... At this point if any store wants to carry the couture line they have to make a real commitment, which is why today, if any department or speciality stores carry it, and it is rare, especially for the men's line, there has to be a designated area, often mimicking one of the designer's boutiques.[48]

The Canadian market would not see its own Giorgio Armani boutique until September 1987 when national retailer Holt Renfrew opened two in-store women's boutiques in both Montreal and Toronto, styled after the Paris location. On hand for the celebrations were Lee Radziwill and Gina DiBernardo, the London, Ontario native who worked as Armani's house model and who confessed to wearing his designs along with Donna Karan in her personal life.[49]

While some retailers were downsized out of existence, others were increasing and accelerating their relationship with the designer. In the USA department stores have always been a crucial facet of the designer business. Barney's as we have already seen was the first to carry the Giorgio Armani collection for both men and women soon after the designer began showing under his own label. Armani was in fact one of the first European designers to consistently force retailers to commit to devoting exclusive floor space and environments which mirrored his own boutiques to ensure continuity. These unique and specially designed in-store boutiques were crucial for the department stores as these spaces provided ideal venues to hold twice-annual shows in the correct and inspired location. These shows have increasingly become important over the years for designers. Usually occurring sometime between the runway presentation in Milan and the beginning of the season, department store trunk events showcase a designer's entire collection, whether they sell the items or not. According to one Giorgio Armani representative: 'Many of the special pieces shown on the runway never even hit the floor. They're all reserved for the trunk shows. We might have 20 of the hot style in various sizes, but there'll be a waiting list of 65 for them'.[50] Customers who stroll into the boutiques throughout the season are often unable to locate or purchase key pieces from the collection, which they might have seen in pictures from the runway presentations.

In October 1985 New York retailer Bergdorf Goodman opened a new, expanded Giorgio Armani boutique, which for the first time coupled womenswear with menswear in one single space. '[B]y combining the two, we will have a stronger Armani business', said Dawn Mello of the department store's unorthodox decision. 'We believe men and women shop together for certain kinds of clothes', she concluded. 'For men's and women's, the point of view is quite similar.'[51] In this retail configuration Armani's notoriety for gender blending and crossing over fashion ideas and textiles is made spatially tangible and compelling. By combining the two previously separate spaces Bergdorf established itself early as a retailer committed to maintaining and advancing a cohesive image for the Giorgio Armani collection, as well as a unified gendered ideal endemic to the designer's ethos. Although today the men's and women's collections are housed in separate spaces (in separate buildings), the exclusive retailer has consistently maintained an excellent relationship with the designer, more often than not enjoying continuous sales growth.

Ensuring his success in North America's most important retail and advertising Mecca was not the only project underway at the end of the 1980s as part of the designer's attempt to consolidate and control his image. In 1988, after seven successful years of collaboration with Hollywood, the house opened a 1,207 square metre (13,000 square foot) boutique on the famed Rodeo Drive in Beverly Hills, a street Armani had previously maintained he would never open a store on. With this spectacular boutique, whose design was luxurious and markedly unlike any of his other stores, Armani set out to establish his

147   Façade of the Giorgio Armani Beverly Hills boutique

image not simply within the city, but around the globe by single-handedly taking the red carpet upmarket through the immense public relations system of Hollywood. Given the location of the boutique and Armani's by then global reputation, the move paid off. Don Tronstein, the owner of the building that both Armani and Ralph Lauren occupy, claims that between 40 and 60 per cent of sales come from tourists,[52] a likely similar number for most Giorgio Armani boutiques in major cities and tourist destinations.

Along with the new boutique, the designer also hired Wanda McDaniel, previously a social columnist and well connected to Hollywood's elite through her film director husband (Albert Ruddy), as a special liaison to Armani's increasing film industry clientele. One year later, both the new store and McDaniel proved to be a brilliant force to be reckoned with. When Billy Crystal hosted the 62nd Academy Awards, he not only wore a Giorgio Armani tuxedo, but four different ones throughout the evening's televised event. Three of the tuxedoes required fittings, while the fourth came from his own closet. Service, beyond simply offering clothing, was premium for his A-list clientele and when Crystal was having troubles with his bow tie, Armani sent along a representative from the new boutique to assist him backstage the night of the awards.[53] By 1991 the annual award event was dubbed the 'Armani Awards' by *Women's Wear Daily*. Turning celebrity marketing into an art form, Armani's use of film stars as human billboards at that precise moment proved to be the most significant in the history of the relationship between designer and actress because it also intersected with, if not propelled, the initial proliferation of red carpet media reporting. Soon Armani and the space of the red carpet became inextricably linked. This conjuncture moved both the designer and the award night celebrity culture into new uncharted global territory. By the 1970s studios no longer gave or lent clothes to their stars, leaving them to fend for themselves, often with extravagantly dire consequences. Armani and his staff, both past and present, have staunchly maintained that he does not pay celebrities to wear his creations. A-list clients who either present at award ceremonies or who are nominated for awards are given their clothes and they are altered in the Rodeo Drive boutique. A second tier of celebrities is given clothing on loan, to be returned in pristine condition after the event. According to McDaniel, originally '[i]t starts out as, "Oh my God, Armani is going to let me wear something!" It was like a privilege coming into the inner sanctum, it has a mystique.'[54] By 1997, however, mystique turned into greed. In that year, things were already out of control when Lauren Holly famously received 56 free dresses from 13 different designers. In fact, the event greatly stimulated the emergence of the celebrity stylist, who would now broker with the designer on behalf of the star client and massage financial kickbacks, a move that would forever alter the direct rapport between designer and wearer.

148   Autumn/winter 1991; autumn/winter 1995. Both outfits were worn by Jodie Foster at the annual Academy Awards, who was not only one of the first to wear his creations on the red carpet, but has remained a faithful devotee of and friend to the designer

For the opening of the Beverly Hills boutique, Armani hosted one of the most eagerly anticipated and coveted black tie events on the Los Angeles social calendar at the Museum of Contemporary Art on 27 January 1988, to which he made a substantial donation. With the art taken down as a protective measure (though clearly also an aesthetic manoeuvre), the first room was devoted to the recreation of his Milan Borgonuovo theatre to showcase his spring/summer 1988 men's and women's collections, a shrewd move given that city's warm clime. Referring to the fashion show, Forte stated the day after: 'Personally, I look at the clothes and I look at the audience, and I see no relation... These things take time and education; little by little they evolve.'[55] What was required was an act of translation on the part of Armani staffers in the USA. Like language, the semantics of a clothing aesthetic can be taught, the skills gained. Sartorial knowledge, like any language, is not inherent, but culturally acquired.

A second space swathed in draping white fabric was devoted to the three-course (Italian) dinner prepared by famed LA restauranteur Wolfgang Puck of Spago followed by a dance reception for the 250 specially invited guests. Leading up to the event, New York-based social coordinator Lee Radziwill who co-hosted the event was criticized in surprisingly numerous articles by dismayed *Los Angeles Times* columnists for not being aware of the city's A-list celebrities. As one columnist reported, the event was 'sending tremors along [the] city's fashionable fault line. It will probably be a very lovely evening – but it becomes much more important to be there when it's clear that you can't buy an invite.'[56] However, those included on the list, it was made clear, were not simply guests from the neighbourhood, but friends of the designer from across the USA and the world, including French socialite and Armani attaché Dreda Mele. Many disgruntled LA A-listers were left without a ticket as a result.

For the Rodeo Drive site, Armani hired London-based restaurateur Mr Chow who claimed responsibility not only for designing the store, but also for hiring staff and setting it up. Chow described the boutique as 'classic modern', where '[n]othing will be cheap'.[57] Indeed it was not, costing $4 million as an investment for a substantial future pay-off beyond anyone's expectations. First-day sales for the first four hours were $70,000, with an equal number of invitations sent out weeks in advance.[58] According to Forte the store generated over $7 million in sales the first year alone.[59] First through the doors were Armani-devotees Arnold Schwarzenegger and his then wife Maria Shriver. The store has a 12 metre (40 foot) exterior façade of glass and steel grids allowing light to pour into the ground and first floor levels, a sharp contrast to the dark and mysterious spaces of the New York boutique. The 464 square metre (5,000 square foot) selling space on the ground level is devoted to womenswear, along with a small mezzanine level located at the far back. Ascending the store's focal point, a dual staircase of painted steel, one initially arrives at a second mezzanine level which showcases accessories for both men and women and from which one has a perfect purview of the entire ground level, a controlling panoptic gaze recurring in a number of the designer's important boutiques. From there one moves to the 464 square metre (5,000 square foot) first floor devoted to menswear. As with the women's floor, suits are hung off steel pegs equidistant along the circumference, each accompanied by two top shelves to display shirts or pullovers, well-matched to the suits hanging below. As with every freestanding and in-shop boutique, Armani stipulates the exact distance between each hanger; a regulation stringently imposed and scrutinized by the New York office. The display shelves and pegs are attached (though movable) to specially designed gold-leafed panels fastened to the wall. These sumptuous panels are set against luminescent white marble floors and plush beige carpets. For the store Armani 'wanted a boutique like his runway and his runway is based on changing light … Los Angeles' natural environment is sunshine all the time, and we wanted to imitate the light outside and inside.'[60] Each carpeted area also contains its own Macassar ebony wood display case, chair and a gold leaf upright shelving unit. These specially designated, intimate shop-within-shop areas are each devoted to a unique facet of the Armani collection: a tuxedo shop, cashmere shop, sportswear and business suit shops, for example. Interesting is that while small furnishings have changed since the boutique's debut, it is the only store never to have undergone any redesign or renovation. In addition to these selling spaces, 278 square metres (3,000 square feet) on the first floor are used for executive offices, a full kitchen and lockers for staff and warehouse facilities. Chow would also later design a Las Vegas boutique for Giorgio Armani which kept to the same design principles as the Beverly Hills store, save for the pod-like chamber display cases and mannequins whose heads were replaced with small television monitors.

With at most two of each garment displayed on any given unit, only 70 per cent of the styles are displayed at any one time, requiring the staff to constantly replenish and re-merchandize the floor. Garments are located in backroom storage spaces, accessed only by way of a security code. In Armani-owned boutiques around the world staff are given two complete regulation Armani navy blue suits, often of wool crepe, and an equally small number of shirts or blouses which are specially designed to represent that season's significant suit and unique shirt, usually worn without tie. Managers are identified by their more formal grey attire. At the end of the season staff is given the choice to purchase the garments at a significantly discounted rate. 'Discreet, quiet' are the terms used to describe the overpowering, omnipresent Armani aesthetic ideal. To this end, salespeople in Armani's boutiques are said to be given a manual outlining 'rules of appearance, down to the hair and makeup' to ensure that the 'Armani image [which] consists of fresh, non-pretentious elegance and ease' is maintained and exhibited.[61] Armani has stated that '[t]he purpose of the Giorgio Armani stores is to put my spirit on display in a concentrated and well-expressed way'.[62] The attractive staff, sporting the latest silhouette, walk in a soft, smooth controlled manner, which coupled with the space itself mimics the runway presentations, an additional layer to the way Armani controls the complete harmonious lifestyle image and empire born in his Milan headquarters and translated across the globe to various outposts.

In 1990, with $1.6 billion worth of Armani products purchased, revenues of $306 million and a global network of 35 Giorgio Armani boutiques (14 wholly owned by the house), in no way did the designer's controlled retail vision relax. Boasting exceptional profit margins of 55 per cent in Europe and between 60 to 70 per cent in the USA, Galeotti's former manoeuvre of pulling the line from low-performing retailers was maintained by Armani himself, much to the surprise of financial analysts. When Saks Fifth Avenue's Houston Giorgio Armani boutique fell short of the designer's minimum sales requirement of $750,000, Armani simply shut the shop down, despite the loss of sales and profits. Meanwhile, in 1991 the department store's Giorgio Armani shop in New York sold $400,000 worth of womenswear in the month of September alone, up from $300,000 from the previous year's same month sales. Notably these significant increases were sharply contrasted with numerous other designers' sagging sales at the tony Fifth Avenue luxury purveyor.[63]

149   The Giorgio Armani Las Vegas boutique with its gold leaf walls and monitor-headed mannequins designed by Michael Chow

150   Interior shot of the Beverly Hills boutique, menswear floor

With the Giorgio Armani boutique at 815 Madison Avenue flourishing, enhanced by a consolidated and controlled network of highly successful department store outlets, Barney's move in 1993 to open a second luxury emporium a mere eight blocks away posed a significant challenge for the designer. The equilibrium on the retail landscape he had spent years contriving was now being threatened by Barney's desire to sell the Giorgio Armani black label men's and women's collections in their new store. What this meant was that the exclusive and expensive men's black label collection would be available in three different doors while the women's sold in five stores in the same district, each blocks away from the other. The ensuing feud between Armani and Barney's reached an arbitration tribunal in Geneva, which in the end ruled in favour of the chic, upscale New York emporium. In a statement following the tribunal's decision, the designer claimed that while he would adhere to the rulings he wished to make clear that he had signed the contract with the retailer in 1979, under entirely different conditions and circumstances. In addition, the tribunal also ruled that he did not have to let them sell in their other stores across the country. As a retaliatory act, Armani discontinued selling his line to the retailer's Houston and Dallas locations. The designer's diffusion white label collection was never a factor in these rulings, given that the contract between them was signed before the label was sold in the USA. As a result nothing was to change according to a spokesperson for GFT. Interestingly the feud between the two parties developed at the same time that Ralph Lauren also pulled its lines from the Barney's Uptown Madison Avenue and legendary 17th Street downtown stores.[64]

As if to compete and mark an ever-greater presence in New York Armani commissioned architect and interior designer Peter Marino in 1996 to design a new and significantly larger boutique at 760 Madison Avenue, a few blocks south of where the original store stood. Marino gained a reputation as a retail architect with an impressive roster of clients within and beyond the fashion industry. He was also responsible for the renovation of the designer's Milan seventeenth-century palazzo in via Borgonuovo; the designer's choice was significant, not only because Marino's spare aesthetic was in keeping with his own minimalist rigour, but also because the designer wanted to translate 'a familiar atmosphere similar to that of a friend's home' into the space of the boutique.[65] However, despite Armani's best efforts to conjure a homely space, the reception of the boutique was less than friendly.

The proposed building designs were presented to Manhattan's Community Board 8 for approval; the Board voted 14 to 12 to send the proposal back for changes. The Board members who voted against the project felt it was ill-suited for its Upper East Side historical surrounding. However, Shelley S. Friedman, a lawyer for the designer, stated that the 'minimalist building reflects the artistic values of Giorgio Armani'.[66] Although minor adjustments were suggested and concessions were made, the final plan kept within

151   Façade of the Peter Marino-designed Madison Avenue Giorgio Armani boutique which drew heavy criticism for its failure to integrate itself more fully with the local architectural culture

Marino's and Armani's minimalist vision. In the end, Marino deferred to the strict codes established by the New York City Landmarks Preservation Commission by keeping the boutique's height at 18 metres (61 feet), flush with those of its neighbouring brownstones. To add some architectural detail or slight decorative flourish, the architect also incorporated a recessed bay and centrally placed terrace on the second and third floors. Critic Ned Cramer claimed that Marino attempted to 'echo the Italian designer's sophisticated clothes through a minimalist wrapper for his new store. But other than adhering to Adolf Loos' axiom that ornament is crime, his rectilinear architecture turns its back on Modernism's basic tenets.' He continued: 'To mask the building's awkwardness, and to relieve his clear discomfort with unadorned surfaces, Marino employs an extravagant material palette on the interior.'[67] Although Cramer spared barely enough ink to mention the boutique's interior as well as its furnishings, like many detractors he saved his hostility for the outside, that is, the façade. Critics such as Cramer suffer from a sort of superficial physiognomic reading of architecture, ignoring the spatial dimension within and beyond the space created by the designer and what it might suggest about the development of minimalist architecture and its relationship to consumption, display and public space. As a method of ascertaining meaning through surfaces, a physiognomic reading, I wish to suggest, is not dissimilar to the minimalist *Geist* itself. Minimalist space and architecture allow for the brand's identity to be clearly articulated, ensuring the consumer-viewer is neither distracted nor dissuaded from the goal, that is, the purchase of a lifestyle. In the New York boutique, boundaries are created – both perceived and material. Heterotopias, Foucault states, 'always presuppose a system of opening and closing that both isolates them and makes them penetrable. In general, the heterotopic site is not freely accessible like a public place ... To get in one must have a certain permission and make certain gestures'.[68] For the New York store the solidity of the cream-coloured repetitive panels of French limestone used for the façade is counterposed with the purported transparency of the glass panels featured in the central portion of the building. Yet, the glass panels located on the ground floor forbid the viewer's visual access to the boutique's interior spaces, due to the wood panelled walls, which serve as a backdrop to the displays. Armani concludes that

> [f]or me the shop window is just a space where you make clothes 'live'. It should be structure-less and the product should be immersed, almost suspended within it [not unlike many of his advertising campaigns]. Lighting is vital: it shouldn't create harsh contrasts. A shop window can be big or small: what's important is to get the right ration between the item on display and its distance to the glass.[69]

On the first to third floors, thick scrims divide the outside from the inside, allowing some light to pour in, while obstructing the view and maintaining the heterotopic exclusivity of the space. The only visibility given to the pedestrian is through the central glass entrance populated by a doorman. While the scrims function as curtains, they remain uncompromising backdrops to the minimalist displays of mannequins featured in the windows on the ground level. By way of the seemingly intrusive minimalist architecture as well as the scrims, the Armani boutique clearly sets itself apart from the neighbourhood and outside public space and is beholden only to its own rules, rituals and regulations. Shop minimalism, with its spare display of objects, is not unlike the minimalism of a modern art gallery; it stands to represent importance through the creation of an aura of originality and exclusivity.

Within a minimalist landscape, as a sort of immediate experience, the embodied subject enters the rarefied realm of fashion and is impelled to create its own narrative, its own sensorial perceptions of the spaces of fashion. The minimalist 'aesthetic of emptiness initially attracts the gaze of passers-by and, as the naked walls offer no further distraction, attracts them magnetically to the strategically placed goods'.[70] Once inside the boutique, luxury, while restrained, is subtly perceived in the ebonized French wood floors which are partially covered with thick and soft custom-made grey or espresso

152 A corner mannequin display of the Madison Avenue boutique focuses attention on the garments rather than on the interior space of the store

woven linen carpets that help to designate unique spaces of consumption, each suggesting its own narrative. The individual sales rooms, which flank either side of each floor's central sales areas, have walls of French limestone, bleached ceruse, curly hickory or bleached anigre against whose surfaces pegs feature complete outfits, hung equidistant from each other. Not unlike the manner in which the critics viewed the design of the building, Armani invites his visitors to participate in a form of surface readings by way of the garments' textiles; after all it is the textiles which tell the story of each season.

To celebrate the opening of this and a new Emporio Armani boutique also located on Madison Avenue, Armani planned a one-week trip to the American city. With numerous special events planned, the week was packed with interviews and parties, including a concert for 900 featuring musical entertainment by the Fugees, D'Angelo, Eric Clapton and the Wallflowers, all received by a glowing, enthusiastic and dancing Armani. To acknowledge and thank the designer for his continued success and high sales, the top four department stores (Barney's, Bergdorf Goodman, Bloomingdales and Saks Fifth Avenue) featured specially designed Armani window displays, 'in what amount[ed] to a rare simultaneous window dressing effort'. When asked if the new mega-store on Madison would put a crimp in department store sales, one spokesperson from Saks believed there were enough Armani customers in or

153   Interior view of the Madison Avenue boutique

visiting the city to warrant more space devoted to the designer stating: 'We all buy Armani differently.'[71] However, the accolades quickly led to controversy and confusion. In a now infamous *New York* magazine cover story of the designer with the bold headline, 'Giorgio Armani says fashion is finished', the designer declared: 'Fashion is finished for me, the diktat is finished'. The declaration was quickly taken up by the press around the world. In a follow-up interview with *The Sunday Telegraph*, Armani attempted damage control by asserting that '[t]his did not mean that I would stop designing. What it did mean was an end to the changing fads of every season, which no longer made sense.'[72] In part the confusion suggested a new era for Armani, one in which his former right-hand Forte was no longer there to insulate and translate Armani's ideas. However, as *The New York Times* made clear,

> no one will ever speak for Mr. Armani again. Or insulate him. The Giorgio Armani who came last week and conquered New York was not a man in a tower. He was a man who wanted to meet Glenn Close, dance with Mira Sorvino and hug Winona Ryder. After years of reclusive power, Mr Armani wants to interact in the world he has worked so hard to create.[73]

While the two store openings were meant to clearly demonstrate Armani's staying power and retail prowess, the publicity and social events initiated by younger Armani aids was a way 'to help overcome the perception that the house was out of touch'.[74] The results were positive, showing a lighter, happier side of Armani. It also announced the end of the Forte era with her tight grip on all forms of communication. 'In the past', Armani said of her power, 'when Gabriella was around, there was a filter. Gabriella would filter information or adopt ideas that came from people in the company as her own.'[75] What the power struggle amounted to was clearly a question of who possessed the rights and control over translation within and beyond the house. However, while Forte's form of translation through filtering was no longer part of the Armani press engine, the designer's own voice was becoming increasingly clearer and more ferocious toward his competing compatriots. When on tour of the recently opened Barney's Madison Avenue location, Armani was less than pleased to find that his menswear shop shared the complete first floor with Prada, who had begun to steal the spotlight away from him. Recognizing that he had fallen from the headlines and spotlight, a very annoyed Armani retaliated once again by attacking the press: 'In the newspapers we read I'm not in fashion. No? Well, I'm very happy to be unfashionable when my clothes fly out the store. Fashion that people don't wear but gets exalted in the press doesn't interest me.'[76] Armani is not alone in this sentiment, as Gene Pressman of Barney's quite correctly pointed out: 'There hasn't been a change since Giorgio Armani.'[77] Armani has continued to dominate the sales at this and other retailers.

$2.95 • SEPTEMBER 16, 1996

NEW YORK

GIORGIO ARMANI

SAYS FASHION IS FINISHED

OTHER PRONOUNCEMENTS FROM THE TOP OF THE HEAP. BY REBECCA MEAD

154   Controversial cover of New York from 1996 featuring Armani declaring the death of fashion

Once again proving his fighting resilience, staying power and vision toward the future, Armani opened a new mega-store at the corner of Fifth Avenue at 56th Street in autumn 2008 amid the worst recession since the 1930s. Dubbed 'Guggenheim Two' by New York Mayor Bloomberg because of its overwhelming spiralling central staircase, designed by Massimiliano and Doriana Fuksas, the store offers all of Armani's lifestyle labels under one roof. Occupying a former Hugo Boss boutique, the 4,366 square metre (47,000 square foot) store is meant as a present to the designer himself as well as to the city of New York on the twenty-fifth anniversary of the creation of his subsidiary American Giorgio Armani Corp. The store is the crowning jewel of the company's three-year $100 million investment in expanding its

USA wholesale and retail operations. Risky, the move dispels the current conventional notion that established brands can no longer experience any substantial retail growth. The mega multi brand boutique features the various Armani lifestyle fashion labels (Giorgio Armani, Emporio Armani, Armani/ Jeans, Armani/Junior and Armani/Casa) as well as restaurant, sweetshop and beauty boutique. Dubbed 'Armani World' by W magazine, the store according to the designer is meant to be 'flexible, open and eclectic'.[78] What is unique about this strategy of bringing together the various family members of the Armani brand under one roof is the creation of a harmonious integrated whole, rather than sell each label as a unique and separated entity as the house did throughout the 1980s and 1990s. 'In 2000 with the opening of Armani/ Via Manzoni in Milan', Armani stated, 'we pioneered a new type of multi-faceted retail destination catering to the growing desire that I noticed among fashion and lifestyle consumers to be able to enjoy an all round experience when they go shopping'.[79] Armani's vertical diversification has allowed him to recreate his own department store, or conceptual epicentre, with its democratizing ethos, which displays the designer's prowess not only with one segment-targeted brand, but with numerous ones displaying his diversity and mainstream appeal. Part of this multi-brand experience is to engender greater access to fashion for a greater number of people. According to Armani:

> One of my guiding principles has always been a sense of democracy through my various collections. Armani/Fifth Avenue will be the retail essence of that sense of Armani democracy, as it will be a space in which customers at every level will be welcomed and where they will feel at home. In many ways the spirit of this new store will reflect the way we increasingly see the world today: international, cosmopolitan, multi-cultural and above all contemporary.[80]

The store allows the customer to consume all aspects of Armani's complex and layered lifestyle brand, while also providing new clients entry into this world by placing lower-priced goods alongside more exclusive items. The strategy seems financially astute and contemporary in keeping with the new fashion ethos of mixing high street and designer goods with low-priced fast-fashion items. In the context of this and other multi-brand outlets, it also offers its clients a complete sensorial experience, where every sense is activated, mobilized and satisfied within this architecture for the care of the self.

While it is still too premature to determine the success of the store, when on a visit to it in January 2010, problems were clearly present. Upon several return visits to the store, sales associates on the menswear floors especially were markedly uninterested in helping me or my shopping companion, ignoring us altogether. Their lack of interest was due in large part to the fact they were busying themselves with chatting, laughing and playing around with each other. On several occasions I rarely saw a salesperson helping a customer, an image which belies not only Armani's desire to conjure the

155 Dubbed 'Guggenheim Two' by New York Mayor Bloomberg, the latest Armani multi-brand boutique in Fifth Avenue is as much a showpiece as an emporium for the various labels which comprise the Armani brand

correct image but also the very real economic situation of the period. Save for the ground level, which benefits from large, expansive windows, the black furnishings, fixtures and ceilings made for a nearly impossible visual experience. According to one of the sales staff, when Armani was at the store over the Christmas holidays the thought was to paint the ceilings white to add some necessary lightness to the space and garments. However, in keeping with his keen and obsessive attention to light and shadow, Armani elected to make the space darker, himself pushing the large display racks away from the light. Seemingly contradictory, he recognized that the only 'true light' was found in the changing rooms. While a rather limited space, it is in this most private of the public space of the boutique that customers' skin tones and body shapes interact directly and intimately with the clothes in the act of trying them on. It is here, therefore, that the light must reveal the true depth of Armani's multi-layered colours. The previously mentioned sales staff also noted how since working at the Fifth Avenue store, he had started wearing sunglasses in the city, even in the subway, given the continued absence of natural or artificial light in the store. With its opening Armani kept his massive four-storey Giorgio Armani boutique on Madison Avenue, while transforming his Emporio Armani boutique into an Armani Collezioni store, the first of its kind in the USA, since closed. However, given the age of this older monobrand boutique, the designer, ever the consummate perfectionist refuses to step foot inside it, and satisfied by limiting himself to waving to his staff as he walks by while in the neighbourhood. The reason, according to another anonymous senior sales associate at the Madison Avenue location, is that the store is in need of serious refurbishment, and given the state of the economy and the expense of the recent opening of the Fifth Avenue store, funds for such a large-scale enterprise at the time were limited.[81] It must also be noted that given Armani's desire to control the number of retailers selling his black label collection in that city, the opening of the Fifth Avenue store has had the effect of cannibalizing the larger Madison Avenue store, despite the fact that the new location only sells 10 per cent of the collection, while the older store sells it in its entirety. The severe economic downturn that hit New York and the USA first has meant that within the span of a year-and-a-half from 2008 to 2009, the number of sales associates at the Madison Avenue boutique decreased from 70 to 30. As a quick response to the situation in the USA, for the 2008–09 season Armani elected to hold end of season sales at 40 per cent off, with an unprecedented additional 20 per cent off at the end of the season. The decision to do this was one which Armani has claimed he would never do again, as it threatens the integrity and perception of Giorgio Armani as a luxury brand. Unsold garments are sent directly to factory outlets (with two in New York State and one located in Vermont) where previous season's garments can be discounted further. In this way, and not unlike the hidden cash registers in each store, any unpleasant economic realities are deferred to 'other' spaces, ensuring that the phantasmagoric illusions of image and spatial uniqueness can be maintained within the highly special spaces of his upscale boutiques.

Asia: The Lure of the East

As part of the house's initial global expansion policy in the late 1980s, it entered into a joint venture to open numerous Giorgio Armani and Emporio Armani boutiques throughout Japan, then the largest consumers of luxury goods. The venture was conceived as a joint collaboration with Armani holding 34 per cent of controlling shares and C. Itoh and Seibu Raika Co. each with 33 per cent. The venture headed by Norimichi Itoh (the Raika president) was as important to Armani as was his entry and expansion in the USA. According to Forte, the house 'didn't want to merely sell licenses. The Japanese market is very important, and Giorgio Armani personally is enamoured of the country.'[82] In addition to opening retail outlets for the two labels, the initial project foresaw producing up to 40 per cent of the Emporio Armani collection in Japan by the second season. The stores, significantly fewer than initially projected, were designed by Ortelli in collaboration with Japanese architect Tadao Ando, who was later commissioned to design Armani's new headquarters in Milan; a strategy to enable the translation of the global image into regional reality. The blueprints followed the respective models for each line already established in Milan. At the time of the joint venture, the Giorgio Armani collection was sold in about 20 Raika's Seibu department store outlets throughout the country.

In the 1980s and 1990s joint ventures such as this one with Itoh and Raika were important ways for Armani to expand into larger markets or initialize new ventures while remaining in control of his distribution network and image. These ventures were also meant to ensure longevity. As Armani stated: 'If the company is to live for more than thirty years, it has to broaden its perspective. There must be some fusion of fashion and finance.'[83] Armani's approach in Japan was unique at the local level while adhering to the global image of his product. Advertising, for example, identical to that produced in Italy and reproduced throughout the world, was not placed in newspapers, but rather on large billboards coupled with more event openings with celebrity guests than anywhere else. The unique approach to the country was important to ensure a smooth transition and translation. Rather than choosing Tokyo to open its first Emporio Armani boutique, the house chose Kobe to mark itself as unique from other Italian labels entering the country. Atsya Tamii, manager of the shop in Kobe, noted how the high prices did not deter the younger generations from buying. In fact, according to him, 'high school boys wash dishes and work at McDonald's to buy Armani'.[84] Italian and French labels fast became hot commodities in Japan throughout the 1980s, especially if acquired while on vacation, as these objects displayed a consumer's status, purchasing power and style cachet. In addition, at the time Italian sizing was better suited to the Japanese unlike the British and American designer labels, which made the clothes both desirable and practical.

Although Armani would be among the first designers to open a shop in mainland China, he would not open there until 1998;[85] in addition two Giorgio Armani boutiques were established in Hong Kong in the late 1980s. The desire to purchase Italian designer fashion began in Hong Kong: mainland China imposed heavy import taxes unlike the formerly British protectorate whose large upwardly mobile classes deploy designer fashion as a means to display status, prestigious and wealth. However, with access to luxury products, often through Hong Kong, Chinese consumers were shedding their Mao jackets and turning to designers to secure their own unique, individual identity. In Shanghai, for example, one consumer Ms Li (a member of the last generation reared in the Mao uniform) noted how '[e]verybody ... likes fashion because you can choose the clothes you wear', while another, Mr Poon, asserted that 'luxury products offer an individual identity'.[86] Here within these bourgeois concepts of identity and individuality, East clashed with West through their perceptions of what Italian designers can and should offer. For Armani to successfully achieve a potent impact on the cultural landscape of fashion and design, he had to make his presence felt in key outposts around the world by way of consistent spaces. Global image (through repetition) is tantamount not simply to the identity of the designer but also, and perhaps more significantly, of the consumer. For his first Beijing boutique, located in the Palace Hotel, which opened its doors in October 1998, the designer wanted to create 'something that will last, not too retro, not too avant-garde, not too classic and not too futuristic'.[87] Originally designed by Ortelli, the boutique featured black granite floors, rice-coloured walls and fitting rooms with red doors with each area divided into different categories of merchandise. For Armani, the boutique achieved an important balance. A few short years later, however, the boutique was refitted no longer to reflect a putative indigenous design, but rather to mirror more exactly the so-called authentic Armani aesthetic showcased in the original Milan boutique: clearly something was lost in these spaces of Armani's cultural translation. 'Modernity,' as Timothy Mitchell has asserted, and we might also insert fashion here, 'has always been associated with a certain place': Europe.[88] Clearly the Chinese customer desired something unique and typically Armani, rather than a quotidian aesthetic endemic to their cultural milieu, effectively staging the designer's boutique as separate and removed from their everyday. For the Chinese, the issue of preciousness comes back to the concern for authenticity, genuineness and maintaining status. As Wu Qiaojuan, a newspaper advertising editor in her early 30s, noted, '[b]uying Italian fashion is a way to show that I have reached a certain level of consumption'.[89]

'In this so-called "China's Century," the examination of the transformation of Chineseness is crucial to our understanding of the transformation of Orientalism in the age of globalization.'[90] Chinese cinema scholar Chu Yiu-Wai argues for a fluid conceptualization of what constitutes Chineseness, and its 'complicity with global modernity'.[91] Actress Zhang Ziyi, along with Gong Li, are China's most successful, prized and global sensations; Ziyi also represents the new 'commercialized' Chineseness in the emerging global order. Both actresses have mastered the art of self-Orientalist characters in Chinese films, destined for a Western audience. Design, architecture and even fashion in their films are used as visual tropes to reinforce an old-styled version of China, one that speaks to older Chinese memories and Western clichéd visions. Ziyi has not only appeared in advertising campaigns for Emporio Armani (before the designer dropped her over a donation scandal in 2010) for the Chinese market, but has also served as the designer's unofficial ambassador in Asia and in North America. This strategy is duplicitous, as it not only services the specificity of the Asian market but also reinforces the notion of a new Hollywood, and its globalization. By collaborating with Ziyi, Armani infused a heavy dose of global modernity by way of Orientalism. Ziyi never wears the designer's more Asian-influenced designs, for to do so would only serve to Orientalize her further. Rather, the modernity by which he transformed the actress situated her within the ever-expanding paradigm of global modernity.

156 Interior entrance to the Giorgio Armani portion of the Hong Kong Armani/Charter House emporium, designed by Claudio Silvestrin

Although it remained a profitable enough venture to warrant maintaining the Beijing store, throughout the 1980s and 1990s Hong Kong remained the pearl of Asian retail success for foreign designers and the gateway to mainland China. In 2002 Armani opened his largest multi-brand, mega-boutique outside of Milan, a 2,787 square metre (30,000 square foot) Armani/Charter House located at the bustling intersection of Charter Road and Pedder Street, with façades on each street devoted to both Giorgio Armani and Emporio Armani. For this unique concept and total lifestyle environment, the designer turned to Silvestrin for the Giorgio Armani boutique, Massimiliano and Doriana Fuksas for the Emporio Armani spaces and his in-house design firm for the Armani/Casa outlet. The mega-store was the first in the world in which both the complete Giorgio Armani and Emporio Armani lines were housed under one roof, in addition to the Armani/Casa, Armani/Dolci, Armani/Fiori, Armani/Libri and an Armani/Bar and Armani/ Caffè Restaurant. Marketing and retail scholar Maurya Wickstrom explains that large concept stores:

> have deemphasized the consumption of specific commodities and instead create experiential environments through which the consumer comes to embody the resonances of the brand as feelings, sensations, and even memories. As if we were actors in the theatre, as consumers in branded spaces we loan the brand's character the phenomenological resources of our bodies. We play out its fictions, making them appear in three dimensions, as if they were real. Embodied, the story the brand is telling feels real.[92]

The concept of the multi-brand flagship in the twenty-first century has come to stand as a vital spatial conceptualization of the total atmosphere, image and identity of a design house in which the consumers are completely immersed by believing themselves to be the acting agents of that world. Armani's own belief in the flagship has been premised on the notion that these stores 'communicate a brand's solidity and seriousness to the consumer'.[93] Space for Armani has come to play a greater significance in his desire to communicate directly with his clientele, sidestepping, if in part, third parties who might re-interpret his steadfast and single-minded vision. As Triefus made clear, however, in this as with all other Giorgio Armani boutiques, space does not simply operate as a shop window, but by 'creating an exciting environment' the company is able 'to do great business'.[94]

After five successful years of collaboration with Silvestrin, Armani worked once again with the architect to refashion and renew his retail space concept with the inauguration of his Shanghai boutique in April 2004 as part of his move to pay more attention to China. Located in the Bund immediately adjoining his cheekier and younger Emporio Armani label, the black label boutique incorporated small spaces for his fledging Armani/

157   Interior shot of the Giorgio Armani boutique at Armani/ Charter House

Fiori (flowers) and Armani/Dolci (sweets) enterprises and a total of 560 square metres (6,027 square feet) for his women's, men's and accessories collections. Both the location and updated style of the boutique at once reveal the designer's affinity for a city's historically rich building sites, while at the same time imposing his distinct modern vision on the landscape of public architecture. According to an Armani press release, the boutique deployed '[u]nique designs that reflect and respect the intrinsic materials used in the building's architecture, while providing pure and simple backdrops for the products on display'.[95] Rather than locating his first boutique in the much busier retail districts of Pudong or Nanking Road,[96] the designer opted to 'focus on the value of urban history and architectural heritage' and was the first designer to open shop on the strip.[97] The Bund boasts some of the city's grandest and most sophisticated architecture such as the Astor House Hotel, known for its equally famous guests such as Albert Einstein and Charlie Chaplin. Located along the Huangpu River, once the centre of the opium trade in the 1930s, the Bund is the heart of the historic foreign presence in Shanghai; its co-ordinates specifically mark out the British Concession dated back to 1846. Built in the 1920s, the substantial Art Deco building perfectly reflects Armani's continued aesthetic interest in the interwar period, especially at a moment when it was reflected directly in his Giorgio Armani and Armani/ Casa collections. These supposed outside influences (from without the West), affect the design, aesthetic and production of fashion in the West, Italy more broadly and Armani more exactly. I need only cite the creation of a logo for his primary collection, a direct response to counterfeiting and Chinese interests in luxury logos. The designer had always vehemently resisted a logo for this label until his recent push into that country when he designed a special streamlined logo with G and A fused together in a spherical shape.

For Armani, the city possesses 'enormous potential and what was once considered a city of small houses has evolved drastically, also thanks to the renovation of beautiful palaces from the Thirties and to futuristic skyscrapers'.[98] In 2004 Armani toured China making stops in Hong Kong, Shanghai and Beijing. The trip was to celebrate the two-year anniversary of Charter House, open his first Shanghai outlet and solidify his presence in a country quickly becoming the largest and most important consumer culture in the world. When the designer arrived in Shanghai accompanied by his usual entourage, in addition to Mira Sorvino, Armani/Ambassador Lady Helen Taylor and current affairs photographer Roger Hutchings, Armani noted how '[i]t was a great revelation to see how China is changing, to see old China next to the new China'.[99] As Suzy Menkes declared in 2004, 'China emerges as the 21st century's promised land'.[100] Armani's push into mainland China following the opening of the first of three eventual Giorgio Armani boutiques he would open in that city, coincided, for example, with the launch of *China Vogue* in August 2005. With an initial print run of 300,000, the inaugural issue sold out almost immediately, despite the fact that the average annual income in China is approximately $1,600, removing magazines from within reach of most.[101] Within just three years Armani had opened 35 boutiques across his various labels in 12 different cities in China. Impressive though this might appear, by 2006 Hugo Boss had 67 while Zegna owned 60.[102] Sales in China for Armani amount to a paltry 5 per cent of sales in pan-Asia, compared with 52 per cent in Europe and 19 per cent in Japan. In comparison, Ferragamo (another Italian house) whose proactive push into China with 20 outlets compared to 59 in Japan boasts pan-Asian sales of 20 per cent and 27 per cent in Japan, while Louis Vuitton claims 20 per cent of its sales comes from Asia, excluding Japan.[103]

For the Shanghai boutique, the then 'traditional' Armani trademark St Maximin stone was replaced with a light grey natural cotton canvas, horizontally pleated over panels spanning the 5 metre (16.5 foot) high walls of the space.[104] The natural, soft and textured effect this has is juxtaposed with the verticality of the stainless steel plated columns which double as mirrors. These elements are reminiscent of the Paris boutique in Place Vendôme he opened in 1987, with its use of light grey and mirrored columns marking out discreet display spaces. Along with the Macassar ebony wood storage and display cabinets 17 metres (56.27 feet) in length, these columns are the only architectural features which attempt any division of what is functionally one large expansive room. The mirrored columns at once block a complete purview of the space, while at the same time, through its reflective surface, prolong and expand parts of the space; in this way, at any given time, certain fashions' presence is repeated while others are occluded. Simple black steel clothing racks are used to display the clothing and are located either along the walls or between the columns. Like the display boxes used to showcase accessories affixed to the walls with horizontal and vertical black steel rods, the garment racks reiterate the vertical and horizontal axes while also emphasizing the constant play between spaces of void and the places of objects: between each garment spaced evenly; between each garment rack; between each mirrored column; and between each display case resting along the floor. The places of fashion and the spaces in between continue the playful choreography, marking out absences and presences. Without succumbing to a modernist structural grid, the boutique precariously balances verticality with horizontality, natural materials with futuristic effects and dark hues with reflective surfaces. Again, importantly like the current Avenue Montaigne boutique in Paris discussed in the first section, the space folds onto itself, and like the fabric along the walls which elongate the space, the horizontal folds conjure a balance between softness and quietness on the one hand and dynamism and vitality on the other.

Much has been made of designers hiring celebrated – or celebrity – architects to design or reinvigorate their retail spaces. In turn, architects themselves have recognized the power, potential and potency of fashion in society and within their own praxis in particular. After all, the architecture of today, produced for the fashion and clothing industry, is an architecture of display and consumption and not that of production. However, within this on-going and renewed dialogue, one thing stands out as a definitive cultural turn: the supremacy of fashion within the arena of high culture, even to the point of looming larger than architecture itself. No longer are fashion designers the feeble little brothers to international bankers, Internet barons and industrial giants, but global powerhouses in their own right with sales, staff and influence no longer easy to measure in strictly monetary terms. I suggest that, with the opening of the Shanghai boutique, a new chapter was penned in the story of Giorgio Armani retail and architecture, which at the same time neatly folds into the larger global cultural trend alluded to above. The material culture of the fabric walls is a result of Armani's introduction one year earlier of his now staple handbag, the plisse, despite the bag's original vertical folds. The bag, introduced as emblematic of summer itself, was initially made with *plongée* plissé nappa leather and featured a round tubular handle. The tacit influence of a female accessory (the quintessential emblem of the ever-increasing fast-paced fashion system) and the move toward textiled walls serve as a metaphor for the dematerialization of architecture in favour of the softness of textiles and the ephemerality of fashion.

The metamorphosis from architectural space to fashioned space iterated in the move from architectural object to clothed subject and the interplay between surface and depth returns us to the nineteenth century, to the influential writings of Gottfried Semper. According to Semper, '[i]n all

Germanic languages the word *Wand* [wall], which has the same root and basic meaning as *Gewand* [garment], directly alludes to the ancient origin and type of the *visible* spatial enclosure'.[105] By exploring the etymological origins and overlaps of wall and garment, Semper makes a claim for the body and space as synonymous ways to engender spatial division. Walls clothe and give shape to space as much as garments clothe and define the contours of the body. This clothing, this shelter, also visibly designates space itself within and around the body and the space within the frame of architecture. As Semper himself clearly states: '[t]he wall is the architectural element that formally represents and makes visible *enclosed space as such*'.[106] In this way, then, the fabric walls of the Shanghai boutique give shape and meaning to the now-layered body. Armani ensures that the body of his customer is not simply clothed, but is clothed in the fabric of space. Both clothing and architecture mark out spatial, territorial and conceptual boundaries, while at the same time providing shelter, safety and comfort to the body. Space is literally, figuratively and materially frame through fashion. In his reading of Semper, architectural historian Mark Wigley asserts that, as part of the construction of space, textiles are the 'mask that dissimulates rather than represents the structure ... As its origin in dissimulation, its essence is no longer construction but the masking of construction... Buildings are worn rather than simply occupied.'[107]

158 Façade of the Armani/Ginza Tower designed by Massimiliano and Doriana Fuksas featuring the LED light bamboo leaves

The vertical folds of the wall's textile covering, like the wrinkles seen in Armani's early menswear suits, are conduits of energy along the surface, here, of architecture. Surface readings once again prove vital to the way Armani plays with textures, light, space and subjectivity itself. The new fabric-walled boutique in Shanghai, where it was first inaugurated, paralleled Armani's move to establish major inroads in the global market, as well as at a moment when his own innovations in textile design and production have been forgotten. Italian textiles mark a long history and distinct economic and cultural phenomena. The move to cover the walls in fabric is as much symbolic as it is aesthetic; a tactile means to stake territory within a country, which increasingly threatens to overtake Italy in the production of textile goods, especially within the luxury market segment. Here, then, the simple repetitiveness of the folds marks out the folds of subjectivity, brand identity and the translation of the Italian idiom of textiles into the global spaces of retail architecture.

By 2001 Armani's new three-storey boutique in the Kioi-cho area of Tokyo was the largest freestanding Giorgio Armani boutique in the world. With the first floor devoted entirely to Armani's aggressively and self-consciously expanded accessory lines, the space was designed by Silvestrin and represented an important part of the $910 million in sales in Japan in 2000. As part of Armani's millennial drive to take greater control over the distribution and production of his fashion, after the nearly decade-and-a-half joint venture with Itoh and Raika, Armani gradually began buying back his retail franchise from them. As if to justify his move, the designer claimed: 'My stores are my windows on the world, which is why they must be my property. It is no longer possible to have franchises. It is the company that has to have the final say on how those windows look'.[108]

By 2007 the house directly owned and operated twelve Giorgio Armani boutiques, fourteen Emporio Armani, two Armani Collezioni stores, two Armani Jeans and two A/X Armani Exchange stores in Japan. It also marked an important year in which the designer attended the grand opening of his nine-storey (in additional to two basement level floors) Armani/Ginza Tower, which according to the press release displayed 'diversified identities' through diversified space'.[109] Developed by Armani in collaboration with Italian architects Doriana and Massimiliano Fuksas, the Armani/Ginza

159   Interior view of the Armani/Ginza Tower, the Giorgio Armani womenswear floor

Tower, located in Japan's most iconic districts, soars high, reaching the area's maximum allowed height of 56 metres (185 feet). The inspiration for the soaring boutique is said to have been the connections he has always believed to be found in Japan: 'pure forms, symbolism of line, the synthesis – where what is taken away, what cannot be seen is as much a part of the creative process as what can be'.[110] Here an interplay between absences and presences is once again integrated into the creation of spatial and design structures. Covering an impressive 6,000 square metres (64,584 square feet) 'Armani has personalised each destination with its own architectural style, developed with the spirit of the city and the location in mind.'[111] As the purported designer of the space Armani commented:

> I have always thought of myself as a democratic designer which I express through the variety of my collections. Locations such as the Armani/Ginza Tower provide the possibility to express this belief in a retail environment where a cross-section of customers can have access to a mix of my designs. I think this reflects the way the world is moving today as it becomes ever more cosmopolitan, international and multi-cultural.[112]

The house's regional offices and showrooms are located on floors six to nine, while the remaining floors are devoted to retail spaces where

> tumbling sensations and indulgence in every sense [are located], from the delights of exquisite fabrics and materials used in the Giorgio Armani and Emporio Armani ready-to-wear collections to the sophisticated comfort of the Armani/Casa home interiors collection and from the culinary pleasures of the Armani/Ristorante to the delicate aromas of the first-ever Armani/Spa.[113]

As fashion journalist and editor Stephano Tonchi has correctly observed:

> Today a fashion brand has to open itself to increasingly variegated markets and to test its value in ever wider circles, so as to become more than a logo: the symbol of a complete way of living. This necessitates using more and more abstract images and techniques steadily less linked to a specific product, while continuously widening its business and applications.[114]

In the glossy photo book published following the opening of the boutique, Armani commented how the Fuksas 'have interpreted the emotions suggested by the clothes with a lightness and a sense of transparency, of light and shade, that link up with the culture of the place'.[115] For Armani the space matches honour and tradition with the future projected dynamism of the city exemplified in the minimalist yet luxurious space of Armani's first spa, replete with Japanese gong. The overall theme, while still keeping within the clearly defined Armani aesthetic ethos, is the subtle motif of bamboo; '[i]ts quality as a delicate yet enduring material is a perfect expression of the seeming contrasts of this country', said the designer. The bamboo motif is utilized as much for the inside along the walls of the restaurant, for example, as for the first three floors of the building's façades. LED backlighting lends a glowing effect while the leaves are covered with a white Plexiglas, also radiating light from behind. The most luxurious spaces are found in the three stories housing the Giorgio Armani collections for men, women and accessories, the latter strategically located on the ground level. The recurring spatial motif of creating smaller, 'salon' environments allows the customer an increased sense of personalized attention and intimacy of experience with the products. This series of compartmentalized environments is achieved through racks and specially designed partitions, both made of a platinum-coloured metal mesh sandwiched between two sheets of clear glass. The black floors are covered in reconstituted marble tiles, while the ceiling reiterates the cover, this time through glossy black-lacquered steel panels. As a sharp and elegant contrast, walls are finished in frosted glass and have gilt metal. Clothes are displayed in transparent Plexiglas units that add to the light, ethereal yet luxurious quality these three floors conjure. The bamboo leaf motif decoratively peppered throughout is used as both utilitarian design element and decorative detail. Here, as with every floor, the designer's ideal of a complete lifestyle, or perhaps more aptly *Gesamtkunstwerk*, is eloquently coupled with his idealized vision of the country that has remained a source of inspiration:

> My dream of Japan is embodied in this palace, with its modernity that transfigures tradition, where it seemed natural to me to construct an itinerary of harmony and wellbeing whose point of arrival is the spa, the first I have created, inspired by the old Roman thermal baths, which utilizes in various forms the obsidian from the island of Pantelleria, a place with which I feel a particularly close attachment.[116]

Perhaps more than any other retail complex that Armani has imagined, the Armani/Ginza Tower represents the growing apogee of his entire lifestyle brands within brand strategy, but also the growing pearl in his empire of the senses.[117]

Conclusions

From afar, many of Armani's designs do not necessarily delight the eye, but titillate, fascinate and provoke haptic fulfilment and maybe even joy. As Riewoldt points out: '[o]nly through real-life experiences, through an unmediated encounter with the tangible attractions of beautiful things, can [retail space] hope to win through against the convenience and efficiency of e-commerce'.[118] Ultimately, I believe Riewoldt is advocating a defence of the phenomenology of shopping which extends visual pleasure into a broader sensory realm. In their conceptualization of the 'experience economy',

B. Joseph Pine II and James H. Gilmore suggest that '[s]taging experiences is not about entertaining customers, it's about engaging them'.[119]

Rooted, once again, in the notion of phantasmagoria is the idea of light and dark, mechanisms to create illusions, the very nature of glamour itself. Various forms of sensorial stimulation coupled with the control of light, ensure certain effects on the spectatorial cum corporeal and cerebral experiences. According to Adorno: 'The product presents itself as self-producing ... In the absence of any glimpse of the underlying forces or conditions of its production, this outer appearance can lay claim to the status of being'.[120] Adorno was specifically referring to Wagner's creation of the *Gesamtkunstwerk*, or total work of art. I have argued that the *Gesamtkunstwerk* conceptualized in the nineteenth century has gradually shifted through the twentieth century to become what we now identify as lifestyle, which designers like Armani have turned into an art form.[121] As Wagner himself believed, the basis of art (or the experience of the aesthetic) is sensation, which is undoubtedly made possible and manifest in the increasingly larger sensory emporia Armani constructs.

Recently designer boutiques have more to do with the business of museums, while museums are redefining themselves as shops. Yet, unlike museums which privilege sight and condemn touch, the ethos of Armani textiles and spatial programmes compel, force even, the customer to touch and enjoy the haptic experience of being in space. Armani, I posit, reinvigorates modernist space by attracting the visitor–consumer by controlling the sensory experience: sound: Emporio Armani Caffè CDs; quiet or specially selected music; scent: the smell of Acqua di Giò, for example, from the menswear cologne collection sprayed throughout the store; taste: Armani restaurants; Armani/Dolci; any beverage is brought to the preferred consumer during the process of selection and fitting; touch: Armani/Spa; one stone, one wood, myriad fabrics; and finally sight: the displayed garments and objects and the often panoptic view of bodies throughout the space. As Wigley points out rather convincingly, modern architecture, seen through the aesthetic lens of whitewashed walls and espoused by architectural giants like Adolf Loos and Le Corbusier, was not so much a renouncing of clothing and its system, but rather very much a part of it; the erratic logic of clothing is projected onto these white walls and the architecture which props fashion up.[122] Patina, as Riewoldt discloses, 'is a vital ingredient of timelessness', an ingredient endemic to Armani's clothing collections, as we have already seen.[123] As the term suggests, patina is characterized as a build up over time, the sediments of longevity, the thickness of haptic layering. Armani reinvests the sensuality lost in the modernist white wall interiors by using a stone or materials whose surfaces are porous, soft, sensual and textured. Within the context of an Armani boutique, spatial articulation comes alive through textiles and provides meaning through haptic discernment and elicits desire and pleasure. However, do garments transcend the retail spaces they occupy or are they simply meant to exist within the rarefied realm of the boutique? Adorno suggests that the phantasmagoria is 'infected from the outset with the seeds of its own destruction. Inside the illusion dwells disillusionment.'[124] Adorno could never have predicted the extent to which designer life-worlds would take over contemporary cultures and refashion every facet of embodied experience. By creating spaces and brands to complete every aspect of the *Gesamtkunstwerk,* the sensory experiences of the Armani boutique can be brought home to be translated, adopted and adapted to each and every environment; these then form the material culture of being-in-the-world.

Notes

1   Although successful freestanding boutiques exist in Australia, South America and the Middle East, these regions have not played important roles in the development of retail strategies or interior design within the expanding Armani empire. For this reason and limited by space these regions will not be discussed here.

2   Wickstrom 2006: 2.

3   Riewoldt 2000: 9.

4   Rietwoldt 2000: 10.

5   Triefus in Turngate 2004: 77.

6   Foucault 1998a: 24.

7   Quinn 2003: 28.

8   'Alluring Armani' 1989: 25.

9   Gilbert 2006: 21.

10   *The Observer* 6 October 1981.

11   *NYT* 8 October 1983.

12   *DNR* 26 January 1987.

13   *DNR* 26 January 1987.

14   *WWD* 26 January 1987.

15   *WWD* 26 January 1987.

16   *WWD* 26 January 1987.

17   Serrats 2004: 112.

18   Armani press release 22 September 2000.

19   See Gronberg 1998: 84.

20   Mostadi 2003: 92.

21   Bertoni 1999: 226.

22   Bertoni 1999: 204.

23   Bertoni 1999: 226.

24   Silvestrin in *The Financial Times* 7 March 2000.

25   Meyer 2000: 15.

26   *The Times* 31 January 1989.

27   Bertoni 1999: 174–5; Merleau-Ponty 1958.

28   Bertoni 1999: 174–5.

29   Armani press release 19 December 2006.

30   Benjamin 1999a: 669.

31   Benjamin 1999a: 804.

32   Drobnik 2005: 272.

33   *Interview* June 1977.

34   *NYT* 26 June 1986.

35   *NYT* 11 December 1983.

36   *WWD* 23 September 1983.

37   *NYT* 11 December 1983.

38   By 1988 the New York boutique was generating $10 million in annual sales. *WWD* 31 August 1988.

39   *NYT* 26 June 1986.

40   *WWD* 15 March 1984.

41   *WWD* 8 October 1984.

42   *W* January 1987.

43   *TS* 3 October 1982.

44   *TS* 3 October 1982.

45   *G & M* 16 April 1985.

46   *G & M* 16 April 1985.

47   *DNR* 1 May 1989.

48   *G & M* 19 March 1985.

49   *G & M* 22 September 1987.

50   *LAT* 12 June 1997.

51   *WWD* 27 September 1985.

52   *LAT* 30 November 1990; this number has been arrived at through numerous news reports on designer boutiques in general and with discussions with sales associates.

53   *LAT* 17 February 1989.

54   *Wall Street Journal* 15 September 1999.

55   Brantley 1988: 130.

56   *LAT* 25 January 1988.

57   *NYT* 24 December 1987.

58   *DNR* 31 August 1988.

59   *DNR* 19 June 1989.

60   *WWD* 31 August 1988.

61   Brantley 1988: 170.

62   *DNR* 19 June 1989.

63   *Forbes* 28 October 1991.

64   *DNR* 15 April 1993.

65   Translation mine, '*Boutiques de Luxe et de Mode*' 1997: 107.

66   *NYT* 19 March 1995.

67   Cramer 1997: 45.

68   Foucault 1998a: 239.

69   Armani in *Uomo Vogue* June 1991: n.p.

70   Ruby 2003: 21–2.

71   *DNR* 20 August 1996.

72   *The Sunday Telegraph* 15 September 1996.

73   *NYT* 17 September 1996.

74   *NYT* 17 September 1996.

75   *NYT* 17 September 1996.

76   *W* November 1996.

77   *NYT* 19 November 1996.

78   *W* August 2007.

79   Armani press release no date.

80   Armani press release no date.

81   As this book was going to press, the Madison Avenue store had completed an extensive renovation scheme keeping with the latest design template established in the Tokyo Roppongi Hills boutique characterized but its use of bamboo as a decorative motif, itself inspired by the Armani/Ginza Tower to be discussed in the final section of this chapter.

82   *WWD* 28 October 1987.

83   *DNR* 27 June 1988.

84   *DNR* 27 June 1988.

85   Luxury goods stores such as Louis Vuitton, for example, had already opened their first store there in 1992. I think it is important to also make a distinction between leather and accessories companies who sell more volume of smaller, easier to transport goods, than fashion labels which are also more susceptible to cyclical and local tastes.

86   *NYT* 20 June 1993.

87   Armani in *WWD* 9 October 1998; see also *La Repubblica* 2 September 1998.

88   Mitchell 2000: 1.

89   *Reuters* 9 June 2006.

90   Yiu-Wai 2008: 184.

91   Yiu-Wai 2008: 184.

92   Wickstrom 2006: 2.

93   Armani in *WWD* 1 November 2002.

94   *WWD* 1 November 2002.

95   Armani press release 17 April 2004.

96   Armani has since opened an additional two boutiques in Shanghai, including one in Nanking Road.

97   Vercelloni 2004: 36.

98   *WWD* 1 November 2002.

99   *Time* 22 November 2004.

100 *IHT* 1 December 2004.

101   *The Independent* 27 May 2006.

102   Armani press release 27 April 2006.

103   *IHT* 1 December 2004.

104   Despite being labelled as 'unsuccessful' by Silvestrin's public relations representative in a brief interview I had with him in May 2006, Armani has elected to continue his use of textilled walls in a new, updated version for his Paris (2007) boutique and subsequent boutique openings and renovations.

105   Semper 2004: 248.

106   Semper 2004: 247.

107   Wigley 1995: 12.

108   *WWD* 7 May 2001.

109   Armani press release 11 July 2007.

110   Armani press release 11 July 2007.

111   Armani press release 11 July 2007.

112   Armani press release 11 July 2007.

113   Armani press release 11 July 2007.

114   Tonchi 2002: 428.

115   Fuksas 2008.

116   Fuksas 2008.

117   For more of a comprehensive discussion of the Armani/Ginza Tower see Potvin 2012b.

118   Riewoldt 2000: 9.

119   B. Joseph Pine II and James H. Gilmore in Riewoldt 2000: 9.

120   Adorno 1981: 85.

121   See Potvin 2010.

122   Wigley 1995: 3.

123   Riewoldt 2000: 22.

124   Adorno 1981: 94.

7

Armani/Theatre: In the 'Church of Armani'

Going to an Armani fashion show is like attending opening night at Milan's La Scala opera house. The usually hassled and haggard buyers and journalists dress up for the event.

Globe & Mail

In 1976, less than one year after founding the company, Armani and Galeotti moved to via Durini 24, a seventeenth-century palazzo designed by architect Francesco Maria Ricini. Filled with mythological and allegorical frescoes, the design of the rooms of the palazzo were antithetical to the pared down, rigorous aesthetic for which Armani was to become internationally recognized. The design studio remained there until 1982, the same year Armani not only famously appeared on the cover of *Time* magazine, but also took up a nineteen-year lease for a larger and equally grand seventeenth-century palazzo at via Borgonuovo 21 where on the second and third floors he set up house and home for himself on one side and Galeotti on the other. Aptly enough the palazzo was originally owned by Franco Marinotti (SNIA Viscosa), the manufacturers of Riva cotton. Not unlike in via Durini, the environment was one in which classical frescoes loomed large, hovering omnipresent above Armani's work and life. This time, however, screens and a drop ceiling were built to cover them, avoiding any and every visual distraction. According to the designer: 'It's necessary to create an ambience for working so nothing disturbs you. The outside world is too complicated and demanding, but geometric forms in clean, open spaces are relaxing and make work easier'.[1] Designed by architect Giancarlo Ortelli, the palazzo also features all-weather and Zen gardens. Three main influences informed Ortelli's designs: Roman classical architecture, Japanese design and the International style of the 1920's. The 'resulting effect is pure form', and was often referred to as a Zen monk's cell.[2]

By the end of the 1980s, Armani commissioned American architect and designer Peter Marino to redesign and bring warmth to the spaces of his via Borgonuovo palazzo. Marino is best known for his work for some of the fashion industry's most celebrated and influential designers, and, as we saw in the previous chapter, also designed Armani's New York Madison Avenue store in 1996. In what became a more richly tactile and sumptuously coloured design, Armani was inspired by and remains an avid collector of furniture by surrealist and modernist designer Jean Michel Frank (1895–1941). The reference for Marino from which to work, therefore, was that of the 1930s and in particular the work of Frank. 'I suggested a period in the past as a point of reference, since the structure of the house was suitable for the kind of atmosphere', Armani stated. This new palazzo, in tandem

160   Armani posing in his via Borgonuovo palazzo, before it was redesigned by architect Peter Marino. The space was likened to a Zen monk's cell, with little decoration save for patterned pillows

with his fashion of the period, represents for him 'simplicity of line, the love of natural materials, modernity without futurism'.[3] The neutral tones and a monochromatic palette, reminiscent of the 1930s and advocated at the time, 'is extremely restful and cool ... and it makes a lovely setting for dresses'.[4] Devoid of pictures, the walls of each room are lined with sycamore (bedroom), oak (library and salon), parchment (dinning room) and goatskin (library). Doors and their casements are fashioned from French polished ebony or in sand and ivory-coloured woods reminiscent of Frank's often pale furniture. Furnishings included wood folding screens, black lacquered tables, desks and a secretary for his private home office, and raw silk beige and sand-coloured sofas. Beyond the interplay between browns, beiges and black, the space is one of neutral and rigorous restraint. The subtlety of detail and surface treatments refer to a play of texture and light that Armani is known for. As Marino puts it: 'It's not about colour, pattern, or decoration. It's a game of textures and finishes.'[5] Perhaps the most revealing feature of the apartment is how a simple, unobtrusive pocket door leading into his private residence upstairs suffices to demarcate and separate the porous spheres of his business downstairs. According to Armani:

> When I thought about my house I wanted it to have the same simple elegance Milan possesses. But I wanted to leave many details unfinished. Anything that is rigidly defined, that's perfect and unchanged irritates me. It gives me the feeling of something too planned. That's a weakness of mine that affects both my life and my work. I'm always thinking about adding something or taking something away. Mostly taking something away. I've always insisted upon simplicity. I can't stand exhibitionism.[6]

Although he purports never to design at home, the separation between home and work in real terms is tenuous at best. Armani is unique in that his various homes have featured prominently in advertising campaigns for his clothing lines, setting the stage through the signifying power of domestic space in the elucidation of meaning for the fashioned garment, and in its wake evoking that all-powerful *Gesamtkunstwerk* of a total style for living.[7] Campaigns for the black label include, for example, the autumn 1986 and spring 1988 (which feature his Milanese home); autumn 1988 (his country home in Forte dei Marmi); spring 1991 (set in a Milanese restaurant, his home, his Milan boutique, the streets of Milan); autumn 2002 (set in the then new Armani/Teatro designed by Japanese architect Tadao Ando). As Armani submits: 'My clothing, in order to be represented at its best, requires large, clean, modern rooms ... It isn't true that a collection can be presented anywhere.'[8] This important symbiosis between Armani's private domestic space and the display of fashion is also apparent when looking through the Fairchild Publication archive, for instance, in which numerous series of editorial photographs deploy Armani's personal interiors of his via

Borgonuovo home as backdrops to his women's collections. By allowing, in fact favouring, trade publications to shoot in his palazzo, Armani is better able to directly control the outcome of the editorial content and visual ideal he seeks to convey, exerting a direct material and visual influence over one sector of the industry's gatekeepers.

When Armani moved from via Durini to via Borgonuovo, the division demarcating private life from public work seemed to fade away. In the basement of the new palazzo are a small private gym and a lap pool wide enough for one man, arms fully outstretched. More significantly, it is here that Armani's theatre is located, the place where Armani presents his twice-yearly men's and women's runway collections. It is here, within the privacy and intimacy of the basement level of what are ultimately the private spaces of his studio and even more intimate spaces of his home, that Armani extends such an intimate invitation to the fashion world, an act no other designer in the last quarter of the twentieth century has done. The space of the theatre marks the site of tension between creativity and commerce, kept at bay through a sophisticated atmosphere of reverence conjured by the designer himself and his staff. The fashion show aims not simply to present the latest collection, but to elevate it to a higher ideal by conjuring an idealized visual image and rarefied material culture. In the case of Armani, the space of his

161   Jean-Michel Frank-designed salon that resembles nearly identically Armani's own, which included numerous pieces from the French designer. The interior is from the Vicomte Charles de Noailles's Paris residence, 1923–26. Picture from: Todd, Dorothy and Raymond Mortimer. *The New Interior Decoration*. London: B. T. Batsford, 1929

theatre is an emotional staging of what is a rather simple event, though cinematic in tone and feel. The staging of the runway collection spatially and conceptually attenuate the designer's identity; every aspect of the space, detail and choreography of an Armani show is determined solely by the designer himself. Unlike many designers who hire external press agents or runway designers and choreographers, Armani determines and orchestrates every single aspect of the presentation of his collections which rarely if ever changes over the seasons, making for a consistent, idiosyncratic and highly identifiable style. Within the space of his theatre, the purity of the Armani aesthetic and vision is honed, perfected and presented to friends, buyers and the fashion press. It is here that Armani, like a director, conjures, even if only for 15 minutes, a theatrical event, complete with stage directions, actors, video and lighting personnel and above all else highly charged emotion. This chapter explores the physical and conceptual spaces Armani has created to present his runway collections to glimpse into how the designer controls this important early stage in the life of a fashion product. In these few minutes the designer must balance the need to entice buyers and elicit desire through the lens of the international press and portray a purity of vision and emotional presence untarnished by outside competing forces.

In the Theatre of Drama

When Armani showed his first men's collection in 1975, he showcased it in a rather plain, uninspired, dimly lit room of the Hotel Palace, where he was hiding behind the door. Gradually, with increased interest from buyers he presented his collections at the ballroom of the Grand Hotel, a much larger facility. As a way to systematize and create an official Milan Fashion Week, Bepe Modenese established a schedule in 1977 featuring a small grouping of around 30 showings at the Fiera di Milano (the Milan fairgrounds). Many of the lesser-known designers continued to show in this venue well into the 1980s. As Modenese would later note of the challenges of staging such an event: 'It's very difficult to keep an Italian group united. There is a tremendous individualism in our blood. Yet, the fact that the French managed to be so successful and united will make the Italians unite and fight back.'[9] While Armani's clothes were heralded as revolutionary, his straightforward and nondescript shows were no more unique than many of his Italian compatriots, who in the 1970s sent the models down the runway in a rather straightforward manner.

In a completely radical and unprecedented departure, for the presentation of his men's spring 1981 show Armani abandoned the Fiera to show it in his own unique venue. The communal space of the Fiera had quickly become the norm, however, and Armani's move had ushered what is today a standard practice for many of the more established Italian houses. Stunned by such a radical departure, journalists were quick to query Armani's move. Armani's reply would forever underpin his ideological and philosophical stance vis-à-vis both runway presentations and his attempt at exerting a more direct influence over the industry's gatekeepers, namely the international buyers.

> Let's just say that runway presentations are just not the ideal medium with which to show the media the things that I have created; runway presentations have become distorted. They are now just huge performances, and they are a way for directors to get paid a lot of money. Where what seems to prevail is the spectacular effect, even if there is no corresponding commercial return. They don't really matter. In the end no one understands a thing, and even the press is disoriented. And in many cases, certain collections aren't matched by a serious industrial reality.[10]

Along with Walter Albini, Armani elected again to present his women's spring 1981 collection elsewhere, and opted for the intimacy his offices in the via Durini palazzo offered. That two of the city's more influential designers elected not to show at the Fiera was 'worrisome' for *Women's Wear Daily* which, among other members of the international press and buyers, considered the overall organization of the Milan shows both 'slick' and a 'comfort'.[11] Again the designer responded to questions regarding his decision in a similar vein to the previous season:

> The idea of huge productions with dozens of models staged for many people who do not have any immediate business with our company is out of date ... The excessive expense, the timely planning and the fact that we show most of our collection in advance simply does not justify such shows. Fashion is not a circus spectacle.[12]

Staged over three days during the regular time frame of the October women's collections, the designer set up a series of small, intimate areas where approximately 20 to 30 buyers and members of the press at a time were shown garments on 8 mannequins and displays. A specially designed area was established for photography while the house also took its own photographs in advance for the press when needed.

Although Armani clearly noted his early dissatisfaction with the fashion system, most notably the press, the desire to move away from the Fiera was surely also a way to set himself apart from the standardized presentations of the Fiera as well as a means to establish greater control over the environment, atmosphere and style of his runway presentations. At the Fiera there was an inescapable sameness to the shows, despite the different fashions and perhaps the energy brought to each. The unprecedented move paralleled what he saw as a 'revolutionary' new look for women. The more feminine Oriental-inspired collection featured kimono jackets coupled with his, according to *The New York Times*, 'waky [sic] pants' were not nearly as exaggerated as the 'more waky [sic] pants' found at Versace.[13] The men's and women's collections were declared successes with both collections sold out in advanced showings, 'making a formal show redundant'.[14]

Not content to stand still, for his spring 1982 women's collection Armani 'invented a new idiom for fashion presentations'.[15] Along with a few models posing throughout the various redesigned presentation spaces of his transformed offices, the garments were displayed in show sequence on rows of black-lacquered poles. Given that the collection was meant to be seen through continuous private showings, presenting the clothes in such close proximity to the buyers displayed them to best effect, underscoring their tactile rather than their purely visual qualities. With frescoes removed from sight, each niche and alcove made up the series of maze-like corridors and enclosed spaces, presenting different aspects of the collection's whole. Each fully composed garment hung on hangers and was lit with pools of light, drenching the brilliant spring colours of the collection. The designer grouped his small eveningwear offering together in the final room. The backlit, black-carpeted space also projected slides showing models wearing the clothes in various forms of action in the city streets as a means to translate and blur the relationship between creative ideal and street culture. Here the visual effect of seeing models moving in the clothes on a runway was given space to express the everyday quality of embodied fashion, that is, clothing that could move directly from showroom into the lives of women's material realities. Despite reporters' obsession with spectacular presentations, emblematized in the Paris fashion system, this presentation was refreshing to many and 'wonderfully effective and, for once, one can see and touch the fabrics, essential in this tactile and gloriously coloured collection', reported the *Toronto Star*. Armani's playful mood meant that with this collection he once again 'surprise[d] and delight[ed] the eye' of those who attended his presentation.[16] Not unlike his previous samurai-inspired collection, Armani attempted to create a *Gesamtkunstwerk*, with tonal music playing overhead to evoke feelings and sensations akin to the garments. The light and music coupled with the display style created an ideal calm environment, where many of the senses were activated. Buyers and press members were left alone to examine each garment freely, allowed to touch and engage directly with the fabrics. In a usual fast-paced runway presentation, the audience is rarely able to glimpse the distinguishing and unique fabrics and true variations of colours endemic to an Armani collection. The designer had already distinguished himself by designing 90 per cent of the patterns and textiles found in each of his numerous collections. Throughout the 1970s and 1980s Armani was already having a significant effect, creating four collections each for Giorgio Armani and Emporio (including Armani Jeans) as well as the collections for Mario Valentino and Erreuno, to say nothing of the numerous freelance consulting and collections he did for various Italian firms. The impact he has had on the development of textiles and fashion cannot be underestimated. In these collections from the early 1980s, presented in such close proximity to its audience, Armani began to forge his identity and reputation as adept in the art of textile design and combinations. With this sort of presentation, Armani also saved buyers time by dispensing with the need for them to come back to the offices to place orders after the runway show had taken place; an affect of thinking through the intimacy between fashion and finance. According to Joan Burstein, owner of London's eponymous boutique Browns which also housed that city's first Giorgio Armani store:

> Fashion's always changing, and that's what's nice about it. I even thought that Armani's decision not to put on a show was new and interesting. The reasons he used were good ones, I thought: he saved money and made the buyers save too. When he showed the collection in the Via Durini showroom he did it in such an exquisite way! But I understand why the press reacted differently. For buyers, though, if the presentation is good and if the accessories are good, then presentation in a showroom is worth more than an actual show.[17]

In these collections, fabrics left to sight alone would have been misleading, as the designer would often develop *tromp l'oeil* fabric patterns and finishes. The *Toronto Star* concluded that although the show lacked the usual 'breathless excitement and theatrical zest of a traditional show' it offered its audience 'a welcome respite' and 'a rare opportunity to really see the fashion in detail. And that, after all' according to the newspaper's reporter, 'is the name of the game'.[18]

162   Image from the controversial *Time* spread featuring the autumn 1982 collection

For autumn, however, Armani would take one final, controversial step in his move to force the fashion system to rethink how it presented and reported collections and did business. Armani decided to show his autumn 1982 women's collection to the media weeks after buyers had a chance to place their orders. In a letter to John Fairchild, president of Fairchild Publications (responsible for publishing the influential trade periodicals *Women's Wear Daily, W* and *Daily News Record*), Armani indicated that the press would not be able to cover his autumn show in March if they did not agree to refrain from showing the collection until the clothes were in stores. In the letter he also claimed that he would only have one show a year, open to the public and in a different city each year.[19] While these ideas never came to fruition, they infuriated Fairchild, who had long been a close supporter and ally of Armani. An irritated Fairchild retaliated by responding that '[w]e will stop covering his collection, and we won't mention the introduction of his new perfume. This business is difficult enough. If someone tries to go negative on me, to hell with him!'[20] Despite Fairchild's annoyance and hostility, Armani was soon after dubbed King George I by *Women's Wear Daily*.

In large measure the move was to protect his designs from being copied and sold at different price points by other retailers. Armani's move, while unheard of in Milan, had very clear historical precedents. Paris-based designers Balenciaga, Givenchy and Courrèges had all attempted to do the same, fuelled by their growing frustration of having their garments copied before they arrived in stores.[21] Armani retorted that while he was not attempting to control the press, neither did he want to be controlled by it. He argued that coverage of the collections occurred too far in advance of when the clothes appeared in stores, and as a result the press was more invested in covering the collections for industry insiders rather than those who purchased it in the stores, the consumer for whom Armani asserted he designed. Fairchild concluded that Armani's actions were those of a man threatened by the ascendancy of his compatriots Luciano Soprani and Gianfranco Ferré. Armani's move was at once to protect himself and his customers, who had already increased significantly, particularly in the USA. His presentation style was in large part fuelled by what he claimed were the realities of the business of fashion. Armani maintained, and continues to do so today, that press coverage does not coincide with reality. Toward this end the designer also mentioned that the reason for the decision was to allow for a greater rapprochement between what was presented on the runway (or in the studio), and what buyers were purchasing for their stores. 'The move', according to Armani,

> is to enable us to provide the press with information we do not have at the time we show to buyers – information such as which designs were favoured by buyers, which were considered less important. Just as we have a choice to decide whom to invite to see our work, Fairchild has the right to decide what he thinks is fair and professional, journalistically.[22]

He thought he had reached a 'compromise' the season before 'by showing clothes on a hanger so journalists and buyers could actually touch the merchandise. That seemed to satisfy half the press.'[23] According to Armani,

> the show became more important than the clothes. Many in the press began to judge the production, not the product. Many designers showed things they did not intend to make ... It's time for a change. I don't want to say the press should not be informed, but for me it is now more important to ... have my clothes seen and judged in the stores and by the people who wear them.[24]

The controversial move on the part of the designer was not intended to prove his originality, but rather 'to follow [his] search for the concrete and realistic in fashion', a move endemic to a modernist collusion between fashion, form and function. As a 'stylist/designer who doubles as a businessman' his goal was to create clothes 'with the precise goal that they are sold, and worn'.[25]

Things got out of hand with Fairchild's and Armani's mutual boycott, however, when a writer for *Time* magazine realized the potential of this relatively new designer and the quiet impact he was having amongst a new constituency of fashion consumers. Jay Cocks wrote one of the most influential

163   While Armani side-stepped the regularity of the runway during the early to mid-1980s for his own collection, he continued to hold wildly successful runway shows for both Erreuno and Mario Valentino. The press and buyers were starving for Armani shows at the time, which only served to heighten the presentations of these other collections. Here an exit from his autumn 1984 Erreuno collection

pieces on the designer for the magazine, and also fuelled an already growing controversy. When the *Time* issue hit newsstands, *The New York Times* quickly entered the fray by asking the following series of questions:

> How did Giorgio Armani manage to win the cover of *Time* magazine's April 5 issue, and how did *Time* manage to photograph Mr. Armani's fall collection when, at the end of January, he had banned the press from seeing anything until after April 1? And was it all, some asked, finally worth it?[26]

Or perhaps it was an April fool's joke, painstakingly orchestrated months before by Armani? Whatever conspiracy theories one can divine, we might safely conclude that it was worth it, regardless of the motivation. Armani recalls:

> That cover made me feel the obligation of my position. We were almost obliged to begin retailing. Not only multibrand stores, but dedicated stores as well, in direct ownership, especially significant in terms of images. We became retailers on the fly, we had no experience.[27]

Response from department store buyers for the collection was overwhelmingly positive, especially given that he managed to offer the garments at prices lower than those of his previous spring collection.[28] So successful was the collection, as were his men's collection that the company's revenue for 1982 tripled.

With the collection having been shown to buyers since 1 March and with the press banned from showing it in their respective venues until 1 April, *The New York Times* continued to query whether Armani had struck a deal with *Time* giving them exclusive rights to showcase the collection and in return receiving the coveted honour of the front cover. According to Martha M. Duffy, senior editor in charge, 'Armani didn't call us. We called him. And we didn't query him about an article until February 23 or 24, whereupon we discovered that he posted his embargo.' According to Gabriella Forte no deal was struck: '*Time* just took the lead while everyone else complained about not seeing the clothes.' In New York at the time when the controversy broke, archrival Versace complained that '[i]t would have been better if Armani didn't show his collection even in *Time* ... It just proved that his secrecy was for nothing.' However, it was Cocks, then a film critic, who later claimed that he 'ha[d] wanted to write something on Armani for the past two years'.[29] Years later Cocks maintained that the article was meant to feature the designer's talents and was not meant as a public relations stunt. Cocks wore an Armani jacket to the interview, which changed the dynamics and provided the designer a sense of calm, realizing he was a fan.[30] According to the author he did not approach the interview from a typical or staid fashion, concerned for such trivial issues as the season's current style or colour, which had plagued most fashion journalism. Rather, his approach was more mundane and quotidian, wondering about Armani's experiences and influences in fashion in more practical terms. Regardless of what exactly went on during the interview, the formula was wildly successful for both men, particularly for Armani. *Time* was the only magazine to see and reproduce images from the collection. The issue with Armani on its cover hit stands the same week as Paris fashion week, upstaging and infuriating French designers. Despite signals of a rapprochement on the part of Armani with *Women's Wear Daily*, going so far as to send the company's fashion editor Etta Froio a bouquet of roses, Fairchild maintained his staunch position and ordered her to '[s]end them back'. Michael Coady, then editor of *Women's Wear Daily* suggested that 'John will never cover Armani again. You can count on it. Never!'[31] In fashion, however, never is a short period of time: although *Women's Wear Daily* banned Armani for the rest of the year, coverage of Armani's shows would resume in 1983; a less than eloquent acknowledgement that the gatekeepers of fashion need designers as much as the latter require the former.

For his spring 1983 collection Armani continued to show in the controlled environment of Palazzo Durini. This time, however, the collection was presented as a film with models moving effortless in his tailored confections. Buyers were then escorted to another room where the clothes were artistically displayed on racks as if in a boutique environment. The fabrics in the film, as they would be in a large runway presentation, were deceiving and what appeared to be a jacket of silk or cotton was in fact made of the softest leather. A reporter claimed that you had to touch it to make certain of what it was.[32] Armani claimed that once again, with the absence of a 'freak show' the collection was 'less about fashion and more about clothes'.[33] His pared-down presentation aesthetic was catching on with fellow designer Mariuccia Mandelli of Krizia, who called it 'a time for re-thinking fashion in simpler, clearer, more defined terms'.[34] Given that Italian designers were anxious over the downturn in the American economy, for autumn 1983, Armani continued to shy away from the runway. With this reduction of costs, the designer presented a subdued collection, in keeping with what his Milanese colleagues 'know how to do best – solid, fine tailoring in handsome fabrics'.[35] As a way to emphasize and attenuate the relationship between runway and retail, Armani opened the Milan season by hosting his collection presentation in his new and first freestanding boutique in 9 via Sant'Andrea. As a thoughtful initiative to promote the new store to buyers and the press, the collection was presented on wooden stands where upon Armani 'lined up his creations along the flesh-coloured walls of his ultramodern shop as though they were paintings, and let everyone ogle and touch and imagine what they would look like on real live models'.[36] Despite the opportunity to get closer and enjoy the haptic and tactile quality of the garments, enthusiasm for such a presentation style was still less than Armani expected. This disappointment is underlined by Silvia Giacomoni, who has offered an interesting perspective on Armani's gestures in those early years of the 1980s:

Armani feels he is the prisoner of the press because this latter exalts or execrates him and refuses to understand the meaning he gives to his gestures. But when he gets angry, Armani hides part of the truth ... In abolishing fashion shows he was convinced he'd dealt the myth of the creator a terrible blow. However, in reality, because he's an extraordinary man, he just wanted to do what he felt like, thus breaking the laws of the fashion system. The funny thing is that Armani used to get angry because the press, whose important function he was in fact denying, didn't take kindly to being excluded. Or because, in view of its efforts to favour the fashion industry, it pretended to interpret his gestures in such a way as to make it fit in with the usual logic of the myth.[37]

164   Still-life presentation style which marked the display of Giorgio Armani collections in the early 1980s. Spring/summer 1984

Rather than visually witness the garments on models on a distanced runway, guests were also invited to view the collection, once again, as a fashion film in the basement level of the boutique. Armani's fashion films presented models strolling down via Montenapoleone, via Manzoni and in public gardens, displaying how women live, move in the clothes and interact in the fabric of the urban landscape. Before fashion films on the Internet became 'fashionable' in the twenty-first century with designers like Alexander McQueen, Gareth Pugh and Stefano Pilatti for YSL, subtle presentations like those Armani devised for his autumn 1983 collection sidestepped the frenzy and mayhem caused by the travelling circus that had become the source of satire for Robert Altman's film *Prêt-à-Porter* (1994). According to Cocks,

> Everyone has to feel important. Armani cut to the heart of this when he remarked, 'Ready-to-wear clothes blew away the pretensions of *haute couture*, but the shows have assumed the same social functions. Where am I sitting? How much time do I get alone with the designer? Will I be invited to dinner? For myself, I want people just to look at the clothes.'[38]

165   Intimate and animated presentation off the runway for his autumn/winter 1984 collection

In the 'Church of Armani'

After slightly more than a two year hiatus, Armani made his triumphant return to the catwalk in July 1983, when he 'dazzled assembled press and retailers' with his men's spring 1984 collection,[39] which garnered a standing ovation for the designer and cries of bravo from buyers and press alike. The designer mused in an interview with Giacomoni on his earlier decision to show his collections in his office headquarters and through fashion films.

> At the outset we, like everyone else, needed to show the collection to the press and the buyers. Then sometimes buyers would find themselves so dazzled by the show that they purchased things which they then couldn't sell. So I began to sell a month before the show, such that what the press saw was the sales collection. And what happened? The garment that I'd designed and that was selling so well didn't make much impact on the press, so I was more or less pushed aside. But since I was sure I'd done the right thing, I broke away from the others and started to hold my parades in my headquarters here in via Durini, so that the sales collection could still be shown to some effect. Then I got to the stage of hanging the collection here in the showroom and showing the press videotapes that gave an idea of how these garments moved when they were worn... I hadn't realized I was the only person who thought the time had come to go on with shows that were over-celebratory, excessively centred on creativity, substantially unaware of the consumer's requirements. And in fact no-one understood what I was up to.[40]

When asked why he returned to the conventional runway format, Armani simply replied: 'Because I am tired of pointless struggles. Giving up shows meant I had to spend far more time talking to journalists, explaining things you don't need to explain when you do put on shows.'[41]

The spring collection was showcased in the basement of the newly renovated palazzo in 21 via Borgonuovo. Armani's deep fascination with light and its effects led him to design a runway made of industrial glass, lit from below with a rear projection system that lends a radiant warmth to the models' complexions and the clothing. The orange honeycombed overhead structure allows for an additional intricate lighting system that can be lowered or raised at will. Seating is provided on three sides, with the far end reserved exclusively for press photographers to give a perfect view of the facing sliding panels from which models exit. This spatial reconfiguration also greatly benefitted buyers, editors and journalists, who are often challenged by the cameras for an unobstructed vantage point from which to view the clothes. Initially the facing wall where models exit was comprised of mirrored panels, an ironic device to be sure on the part of Armani, given his more recent fracas with the press who were now forced to see themselves in the mirrored space of fashion he presented them. The panels, which would eventually be replaced with various materials over the years, conjure Japanese shoji screens, a recurring motif in Armani's stores and home, located two floors above this former ballroom turned fashion theatre. Armani later described his office spaces as 'Un po' Zen' (A little Zen). According to him, '[y]ou can add on to simplicity, the Japanese style. You cannot add on to the baroque.'[42]

In an article entitled 'It's Armani all the way in Milan', the *Daily News Record* touted the collection shown on the night of the unveiling of his new theatre as having, 'once again, laid the groundwork for a tailored clothing revolution with his supple, slouchy, very wide lapelled suits for next season'.[43] The article noted how the male models' hands were tucked snugly into their pockets of jackets whose 'fabrics were inspirational'.[44] For his women's spring 1984 collection the designer had his theatre refitted to accommodate a double seating capacity and constructed a longer runway. Again *Women's Wear Daily* reported, '[a]long with the clothes, Armani wowed his audience with a sparkling new plushly carpeted theatre in his new very expensive palazzo'.[45] Soon the spaces of via Borgonuovo, the gardens, offices, his apartment and in particular the specially constructed theatre began to manifest an aura of quiet elegance and an atmosphere of control and restraint. There is little noticeable or qualitative difference between the spaces of work and the spaces carved out for living. Employees who occupy the various spaces of the palazzo, whether craftsmen, seamstresses or secretaries, know and willingly enforce the laws of the Armani atmosphere. Apart from Ralph Lauren, no other designer in the world projects such a consistent image and in such an emphatic way. To this end, when Armani ever stages a runway presentation outside of Milan, he has his runway and seating shipped to recreate the environment and atmosphere of his Milan theatre ensuring a steadfast consistency.

The staff coupled with the atmospheric spaces has led reporters to describe their experiences of being invited into the inner sanctum of Armani's realm, always entering the space 'with a kind of reverence'.[46] For others, like Ellin Saltzman of Saks, attending a runway show in via Borgonuovo is 'like going to church'.[47] Part of the intense mystique hovering around Armani is invoked in this theatre where emotions run high, and where the audience applauds not only at the end, but regularly throughout the presentation, unprecedented and unheard of among his peers. Despite their simplicity, Armani's fashion shows have caused some in the audience to shed tears, particularly in the 1980s and early 1990s.

Staging 'Made in Italy'

Here I wish to consider Armani's presentation of his spring 1997 menswear collection at the Pitti Imagine Uomo twice-annual trade show. While some might dismiss it as merely celebrity fashion endorsement, the political and economic factors were clearly invested and maintained by this invitation. On 1 May 1996, *Daily News Record* announced that the Pitti Imagine Uomo

166   From the September issue of *Esquire*: Armani poses with models displaying his autumn/winter 1987 collection on his basement runway in via Borgonuovo

had pulled off a major coup by getting the Milan-based designer to show his men's spring collection there rather than in Milan. It was also noted, however, that the effect would be devastating for those Paris designers showing their collections in the early days of that city's calendar, given that many buyers and members of the press would be forced to stay longer in Italy to attend Florence following the Milan shows. The *G. A. Story*, the special hybrid runway show, theatrical and retrospective event, was held in Florence's then derelict nineteenth-century Stazione Leopolda. Staged and directed by American Robert Wilson, the event was meant to purposefully coincide with the twenty-fifth anniversary of the Florentine tradeshow organization, giving it a much-needed shot in the arm. Heavily subsidized by the Italian government, the train station was renovated by Gae Aulenti. The choice to employ Aulenti underscores Armani's desire for consistency even in his collaborations and reveals his need to stay within his comfort zone. In 1992 Aulenti also curated a retrospective installation of 100 pieces of Armani's work. Not unlike the *G. A. Story*, the 1992 installation coincided with the fortieth anniversary of the Sala Bianca at the Palazzo Pitti in Florence, an event meant to celebrate the history of Made in Italy since its inception in the immediate post-war period.

According to the designer, Wilson's work is 'magical, metaphysical'.[48] In a rare decision, Armani left Wilson a considerable amount of freedom to interpret his fashion, asserting: 'I am very happy to be changing my means of presenting the collections ... and I think my clothes will speak for themselves.'[49] In order for them to 'speak for themselves', chronology was dismissed in favour of thematic spaces where the line between mythical landscapes and real spaces of the quotidian blurred and became imperceptible. The train station was divided into three stages with eleven additional smaller, off-stage venues where 30 dancers and 50 models performed various *tableaux vivants*. Unclear how to navigate the space on their own, the audience was directed through the various spaces over 90 minutes. *Daily News Record* described the event as a 'gargantuan performance art piece cum fashion show'.[50] In addition to the performers, video projections featured images from previous campaigns as well as celebrity friends photographed over the years sporting his creations. The first of the spaces guided the visitors through the four seasons. Light rain, green grass and trees helped to conjure a mystical spring garden. This merged into a dreamy summer beach scene where models displayed the spring 1997 collection by moving at a trance-like pace, typical of Wilson's choreography. The background's blue colour not only referred to the designer's favourite colour, but also to Wilson's own signature. Within the blue-hued scene, a man jogged in the background while a boy played in the sand and a woman sat, dazed, in a chair. An additional section of the summer scene was a fairy-tale garden, where male models stood among the bushes while a sleeping beauty lay in an alcove bathed in golden yellow light wearing a diamond-

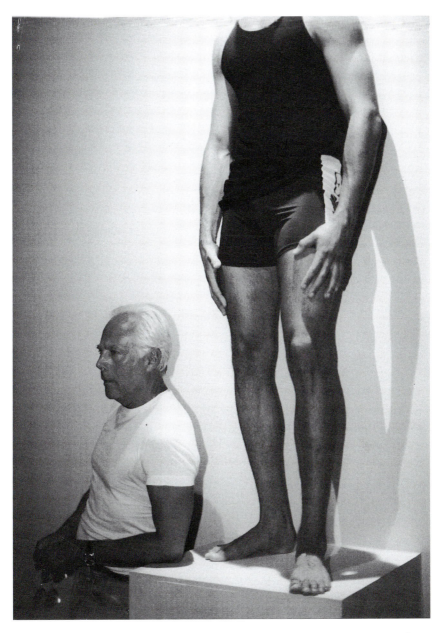

167 The designer posing in front of one of his models cum Adonis cum living sculpture from the spring 1997 presentation at the Stazione Leopolda in Florence as part of the G. A. Story, the showcase of the Pitti Imagine Uomo

encrusted floor-length dress. An office space was constructed to represent daywear, where models performed the rituals of work, again in slow motion. For eveningwear, two levels were connected by way of a staircase silhouetted by a blue-lit backdrop. In one of the final sections of the long station, male models with paste combed through their hair posed on pedestals reminiscent of Grecian statues wearing the latest underwear and swimwear collections. *Le Monde* noted the clear homoeroticism of the live installation, situating them within a transhistorical relationship to statues from the Renaissance, drawings by Cocteau and photographs by Bruce Weber.[51]

The premiere showing for the political leaders was meant to showcase the theatrical component of the show, rather than simply the designer's latest menswear collection. To train the models and actors, Wilson ran through his rigorous routine of concentrating strictly on their movements. The absence of a grand narrative meant that Wilson was free to focus on what he does best, visual affect and choreography. Wilson in tenor, Armani in ambience, the model's careful, slow and methodical movements, not unlike that seen on an Armani runway, were slowed down to a snail's pace by Wilson, analogous to his own theatrical staging style. However, Wilson noted the important difference between theatre and a fashion show when he pointed to the speed by which the latter event takes place; the effect is therefore quite different when working with models. 'This marks the first time that I have worked with models. Rather than walk as they are used to,' Wilson submitted, 'I asked them to listen to the movement inside themselves, to find the line. Above all one must not think about it. The gesture follows.'[52] Without words and only through their bodies models are limited to the language of movement and gesture to translate the essential idea of a garment or express the vision of a designer. Wilson's particular slow-moving choreography for the *G. A. Story* was received with mixed reviews. *Le Monde*, for example, bemoaned the slower tempo and the absence of 'dramatic tension'. The office scene mimicking the material conditions of contemporary life, however, was described by the French paper as 'an assembly of directors transformed into a seminary of apostles'.[53] *Daily News Record* claimed that the Wilsonian slowed-down movements and gestures were well suited to the beach scene showcasing the latest swimwear collections, however, 'Wilson's staging worked less well with an evening-wear grouping that was more funereal (replete with widow) than festive.'[54]

In this fashion show cum installation cum performance, economics, politics, theatre and fashion cavorted, engendering a cultural performance that placed Armani as a, if not *the*, central powerhouse of the economic and aesthetic success of the Made in Italy label. While Armani was not alone in his showcasing of his latest collection at the Pitti, its managing director, Raffaello Napoleone, submitted that '[e]veryone will benefit from [Armani's] presence here because he represents Italian creativity and has the support

168   Various scenes from the G. A. Story choreographed and orchestrated by American theatre director Robert Wilson, with whom the designer has collaborated several times

of the fabric and manufacturing industry behind him'.[55] However, rumours were circulating that having Armani show in Florence rather than in Milan was simply a tactic to have the delegates, , buyers and press stay longer in Italy. Like his French namesake, Napoleone defiantly denied the rumours, asserting:

> We're not declaring war on anyone; we think there is space for everyone this season. We naturally chose Armani because we think he best represents the progress Italian fashion has made over the past 25 years ... We are not trying to compete with the Camera Nazionale [in Milan] – instead our relationship is becoming stronger and we think this event will benefit the whole industry.[56]

It did, however, require Modenese to readjust Milan's menswear fashion week to accommodate Armani's flight to Florence. The show's economic and political significance cannot be underestimated, given that it was staged twice to two very different constituencies. The first showing on 21 June, slightly different to that on 3 July for the fashion pack, was attended by an exclusive group of 300 European government delegates already in the Tuscan capital taking part in the closing summit conference of Italy's EU presidency. Although they were barred from the actual event, the media's coverage was widespread throughout Italy and further abroad, giving additional exposure for the talents of Wilson and Armani as well as garnering much-needed attention to the Florence shows, which had lost considerable ground to Milan when it gained cultural ascendency as the headquarters of Italy's media and fashion industries in the 1970s. Armani's participation in such an event coupled with it also servicing as a retrospective of sorts situated the Milan-based designer at the centre of the history and lineage of Made in Italy. No similar or equivalent show has taken place at the Pitti showings on such a vast scale and within such an important political and economic context.

Repetition and the Model: The Performing Armani Body

When Armani moved his design studios and theatre to via Borgonuovo he also began to systematize and codify his presentation style; a style which would forever be identified with the designer. In the days leading up to a show, at Armani controlled diligence serves to ensure that every member of the production is willing to stay in the theatre until the morning hours.[57] Armani himself orchestrates all fittings, last-minute alterations and model walk-throughs. In the early 1980s Armani usually kicked off the Milan season, with his archrival Versace left to close it. Gradually as both rose to international prominence, both vied equally to close Milan fashion week and assume the honorific role of producing the final image of the season. In the end, it was Armani who won out,. However, by the early 1990s, when the

169   Armani is no stranger to working directly with the theatre and opera. These are costumes from the successful 1995 Covent Garden production of Mozart's *Cosi fan tutte*. Armani took garments from his Giorgio and Emporio Armani collections which not only lent a modern, but also decidedly North African feel to the characters

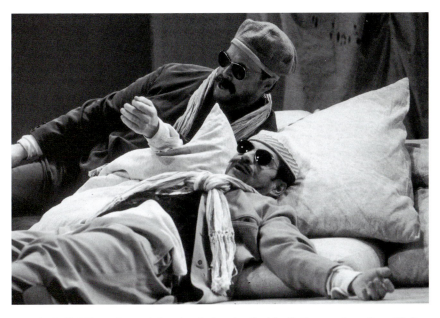

170   *The Daily Telegraph* noted that the clothes for *Cosi fan Tutte* were done 'beautifully, tastefully and wittily'. Overall the clothes were widely praised by critics

rivalry between Versace and Armani hit its peak, both designers entered into regular seasonal duals. For the spring/summer 1993 womenswear season, for example, Armani decided to move his show's time slot twice. According to Modenese the designer was simply allowing more time for buyers to catch the last plane out of Milan to Paris by presenting his show earlier in the evening.[58] However, the changes were caught by the press and by September headlines were reading 'Gianni Versace, Giorgio Armani fight to the finish'.[59] The previous season Armani chose to leave the coveted last spot, opting to open fashion week. The problem was that he wanted the spot back. The reason for the previous season's change was that Armani wanted to showcase his Giorgio and Emporio Armani collections together to celebrate Carnevale and host a special seasonal party. Forte noted, now 'we're simply going back to our usual spot'.[60] The people at Giorgio Armani confirmed that they had requested to do their show at 7.30 and 9.00 on the last evening. 'It's a big fight', said one member of the Versace camp, '[w]e don't know what's going to happen.'[61] With both houses vying to show at 7.30, Versace in the end opted to show at 6.30. The decision, seen by Rosanna Armani, then head of the press office, as an act of goodwill on the part of the house, still left buyers and member of the press to worry about having enough time to get from one show to the next, ostensibly forcing them to choose between the two. Although Armani was due to hold a second show, space and time would not guarantee the press a spot. Annoyed by his compatriots, Ferré simply boiled down the conflict to attention-seeking behaviour: 'It's the same old thing – making people talk about them.'[62]

171   The Versace woman (Dalma at left) versus the Armani women (centre and right) for spring 1991

By the early 1990s, Versace had already claimed himself king of the catwalk, having ushered in the era of the supermodel. Before the arrival of the supermodels, and a certain Canadian claiming $10,000 before she would opt to leave her bed, Milan fashion shows were still big business. In the early 1980s models could make three times what they did in Paris ($1,500 versus $500), and could walk as many as 30 runways a season.[63] Armani maintained a clear vision for his models and usually opted to forgo the industry's now celebrated names and faces. The body under the clothes has always been a sore point for the designer. More often than not models are chosen for their bodies and not their faces; he believes the right body displays his clothes in the best possible light. Over the years this has meant very thin, small-breasted women and chiselled, decidedly well-toned men. In response to the so-called 'perversity' of using such thin androgynous models, Armani asserts:

> It's very gratifying to see my clothes being worn by bigger women. But for the catwalk the jackets hang better on thin women. It's not that I don't like breasts, it's not that I'm saying only one shape is attractive, but it's easier to show the design on a flat chest.[64]

Armani later addressed his detractors when he conceded that 'everyone says that the fashion of Armani is androgynous. Without breasts, without hair. And it's true, sometimes when I watch the fashion show, I realize that there is a gorgeous body in place of a beautiful face.'[65] In 2006, Armani edited a special issue of *The Independent* featuring a black-faced Kate Moss on its cover. The proceeds of the issue went in aid of Bono and Bobby Shriver's Project Red campaign supporting African AIDS relief. In the issue Armani wrote three independent letters from the editor, the third, worth quoting at length, states how the designer's use of a certain type of model was largely the result of the relationship between textiles and the body. He claims:

> Ever since I started out as a fashion designer, I chose to use models that were on the slender side. This was because the clothes I design and the sort of fabrics I use need to hang correctly on the body, I want the dresses to seem to float and flow with the body. Gianni Versace was a very different kind of designer. He used jerseys and chiffons, which needed a body of a certain shape to hold the fabric. He used more voluptuous models. The particular styles I designed were quite different, and this is why, maybe, I was regarded as being among those designers who used slim women as models ... But I do not feel responsible for setting a trend toward models that look anorexic.[66]

Armani was the first designer to give outright support to ejecting super-skinny models from all the main fashion shows, imposing a minimum BMI on the models he hires. Armani's quick response came immediately following the death of Brazilian model Ana Carolina Reston from anorexia. The story surrounding her death was made more unfortunate and tragic when it was reported that a member of Giorgio Armani's team had complained that she was too skinny. Reston was photographed for an Armani catalogue in 2005, and a spokesperson for the house, concerned about the model's appearance during the shoot, telephoned Lica Kohlraush, director of her agency L'Equipe in São Paulo, to voice concerns over the model's health and thinness. No action was apparently taken by the agency.[67]

172   Thin and androgynous models dominated Armani's catwalk throughout the 1980s and 1990s. Here, an example from his spring/summer 1988 collection

173 An androgynous siren from his spring 1989 collection inspired in part by the Ballet Russes

At each show Armani walks through the paces with his models, and demonstrates how the model is expected to walk. In a scene from *Made in Milan*, he uses house model Laura to establish the correct pace and motions each model will have to perform on the runway. 'Try walking like a woman who moves down the street feeling natural as if she's in the centre of the world. Go. Slowly, Laura. Even when you turn, do it gently. Now stop, as if you were window-shopping. Not as if you were on a runway.'[68] Here Armani flips the scopic order, by placing the mannequin who is on display to appropriate the power of the gaze, as if she were in the world outside of the runway. The woman Armani attempts to articulate in the rarefied space of the runway is one that posses power, a mastery over self and her domain, but one whose corporeality is controlled and surveyed by the designer himself. She, through Armani's dictates only, is the mistress of movement. Montreal-based model Kate Rusko noted how in 1994 Armani hired older models, not for their looks but for their ability to command presence for his clothes on the runway. After rehearsals, she recalled, Armani reminded them: 'No posing! Smile a little! Do a full turn when wearing a dress so that the fabric can billow out!'[69]

Like the lighting system he uses in his theatre to direct attention to each individual garment, through a tacit yet palpable script Armani suppresses his models' individuality, ensuring that at no point in the show do they upstage his clothing. Little has changed over the years and before every show, Armani gathers his models together and reminds them of their job. 'I tell them', Armani states, 'to remember that the audience is not there to sleep with them. I tell them the point is the clothes. I tell them not to walk in a sexy way.' When asked whether they comply with his instructions, Armani responded: 'All except for Dalma.'[70] The model, seen on every major catwalk, embodied the fashion of the late 1980s and 1990s long before the supermodels took the job to new heights. After he instructs his hair and make-up team on how he wants his models groomed, the designer checks each model, usually only to redo it all himself, often by simplifying and removing make-up. On the occasion of one show, he was horrified to see that the make-up was 'Troppo Dallas', 'Troppo Miami Vice', 'Troppo Joan Collins'.[71] According to Forte, '[b]ecause every decision goes back to him, the image has a clarity that transcends what you think of it. What I am doing today I do only because he thought about it five years ago.' This is the formula to his on-going success.[72] Often devoid of jewellery and with little make-up, the Armani woman who appears on the runway and in the advertisements forces the audience to focus its attention entirely on the clothes and according to *The New York Times*, 'the effect is electric. He has a strong point of view that is projected in all his clothes and gives power to his presentation.'[73] Josie Borian, a popular androgynous model in the 1990s and a favourite for Armani for over 12 years, claims that '[h]e probably is a bit of a control freak. But he knows what he's doing. It's a serious business being in his shows.' Bodily control invades even the casting process when 'he makes all the girls wear strange flesh-coloured body stockings so that he can see the outline of their bodies, but they're not actually naked. Sometimes the younger ones get very nervous. But', as Borian attests, 'there's a great buzz to doing an Armani show.'[74]

174   Billowing sheer fabric, best seen either up close or through the choreographed turns made by models seen here at the spring 1988 collection

175   Even suits and jackets are made to convey movement and effortlessness, as seen in the spring 1988 collection

For his women's collection models usually walk a few metres, spin around quickly, often dramatically leaving the fabric of their jackets, skirts or dresses to billow out. The turning allows those in the theatre to visually grasp, even if only fleetingly, the effect textiles have on the silhouette and its relationship to the body. Models who are often paired to walk down the runway side by side turn in a perfect synchronization of movement toward the entrance, pause and turn again as they continue to move forward anew. The same is true if they walk in a sequence, an act of repetition set to establish recurring design motifs. Hand movements are special in an Armani show and are also choreographed and regulated. Loosely hanging, almost lifelessly, by their sides, often with one or two fingers elegantly separated and pointed downward. After seeing one of his shows, actor Donald Sutherland turned to a *Vogue* reporter and asked, '[d]id you notice the model's hands? ... Their hands were perfectly relaxed, yet full of energy. There's something about those clothes, and Armani himself, that conveys a self-assurance even to the models.'[75]

Female models are also, at times, seen with their hands or thumbs peeking out of a pockets, slightly and effortlessly dangling out, as if nearly falling out, giving a *soupçon* of haughty indifference and nonchalance. They also hold their hands up around their waist, bosom or simply in the air, suggesting a degree of artificial femininity and attenuated elegance. Every step taken is rhythmic, subtly choreographed down to the slightest movement. Nothing distracts from the purity of line, textiles and the auratic presence Armani wishes his garments to convey. For this reason he rarely uses supermodels, and if he does it is often difficult to identify them because their iconic status and flamboyance, instilled in them by his competitor Versace, is suppressed and reigned in, deferring to Armani's corporeal programme. Supermodel Yasmin Ghauri once claimed: 'He's trying to achieve a dreamlike state. But it can be very boring for us.'[76] Music also increasingly began to be used by the designer to achieve the rarefied realm he is known for, opting for techno, ambient and ethnic tunes, replacing the softer pop music he used well into the mid-1980s. By 2005, as part of a continued solidification of his complete sensorial empire, Armani began to release CDs through the Emporio Armani Caffè label that featured music used in various runway shows. Over time these five compilations in turn have served to reinforce the ambient and atmospheric quality of Armani events, with many of the songs reused in runway show DVDs included in catalogues or youtube.com video clips of special events recorded by the house. These reissued runway presentations are also sound edited, with clapping often replayed at distinctly different times than is seen in the original video. Sound, then, also became elemental in the quest to forge a cohesive lifestyle identity. For Armani himself claims: 'My atmosphere is everything.'[77]

176 Every detail is choreographed, even down to the placement of hands and thumbs. Autumn/winter 1987

177   Autumn/winter 1988

Given that Armani states he 'read[s] people through their body movements' claiming 'it's my work',[78] bodily movement on the runway has to be precise and exact a specific idea; they are after all, 'carriers of a message'.[79] To this end, male models, unlike female models that often hang only their thumbs in the pockets, decadently plunge their hands in their pockets, often exposing the amplitude of the fabric and silhouette lending a sense of informal ease. Male models are masculine, with chiselled features, and not unlike their female cohorts they spin around or turn to the side, stare deep into the audience and return to their steady gait. In the 1980s male models also possessed a more carefree insouciance to their walk, smiling and at times interacting more visibly with each other and the audience. By the 1990s, Armani's men became decidedly more serious, walking side by side without acknowledging their neighbour, not unlike the sense of dislocation felt in metropolitan urban centres, creating a greater distance between audience and stage while also enhancing the intensity and auratic atmosphere of the event. In the 1980s and early 1990s Armani would often send his models in a series of precise formations depending on the garments; three were presented one after the other, while four were sent out in two pairs.

These short sequences displayed either virtually identical outfits or slight variations on the same theme, often giving his buyers three options in both colour and fabric. What it meant, however, was significantly longer than usual shows, running well over 30 minutes by the mid-1990s, especially for

178   The relationship between body and textiles is crucial to understanding the runway and the ideal Armani body. Spring/summer 1990

his menswear collections that presented his Giorgio and Emporio Armani collections together. Here the notion of repetition is useful in understanding the Armani aesthetic and aura his presentations had in the 1980s and 1990s. By the mid-1990s, the size and time of an Armani show grew out of proportion and took on a decidedly more serious tone and mood. At the time, the designer stated that

> [f]or me the fashion show is an extremely serious thing, and that is why I approach it so intensely. It's important to send a clear message. And that's why at the end of the show I don't want the girls to applaud or make a lot of noise. I want people to leave my show convinced they have seen something that has been thought out very carefully, down to the last detail.[80]

For his autumn 1995 women's collection, while everyone else in Milan had headed to a minimalist haven, Armani showed his collection in the specially renovated Padiglione 36, a massive industrial warehouse in the southern outskirts of Milan. Rather than create an entirely different and unique stage for his runway show in this new temporary space, Armani imposed his steadfast spatial regime to ensure the continuity and quiet evolution of the house's identity he has honed. The cost to renovate the warehouse for discrete spaces for runway, dinner and dance floor was enormous. The vision, not surprisingly, was that of a movie studio, replete with cinematic scale and intensity. To an audience of 1,200, seventy male and female models presented what was an austere late 1930s and 1940s inspired collection of 400 exits on a 47.4 metre (157 foot) long catwalk. The silhouettes of vintage lamps were projected onto the walls, with palm trees seen through the large windows. The collection was at once austere yet highly sensual, reminiscent of 1930s embroideries and appliqués; some outfits were harsh with severe lines and a restricted colour palette of neutrals, blacks and browns in rich, soft fabrics, while others were light and radiant with rich and elaborate embroideries. Peter Lindberg also subsequently photographed the advertising campaign in this special runway space, with the models featured in the various areas that comprised the evening's spectacle. For his summer 1996 men's collection Armani continued his theme of bigger is better when he sent out a staggering 400 exists on 75 models along a specially designer 60 metre (199 foot) runway he had designed in the Ansaldo, a former factory he had renovated for the special showing.[81] He sent out around 20 models at once, as a way to 'convey an emotion', and of course overwhelm those present by his sheer creative output.[82] The largess of the space and show, like the trousers he showed that evening, conjured the 1930s and 1940s. At the end of the presentation, Armani had his army of models kneel before him as he waved to the audience. Despite the overwhelming display and vastness of the message, in which by Armani's own admission '[s]ubtle research is out', *The New York Times* heralded it as 'the sexiest Armani show in recent memory, with a body-conscious allure missing in the draped disguises of the past'.[83]

Armani/Teatro

Armani's shows expose an evolution largely informed and conditioned by the theatrical spaces he has used over the years. As part of his numerous millennial projects, Giorgio Armani inaugurated a new theatre and display space, Armani/Teatro, in Milan's industrial cum artist enclave of Porta Genova. Designed by Japanese minimalist architect Tadao Ando, Armani's signature turns, hands in pockets and walk were simplified even further, seemingly as the result of or in the very least in tandem with the new and austere concrete space. Since the inauguration of the Teatro models are sent down the runway either in single file or in pairs, devoid of turns, glances or playfulness. The result of the albeit slightly altered pattern has lent a perceptible detachment to the event, clothes and models, and I wish to highlight the textiles. He has retained his signature illuminated panelled runway, and the warmth it once lent to his basement theatre in via Borgonuovo is still present in what is a rather industrial and cold space designed by Ando. The clothing on the runway is to give warmth and texture to a space not meant to upstage the designer's creations.

The vast entrance of the building leads upward on a slight sloping incline along a cavernous 100 metre (331 foot) corridor broken up only by way of a centrally positioned series of concrete columns that bisect the axis. The semi-circular foyer directly opposite the theatre conceals the lavatories and cloakrooms for guests. The three reception desks are made of backlit

179   Autumn/winter 1995

glass. The theatre seats nearly 700 guests comfortably on white upholstered armchairs arranged on other side of the polished runway on high-rising bleachers. These seats can be rearranged to accommodate four different spatial configurations and event types, more ideally suited to fashion shows, ballets, movie screenings or conferences. Along the way to the theatre, the inner sanctum of the former factory, are numerous offices, showrooms and storage facilities whose access is concealed; again the labour or crass business of fashion, such as the monetary transaction at the cash register, is occluded from the initial fantasy that fashion presents. Throughout the space the visitor is afforded few liberties and movement is controlled and guided by the architecture. As is often the case with the spaces of Armani's empire, there is a purposeful interplay and

180   Modernist repetition colludes with corporeal choreography on Armani's runway to create a distinct aesthetic vision. Autumn/winter 1989

control of the relationship between light and dark, concealment and revelation, labour and performance, movement and confinement.

Ando is known for his ability to create 'spaces that defy trends and styles'.[84] Of the space Armani concedes that 'it has something lasting about it; it is not tied to the present, but has a substance that will allow it to be used for a long time to come, and maintain its rather ascetic atmosphere'.[85] Given Armani's more recent pretentions to safeguard his patrimony, it is fitting that the designer opted to commission an architect known for blueprints premised on longevity, permanence and solidity, as well as a desire to use simple materials which in no way conceal their industrial origins. In both the material and space of this architecture, aesthetics and industry enter into dialogue. Communication is also integral to the way Ando conceptualized the need and use of the space. According to the architect:

> During a show, a lot of people come together here. There is a strong feeling of interaction, a feeling of communication between people. That's the moment when you can really feel what this space has to offer, and the way in which it can boost the energy of those meeting in it, for a specific purpose.[86]

Armani sees the building and theatre as a gift back to Milan, given that the theatre also contains an exhibition space opened up to the public and for special events.

In a specially commissioned book, *Armani Backstage*, to commemorate the inauguration and first collection presented in the Armani/Teatro, the designer spoke of the necessity and implications of spatial confinement when developing and thinking through the final stages of a collection.

> When I am busy with the fittings for the collection, I can concentrate without distraction, and see the clothes in the same environment they will be shown in. I can refine them, rework them. And so, the theatre really becomes a laboratory which allows me to express what I feel without any inhibitions.[87]

In 1994 he said it best when he avowed:

> I believe firmly in the value of a fashion show, in the advantage of a fashion show, both for the person who creates fashion and for the person who sees it. A fashion show gives you a precise sensation. But it is one thing to put on a fashion show and another thing to put on a 'specttacolo'. I detest fashion when it becomes grotesque.[88]

Noteworthy is how 'specttacolo' is singled out in the translation (likely performed by an Armani aide) to remain in the 'original' language. Its importance then, that is, Armani's anti-theatrical, or anti-'specttacolo', stance can be traced as far back as Plato, who maintained that theatre is a cheap imitation of the realm of reality and the higher realm of pure ideas. Like the shadows on the walls in Plato's cave, Armani attempts to shed light on the erroneous ways of the fashion system, first through the way he presents his collections and secondly by refusing to create runway shows with no relation to the way men and women live their lives. Since Plato there has been a distrust of theatricality, generally because the term is consumed by notions of artifice. In art history, this rejection of theatricality, often conflated with spectacle and hyperbole, becomes most palpable within the long modernist tradition of seeing theatricality as artificial and negative. Theatricality as a form of representation and mode of expression has long been conflated in everyday life with notions of artifice, trickery and dishonesty and is charged with residing solely within the world of fiction.[89] In this vein, Armani has viewed theatricality and the spectacularization of fashion as deceptive and against the desires and needs of the customers who, in the end, are burdened with having to pay for the runway presentations and hyperbolic styles that do not sell. Undoubtedly one of the most infamous and often-cited modernist critiques teasing out the fraught relationship between theatricality and performance is Michael Fried's essay from 1967 in which his distaste for the purported fakery of theatre is made clear when he argues that '[a]rt degenerates as it approaches the condition of theater'.[90] Not unlike Armani, Aristotle, on the other hand, observed that theatre presents things not as they are, but as they ought to be, an idealist venue for translation and hence for transformation.

However, theatre scholar Josette Féral has theorized two important conditions of theatricality. First, it is a mode particular to theatre, which marks it as distinct from other aesthetic enterprises. Second, it is not bound by what we traditionally understand as 'theatre', but also resides within the realm of the quotidian, or the everyday.[91] It is precisely this everydayness of theatricality that marks the site of irony in Armani's anti-specttacolo statement in what amounts to a misreading of the term in the wake of a desire to criticize the fashion system. As a result of wanting to remain in control of his image, Armani has sought out numerous and various venues to stage what are repetitive and near-identical performances of his fashion, whether in his via Borgonuovo theatre, renovated factories, exhibitions, ambassadors' movements, cinema and the red carpet, ensuring his power remains greater than the fashion system's gatekeepers. It is precisely in these theatres of fashion, as Armani has devised them, that the tension between theatrical performance and his desire to have his clothes worn by people in the real world of the everyday is ennobled and embodied. As we have already seen, Armani has claimed that '[l]ife is the movie and my clothes are the costumes'.[92] While movies are not theatre, his statement draws spectacle and embodied everydayness close together through his clothes. At the centre of the conditions of theatricality is the gaze of the audience, which, through perception enacts the space as an 'other' space, no longer subject to the laws of the quotidian, and in this space he inscribes what he observes, perceiving it as belonging to a space where he has no place except as external observer. Without this gaze, indispensable for the emergence of theatricality and for its recognition as such, the other would share the spectator's space and remain part of his daily reality.[93]

The theatres of fashion (broadly understood as the various and multiple venues Armani has employed to stage a live event), foregrounds a mode of communication through which the body of the model, controlled by the designer, functions as the embodied mediators of the message, that is, the theatricality of the aura itself. This control can only be achieved through repetition.

Lacking the over-the-top spectacular scenarios of Alexander McQueen, Viktor & Rolf or John Galliano, Armani's highly controlled, streamlined spaces and seemingly endless and repetitive performances has meant that scholars have neglected to understand that performance and performativity do exist without the hyperbolic or the avant-garde, and as such is equally worthy of investigation as spaces and utterances which in actuality affect change precisely through subtlety, aura and controlling representation. Feminist performance scholar Elin Diamond contends that '[w]hen performativity

181   Spring/summer 1996

materializes as performance in that risky and dangerous negotiation between a doing (a reiteration of norms) and a thing done (discursive conventions that frame our interpretations), between someone's body and the conventions of embodiment, we have access to cultural meanings and critique.'[94] The body in a fashion show (whether live or in film) becomes crucial as both the site of the aura, the phenomenological experiences of the clothing and the representation of identity. Askesis, as inspired by its Ancient Greek origins, is as much about a discipline of the body as it is a 'control of representations'.[95] The techniques and technologies of askesis (an ascetic denial of worldly pleasures in favour of moral, spiritual or ethical codes), is given space in Ando's concrete austerity and Armani's utopian vision through a control of the body and representation contra the realm outside the latter's empire. In an Armani show, as I have noted, models turn or spin, creating a heightened sensory experience of the tactile element of the textiles. Sensorial memory becomes endemic to the way an audience experiences a runway show, often through quiet and unassuming repetition rather than through grand hyperbolic gestures. The serialization of the (non-super) models down the runway, the way they turn in a nearly identical way, at exact intervals, removes thinking from the experiences and replaces it with sensory perception, the phenomenological.

Unlike any other contemporary designer, in an Armani show a design idea or sartorial proposition is achieved through repetition. Whether by having ten models wearing the same outfit strutting down the runway at the same time, or models walking in a sequence of three, the message is always articulated through a clarity that at times verges into the dogmatic. The subtle, yet theatrical gestures and bodily restrictions Armani imposes on his models, what theatre scholar Willmar Sauter would describe as 'encoded gestures',[96] suggests that in order for the performative to affect and embody real change, the idealized and even romanticized propositions Armani sends down his runway deploy repetition as a theatrical device to underscore what has a heavily modernist ideological underpinning of what he sees as a response to the vulgarity in design. Armani's repetition, used in any of the theatrical settings he has devised, allows for imitative and emulative potential. His models' signature poses, postures and movements, because they are only slightly different one from the next, are highly effective as affective translations of his utopian ideal, and serve to reinforce how identity is made possible though performance, rather than a product of an essential essence.[97] While Armani encourages his models to repeat and perform in a certain, codified way, things can definitely go wrong: such as Dalma, for example, refusing to conform to his dictates. Between its scripted gestures and clear sartorial propositions, his models trouble our own relationship with and to the body as we continue to stake a claim for its agency in identity-formation and subject-actualization. Here we might think, however, of the inherent and vital difference between embodiment and representation. Embodiment offers not a distance from the

object, as representation suggests through the Cartesian mind–body split and Kantian act of aesthetic disinterest, but rather a living presence activated by materiality through the commingling of the subject with the object; for example, between textile surfaces and body's shape. It hints at sensorial acts beyond the opticality of visual images, by suggesting a sophisticated haptic knowledge of the different materials and ways these react to different sources of light and environments. Armani's runway is coded as not simply a semiotic space of theatre in which knowledge of a new collection is achieved, but one which facilitates embodiment itself. Armani's self-professed modernist vision reduced to the notion of repetition should turn our attention to Rosalind Krauss who made the term current in her infamous essay, 'The Originality of the Avant-garde'. Krauss contends that within the aesthetic economy of modernism, repetition is suppressed in favour of originality, a continuous and – dare I say – pathological desire for newness, shock and spectacle on the part of the avant-garde.[98] Armani defies the logic of the avant-garde, for within his vision, design seriality through theatricality becomes an embodied practice that enables his global modernity and the empire of the senses. A leitmotif throughout this book has been Armani's utopian ideals as a means to move from studio to runway to boutique to street. In this formulation there is no inherent contradiction for the designer, for his fashion, *the empire of the senses* he has built through his various brands and enterprises is meant to integrate into and yet transform the world, a desire held firm by modernist painters, architects, designers and writers in the early decades of the twentieth century. 'It's really very straightforward', states Armani. 'I design for real people. I think of our customers all the time. There is no virtue whatsoever in creating clothing or accessories that are not practical.'[99] In the final sequence of *Made in Milan*, house model Laura walks the runway, showcasing the exquisite evening creation Armani has been working on throughout the film. As she continues to walk, the runway is gradually transformed, through the trickery of film, into the street of via Borgonuovo. From runway to street, Armani has always maintained that what is presented in his theatre must be able to translate and walk out into real streets whether in Milan, Tokyo, Sydney or Montreal.

183   Giorgio Armani takes a final bow

Notes

1   *DNR*: The Magazine September 1983.

2   *DNR*: The Magazine September 1983.

3   Grandee 1990: 151.

4   *The Star* (UK) 22 June 1933.

5   Grandee 1990: 152.

6   Armani in *Made in Milan* 1990.

7   Ralph Lauren has also used some of his homes as advertising backdrops. However, unlike Armani who has created his own unique and highly identifiable spaces, Lauren's spaces are more in keeping with a broad English WASP aesthetic, blend easily within this larger idiom and are not strictly understood as his private domestic sphere. As a result, Armani's spaces are all of his own design and have become endemic to the aura, lifestyle and aesthetic he has fashioned himself.

8   Armani in Molho 2007: 217.

9   *NYT* 20 June 1982.

10   Armani in Molho 2007: 90.

11   *WWD* 18 June 1980.

12   *WWD* 18 June 1980.

13   *NYT* 5 October 1980.

14   *TS* 28 November 1980.

15   *TS* 6 October 1981.

16   *TS* 6 October 1981.

17   Burstein in Giacomoni 1984: 126.

18   *TS* 3 December 1981.

19   *NYT* 9 February 1982.

20   Armani in Molho 2007: 95.

21   For more on this issue see for example Palmer 2001; Palmer 2009; Wilcox 2007.

22   *LAT* 19 February 1982.

23   *LAT* 2 April 1982.

24   *LAT* 19 February 1982.

25   Poux 1982: n.p.

26   *NYT* 6 April 1982.

27   Armani in Molho 2007: 99.

28   *NYT* 9 March 1982.

29   *NYT* 6 April 1982.

30   I wish to point out that Jay Cocks and his wife have become devoted collectors of Armani garments over the decades. A significant number of the garments held by the FIT Museum were given by Jay Cocks and Verna Bloom Cocks. In addition, their own private collection was borrowed from for the Guggenheim exhibition. Looking at the FIT list of garments held by the museum, it is clear the Cocks were avid collectors of the designer's work early on and have continued to buy his fashions well into the present. Cocks has been a close collaborator and supporter of Armani, working on several projects with him.

31   *NYT* 9 March 1982.

32   *NYT* 7 October 1982.

33   *LAT* 11 October 1982.

34   *LAT* 11 October 1982.

35   *WWD* 7 March 1983.

36   BG 7 March 1983.

37   Giaconomi 1984: 21.

38   *Time* 9 May 1983.

39   *DNR* 8 July 1983.

40   Armani in Giacomoni 1984: 70.

41   Armani in Giacomoni 1984: 73.

42   *The Times Magazine* 22 August 1998.

43   *DNR* 8 July 1983.

44   *DNR* 8 July 1983.

45   *WWD* 8 October 1983.

46   *The Times Magazine* 22 August 1998.

47   Brantley 1988: 170.

48   *DNR* 17 June 1996.

49   Armani in *DNR* 9 May 1996.

50   *DNR* 8 July 1996: 8.

51   *Le Monde* 6 July 1996.

52   *Le Monde* 6 July 1996.

53   *Le Monde* 6 July 1996.

54   *DNR* July 8, 1996.

55   *DNR* 9 May 1996.

56   Napoleone *DNR* 3 May 1996.

57   According to the *G & M*, the average cost of an Armani runway show in the 1980s was around $350,000 (16 December 1986).

58   *DNR* 25 June 1992.

59   *WWD* 11 September 1992.

60   *CDS* 15 September 1992.

61   *WWD* 11 September 1992.

62   *WWD* 15 September 1992.

63   *NYT* 28 March 1984.

64   'In the court of Armani' June 1994: 191.

65   Bachrach 2000: 364.

66   *I* 21 September 2006.

67   *I* 19 November 2006.

68   Armani in *Made in Milan* 1990.

69   Armani in *MG* 14 June 1994.

70   Armani in Howell 1990: 123.

71   Armani in Brantley 1988: 130.

72   Howell 1990: 125.

73   *NYT* 10 October 1985.

74   'In the Court of Armani' 1994: 189.

75   'The Armani Edge' 1992: 318–19.

76   'The Armani Edge' 1992: 320.

77   'The Armani Edge' 1992: 322.

78   'The Armani Edge' 1992: 323.

79   *WWD* 25 October 1994.

80   *WWD* 25 October 1994.

81   The Ansaldo factory complex would later be transformed into the *Città delle culture* (City of Culture).

82   *DNR* 28 June 1995.

83   *NYT* July 1995.

84   Quick 2002: 125.

85   Casciani 2001: 51.

86   Casciani 2001: 51.

87   Hutchings 2002: n.p.

88   *WWD* 25 October 1994.

89   For a detailed discussion of the long-held negative associations to theatricality see Carlsson 2002.

90   Fried 1969: 139.

91   Féral 2002: 3.

92   Armani in *Made in Milan*, 1990.

93   Féral 2002: 105.

94   Diamond 1996: 5.

95   Foucault 1990b: 74.

96   Sauter 2000.

97   Here I refer to Butler's core argument that gender is performative, and as such it is an act of doing rather than one of being. See Butler 1990.

98   Krauss 1986.

99   Armani in Andrews 2007: 360.

Select Bibliography

Given the sheer number used, articles in daily and weekly periodicals are not listed in the bibliography nor are their page numbers given in the text.

Periodicals consulted (with abbreviations used in the endnotes)

Boston Globe (BG)
Corriere della Sera (Corriere)
Daily New Record (DNR)
Fashion Wire Daily (FWD)
The Guardian
Globe and Mail (G & M)
The Independent
International Herald Tribune (IHT)
Los Angeles Times (LAT)
Le Monde
The New York Times (NYT)
The Observer
La Repubblica
The Times (London)
Telegraph
Toronto Star (TS)
Women's Wear Daily (WWD)

Catalogues

Giorgio Armani since autumn/winter 1989

Films

Altman, Robert. *Prêt-à-Porter*. 1994.

Beresford, Bruce. *Double Jeopardy*. 1999.
Schrader, Paul. *American Gigolo*. 1980.
_____ . *The Comfort of Strangers*. 1990.
Scorsese, Martin. *Made in Milan*. 1990.
Scoot, Tom. *Top Gun*. 1986.
Shanley, John Patrick. *Joe Versus the Volcano*. 1990.
Tucker, Anand. *Shop Girl*. 2005.
Von Sternberg, Josef. *Shanghai Express*. 1932.
Wender, Wim. *Notebook on Cities and Clothes*. 1989.
Winkler, Irwin. *De-Lovely*. 2004.

Articles and Books

Adorno, Theodor. *In Search of Wagner*. London: NLB, 1981.
Alhadeff, Gini. *Diary of a Djinn*. New York: Anchor, 2004.
Allen, Beverly. 'The Novel, the Body, and Giorgio Armani: Rethinking National "Identity" in a Postnational World', in Giovanna Miceli Jefferies (ed.). *Feminine Feminist: Cultural Practices in Italy*. Minneapolis and London: University of Minnesota Press, 1994: 153–70.
'Alluring Armani'. *Interior Design* (May 1989): 25.
Anderson, Fiona. 'Museums as Fashion Media', in Stella Bruzzi and Pamela Church Gibson (eds.). *Fashion Cultures: Theories, Explorations and Analysis*. London, New York: Routledge, 2000: 371–89.
Andrews, John. 'Business Sense: It Takes a Lot More than Individual Flair to Stay at the Top', in Linda Welters and Abby Lillethun (eds.). *Fashion Reader*. Oxford, New York: Berg, 2007: 356–60.
Annunziato, Lisa. 'Armani's Atelier'. *Contract* (July 2001): 62.
Appadurai, Arjun. *Modernity at Large: Cultural Dimensions of Globalization*. Minneapolis: University of Minnesota Press, 1996.
Aragno, Bonizza Giordani (ed.). *Moda Italia: Creativity and Technology in the Italian Fashion System*. Milan: Editoriale Domus, 1988.
'Architectural Digest Visits Giorgio Armani'. *Architectural Digest* (November 2006): 174–83.
Armani, Giorgio. 'Foreword', in Grant Camden Kirkpatrick. *Shops and Boutique*. New York: Rizzoli International Publications, 1994.
_____ . 'Die Klarheit der Linie', in Herausgeben von Walfgang Jacobsen et al. (eds.). *Kino, Movie, Cinema*. Berlin: Argon Verlag GmbH, 1995: 103–10.
_____ . 'Away from Catwalks'. *Flash Art* (January/February 1997): 78.
_____ . 'Foro Italico'. *Out* (June 2002): 40–1.
'Armani/Architecture'. *Abitare* (February 2002): 97–107.
'Armani Disarmed'. *Emporio Armani Magazine* 14 (September 1995–February 1996): ii–xvi.
'The Armani Edge'. *Vogue* (USA) (March 1992): 317–23.
'Armani e Bob Wilson Alle Terme De Diocleziano'. *Abitare* 441 (July/August 2004): 96–104.
'Armani, Inc'. *Esquire* (October 1997): 84–7.
'Armani on the Loose'. *GQ* (August 1978): 120.
'Armani/Teatro'. *The Japan Architect* (Winter 2002): 58–61.
Armstrong, Lisa. 'In the Court of Armani'. *Vogue* (UK) (June 1994): 148–51,190–1.

Arvidsson, Adam. *Marketing Modernity: Italian Advertising from Fascism to Postmodernity*. New York and London: Routledge, 2003.

Attfeild, Judy. *Wild Things: The Material Culture of Everyday Life*. Oxford and New York: Berg, 2000.

Bachrach, Judy. 'Armani in Full'. *Vanity Fair* (October 2000): 360–5, 395–8.

Bakhtin, M. M. *The Dialogic Imagination: Four Essays*. Austin and London: University of Texas Press, 1981.

Ball, Deborah. *House of Versace*. New York: Crown Publishers, 2010.

Barthes, Roland. *Système de la mode*. Paris: Seuil: 1967.

_____ . *The Language of Fashion*. Translated by Andy Stafford; Andy Stafford and Michael Carter (eds.). Oxford and New York: Berg, 2006.

Baudelaire, Charles. *The Painter of Modern Life and other Essays*. London: Phaidon, 1970.

Baumgold, Julie. 'Armani Explains it All'. *Esquire* (October 1995): 176.

Beker, Jeanne. 'Dressed to Kill'. *GQ* (Fall 2005): 67.

Belk, R.W. and M. Wallendorf. 'Of Mice and Men: Gender Identity in Collecting', in Susan M. Pearce (ed.). *Interpreting Objects and Collections*. London and New York: Routledge, 1994: 240–53.

Beng Huat, Chua. 'Shopping for women's fashion in Singapore', in Rob Shields (ed.). *Lifestyle Shopping: The Subject of Consumption*. London and New York: Routledge: 1992: 114–35.

Benjamin, Walter. *The Arcades Project*. Howard Eiland and Kevin McLaughlin (trans.). Cambridge: Harvard University Press, 1999a.

_____ . *Illuminations*. London: Pimlico, 1999b.

Bertoni, Franco. *Claudio Silvestrin*. Basel, Boston and Berlin: Birkhausen. 1999.

Betsky, Aaron. 'Minimalism: Design's Disappearing Act'. *Architecture* (February 1997): 47–51.

Bhabha, Homi. 'The Third Space', in J. Rutherford (ed.). *Identity: Community, Culture, Difference*. London: Lawrence and Wishart, 1990: 207–21.

_____ . *The Location of Culture*. New York and London: Routledge, 2004.

Biachino, Gloria (ed.). *Italian Fashion Volume I: The Origins of High Fashion and Knitwear*. New York: Rizzoli International, 1987.

_____ . *Italian Fashion Volume II: From Anti-Fashion to Stylism*. New York: Rizzoli International, 1987.

Bingham, Neil. *The New Boutique: Fashion and Design*. London and New York: Merrell, 2005.

Bingham, Neil and Michael Gabellini. 'The New Boutique'. *Fashion and Design* (2005): 52.

Blonsky, Marshall. *American Mythologies*. New York; Oxford: Oxford University Press, 1992.

Bocca, Nicolettea. *Moda: Poesia e Progetto*. Milan: Domus Academy, 1990: n.p.

Bonami, Francesco. 'Fashion, Wine, and Olive Oil'. *Flash Art* (January/February 1997): 76.

'Boutiques de Luxe et de Mode'. *Architecture Interieure Crée* 275 (1997): 106–7.

Boyd, Suzanne. 'Mass Mania'. *Flare* (September 2000): 84.

Boym, Svetlana. *The Future of Nostalgia*. New York: Basic Books, 2001.

Brampton, Sally. 'Armani's Island'. *Elle Decoration* (UK) (1989): 120–5.

Brantley, Ben. 'The Armani Mystique'. *Vanity Fair* (June 1988): 126–30, 170–3.

Breward, Christopher. *The Culture of Fashion*. Manchester: Manchester University Press, 1995.

_____ . *The Hidden Consumer: Masculinities, Fashion and City Life*. Manchester and New York: Manchester University Press, 1999.

_____ . 'Cultures, Identities, Histories: Fashioning a Cultural Approach to Dress', in Nicola White and Ian Griffiths (eds.). *The Fashion Business: Theory, Practice, Image*. Oxford and New York: Berg, 2000: 23–35.

Brunisi, Lucy and Kicki Wehlou. 'When Armani Makes Pants'. *Threads* (February/ March 1995): 38–43.

Brunel, Jacques. 'La Precision Du Flou Armani'. *Vogue* (Paris) 806 (April 2000): 184–6.

Bruzzi, Stella. *Undressing Cinema: Clothing and Identity in the Movies*. London and New York: Routledge, 1997.

Buck-Morss, Susan. 'The Cinema Screen as Prosthesis of Perception: A Historical Account', in C. Nadia Seremetakis (ed.). *The Senses Still*. Boulder: Westview Press, 1994: 45–62.

Burger, Peter. *Theory of the Avant-Garde*. Minneapolis: University of Minnesota Press, 1984.

Burke, Peter. 'Cultures of Translation in early Modern Europe', in Peter Burke and R. Po-Chia Hsia (eds.). *Cultural Translation in Early Modern Europe*. Cambridge: Cambridge University Press, 2007: 7-38.

Butler, Judith. *Gender Trouble: Feminism and the Subversion of Identity*. New York: Routledge, 1990.

Calefato, Patrizia. *The Clothed Body*. Oxford and New York: Berg, 2004.

Carlsson, Marvin. 'The Resistance to Theatricality'. *SubStance* (2002): 238–50.

Caracciolo, Marella. 'Armani's Country Look'. *The World of Interiors* (February 1990): 67–75.

Casciani, Stefano. 'Ando e Armani'. *Domus Fashion* (2001): 48–63.

_____ . 'Armani Hong Kong'. *Domus Fashion* (2003): 44–9.

Chapman, Rowena. 'The Great Pretender: Variations on the New Man Theme', in Rowena Chapman and Jonathan Rutherford (eds.). *Male Order: Unwrapping Masculinity*. London: Lawrence & Wishart, 1988: 225–48.

Chenoune, Farid. *A History of Men's Fashion*. New York and Paris: Flammarion, 1996.

Cliff, Stafford. 'Emporio Armani'. *50 Trade Secrets of Great Design Retail Spaces*. Bervely MA: Rockport Publishers, 1999: 218–9.

Clifford, James 'Museums as Contact Zones', in James Clifford (ed.). *Routes: Travel and Translation in the Late Twentieth Century*. Cambridge, MA: Harvard University Press, 1997: 188–219.

Clifton-Mogg, Caroline. 'Insider Lifestyle'. *House and Garden* (March 2006): 32–8.

Colavita, Courtney. 'This Time, it's Personal'. *W* (December 2004): 144.

Collings, Matthew. 'The Art of Not Offending Anyone. The Road to Relativism. Or Maybe Not'. *Modern Painters* (2001): 14, 100–2.

Colomina, Beatriz. 'The Split Wall: Domestic Voyeurism', in Beatriz Colomina (ed.). *Sexuality and Space*. Princeton: Princeton Architectural Press, 1992: 73–128.

Comita, Jenny. 'Natural Light'. *WWD Magazine* (April 2001): 98–100.

_____ . 'The Ambassadors'. *W* (August 2004): 77–8.

'Concrete Couture'. *The Architectural Review* CCXI, 1260 (February 2002): 74–8.

Craik, Jennifer. *The Face of Fashion: Cultural Studies in Fashion*. New York and London: Routledge, 1994.

Cramer, Ned. 'Fashion Victim'. *Architecture* (February 1997): 45.

Crow, Thomas. *Modern Art in the Common Culture*. New Haven and London: Yale University Press, 1996.

D'Arcy, David. *Profile: Guggenheim Museum's Exhibit of Giorgio Armani Fashions*. 2000. (transcript).

Davis, Fred. *Fashion, Culture, and Identity*. Chicago and London: University of Chicago Press, 1992.

de Combray, Richard. 'Giorgio Armani', in Richard de Combray. *Luxe, Calm et Volupté*. Milan: Franco Maria Ricci Editore, 1982: 143–208.

de la Haye, Amy. 'Ethnic Minimalism: A Strand of 1990s British Identity Explored via a Contextual Analysis of Designs by Shirin Guild', in Nicola White and Ian Griffiths (eds.). *The Fashion Business: Theory, Practice, Image*. Oxford and New York: Berg, 2000: 55–66.

Deleuze, Gilles. *The Fold: Leibniz and the Baroque*. Minneapolis: University of Minnesota Press, 1993.

Diamond, Elin. (ed.). *Performance and Cultural Politics*. New York and London: Routledge, 1996.

Dorleans, Francis. 'Armani'. *L'Officiel* (March 2000): 2.

Drobnik, Jim. 'Volatile Effects: Olfactory Dimensions of Art and Architecture', in David Howes (ed.). *Empire of the Senses: The Sensual Culture Reader*. Oxford and New York: Berg, 2005: 264–80.

Edwards, Tim. *Men in Mirror: Men's Fashion, Masculinity and Consumer Society*. London: Cassell, 1997.

Entwistle, Joanne. '"Power Dressing" and the Construction of the Career Woman', in Malcolm Barnard (ed.). *Fashion Theory: A Reader*. London and New York: Routledge, 2007: 208-19.

_____ . *The Fashioned Body: Fashion, Dress and Modern Social Theory*. Cambridge: Polity Press, 2000.

Evans, Caroline. *Fashion at the Edge: Spectacle, Modernity and Deathliness*. New Haven and London: Yale University Press, 2003.

_____ . 'The Enchanted Spectacle'. *Fashion Theory* 5, 3 (August 2001): 271–310.

'Fall Style Preview: The Collections'. *Esquire* (August 2005): 132.

Fallaci, Paola. 'Giorgio Armani'. *L'Officiel* (April 1981): 164, 176.

'Fashion Show'. *Architectural Review* (June 2001): 78–80.

'Fashion Victim: A New Madison Avenue Boutique Maxes Out on Minimalism'. *Architecture* (February 1997): 45.

Féral, Josette. 'Theatricality: The Specificity of Theatrical Language'. *SubStance* 31, 2 & 3 (2002): 2–7, 94–107.

Ferrero-Regis, Tiziana. 'Fatto in Italia: Refashioning Fashion'. *Journal of Multidisciplinary International Studies* 5, 2 (July 2008): 1–17.

Field, Tiffany. *Touch*. Cambridge and London: MIT Press, 2001.

Finkelstein, Joanne. *The Fashioned Self*. Cambridge and Oxford: Polity Press, 1991.

Fiori, Pamela. 'The Quiet Man'. *Town & Country* (January 1998): 70–7, 125–7.

Fischer, Lucy. *Designing Women: Cinema, Art Deco and the Female Form*. New York: Columbia University Press, 2003.

Foley, Bridget. 'Master Armani'. *W* (October 2000): 382.

Foot, John. *Milan Since the Miracle: City, Culture and Identity*. Berg: Oxford and New York, 2001.

Forden, Sara Gay. 'Numero Uno'. *W* (January 1995): 48–53.

Forgacs, David and Stephen Gundle. *Mass Culture and Italian Society: From Fascism to the Cold War*. Bloomington: Indiana University Press, 2007.

Foucault, Michel. *Language, Counter-Memory, Practice: Selected Essays and Interviews*. Oxford: Blackwell, 1977.

_____ . *History of Sexuality Volume* I: *The Will to Knowledge*. New York: Vintage Books, 1990a.

_____ . *History of Sexuality Volume 2: The Uses of Pleasure*. New York: Vintage Books, 1990b.

_____ . 'Of Other Places', in Nicholas Mirzoeff (ed.). *Visual Culture Reader*. London and New York: Routledge, 1998a: 238–44.

_____ . What is an Author?', in James D. Faubion (ed.). *Aesthetics, Method and Epistemology Vol. 2*. New York: New Press, 1998b: 205–22.

_____ . 'What is Enlightenment?' *The Foucault Reader*. London: Pantheon Books, [1978] 2004: 32–50.

Franceschetti, Roberta. 'L'Anno Di Re Giorgio'. *Arte* 328 (December 2000): 156–61.

Freud, Sigmund. *Leonardo da Vinci and a Memory of his Childhood*. Harmondsworth: Penguin Books, [1910] 1985.

Fried Michael. 'Art and Objecthood', in Gregory Battock (ed.). *Minimal Art*. New York: Dutton, 1969: 116–47.

Frisa, Maria Luisa and Stefano Tonchi (eds.). *Walter Albini and his Times: All Power to the Imagination*. Venice: Marsilio, 2010.

Fuksas, Doriana and Massimiliano Fuksas. *Armani Ginza Tower*. New York and Barcelona: Actar, 2008.

Gale, Colin and Jasbir Kaur. *The Textile Book*. Oxford and New York: Berg, 2002.

Ganem, Mark. 'Hurricane Giorgio'. *W* (November 1996): 248–52.

Garafola, Lynn. *Diaghilev's Ballets Russes*. New York: Oxford University Press, 1989.

Garber, Marjorie. *Vested Interests: Cross-Dressing and Cultural Anxiety*. New York: Routledge, 1997.

Gaudoin, Tina. 'Amore Armani'. *Elle* (UK) (July 1995): 44–8.

Giacomoni, Silvia. *The Italian Look Reflected*. Milan: Mazzotta, 1984.

Gibson, Pamela Church. *Fashion and Celebrity Culture*. Oxford and New York: Berg.

Gilbert, David. 'Introduction: From Paris to Shanghai', in Christopher Breward and David Gilbert (eds.). *The Changing Geographies of Fashion's World Cities*. Oxford and New York: Berg, 2006: 3–32.

Gili, Oberto. 'The House of Armani'. *House and Home* (UK) (April 1990): 144.

'Giorgio Armani'. *Toronto Life's Fashion* (Winter 1986): 107–8.

'Giorgio Armani'. *Metropolitan Home* (October 2006): 130.

Giorgio Armani. (exh. cat.) New York: Guggenheim Museum, 2000.

'Giorgio Armani on What's Sexy'. *Details* (September 2005): 129.

Goulet, Anne Laure. 'Boutiques de Luxe et de Mode'. *Architecture Interieure* 275 (1997): 184–7.

Grandee, Charles. 'The House of Armani'. *House and Garden* (UK) (April 1990): 144–53.

Greer, Bonnie. 'Cut from the Same Cloth'. *RA Magazine* (Autumn 2003): 58–61.

Grignaffini, Giovanna. 'A Question of Performance', in Glorai Bianchino and Paul Blancharel (eds.). *Italian Fashion: The Origins of High Fashion and Kintwear*. Milan: Rizzoli, 1987: 6–26.

Gronberg, Tag. *Designs on Modernity: Exhibiting the City in 1920s Paris*. Manchester and New York: Manchester University Press, 1998.

Gundle, Stephen. 'Hollywood Glamour and Mass Consumption in Postwar Italy'. *Journal of Cold War Studies* 4, 3 (Summer 2002): 95–118.

Hale, Sheila. 'King Giorgio'. *Harper's and Queen* (October 1992): 97–9.

Harris, Sarah. 'Amazing Grace'. *Vogue* (UK) (March 2005): 316–9.

Harvey, John. 'Loose Living'. *RA Magazine* (Autumn 2003): 54–6.

Heartney, Eleanor. 'The Guggenheim's New Clothes'. *Art in America* (2 January 2001): 61–2.

Himelfarb, Ellen. 'Armani's Smooth Sailing'. *Sir* (Fall 2005): 45–8.

Hirschberg, Lynn. 'Giorgio on My Mind'. *Harper's Bazaar* (October 2000): 188.

Hochswender, Woody. 'Armani Classico'. *Esquire* (February 1996): 101–2.

Hollander, Anne. *Seeing Through Clothes*. Berkeley and Los Angeles: University of California Press, 1975.

_____ . *Sex and Suits: The Evolution of Modern Dress*. New York: Kodansha International, 1994.

Holley, Brandon. 'Bravo, Giorgio!' *GQ* (April 2000): 231.

Hooper-Greenhill, Eileen. *Museums and the Interpretation of Visual Culture*. London and New York: Routledge, 2000.

Howarth, Peter. 'A Cut Above'. *GQ* (UK) (January 1994): 9.

_____ . 'Armani Takes a Bow'. *GQ* (March 1994): 21–2.

_____ . 'Giorgio Armani Esq'. *Esquire* (UK) (October 2002): 64–70.

_____ . 'Giorgio Armani'. *GQ* (March 2005): 129–33.

Howell, Georgina. 'Giorgio Armani: The Man who Fell to Earth', in Georgina Howell. *Sultans of Style: Thirty Years of Fashion Passion, 1960–1990*. London: Ebury Press, 1990: 121–7.

Hutchings, Roger. *Armani Backstage*. Milan: Frederico Motta, 2002.

Hyde, Ann. 'Inside an Armani Jacket: Exploring the Secrets of the Master of Milan'. *Threads* (August/September 1990): 24–7.

Ilari, Alessandra. 'Armani the Eccentric?' *WWD Magazine* (Fall 2004): 80.

'Interview with Giorgio Armani at Armani Teatro in Milan'. *Architecture + Urbanism* (July 2004): 10–1, 18–21.

'In the Court of Armani'. *Vogue* (UK) (June 1994): 148–50, 189, 191.

Irigaray, Luce. *Speculum of the Other Woman*. Ithaca: Cornell University Press, 1985.

'Italian Fabrics '78'. *Vogue* (USA) (January 1978): 119–21.

Jones, Carla and Ann Marie Leshkowich. *Re-Orienting Fashion: The Globalization of Asian Dress*. Oxford and New York: Berg, 2003.

Jones, Dylan. 'Giorgio Armani: The Modernist'. *Arena* (April 1996): 159.

Jones, Rose Apodaca. 'Armaniwood'. *W* (November 2003): 308–11.

Katz, David and Lester E. Kruger (eds.). *The World of Touch*. Hillsdale: Lawrence Erblaum Associates, 1989.

Kazanjian, Dodie. 'Finally Buying Armani'. *Vogue* (USA) (May 1994): 126, 128, 140.

Khan, Nathalie. 'Catwalk Politics', in Stella Bruzzi and Pamela Church Gibson (eds.). *Fashion Cultures: Theories, Exploration and Analysis*. London and New York: Routledge, 2000: 114–27.

Kirkham, Pat (ed.). *The Gendered Object*. Manchester and New York: Manchester University Press, 1996.

Kirkpatrick, Grant Camden. *Shops and Boutiques* (Foreword by Giorgio Armani). New York: Rizzoli International Relations Inc., 1994.

Kondo, Dorinne. *About Face: Performing Race in Fashion and Theatre*. New York and London: Routledge, 1997.

Krauss, Rosalind. 'Originality of the Avant-Garde', in Rosalind Krauss. *The Originality of the Avant-Garde and Other Modernist Myths*. Cambridge: MIT Press, 1986: 151–70.

Kuhn, Annette. *The Power of Image: Essays on Representation and Sexuality*. London: Routledge and Paul Kegan, 1985.

'Ladies and Gentlemen Armani!' Esquire (May 2002): 40–1.

Lalanne, Olivier. 'Corps D'Elite'. *Vogue (Paris)* (November 2004): 166–71.

Lamacraft, Jane. 'Italian Growth'. *Interior Design* (May 1989): 25, 28–9.

Law, John. 'Notes on the Theory of the Actor Network: Ordering, Strategy and Heterogeneity', published by the Centre for Science Studies, Lancaster University, Lancaster LA1 4YN, at http://www.comp.lancs.ac.uk/sociology/papers/Law-Notes-on-ANT.pdf (accessed 18 November 2010): 2003.

Lehmann, Ulrich. *Tigersprung: Fashion and Modernity*. Cambridge and London: The MIT Press, 2000.

Linn, Charles. 'The very Fine Art of Lighting Basic Black'. *Architectural Record* (November 1997): 158–9.

Lipovetsky, Gilles. *The Empire of Fashion: Dressing Modern Democracy*. Princeton and Oxford: Princeton University Press, 1994.

Loos, Ted. 'Armani Artfully'. *Town and Country* (October 2000): 142.

Loratt-Smith, Lisa. *The Fashion House: Inside the Homes of Leading Designers*. London: Conran Octopus Limited: 1997.

Lukács, George. 'Realism in the Balance', in Ernst Bloch et al. (eds.). *Aesthetics and Politics*. London: NLB, 1977.

'Man about Town'. *W* (January 2005): 68.

Manvelli, Sara. *Design for Shopping: New Retail Interiors*. London: Lawrence King Publishing, 2006.

Marks, Laura. *The Skin of the Film: Intercultural Cinema, Embodiment and the Senses*. Durham; London: Duke University Press 2000.

Martin, J.J. 'What Makes Giorgio Armani Tick?' *Harper's Bazaar* (August 2005): 158, 160–2.

Martin, Richard. 'Cine-Mode: Fashion and the Movie Metaphor in the Art of Giorgio Armani'. *Textile and Text* 14, 2 (1991): 22–31.

_____ . 'Fashion and a Sense of Place: Emporio Armani's European Grand Tour'. *Textile and Text* 13, 2 (1990a): 14–21.

_____ . 'Giorgio Armani's Encyclopedia of Man in 1986'. *Textile and Text* 13, 2 (1990b): 3–13.

_____ . '"What is Man!" – the Imagery of Male Style of J. C. Leyendecker and Giorgio Armani'. *Textile and Text* 13, 1 (1990c): 3–27.

Martin, Richard and Harold Koda. *Giorgio Armani: Images of Man*. New York: Rizzoli International Publications, 1990.

_____ . *Orientalism: Visions of the East in Western Dress*. New York: Metropolitan Museum of Art and Harry N. Abrams, Inc.: 1994.

McBride, Patrizia C. '"In Praise of the Present": Adolf Loos on Style and Fashion'. *Modernism/Modernity* 11, 4 (2004): 745–67.

Merleau-Ponty, Maurice. *The Phenomenology of Perception*. London and New York: Routledge, 1958.

Merlo, Elisabeth and Francesca Polese. 'Turning Fashion Business: The Emergence of Milan as an International Fashion Hub'. *Business History Review* 80 (Autumn 2006): 415–47.

Meyer, James (ed.). *Minimalism*. London: Phaidon, 2000.

Miceli Jefferies, Giovanna (ed.). *Feminine Feminists*. Minneapolis and London: University of Minnesota Press, 1994.

Miller, Sanda. 'Fashion as Art; is Fashion Art?' *Fashion Theory* 11, 1 (March 2007): 25–40.

Mitchell, Timothy. *Questions of Modernity (Contradictions of Modernity)*. Minneapolis and London: University of Minnesota Press, 2000.

Molho, Renata. *Being Armani*. Milan: Baldini Castoldi Dalai, 2007.

Mort, Frank. 'New Men and New Markets', in Peter McNeil and Vicki Karaminas (eds.). *The Men's Fashion Reader*. Berg: Oxford and New York, 2009: 454–9.

Mostadi, Arian. *Hotshops*. Barcelona: Carlos Broto and Josep M. Minguet, 2003.

Mower, Sarah. 'Emperor Armani'. *Vogue* (UK) (March 1989): 248–9, 342.

_____ . 'Armani After Dark'. *Harper's Bazaar* (February 1993): 142–3, 200.

Muscau, Francesca. 'The City Boutique: Milan and the Spaces of Fashion', in John Potvin (ed.). *The Places and Spaces of Fashion*. London and New York: Routledge, 2009: 121–38.

Nixon, Sean. *Hard Looks: Masculinities, Spectatorship and Contemporary Consumption*. London: University College London Press, 1996.

Palmer, Alexandra. *Couture and Commerce: The Transatlantic Fashion trade in the 1950s*. Washington: University of Washington Press, 2001.

_____ . *Dior*. London: V & A Publishing, 2009.

Paulicelli, Eugenia. 'Fashion, the Politics of Style and National Identity in Pre-Fascist and Fascist Italy'. *Gender and History* (November 2002): 537–59.

Pener, Degen. 'Italian Lessons: Giorgio Armani's Design for Living'. *Elle* (March 1993): 182–6.

Petridou, Elia. 'The Taste of Home', in Daniel Miller (ed.). *Home Possessions: Material Culture behind Closed Doors*. Oxford and New York: Berg, 2001: 87–104.

'Photographs'. *Moda* (October 1992): 244–5.

Piaggi, Anna. 'Armani' and 'Designs of Influence No. 3: Armani'. *Vogue* (UK) (June 1979): 235, 236.

'Poesia e Progetto'. *Moda* (1990): 17–8.

Poiblanc, Ludivine. 'Chic, La Nuit'. *Vogue (Paris)* (November 2004): 50.

Polan, Brenda. *Fashion 84*. New York: St. Martin's Press, 1983.

Pollock, Griselda. *Differencing the Canon: Feminist Desire and the Writing of Art's Histories*. London & New York: Routledge, 1990.

Postrel, Virginia. *The Substance of Style*. New York: Harper Collins, 2003.

Potvin, John. 'Lost in Translation?: Giorgio Armani and the Textualities of Touch', in Sandra Alfoldi (ed.). *NeoCraft: Modernity and the Crafts*. Halifax: Nova Scotia College of Art and Design University Press, 2007: 83–98.

_____ . 'Cross-Dressing Fashion and Furniture: Giorgio Armani, Orientalism and Nostalgia', in John Potvin and Alla Myzelev (eds.). *Fashion, Interior Design and the Contours of Modern Identity*. Aldershot and Burlington: Ashgate, 2010: 225–44.

_____ . 'Fashion and the Art Museum: When Giorgio Armani went to the Guggenheim'.. *The Journal of Curatorial Studies* 1, 1 (January 2012a): 47-63.

_____ . 'The Emporium of the Senses and Multi-label Retailing: The Case of Armani/ Ginza'. *Senses and Society* 7, 2 (July 2012b): 236-50.

Potvin, John and Dirk Gindt. 'Creativity, Corporeality and Collaboration: Staging Fashion with Giorgio Armani and Robert Wilson'. *Studies in Theatre and Performance* (forthcoming 2013).

Poux, Michèle. 'Giorgio Armani: Le Couturier de L'anticonformisms'. *Elle* (France) (3 August 1982): n.p.

'The Power of Armani'. *Esquire* (March 1993): 161–71.

'Power Couples: Giorgio Armani and Tadao Ando'. *Wallpaper* (18 September 2006): http://www.wallpaper.com/design/Power%20couples:%20day%205/1075 (accessed 21 October 2008).

Quick, Harriet. 'Better by Design'. *Vogue* (UK) (January 2002): 124–7.

_____ . 'Silver Fox'. *Vogue* (UK) (November 2003): 282–9.

Quinn, Bradley. *The Fashion of Architecture*. Oxford and New York: Berg, 2003.

Quintavalle, Arturo Carlo. 'The Story of Giorgio Armani', in Richard de Combray. *Luxe, Calm et Volupté*. Milan: Franco Maria Ricci Editore, 1982: 119–41.

Reiwoldt, Otto. *Retail Design*. London: Laurence King Publishing, 2000.

Rivetti, Carlo. EBHA Plenary: Fashion and Fashions between Business and Creativity. Fashions: Business Practices in Historical Perspective. Bocconi University, Milan. (11–13 June 2009).

Riviere, Joan. 'Womanliness as Masquerade', in Victor Burgin, James Donald and Cora Kaplan (eds.). *Formations of Fantasy*. New York: Routledge, [1929] 1986: 45–61.

Romanelli, Marco. 'Il progetto Dell'Abito 1988'. *Domus* 690 (January 1988): 62–9.

Ruby, Ilka, Andreas Ruby and Angeli Sachs. *Minimal Architecture*. Munich, New York, Berlin and London: Prestel, 2003

Said, Edward. *Orientalism*. New York: Vintage, 1979.

Sauter, Willmar. *The Theatrical Event: Dynamics of Performance and Perception*. Iowa City: University of Iowa Press, 2000.

Sedgwick, Eve Kosofsky. *Novel Gazing: Queer Readings in Fiction*. Durham: Duke University Press, 1997.

Segre Reinach, Simona. 'The Material Speaks for Itself', in Valerie Steele. *Fashion: Italian Style*. New Haven and London: Yale University Press, 2003: 121–9.

_____ . 'China and Italy: Fast Fashion versus Prêt-à-Porter: Towards a New Culture of Fashion'. *Fashion Theory* 9, 1 (March 2005): 43–56.

Semper, Gotfried. *Style in the Technical and Tectonic Arts, or, Practical Aesthetics*. Los Angeles: Getty Research Institute, 2004.

Seremetakis, Nadia C. *The Senses Still: Perception and Memory as Material Culture in Modernity*. Philadelphia: Westview Press, 2001.

Serrats, Marta. *New Shops and Boutiques*. New York: Harper Design, 2004.

Sharma, Sanjay and Ashwani Sharma. 'White Paranoia: Orientalism in the Age of Empire'. *Fashion Theory* 7, 3/4 (September 2003): 301–18.

Slater, Don. *Consumer Culture and Modernity*. Cambridge: Polity Press, 1997.

Smith MacIsaac, Heather. 'Milan by Armani'. *Travel & Leisure* (October 1996): 161–72.

Solomon-Godeau, Abigail. 'Going Native: Paul Gauguin and the Invention of Primitivist Modernism'. *Art in America* 77 (July 1989): 118–29.

Sozzani, France. 'On Womenswear', in *Giorgio Armani*. New York: Guggenheim Museum Publications, 2000.

Sparke, Penny. *As Long as it's Pink: The Sexual Politics of Taste*. London and New York: HarperCollins Publishers, 1995.

Steele, Valerie. *Fetish: Fashion, Sex, and Power*. New York: Oxford University Press, 1996.

_____ . *Fashion, Italian Style*. New Haven and London: Yale University Press, 2003.

_____ . 'Museum Quality: The Rise of the Fashion Exhibition'. *Fashion Theory* 12, 1 (March 2008): 7–30.

Sturdza, Marina. 'A Conversation with Armani'. *Toronto Life* (Winter 1987): 66–70.

'Sur un Portrait de Gabriel d'Annunzio Dandy'. *Monsieur* 18 (June 1921): 141–2.

Svendsen, Lars. *Fashion: A Philosophy*. London: Reaktion Books: 2005.

Thomas, Dana. *How Luxury Lost its Luster*. New York: Penguin Books, 2007.

Thurman, Judith. 'A Cut Above: Giorgio Armani's Cool, Cool Elegance'. *Connoisseur* (August 1988): 86–93.

Tickner, Lisa. *Modern Life and Modern Subjects: British Art in the Early Twentieth Century*. New Haven and London: Yale University Press, 2000.

Tilton, Marcy. 'The Armani Effect'. *Threads* (April/May 1999): 31–5.

Tonchi, Stephano. 'At the Court of King Fashion', in Maria Luisa Frisa, Mario Lupano and Stefano Tonchi (eds.). *Total Living*. Milan: Edizione Charta, 2002: 426–31.

Tournier, F. 'Armani Plays Prospero'. *Elle Decor* (March 1990): 83–93.

Troy, Nancy J. *Couture Culture: A Study in Modern Art and Fashion*. Cambridge and London: The MIT Press, 2003.

Turngate, Mark. *Fashion Brands: Branding Style from Armani to Zara*. London: Kogan Page, 2004.

'Twist and Shoot'. *W* (September 1996): 191–2.

Venuti, Lawrence (ed.). *Rethinking Translation: Discourse, Subjectivity, Ideology*. New York: Routledge, 1992.

Vercelloni, Matteo. 'Sul Bund Di Shanghai'. *Interni* 544 (September 2004): 34–9.

von Fürstenberg, Egon with Camille Duhé. *The Power Look*. New York: Fawcett Columbine, 1978.

Warwick, Alexandra and Dani Cavallaro. *Fashioning the Frame: Boundaries, Dress and the Body*. Oxford and New York: Berg, 2001.

Webb, Iain R. 'Empire Armani'. *Elle* (UK) (April 2000): 259, 163–4.

Webb, Michael. 'Concrete Couture'. *The Architectural Review* CCXI, 1260 (February 2002): 74–8.

White, Nicola. *Giorgio Armani*. London: Carlton Books, 2000a.

_____ . *Reconstructing Italian Fashion: America and the Development of the Italian Fashion Industry*. Oxford and New York: Berg, 2000b.

White, Nicola and Ian Griffiths (eds.). *The Fashion Business: Theory, Practice, Image*. Oxford and New York: Berg, 2000.

Wickstrom, Maurya. *Performing Consumers: Global Capital and its Theatrical Seduction*. London and New York: Routledge, 2006.

Wigley, Mark. *White Walls, Designer Dresses: The Fashioning of Modern Architecture*. Cambridge and London: The MIT Press, 1995.

Wilcox, Claire (ed.). *The Golden Age of Couture: Paris and London 1947–57*. London: V&A Publications, 2007.

Wilson, Catherine. 'My Deft Cut'. *Harper's & Queen* (July 1994): 89–93.

Wilson, Elizabeth. *Adorned in Dreams: Fashion and Modernity*. New Brunswick: Rutgers University Press, 2003.

Witter, Simon. 'The Emporio Strikes Back'. *Sky* (March 1989): 96–102.

Wojciechowski, Ena. 'Showroom Dummies'. *Frieze Magazine* (April 2001): 52–3.

Wollen, Peter. 'Out of the Past: Fashion/Orientalism/The Body', in Peter Wollen. *Raiding the Icebox: Reflections on Twentieth-Century Culture*. Bloomington and Indianapolis: Indiana University Press, 1993: 1–34.

_____ . 'Strike a Pose'. *Sight and Sound* 15, 3 (1995): 10–5.

Yiu-Wai, Chu. 'The Importance of Being Chinese: Orientalism Reconfigured in the Age of Global Modernity'. *Boundary* 2 (Summer 2008): 183–206.

York, Peter. 'On Armani Men'. *RA Magazine* (Autumn 2003): 57.

Index